HENRY LLOYD
AND THE MILITARY ENLIGHTENMENT
OF EIGHTEENTH-CENTURY EUROPE

General Henry Lloyd. Reproduction by permission of the Syndics of the Fitzwilliam Museum, Cambridge.

HENRY LLOYD
AND THE MILITARY ENLIGHTENMENT
OF EIGHTEENTH-CENTURY EUROPE

PATRICK J. SPEELMAN

Foreword by Dennis Showalter

Contributions in Military Studies, Number 221

Greenwood Press
Westport, Connecticut • London

Library of Congress Cataloging-in-Publication Data

Speelman, Patrick J.
　　Henry Lloyd and the military enlightenment of eighteenth-century Europe /
　　Patrick J. Speelman ; foreword by Dennis Showalter.
　　　　p.　cm.—(Contributions in military studies, ISSN 0883–6884 ; no 221)
　　Includes bibliographical references (p.) and index.
　　ISBN 0–313–32160–4 (alk. paper)
　　1. Lloyd, Henry, ca. 1720–1783.　2. Soldiers—Europe—Biography.
　　3. Europe—History, Military—18th century　4. Europe—Intellectual life—
　　18th century.　5. Military art and science—Europe—History—18th century.
　　6. War—Philosophy. I. Title. II. Series.
　　D285.8.L62 S64　2002
　　355'.0092—dc21
　　[B]　　　2002021618

British Library Cataloguing in Publication Data is available.

Library of Congress Catalog Card Number: 2002021618
ISBN: 0–313–32160–4
ISSN: 0883–6884

First published in 2002

Greenwood Press, 88 Post Road West, Westport, CT 06881
An imprint of Greenwood Publishing Group, Inc.
www.greenwood.com

Printed in the United States of America

The paper used in this book complies with the
Permanent Paper Standard issued by the National
Information Standards Organization (Z39.48–1984).

10　9　8　7　6　5　4　3　2　1

To my parents, David and Nancy

Contents

Illustrations   ix

Foreword *by Dennis Showalter*   xi

Acknowledgments   xiii

Introduction: An Eighteenth-Century Odyssey   1

1   Genesis of Genius   5

2   The School of War   19

3   Toward a Theory of Principles   39

4   Henry Lloyd's Enlightenment   61

5   Servant of Mars   79

6   Philosopher of War   95

Conclusion: The Death of General Lloyd   117

Appendix A: Lloyd's Principles of War   123

Appendix B: Publishing History of Lloyd's Works   129

Notes   133

Selected Bibliography   193

Index   213

Illustrations

The Battle of Fontenoy   23

The Battle of Prestonpans   30

The Siege of Bergen-op-Zoom   36

The Battle of Maxen   54

The Battle of Hochkirch   56

The Siege of Silistria   86

Lloyd's New System   107

Foreword

Henry Humphrey Evans Lloyd is a footnote. In a career that spanned four decades in the middle of the eighteenth century, he served in the French, Prussian, and Austrian armies. He participated in the Young Pretender's 1745 invasion of Britain. Lloyd commanded a Russian division against the Turks in 1773–1774. His history of the Seven Year's War appeared in a half-dozen French and German translations. Lloyd's theoretical writings influenced the development of continental military thought. Yet he is relegated to pigeonholes in histories of military thought as a secondary figure whose understanding of war's nature and history was limited by his blinkered Enlightenment adherence to systems and principles.

Patrick Speelman's biography brings Lloyd to center stage as a military thinker far more significant than his German counterparts Dietrich von Buelow and Georg von Berenhorst. Like any another prolific writer, Lloyd periodically contradicted himself. His body of work is sufficiently extensive that it is possible to discover what one wishes to find, and critics from Jomini and Clausewitz to Azar Gat have insisted that Lloyd sought to create a science of war, an abstraction out of touch with the actual fog and friction of combat. Speelman, by contrast, makes clear the connection between Lloyd's wide-ranging operational experience and his developing theories on the nature and practice of war. Lloyd's writing rests on a well-established basis of empirical data, much of it gained at first hand and at direct risk. Principles, he asserted, structured events and enabled analysis. Chance and passion nevertheless balanced reason with contingency.

As he developed that insight in the context of the late Enlightenment, Lloyd matured into a true military intellectual—not just a field soldier who picked up a few basic current ideas, then repeated them in narratives. Lloyd was the first to integrate the study of military history with the development of military theory, establishing a synergy between the two disciplines that endures to this day. Lloyd was among the first "practical soldier," who challenged the prevailing myth that the craft of war could be mastered only by experience and apprenticeship. He called as well for the creation of a formal educational structure for officers. Ultimately Lloyd came to understand warfare as a product of human behavior and human societies. Through his analysis of the role of moral and emotional force in war, and by addressing their various manifestations in different cultures he became one of the founders of military sociology. He merits recognition, too, for being one of the first modern strategic thinkers for his insistence that military planning needed to conform to social systems and seek political solutions.

While establishing Lloyd's achievements, Speelman avoids the usual biographer's temptation to make his subject more than he was. This avoidance of overstatement, the painstaking contextualization of Lloyd's work in the broader military and intellectual contexts of the Enlightenment, has a paradoxical result. It restores Henry Lloyd to his legitimate place at the forefront of military historians and theorists in the second half of the eighteenth century: those who established the matrices for Jomini, Clausewitz, and their successors to the present day. In this important analysis of a pathbreaking military intellectual, the scholar and the subject are well matched.

Dennis Showalter
Colorado College

Acknowledgments

Countless people have contributed to this book's completion. Chief among them is Dr. Russell F. Weigley, whose tutelage and instruction enriched the final product in innumerable ways. Drs. Barbara Day-Hickman and Allen F. Davis of Temple University, and Dr. Henry G. Gole of the U. S. Army War College offered sagacious advice and criticism during the formative stages. Dr. Allen F. Davis of Temple University possibly gave the most poignant counsel of all with the question: "Do we really need another biography of a general?" I took his point seriously, and hope that the result of my labor addresses his concern. My gratitude also extends to Dr. Jay B. Lockenour and Dr. Ernst L. Presseisen of Temple University for their comments and suggestions along the way. I want to express appreciation to Dr. Dennis E. Showalter of Colorado College for his support and encouragement.

Any work of scholarship depends on the support of educational institutions. I wish to extend my thanks to Temple University's Graduate School for the Dissertation Completion Grant I received for the 1999–2000 academic year, which greatly expedited the completion of this manuscript's early form and my graduation. Also, Temple University's Center for the Study of Force and Diplomacy provided necessary funding for research in London and elsewhere. To Catherine Meaney and Betty Denkins of Paley Library's Inter-Library Loan Department, I express my deepest gratitude and respect for all their efforts and tireless pursuit of my unending and often esoteric requests. John Oram of Paley Library provided essential support and service in an all-too-often difficult environment.

At the risk of omitting persons responsible for the countless hours of research I employed in the pursuit of a shadowy figure named Henry Lloyd, I want to thank the staffs at the William L. Clements Library, Ann Arbor, Michigan, and the Niedersächsisches Staatsarchiv in Bückeburg, Germany. My gratitude also extends to Elizabeth M. Fielden of the Fitzwilliam Museum, Cambridge; Aniceto Henrique Alfonso of the Arquivo Histórico Militar, Lisbon; Peter McNiven of the John Rylands University Library, Manchester; Elizabeth Archer of the Hallward Library of the University of Nottingham; Alexander P. Romanov of the National Library of Russia, St. Petersburg; Dr. Peter Broucek of the Kriegsarchiv, Vienna; and the staff of the Trinity College Library of the University of Dublin, the British Library, and the Public Record Office at Kew for all their help. The book would be lacking without their professional dedication and interest.

To Dr. John A. Lynn of the University of Illinois at Urbana-Champaign and Dr. Ira D. Gruber of Rice University goes my appreciation for all the interest and information they provided. Special thanks go to Mark H. Danley of Kansas State University, who shares my fascination with eighteenth-century Europe. Without the continuous aid and assistance of Joanne Follmer, Graduate Secretary for the History Department at Temple University, I would still be mired in a bureaucratic imbroglio. And last but not least, I want to express my unending appreciation to my wife and colleague, Dr. Jennifer Speelman, for her encouragement, criticism, and support. Without her this book would not exist. All errors in fact and interpretation are mine alone.

Introduction: An Eighteenth-Century Odyssey

Brussels, circa 1776. A traveler arrived at the Imperial residence seeking an audience with the Governor-General of the Austrian Netherlands, Prince Karl Alexander of Lorraine. Despite the man's polished French and cultivated demeanor this middle-aged, portly figure in a scarlet uniform made little impression on the valets. They denied his request and asked what he wanted. The stranger curtly replied that he did not desire a thing and departed, vexed at their insolence, yet unwilling to damage his name with a public display of acrimony.[1] That dejected caller, the Welshman Henry Lloyd, had returned recently from Russia and wished to relate his adventures in that country's late war with Turkey to Karl, an acquaintance from the Seven Years' War. But the treatment by the royal valets came as no surprise. Lacking noble credentials, he had endured similar humiliations. This latest incident intensified his rancor toward the inequities of European society. It also represents the confluence of Europe's aristocratic military culture and the intellectual fermentation of the Enlightenment: an underlying theme running through Lloyd's life and this book.

Henry Humphrey Evans Lloyd (c.1729–83) had abandoned his native land at an early age to search for adventure on the European continent. He served in the French army during the War of the Austrian Succession (1740–48); in the Austrian and Brunswickian armies during the Seven Years' War (1756–63); and in the Russian army during the Russo-Turkish War (1768–74). Extensive experience endowed him with expertise in the theory and practice of war that he synthesized into several volumes on military history and philosophy. More specifically his writings gave birth to the modern fields of military history, theory, and criticism, and with some justification he stands as the father of military sociology.[2] Possibly the most important military intellectual of his era, Lloyd remains an obscure and misunderstood character. The explanation for this state of affairs is found in the traditional interpretation of eighteenth-century warfare in general and the study of the Enlightenment in particular.

Limited war for limited objectives became the predominant view of warfare in Europe under the *Ancien Régime*. Monarchs waged war for dynastic reasons with small professional armies recruited from the large pool of Europe's rabble and social miscreants. Generals rarely sought battle, rather they followed the direction of their sovereigns who viewed armed conflict as a means to occupy adjacent territories and further their own narrow dynastic interests. War was not an expression of the entirety of society; it was limited therefore in practice as well as theory. The French Revolution and Napoleon Bonaparte demolished this model by unleashing national war based upon an armed citizenry, thereby exposing the inefficacy of the preceding age both politically and militarily. The era's great theorists, Maurice de Saxe, Frederick the Great, Jacques Antoine Hippolyte, comte de Guibert, and Adam Heinrich Dietrich, Freiherr von Bülow, personified this interpretation. Such is the "republican synthesis" of military history initially articulated by Carl von Clausewitz, which exhorted the accomplishments of the post-1789 world.[3]

Lloyd did not escape the scathing criticism aimed at the supposedly defunct mode of war. Nineteenth-century detractors argued the following: animated by the spirit of the age, the Welshman and his contemporaries had tried to reduce war to an exact science in which battle was optional. For them his writings firmly justified the cautious, defensive-minded maneuver strategy characteristic of that backward mode of waging war.[4] And Lloyd's status as a mercenary officer did not help his image for posterity. A man without a country was doubly damned in the post-1789 context, when the universal soldier became suspected of a certain lack of virtue. This critique remained for too long unchallenged and failed to take into account any study of his life or analyze his writings within their historical context. Only recently have historians begun to reorient their focus on military theory in early modern Europe, a change that reflects a renewed interest in and interpretation of the period in general.[5]

The greatest limitation eighteenth-century military history imposed on itself was the soldier's preoccupation with the study of "Great Captains" at the expense of such figures as Henry Lloyd. Instead, Marlborough, Saxe, and Frederick the Great, all of whom appeared to nineteenth-century writers as the precursors of Napoleon Bonaparte, dominated the traditional literature. Their campaigns and battles attracted much attention and publication. It was not the aristocratic century itself, but its interpreters who tended to neglect all but the greatest wars and campaigns while relegating the lesser known figures and events to the periphery. This ossified frame of reference has undergone significant change with the emergence of "war and society" studies; now it is the "Great Captains" who are the objects of neglect.

The notion that the commanders of the era did not seek decisive battle or complete victory has a long life in historical studies and still persists in the imagination of non-specialists. This stereotype requires significant revision as well as it no longer adequately characterizes warfare of the period.[6]

Historians need to examine this era with a new set of questions. Rather than lament the inability of armies to totally annihilate one another or bemoan the inept political control or the dynastic aims of those armies, several pressing queries suggest a new critique of that epoch of arms. What restraints hindered the realization of the great decisive battle long sought for its perceived connection to Greco-Roman warfare? What technical developments promoted the defense, thus rendering the offense a precarious enterprise? Finally, what did the soldiers, commanders, and military intellectuals think and do about these restraints and developments, which appeared to them not a part of a military revolution, but a retreat from a nostalgic decisive war archetype? Henry Lloyd and other military writers explored these questions in order to solve battlefield dilemmas that rendered tactical and operational war less than decisive. The lengthy debate within the French military establishment concerning column versus linear tactics marked the first true institutional change realized through professional military discourse.[7] Lloyd also entered these debates, but he took the quest to improve the efficacy of war-making a step further. By applying Immanuel Kant's later motto, "Dare to know," to military history and theory, Lloyd became a central figure, a *philosophe,* of the Military Enlightenment of eighteenth-century Europe.

Was there a Military Enlightenment? The historiography of philosophy during the Age of Reason lacks reference to such an intellectual construct because it suffers from a traditional bias towards military affairs in general. Conventional wisdom holds that the so-called program of the Enlightenment was pacifist and opposed to the *Ancien Régime* that perpetuated conflict to the detriment of society. The Abbé St. Pierre, Voltaire, and Jean-Jacques Rousseau are the standard bearers of this enlightened opposition to war.[8] Absent in the literature is any serious discussion of the relationship between the military profession and enlightened philosophy. Warfare, it seems, entered the minds of *philosophes* and their sympathizers only when attacking the established church or condemning the vanity of kings.[9] But an ambiguity weakens this point of view. The same Voltaire who in *Candide* lamented the insanity of war also urged Catherine the Great of Russia to exterminate as many Turks as possible.[10] Several of the leading thinkers, Edward Gibbon and Montesquieu for example, actually served as soldiers out of patriotism or a sense of duty. Denis Diderot's *Encyclopédie,* itself the popular embodiment of enlightened ideals, contains over 1,200 entries about warfare, and thereby exposed a wider reading public to the workings of the military profession.[11] It is increasingly difficult to contend that the enlightened thinkers were the academic pacifists of their day. They accepted war and hoped the leaders of Europe would resort to it only to benefit the interest of the entire political community.

Supposing the *philosophes* understood war as a permanent state of human affairs and hoped their enlightened despots might use it for the benefit of mankind, there stills remains a gulf between the traditional culture of the Enlightenment and the military profession.[12] Henry Lloyd, a military officer and a *philosophe,* was a conduit through which the Enlightenment and European armed forces converged. Incorporating the growing secular and materialistic interpretation of the universe and mankind, Lloyd studied human nature and society in order to apply general principles to its organization and function as it pertained to warfare. In this endeavor he would formulate a new philosophy of war that incorporated the human and material elements of combat and military organization, and in the role of a military Voltaire censure traditional methods and prejudices. During this lifelong process his inquiries led to a formulation of constitutional theory, sociology, and modern capitalist economics as offshoots of his general study of war and society.[13] His life and writings reflect the Military Enlightenment that cut through the largely aristocratic military culture of Europe and attempted to make war an empirical science.

The following study is a biographical account and analysis of Henry Lloyd's military service, intellectual development and relationship with the Enlightenment. How that intellectual conflagration effected and influenced his ideas and outlook on the world and how then he contoured his military theory using those ideas and concepts is the core objective of this book. For Henry Lloyd the eighteenth century was an intellectual odyssey that took him from the grip of religious orthodoxy to the uneasy liberation of materialism and agnosticism. But this transformation mirrored a personal odyssey motivated and energized by his middling status that hindered professional military advancement and his own desire for glory and renown. For all the attention given to the rationalism, empiricism, and cold, calculating reason of the enlightened mind, Lloyd also exhibited an uncompromising romanticism, which he understood as his nemesis. Friends and observers referred to this restlessness as a manifestation of his inner "spring" that compelled him to seek conflict, whether personal or martial. Without an appreciation of the dual-nature of Lloyd's character and personal sentiment his adventures and career decisions appear unprincipled if not hypocritical and mercenary. However, for all the merit of his modern enlightened outlook, Henry Lloyd remained the prototypical Greek hero seeking fame and fortune for their own sake.

Genesis of Genius

So true is it that the gods do not give gracious gifts to all alike, not form
nor mind nor eloquence.

—*Homer,* The Odyssey

A backwater of eighteenth-century Europe, Wales remained on the periphery of Great Britain because its primitive road network and mountainous landscape restricted contact with more commercial areas such as London. The countryside yielded few resources, and subsistence farming barely supported the small populace ravaged periodically by hunger and disease.[1] Repetitive daily toil dominated the peasantry's existence as mountains and myths permeated their culture. The Llwyd, or Lloyd, family was of middling status, but it claimed an ancient, martial lineage. Family lore asserted that its founder Cadwaladr conquered the county of Merioneth in the twelfth century.[2] Over time this family myth may have fused with another Cadwaladr, the fictional medieval warrior-king destined to lead the Britons in victory over the Saxons.[3] Henry Humphrey Evans Lloyd was born into this pedigree circa 1720 to a respected Anglican cleric, the Reverend John Lloyd of Wrexham.[4] Welsh heritage, family history, and the rugged topography invariably played a significant role in the young boy's cognitive development and personal proclivities. In turn his experience at Oxford would provide a vital knowledge base and foundation for the education of a *philosophe.* From his Welsh lineage, Lloyd developed his sense of personal destiny and the military talent, *coup d'œil;*[5] from his Oxford education he acquired a thorough grounding in classical and military history.

Mytho-history comprised a fundamental romantic element in Henry's upbringing. Especially important in Celtic society was family lineage, which served as a powerful vehicle for status.[6] As noted, Henry's family traced its roots to a revered prince and warrior-king, and perhaps these myths captured his imagination and ignited his ambition. Much-recounted Welsh traditions and history (especially military history) reinforced the family lore. The countryside abounded with reminders of a glorious past. Harlech Castle stood on the western coast. Built by Maelgwyn Gwynedd in 547 and refurbished by Edward I in 1286, it was the last castle to surrender to the Yorkists during the War of the Roses and the final Stuart stronghold to yield to Oliver Cromwell during the Puritan Revolution.[7] Older still the Roman ruins, roads, and the ancient Briton circular camps called *caers* further stirred boyish fascination. No doubt ancient Welsh history from such well-known sources as Cornelius Tacitus' *Agricola* also fired Henry's imagination. Knowledge of the past fueled his appetite and desire for the adventure of a military career. The difference between the romance of war and its grim realities is indistinguishable to youthful comprehension.

The influence of Wales's rugged terrain on Henry's understanding of the physical world cannot be quantified but must not be underrated. One of the more mountainous counties, Merioneth contains peaks rising to nearly 3,000 feet on all sides. He and his Welsh contemporaries confronted these barriers daily. Contours of valleys, waterways, travel routes, and the ensuing general appreciation of space and time affected them deeply. The landscape invited him to envisage the land from a three-dimensional rather than linear perspective. Enclosed areas encouraged spatial abstraction, thus bolstering the talent called *coup d'œil* and military attributes in general. For instance, the quintessential skill of a contemporary military commander was arranging soldiers in enclosed spaces and maneuvering them. Henry's youth was spent in an environment that inculcated a military outlook within him. Yet, had he been a peasant or even a wealthy peer, the application of this knowledge would have been limited to the fields, pastures or drawing room. Henry's middling status as the son of a clergyman bolstered by his father's belief in the value of education enabled him to hone his intellectual and budding military acumen at Oxford University.

John Lloyd's position in society opened the gate to education, the most important element in Henry's intellectual development. The gentry of north Wales exhibited great discrepancies in wealth and status. Henry's father was not an affluent squire, but the perquisites of the clerical profession still provided an upbringing far above that of the average child.[8] Since 1100 the family owned an estate at Cwm Bychan, a scenic vale near the River Artro that covered a four-mile radius encircling a lake, a woods, and several rocky crags. Contemporaries considered the isolated locale and its manor house indicative of the holdings of a Welsh gentleman.[9] Although their annual income never propelled the family into the peerage the Lloyds enjoyed a relatively stable existence. But the Welsh gentry including John Lloyd expected their sons to enter the legal or religious professions and disavow the common life of farming and herding. A successful professional career would solidify their social standing and make them more acceptable to their English comrades. In short, the future lay in England, not Wales. Attending an English university further enhanced a family's economic and social standing. Henry probably first studied a local grammar school, but it is likely that he received a basic education from his father before enrolling in Oxford's Jesus College for religious training.[10]

Oxford might appear as infertile ground for a future enlightened *philosophe*. A poor reputation indicated by declining enrollment vexed the university throughout the eighteenth century. Much criticism was political. Whig detractors considered it medieval, reactionary, and backward. Oxford served the country gentry and produced Anglican clerics who supported Toryism. But its support of the Anglican Church and its conservative political orientation in hindsight was particularly important to Henry. Since the Glorious Revolution of 1688 it clashed with the establishment, ever defiant toward the Hanoverians and defending itself against accusations of Jacobitism. Here Henry fraternized with partisans of the exiled Stuarts and their Tory supporters, and if his later exploits in the Forty-Five reflect his early political leaning, Oxford transformed him into a Jacobite sympathizer. Whig charges were overblown, but sentimental attachment to the lost cause of Jacobitism helped socialize Oxford's students.[11] The time spent there, whether or not it merely reinforced existing beliefs, directly shaped the first half of Henry's life.

No less important than Oxford's political incorrectness was its orthodoxy. Learned critics claimed its religious orientation bred ignorance, bigotry and promoted clericalism. Papist, monkish, and out of step with the times, the well-known and often disregarded rule of celibacy in particular was ridiculed. But not all commentators disliked Oxford's religious outlook. Samuel Johnson glorified its tradition and cherished the discipline and order of its formal system. The problem was lack of funding, which diminished the quality of its academic reputation in general. Notwithstanding Johnson's sentiment, Oxford continued to languish under a tainted image. Edward Gibbon personified the antipathy by frankly admitting the utter uselessness of his fourteen-month tenure. He renounced it as he cheerfully believed it would disregard him.[12] Perception, however, is hardly a sound substitute for reality. Underneath the polemical rhetoric lay a fine institution of learning that was respected internationally if not in England.[13]

Jesus College was a Welsh entrepôt that proudly wore the clerical label. Queen Elizabeth I established it in 1571 "to spread and maintain Christian religion in its sincere form, to eradicate errors and heresies . . . for education of youth in loyalty, morality and methodical learning."[14] Supporters believed it provided the ideal environment for those wishing to enter the priesthood, defend the traditional order, and become gentlemen. Shedding the drunken, crude and vulgar stereotype was vital for a Welshman's future career in England where he occupied a much lower social standing than his English equivalent. Henry's father expected him to use this time to polish his manners and make a reputation among the Welsh country-gentry. That network of associations would then serve him throughout his life in Great Britain. The ways of the gentleman had the potential to further Henry's ambitions in a military career as well. Like Gibbon before him and numerous other figures of the Enlightenment, Lloyd would later become an avowed enemy of orthodox Christianity even though he was a product of that milieu.

Little is known firsthand of Henry's academic performance. He matriculated in March 1740 with, as an admirer noted, a mind made large by nature.[15] He did not take a degree for reasons that remain unknown. As for his position in the school hierarchy, he probably wore the round cap and silk gown of the Commoner class reserved for sons of the clergy and country gentlemen.[16] In order to graduate the university mandated a four-year course of study and successful completion of three disputations and one oral examination. This curriculum conformed to an official body of regulations, the Laudian Statutes.[17] Albeit rigid and altered only by royal decree, students regularly supplemented it with fee-based lectures in modern science and European languages. Outside lecturers provided these services, thus juxtaposing the religious categories of instruction with the philosophy of John Locke, René Descartes, and Isaac Newton. Oxford also possessed a prestigious program of scientific learning grounded in geometry and astronomy. For instance, Edmond Halley (1656–1742) occupied the chair of geometry throughout the 1730s. The typical student received refinement and digested the new trends and methods of eighteenth-century philosophers, deists, and scientists. Instead of producing ignorant religious bigots, Oxford could boast that it formed cosmopolitan, albeit orthodox, English gentlemen. For his part, Henry received a well-rounded education grounded in languages, letters, philosophy, and mathematics.[18]

The core component of Lloyd's studies, and the most pertinent feature of his Oxford education, focused on classical literature. Students immersed themselves in the writings of Herodotus, Aristotle, and Plato with daily translations from Latin or Greek to English and back again in order to master the ancient languages.[19] Lloyd's exposure to classical writers formed the basis of his early intellectual development. The canon included Thucydides, Arrian, Xenophon, and Polybius. Especially significant is the fact that many if not most classical authors wrote about military history. Wars of the Greeks and Persians, Alexander the Great, and Hannibal provided a solid historical foundation. He particularly revered histories written by actual participants or persons with military experience because "this enabled them to write on those transactions with judgment and propriety."[20] Lloyd's general impressions were preoccupied in all probability with the role of the heroic or noble leader and the valor of the great commander. Julius Caesar, an ancient writer he especially admired, presented military history in that fashion.[21]

Instructional texts complemented the historical literature. The foremost classical authority on military affairs was the Athenian expatriate Xenophon (c.430–c.354 B.C.), whose *Anabasis* served as a virtual textbook for military operations. He also wrote on Cyrus the Great, the Peloponnesian War, and the subject of generalship.[22] Other well-known writers as Onasander and Frontinus provided useful manuals on military topics including the cavalry, strategy, and the personality of the ideal commander.[23] From like authors Henry discovered the "art of war" based upon principles and rules, which provided form, structure, and context to his future ideas on war. Like most enlightened thinkers he appreciated the military lessons and principles that one could distill from Greco-Roman prose. He wrote: "[T]heir works will ever be regarded, by military men in particular, as a pure spring from whence the general principles of war may be deduced."[24] The specific and particular facets of the ancient military literature might lack utility and relevance to modern times, but the generalities and basic assumptions remained unaltered. Therefore Lloyd's classical inheritance was substantial. With this arsenal of learning he would base his military thought on the authority of the ancients while blending it with the new thinking of the Enlightenment in order to synthesize a modern philosophy of warfare.[25]

Books alone cannot account for Lloyd's decision to forsake a clerical career for a martial one, nor can the social benefits, if any, of joining the British army. It was far more profitable to enter politics or the legal profession. Lloyd's middling status did not bode well for such opportunities and should have deterred him. The middle-rank gentry, especially if one were not English, found it difficult to enter and rise through the ranks without substantial income or political connections. An inheritance might make a commission possible, but the army's upper echelons remained all but closed to him.[26] A more elemental reason explains his lifelong desire for a military career. He simply possessed an affinity for war, romantic in nature, combined with intellectual pretensions described by Pietro Verri as the perfect combination of Aristotle and Alexander.[27] Such affinity was considered in his day a sign of 'genius' in both the general and specific sense. One popular eighteenth-century connotation argued that genius indicated a bias towards one art (such as war) over another, which surfaced early in a person's life and marked out their station and destiny.[28] Using a similar definition, but with an eye toward understanding its origin, modern science suggests genius may have familial roots.[29] Regardless of the source, his passion for adventure, prefigured by a streak of romanticism, was untiring, and it propelled him into a life of insecurity, upheaval, and poverty.[30] Such was the price he paid for his nemesis.

Henry left Jesus College around Easter 1741 perhaps due to the unexpected death of his father. He practiced law for a time and suffered additional misfortune when his mother remarried a gentleman who defrauded him of an estate worth £2000.[31] Any hope of entering the British army vanished with his property. Restless and distraught he left his home to seek adventure on the continent. For nearly thirty years he lived as a voluntary expatriate.

Europe appeared a promising place for gentleman adventurers at this time. After nearly two decades of general peace, war again was afoot. International tensions revolved around dynastic politics, colonial trade, and symbolic *causus belli* like Master Mariner Robert Jenkins' dismembered ear. Nearly every state attracted its share of mercenaries. France was one logical destination since it had once nurtured a tradition established by Louis XIV (r.1643–1715) of allowing non-nobles to serve in its officer corps albeit as subalterns. The Spanish and Austrian armies also commissioned foreigners, especially Irish Catholics and other Jacobites exiled after the failed 1715 rebellion. Overall, however, the seventeenth-century tradition of hiring foreign and non-noble military figures was waning throughout most of Europe. Armies increasingly incorporated native nobles rather than employ foreigners. The trend continued unabated throughout the eighteenth-century until the European officer corps could be termed an aristocratic caste.[32] Lloyd first tried his hand at fortune by traveling to the remote region of Prussia.

By the 1730s Prussia, a Protestant state, had achieved near military parity with the traditional Catholic powers of Europe. Its population ranked twelfth but its army ranked fourth in size among European powers.[33] A Prussian officer was considered a member of the most highly regarded and proficient military establishment in Europe. Frederick William I (r.1713–40) had welcomed non-Junkers into the lower ranks of his officer corps. Frederick II (r.1740–86) discontinued his father's policy because he believed the Junker nobility was the only estate suited for military service.[34] Henry traveled to the small, beautiful capital of Berlin, known for its large garrison, but he failed to acquire a military commission. The quest for status within the noble-dominated military profession became a recurring theme throughout his life. Lloyd's lack of noble lineage, merit, and wealth impressed no one at this time. Instead he turned to Berlin's social recreation, fell in love with a ballerina, and incurred substantial debt. He fled his creditors and traveled south into Italy where he found refuge in Venice. Once a great maritime power but now an ossified oligarchy, Venice fielded a small 4,000-man provincial army. For all the romance of past glory it could no longer be considered the queen of the Adriatic Sea. Stagnant waters caused chronic sickness and virtuous onlookers considered it the "brothel of Europe."[35] A high crime rate also made it an uninviting place for the young, destitute refugee from Prussia. Due to chance or good fortune Lloyd's Anglo-Catholic credentials and desperate situation attracted a group of Jesuits who settled his debts. In return for their act of mercy they expected him to join the order.[36] In hindsight it was a pivotal event in his life.

The one-time soldier, Ignatius of Loyola, founded the Jesuit order in the sixteenth century. Known as the Society of Jesus, it carried the Pope's banner and assumed the vanguard of Roman Catholicism across the globe. Perhaps the order's military character attracted Lloyd, but in reality he had no choice but to join them. To his benefit the Jesuits more than just proselytized unbelievers; they manned the educational system of Catholic Europe. In 1551, Ignatius had recommended the establishment of colleges to teach the Greco-Roman classics, logic, and theology. By 1730 the Society administered dozens of schools across Europe that educated the sons of nobles, artisans, and laborers. A Jesuit education allowed men of lesser social status to gain government positions and attain some level of distinction in Europe's hierarchical society.[37] Lloyd's patrons sent him to the prestigious Roman College, which catered to Englishmen.[38] With a renowned faculty and scientific curriculum, the school inculcated Henry with Newtonian-based subjects like physics and astronomy. He may well have studied under Ruggiero Giuseppe Boškovíc (1711–87), a polymath who published over sixty books on science between 1730–60.[39] The school also offered courses in the science of mapping and cartography, which appealed to the more educated soldiers in European armies: the engineers.[40] A strong mathematics tradition attracted nobles destined for military service as well. Here Lloyd no doubt first encountered the quasi-cadets of the military profession. Education rather than landed or commercial wealth would assist his path of advancement.

Again it is ironic that a future *philosophe* would receive aid from the standard-bearers of religious orthodoxy. The Jesuits did uphold Papal authority, but they also forged a loose association with enlightened writers. Although it was an expedient relationship, even the most anti-religious writer could respect the Jesuit order's social utility. First, they educated the poor and provided valuable skills to persons seeking higher status. The Jesuits also tutored and instructed leading figures of the Enlightenment such as François-Marie Arouet de Voltaire, Denis Diderot, and Marie-Jean-Antoine-Nicholas de Caritat, marquis de Condorcet. As the "schoolmasters" of the early Enlightenment the Jesuits exerted great influence on those who considered themselves enlightened. However the entente was uneasy and often strained. Neither camp reconciled its diverging beliefs over the supernatural, but a mutual amity did develop between these unlikely allies. Even Voltaire regretted their suppression in Portugal (1759), France (1764), and Spain (1767). When Pope Clement XIV's brief *Dominus ac Redemptor* (1773) dissolved the order altogether many, including Lloyd, lamented their downfall.[41]

Another thread bound the Jesuits and enlightened thinkers. Jesuit intellectuals, immune from the Inquisitors of Portugal and Spain or the censors in France, openly discussed controversial literature. They rigorously ana-lyzed a text's theological consistency in popular, widely read publications like the *Journal de Trévoux,* thereby exposing the general reading public to the contemporary philosophy of enlightened writers.[42] The Jesuits did not generally support those writers. They wanted to save souls and reform the minds of lapsed or heretical Roman Catholics. Using unorthodox means (the Jesuits were always flexible toward liturgical and doctrinal practices) these journals and colleges served as instruments of an "evangelical" Roman Catholicism seeking to conjoin the Enlightenment's scientific world-view with that of religious doctrine.[43]

By mere circumstance Lloyd received an education similar to such lead-ing *philosophes* as Voltaire: one immersed in the classics, modern science, and theology. His Jesuit experience not only deepened the base of his knowledge but also exposed him to the larger world of European intellec-tual life. In an age where intellectuals first formed a professional class, knowledge had the potential to open doors for advancement even for com-moners. Yet after a year or two of study Lloyd left his Jesuit protectors. He was once again eager to search for a military career and his interests did not coincide with their religious mission. After returning to Venice, he became the residing Spanish ambassador's secretary. The ambassador recommended his protégé to Jaime Miguel Guzmán, marqués de la Mina (1690–1767), then interim captain-general of Catalonia. The Marqués owned a celebrated military record; he had won the Order of St. Gennaro with his decisive vic-tory at Monte de Santo during Spain's invasion of Oran in 1732 and served as Madrid's ambassador to Paris (1736–40).[44] Unfortunately, Guzmán could not commission Lloyd in the military, so he traveled to Madrid and impressed King Felipe's cabinet secretary, the Irishman Ricardo Wall, for whom he worked as a secretary.

War loomed on the horizon even though Spain hovered on the periphery of European politics.[45] A veritable shadow of the empire of Charles V (r.1519–56), onlookers viewed the kingdom of Felipe V (r.1700–46) as a geographic and political appendage of France. Most of its activity involved its New World colonies from which it received an annual gold and silver convoy. At its base, however, Spain was a poor, stagnant country. King Felipe and his wife Elisabeta Farnese had abandoned an aggressive colonial policy and shifted their focus to the Mediterranean in order to place their sons on the thrones of various Italian kingdoms.[46] Don Carlos took the Neapolitan throne, traded for Elisabeta's initial goals of Parma and Tus-cany. Spain entered the War of the Austrian Succession (1740–48) to advance the careers of the Queen's other children. But in Madrid Lloyd became frustrated by the lack of promotion and inability to participate in the conflict. He rejoined the Marqués de la Mina, who introduced him to military and technical education via an engineers school.[47]

Traditional military education imparted a specialized knowledge of war to noble cadets. The military academy as understood today did not exist. Training camps and vocational institutes inculcated youth with proficiency in weapons, riding skills, and military ethos. However, these schools grew slowly in number over time and cost a great deal of money to maintain. France and Prussia pioneered the trend. Louis XIV and his war minister François Michel le Tellier, marquis de Louvois (1630–91) established nine provincial cadet companies in 1682. Frederick William, the Great Elector (r.1640–88) of Brandenburg-Prussia that same year created the first official cadet company designed solely to concentrate and educate his future officers, the sons of the Junkers of East Prussia. Only a state that farmed large revenues like France or efficiently managed its meager resources like Prussia could support noble cadet companies and schools. For most European states the cost of these institutions outstripped their resources.[48] Most noble cadets, if no company or regional school existed, directly joined a regiment. They usually attached themselves as apprentices to high-ranking officers (often their relatives) and learned by experience. The regiment, not central authority, educated the majority of cadets, and was both cost and time effective. This method introduced the young nobleman to the rigors and dangers of regimental life even though it did not promote subordination or loyalty to state authority. Because the regiment's traditions and myths formed a cadet's outlook and sculpted his sense of honor and duty, an officer's loyalty was first to the regiment and then to the state. Additionally, a regiment's internal politics and dynamics could present obstacles to soldiers and officers seeking advancement.

Lloyd again faced the chief obstacle that became the bane of his existence: the disadvantage of a low birth. Since the prerequisite for military service was aristocratic lineage, most cadets were predominately sons of nobles and great landowners. Society considered them a different class if not race of people who supposedly held a high aptitude for warfare. As the natural leaders of society they received special privileges that set them apart from the common people in civil and public life. Nobles officered the armies and in most countries manned the state bureaucracies. Commoners and lesser adventurers constituted a small proportion of officers in European armies, though their numbers varied from state to state. Of these select few most were commissioned on merit or due to unusual circumstances.[49] Lloyd faced almost insurmountable institutional barriers that later he attacked in his enlightened philosophy of war.

Gradual change transformed this system during the eighteenth century. Spurred by the French and Prussian examples states began to centralize officer education. Despite the cost European rulers found it attractive because it standardized the knowledge and skill of cadets and also helped subordinate the officer class by undercutting the all-powerful colonel-proprietors who managed the regiment like a private enterprise. A king demanded loyalty and duty to the state. Viewed in this context, the creation of professional officers in the eighteenth century marked the erosion of the proprietary and semi-private nature of regiments. The process did not always lead to the desired results. For instance, the Prussian king bound the Junker officers more or less to his will, yet their monopolistic control over the officer corps made them a potential threat to the Hohenzollern control of state policy.[50] Not until the nineteenth century (far too late for Lloyd) would the expansion of armies based on national conscription weaken the aristocratic control of the officer corps.

Because he was barred from traditional methods of military training Lloyd received his military education from another relatively new form and style of instruction, artillery and engineering schools. From quasi-mystical origins of alchemists and proto-scientists, military engineers emerged as important auxiliary troops, first organized in France to construct border fortresses. The *Corps des Ingénieurs de Génie Militaire* as it was known also conducted sieges, paved roads, built bridges, surveyed frontiers, and invented the science of mapping.[51] Often educated by Jesuits in France, Holland or Italy, engineers represented the most formally trained of all the units in an army, who typically served during wartime as units attached to the artillery corps. Over time it became clear that a permanent organization would alleviate scraping together skilled personnel during war. The problem was especially acute in France during the War of the Spanish Succession. Louis XIV had cut costs by decommissioning France's military engineers after the Peace of Ryswick (1697). The Sun King's parsimony exiled thousands of skilled engineers, mostly Huguenots, to all corners of Europe and led to the establishment of engineering services in rival states.[52]

A strong, well-trained engineering corps along the Bourbon model became the hallmark of an effective and sophisticated military establishment. A ready reserve of skilled personnel made an army a flexible war machine: it could conduct sieges as well as fight in the field. Peter the Great (r.1682–1725) established both artillery and engineering schools as part of his modernization program during the Great Northern War (1700–21). Unlike traditional military education, technical training grew solely from practical concerns. Louis XIV and Sébastien le Prestre, marquis de Vauban (1633–1707) as well as Czar Peter understood that the growth of armies and the sophistication of siege warfare demanded specialized troops. Historians view this process as the stirrings of officer professionalism, but engineers were no more or less professional than the career-oriented noble officer class.[53] Both groups required advanced training and expertise to translate their skills into practice. What differentiated *la genie* was their non-noble social lineage and base of knowledge. It was scientific and wholly secular. Modern knowledge, or the scientific understanding of a

Newtonian universe, had become an important commodity and facet in conducting successful wars.

The importance of scientific knowledge grew as armies increasingly relied upon artillery and fortifications. By the mid-eighteenth century most European powers had established technical schools for engineers and artillerists. The Austrian army even began infusing the scientific or problem-solving outlook into small groups of their officers via staff organizations. The French École Militaire reinvigorated officers' skills and provided them with a basic technical education.[54] In due time this structural transformation exposed the traditional army system based upon noble lineage and seniority to a system based upon merit and special knowledge. A deeply felt antagonism emerged between members of the two groups based respectively on privilege and performance.[55] Nonetheless sovereigns soon organized engineers into regiments and gave them military commissions like all other officers. Napoleon Bonaparte, himself an artillerist, benefited from this transformation early in his career.

In Spain the inherent prejudices of European society toward non-nobles compelled Lloyd to enter an organization from which few advanced. As an engineer he received his first formal training in military science, a benefit of larger trends begun years earlier. The much-maligned Spanish army was the product of a series of Bourbon reforms enacted after the War of the Spanish Succession (1701–14). On paper it was a formidable and cosmopolitan force organized in regiments that consumed over sixty percent of the state budget. Foreigners comprised one-third of its officer corps, and its regiments included Swiss, Italian, Flemish, and Irish units. A key reform in 1711 created an engineer corps headed by the Fleming Jorge Prospero de Verboom, who wrote its first regulations. As in other European armies at that time, the Spanish engineers remained outside the regimental system and did not hold formal military rank: they served as auxiliary units within the army itself during wartime. Even so, the Bourbons created provincial military schools to educate and train the engineers by the time Lloyd joined the corps.[56] His training provided him with a sound military and technical education based upon engineering and the study of the military masters and their authoritative treatises. He took the first step from military engineer to military philosopher.

The foremost military theorist Sébastien le Prestre, marquis de Vauban, permanently implanted the scientific spirit in western warfare.[57] His methods remained an integral part of military education into the nineteenth century and beyond. Contemporaries within and outside France avidly digested his maxims and put his methods into practice. Simply put, he transformed siege warfare into a near science, and when properly followed his procedures could force any citadel to surrender within fifty days. Not only did his methods craft war into a deliberate and more logistically based operation, but they also helped limit its effects upon the civilian population. Vauban was sensitive to the bloodletting of war and wanted to ritualize conflict in areas where fortifications abounded and geography channeled military forces close together as on the Rhine frontier, in the Low Countries, and Italy. Such concerns did not affect Baron Emmo van Coehoorn (1641–1704), known as the "Dutch Vauban" and the "Fighting Engineer." His method of siege warfare, the antithesis of Vauban, emphasized simplicity in fortification design and advocated storming recalcitrant fortresses. These tactics typically caused great loss of life.[58] Smaller, poorer states tended to use them. For instance, Prussian siege operations in the Seven Years' War followed this pattern more than Vauban's capital-intensive technique. From these two men Lloyd and his contemporaries learned the basic structure of siege warfare. The inheritance was noteworthy. Vauban and Coehoorn strengthened Lloyd's already developed sense of rules and principles that allowed for a more rational practice of war where victory if not completely assured could be envisioned in quantitative terms.

One of the more popular writers on war, Raimondo Montecuccoli, duca di Melfi (1608–80),[59] also reinforced that outlook. He had served in the Imperial army during the later stages of the Thirty Years' War and became *generalissimo* of all Austrian forces after his victory against the Turks at the Raab River (1 August 1664). More important was his interest in the study of war, which he believed to be a science that could be mastered through intense study. He wrote several works on his own theory of warfare and military campaigns and is credited with putting its study on a scientific basis. He intended to reveal war's near-mystical mechanics, symbolized by universal principles, rules, and maxims that anyone could use when conducting military campaigns. Noteworthy is the fact that Henry Lloyd's fundamental methodology would follow this quest for rules and principles.[60] Furthermore, Montecuccoli's thought particularly enticed engineers because it emphasized the utility of military geometry, trigonometry, and arithmetic.

The foremost French authority on war was Antoine de Pas, marquis de Feuquières (1648–1711). Soldiers widely read his memoirs when published in the 1730s, for they were filled with vehement criticism of the French marshals who conducted the wars of Louis XIV.[61] To him human fallibility and ignorance, especially ignorance of geography, bred military defeat. "Almost every unsuccessful Event may be imputed," he wrote, "to a defective Disposition, and the Timidity, or want of Judgment in the General who is defeated."[62] Feuquières stressed that war was based upon aggression and should be waged aggressively. His was a field officer's response to Vauban, whose methods slowed the speed and rapidity of strategic and operational movement. An attractive alternative approach, Frederick II of Prussia admired Feuquières' audacious recommendation for offensive action.[63] Lloyd also argued that war was a state of action, rapid movement, and decision; a view nurtured by his experience in the Austrian army during the Seven Years' War and supported by his study of military philosophy.[64]

Closer to Lloyd at this time were two Spanish contemporaries. The first, Alvaro Navia Osorio, marqués de Santa Cruz de Marcenado (1684–1732), gained fame for leading the Spanish expedition against Sicily in 1718.[65] Santa Cruz wrote primarily to instruct future generations of officers and his *Reflexiones militares* appeared condensed and translated into French not long after his death. The original eleven-volume treatise was an encyclopedic account of his various military undertakings. Santa Cruz placed special emphasis on the interplay between moral forces and tactics and the importance of understanding battlefield psychology. Lloyd did not ignore him in this respect as his own philosophy of war would demonstrate.[66] In addition, Lloyd was privy to the military thought of none other than the Marqués de la Mina, who later published his ideas as *Maximas para la guerre*.[67] As the title suggests, he too sought to uncover and illustrate the universal principles and maxims of war. He is noted for criticizing Jean-Charles, chevalier de Folard's (1669–1752) revival of the Greek and Macedonian phalanx as a viable tactical system.[68] In his later writings Lloyd also criticized Folard's "new" infantry column, suggesting that it could not operate against smaller units armed with firearms.[69] His own experience with the French army at Fontenoy in 1745 would strengthen this conviction against deep, massed formations.

Lloyd's Spanish tenure ended without distinction. The Marqués de la Mina neither took him on his Italian campaigns nor promoted him. The frustrated young engineer left Barcelona in 1744 and ventured north into the kingdom of Louis XV (r.1715–74). During his youth and from his education, Lloyd had obtained the tools with which he would become an enlightened thinker and military theorist. By the time he joined the Austrian army in 1758 he was erudite in contemporary military literature. His knowledge of European languages including Welsh, English, Latin, French, German, Italian, and Spanish enabled him to digest such a wide array of sources.[70] Judging from these educational experiences it is evident that his ideas on war, while original in their own right, developed in accordance with existing patterns. Both classical writers and contemporaries made their mark on his impressionable and eager intellect. Basic themes emerged at this time: the idea of universal rules and principles, the predominance of moral factors, and the necessity for aggressive action. Authority personified by Montecuccoli and others validated that outlook. In the meantime, the Jacobites, adherents to the House of Stuart, were planning another strike at the Hanoverian dynasty. Lloyd soon found his school of war on the fields of Flanders.

The School of War

And experience . . . provides the starting point of art and science: art in the world of process and science in the world of facts.
—*Aristotle,* Posterior Analytics

Lloyd's formative military experience comprised three main phases. In 1745 he fought at Fontenoy with the French army under Hermann Maurice, comte de Saxe (1696–1750). Next, he joined the Jacobite Rebellion known as the Forty-Five. Last, he faced the grim realities of combat unfettered by the social and legal conventions of limited war at the siege of Bergen-op-Zoom in 1747. Apart from experiencing the carnage of war, Lloyd's presence in France during the 1740s also exposed him to the main currents of Enlightenment philosophy. The works of Voltaire and Montesquieu, the twin pillars of French thought, circulated clandestinely along the trade routes with the Netherlands, a virtual "bookstore" of the Enlightenment. Warfare contoured the transmission of these ideas across national boundaries. Interested aristocrats and military officers carried all sorts of literature across Europe's war-torn landscape. Prince Eugene of Savoy for example had collected a vast library of seditious and proscribed literature during his many military campaigns. In addition, enlightened writers and philosophers often served in the armed forces. For instance the materialist philosopher Julian Offray de La Mettrie (1709–51) served as a French military surgeon in Flanders. For the next ten years Lloyd traveled across Europe and added to his knowledge of Enlightened and often censored literature. He personified the nexus between *philosophe* and military professional.

France's entry into the War of the Austrian Succession in November 1743 inadvertently launched Lloyd's military career. Policy-makers hoped to facilitate a favorable peace by restoring the defunct House of Stuart to the English throne.[1] From Dunkirk they planned a cross-channel invasion to be led by Marshal Saxe: they would first land at Maldon and then advance on London. The army collected ships, supplies, and men at Dunkirk and a battle fleet at Brest for the invasion scheduled for early 1744. To augment the army, Louis XV had raised a new regiment, the Royal Écossais, from a group of Scottish Jacobites.[2] But the French fleet did not leave Brest until 8 February, one month behind schedule. Delays allowed scattered British naval forces under Admiral John Norris (1660–1749) to concentrate and prepare for the invasion. Misfortune struck *chef d'escadre* Jacques-Aymar, comte de Roquefeuil (1665–1744) on 7 March when a violent gale blew his ships away from the British fleet. Worse still, the same storm wreaked havoc on the troop transports at Dunkirk. The "Protestant Wind" sank a dozen ships loaded with men, ammunition, and supplies. Saxe cancelled the invasion and the French government officially abandoned the operation on 13 March after spending nearly 900,000 *livres*.[3] Two weeks later King Louis XV (r.1715–74) declared war on Great Britain; on 27 April he declared war on Austria.

The aborted Jacobite invasion caused a chain reaction that swept Henry Lloyd into the great events of that war. In 1744 he was serving as a lay brother in a Jesuit college in northeast France where he taught military subjects to Irish and Scots in French service. He was recommended as a tutor to Lord John Drummond, the commander of the new Royal Écossais regiment and an exiled member of the Associators, a clandestine Scottish Jacobite organization.[4] Lord Drummond sent his son John, an engineering cadet, to Lloyd for military instruction to prepare him for the Jacobite crusade. With the failure of the proposed invasion, Drummond departed to join Saxe's army forming for a Flanders campaign slated for early 1745. He needed little effort to persuade his schoolmaster to accompany him, because Lloyd's "genius" compelled him to go.[5] He finally would see war first-hand under the command of the Comte de Saxe, the most celebrated officer in Europe, who was planning to wrest control of the Austrian Netherlands from the Habsburgs. His Army of Flanders consisted of two large corps: his own consisting of 37,000 men and a second of 50,000 soldiers commanded by Louis XV. The offensive continued unabated throughout the summer and autumn of 1744. Menin surrendered on 5 June, Ypres on 24 June, and Knocke on 29 June after one day's resistance.[6] The path lay open for a general invasion of Flanders, the United Provinces, and the Electorate of Hanover. Great Britain, the Netherlands, Austria, and Saxony opposed the French advance with an expeditionary force of 47,000 commanded by William Augustus, duke of Cumberland (1721–65), a son of King George II (r.1727–60).[7] In the spring of 1745 the allies (mostly British, Hanoverian, and Dutch soldiers with small detachments of Austrians) concentrated near Brussels to oppose Marshal Saxe's 95,000 soldiers stationed near Courtrai on the Lys River.

Saxe targeted the border fortress of Tournai because it would provide control of the Scheldt River that traversed the entire region. He sent his able Danish assistant Ulric Frédéric Waldemar, comte de Lowendal (1700–55) to seize the town.[8] Saxe planned to take a detached corps down the right bank of the Scheldt and force a battle with the allied army advancing from Brussels. On 30 April Lowendal opened the trenches at Tournai. Saxe clearly had gained the initiative and achieved operational surprise over Cumberland.[9] Designed by Vauban, Tournai was a strong fortress with a garrison of 7,000 Dutch under Johan Adolf, Baron van Dorth (d. 1747). On 9 May, Cumberland's army encamped five miles southeast of Saxe between the villages of Maubray and Baugnies, a move that forced the French commander to pull 66,000 of the 81,000 troops from Tournai to meet it. The next day Saxe surveyed the landscape between Tournai and the allied camp. John Drummond, an engineer cadet and lieutenant in the Royal Écossais, joined the advance guard along with Lloyd, who subsequently impressed the chief engineer de Rochauard with his sketches of the proposed battleground. For his skill, Lloyd received an order from Saxe to wear the uniform of the Royal Écossais, a blue coat with red cuffs and lapels. In this guise he attended Drummond on horseback as an assistant "draughtsman." The position inaugurated Lloyd's military career.[10]

Lloyd's drawings possibly aided Saxe's choice of the battlefield on the small inclined plain around the village of Fontenoy. More conceivable is that his sketches helped confirm Saxe's positions. On the French left stood the wood of Barré, in the middle Fontenoy, and adjacent to the Scheldt on the right the small village of Antoing. Saxe garrisoned these strong points and built several redoubts between them, which he manned with a small portion of his army. Influenced by the Russian use of fortified positions at the battle of Poltava (28 June 1709), Saxe expected them to repel and inflict severe losses on the allied army, thus rendering "fortune favorable by skillful dispositions."[11] A cautious man, he strengthened the French line with over 200 artillery pieces, but the 800-yard space between Fontenoy and the Barré woods lay open.[12] Some thirteen years earlier Saxe wrote: "There is more skill than one might think in making poor dispositions intentionally."[13] Perhaps he planned to ensnare Cumberland in a tactical quagmire. In the gap he dug two trench lines manned respectively by nine and eleven infantry battalions. If the allies overran these trenches Saxe would annihilate them with crossfire and counterattacks by his reserves. The plan fully exploited the ground in this somewhat small, congested plain.[14] "Nature," he wrote, "is infinitely stronger than the works of man."[15] Ignorant of these strong positions, Cumberland decided to launch a direct attack across the entire mile-long front. The plan was simple. He would capture the French left flank anchored on the Barré woods, sweep over the Fontenoy plain, and rout the French reserves in the rear. Success depended upon the speed and coordination of the attacks. If the allies failed to silence the French artillery, any assault into the rear areas would be pure folly. Cumberland's plan left no room for error or chance as his army unwittingly began its march into the tiger's teeth. Early in the morning of 11 May he signaled the advance. His army assembled into four lines and marched up the plain.

Skirmishing began around 6:00 A.M. when Brigadier-General Richard Ingoldsby (d.1759) attacked the French left. To his surprise he encountered the first of Saxe's strong points, the redoubt d'Eu. Within minutes the advance bogged down near the Barré woods as sharpshooters, the *Grissons*, unleashed a murderous musket fire. Ingoldsby hesitated, resumed the attack and paused once more. When he learned a half an hour later that cavalry support was not forthcoming (the cavalry commander Lieutenant-General Sir James Campbell having been killed) his assault was already in disarray. Forces of contingency had wrecked Cumberland's plan. Lloyd later acknowledged the role of unforeseen events when he admitted "chance has generally much more influence, on the events of battles, than human prudence."[16] At 7:00 A.M. Cumberland ordered the Austrians under Lothar Dominik, Graf von Königsegg und Rothenfels (1673–1751) and Karl August Friedrich, Fürst von Waldeck's (1704–63) Dutch forces to attack both Antoing and Fontenoy. The first village withstood the Austrian assault. The Dutch, later accused of incompetence, retreated from Fontenoy under heavy fire from the artillery stationed across the river.[17]

Notwithstanding the failure of Cumberland's opening gambit, Sir John Ligonier (1680–1770) began his scripted advance on Fontenoy. Lack of coordination doomed his troops as they marched up the slope between the cross fire of muskets and cannon. For an hour his force pushed onward under a "murderous cannonade" still 400 yards from Fontenoy.[18] The Austro-Dutch failure to overrun the French right rendered any flank support a chimera. By 9:00 A.M. dark clouds of expended black powder smoke blanketed the battlefield causing a pessimistic Saxe to fear the battle nearly lost as he was carried about in a wicker litter.[19] For the next two hours the fight settled into an intense bout of volley and counter-volley. At 11:00 A.M. Cumberland stopped the futile assaults on Antoing. He resolved to take command himself, overrun the trenches between Fontenoy and the Barré woods, and attack the French rear. His troops had endured five hours of continual combat, but the duke stood firm because he feared defeat more than he sensed victory. The Dutch charged Fontenoy in support of the revised plan, but they again failed to break through Saxe's fortifications. Cumberland advanced toward the trenches under heavy artillery fire on his right (the redoubt d'Eu) and left (Fontenoy).

As Cumberland advanced, the gap near Fontenoy narrowed into a bottleneck, which forced his column to form closer and closer ranks until it

The Battle of Fontenoy

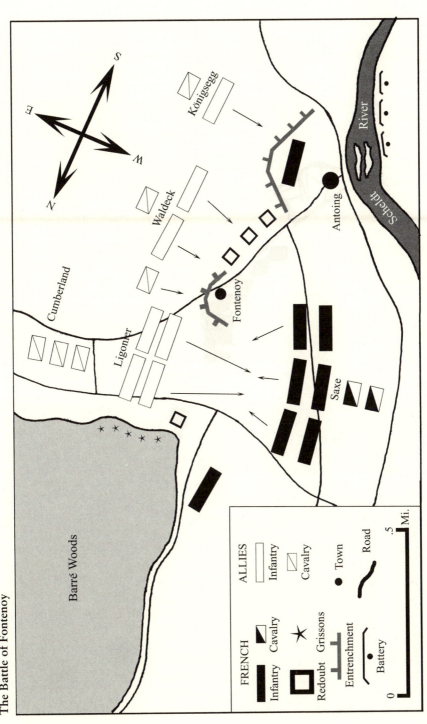

FRENCH

Infantry

Cavalry

Redoubt

Entrenchment

Battery

Grissons

ALLIES

Infantry

Cavalry

Town

Road

0   .5   Mi.

Barré Woods

Cumberland

Ligonier

Waldeck

Königsegg

Fontenoy

Antoing

Saxe

Scheldt

River

resembled a Swiss phalanx of old.[20] The column charged twice and dislodged the French Guard units covering the trenches. Victory seemed within Cumberland's grasp as he pressed on toward the French reserves. Now 1:00 P.M., Saxe feared defeat as his troops in Fontenoy ran out of ammunition. Nothing seemed to slow the British phalanx. But having advanced past the trenches, it was enveloped by the French reserves. When it halted, the enemy unleashed a volley of grapeshot into its front and attacked its left flank. The British soldiers stood firm and traded musket volleys until fatigue, artillery barrages, and common sense forced them to slowly reverse course and withdrawal. With his army "miserably galled by the cannon," Cumberland ordered a general retreat at 3:00 P.M. Saxe did not pursue because his soldiers were fatigued and he knew the Dutch army and British cavalry lurked somewhere beyond the clouds of smoke that engulfed the battlefield.[21] A beaten but not shattered allied army first limped back to Ath and then to Brussels. Tournai surrendered to the French army on 21 May.

With 7,000 French casualties Saxe celebrated a marginal victory. The allied forces suffered over 7,500 casualties, most of who belonged to the British and Hanoverian contingents. Cumberland did not receive the brunt of the blame. Many observers and commentators censured the Dutch or Ingoldsby's failure to capture the Redoubt d'Eu.[22] The exasperated Horace Walpole argued the loss was attributable to the French predominance in cannon.[23] His sentiment became the standard interpretation of the battle particularly for the Dutch. "If we had fought against men," claimed a Dutch participant, "I can assure you . . . there would not have escap'd [sic] a third part of the French army . . . we fought against 266 pieces of cannon."[24] The explanation was a rationalization, if not an excuse. French artillery did inflict severe damage, but it did not cause Saxe's victory. Instead of making a coordinated assault along Saxe's front, the allies attempted a series of smaller attacks at different locations, all with little cumulative effect. Lloyd understood this tactical lesson and later condemned faulty battle plans and their poor execution.[25] What the situation required, as Cumberland well understood, was an overwhelming shock along the entire French front that would prohibit any one sector from mutually supporting adjacent positions. Had the allies captured any number of positions they could have threatened the entire French army in the rear. Due to misfortune and impatience, Cumberland allowed and then ordered his army into positions that drew overlapping crossing fire from enemy artillery. His ineffective command and inflexible plan contributed considerably to the defeat. There was valor on the battlefield, but little prudence.

Lloyd learned the art and science of tactics from Saxe and the battle of Fontenoy. Saxe's use of terrain was the chief lesson of Fontenoy. Lloyd later wrote: "The next, and indeed most important object of any, to those who aspire to the command of armies, is geography; not only *that* which consists in a general knowledge of a country, but a local one: a man must be thoroughly acquainted with the face of the country, and its productions; and particularly with those objects which are immediately connected with military operations."[26] Cumberland had failed to survey the area and thereby suffered from his lack of intelligence. On the contrary, Saxe exploited the landscape and made nature work to his advantage and to Cumberland's disadvantage. Topographic and geographic knowledge formed the core of Lloyd's tactical doctrine because he believed it enabled one to make war with prudence and precision. "Not only an exact knowledge must be had of all fortified towns, but even of all the villages . . . because they form defiles, which being occupied, put an effectual stop to an enemy," Lloyd professed, coming close to explaining the problems Cumberland faced at Fontenoy.[27] He took this principle one step farther: "If you possess these points [i.e. geographically advantageous], you may reduce military operations to geometrical precision, and may for ever make war without ever being obliged to fight."[28] Whatever the validity of this sweeping statement, it gained credibility and momentum after his experience at Fontenoy. English apologists blamed the French artillery or the Dutch, but Lloyd sought to discover the principles behind battlefield effectiveness and success.

A second, no-less important lesson learned at Fontenoy was the futility of attacking without flank support, and conversely the advantage of attacking the enemy's flank. The lesson was not lost on Lloyd, who developed an axiom "that no manœuvre whatever be executed, especially when near the enemy, unless it be protected by some division of the troops."[29] Even with support any assault was dangerous to the attacker; without support it was folly. For this reason he urged rapidity in maneuver and attack rather than reliance on firepower, an insight especially valid when storming entrenchments.[30] But underneath this quantitative assessment of battle, Fontenoy also reminded Lloyd of the "instantaneous and transitory" nature of human combat.[31] One could not simply reduce battle to basic mechanics or tactical evolutions without first appreciating the chaos implicit in waging war.

These sample reflections were buttressed by Lloyd's subsequent emulation of the first military genius under whom he served, Hermann Maurice, comte de Saxe. A German-born French hero, Saxe was the most revered soldier of his day. He received accolades from Louis XV bestowed previously only upon Henri de la Tour d'Auvergne, vicomte de Turenne (1611–75).[32] He also theorized about war. His famous military testament *Mes Rêveries* was written in 1732, although the book was not published until after his death in 1750. This short, idiosyncratic essay is probably the best known and most widely read military treatise produced during the eighteenth century. In it Saxe emphasized understanding the human variable in addition to the traditional mechanical analysis of arms, tactics, and battlefield formations. He believed the solution to unlocking the mysteries and perfecting the practice of war lay in the human heart.[33] Saxe's theory anticipated the study of human psychology in war, yet it did not embrace a Lockean outlook. He argued that military discipline, tactics, and training should complement rather than counter human nature. "It is much easier to take men as they are than to make them as they should be," he quipped.[34] His military humanism was not lost on the impressionable Lloyd, who developed Saxe's theme further with the concept of National Character and his analysis of the role of passions on human conduct in battle. He later used his conclusions to criticize the fashion of introducing Prussian drill after the Seven Years' War; it was too harsh for non-Prussians. "Nature must be improved," Lloyd warned, "not anihilated [sic]."[35]

Lloyd borrowed liberally from other parts of Saxe's theory and would develop them further in his own writings. He adopted his mentor's commentary on soldiers' contemporary clothing and equipment and made those criticisms the basis of his principles of war and the operational system. Like Saxe, Lloyd called for the introduction of helmets, sandals, and leather armor for the infantry, breech-loading muskets, and the reintroduction of the pike.[36] Each writer in turn developed speculative military formations: Saxe and his Legion, Lloyd and his New System.[37] Both men emphasized similar qualities of command,[38] and moreover each held a Fabian dislike of battle. For Saxe they were anathema: "I do not favor pitched battles, especially at the beginning of a war, and I am convinced that a skillful general could make war all his life without being forced into one."[39] Lloyd echoed that sentiment with reference to defensive war.[40] But his interest in Saxe's ideas should not be construed simply as slavish imitation; it was more like hero-worship. After Fontenoy, Saxe attained near mythic proportions. His military theory, well-known and distributed within the French army, provided Lloyd with a model that embraced the technical facets of war as well as more sublime concepts rarely discussed in existing literature. Over the course of the next decade he absorbed these ideas and published in 1766 his first attempt at defining and explaining the principles of warfare. From these first principles his entire corpus of military and political writings came into fruition.

Fontenoy's immediate impact reverberated throughout Great Britain. Saxe continued the thrust into Flanders and the Low Countries with the express intention of entrapping the enemy against the coast. Outnumbered and reeling from their defeat, the allies scrambled to regain control of the areas around Brussels. Compelled by this dire situation, the British government reinforced Cumberland's army with a large portion of its home garrison. The transfer denuded Great Britain of troops and left fewer than 10,000 men, mostly militia and raw recruits, for home defense. It also inspired Charles Edward Stuart (1720–88), the son of James Francis Edward Stuart, the Old Pretender. From Rome Charles secretly journeyed to France in violation of the treaty with Great Britain that barred the Stuarts from French soil. He came without his father's knowledge to lead a new Jacobite invasion that would take advantage of Britain's military anemia. Charles's rash action unwittingly propelled Lloyd into that great romantic adventure called the Forty-Five.

The Jacobites, pro-Stuart opponents of the Glorious Revolution of 1689 and the Hanoverian Succession of 1714, had failed to overthrow the English monarchy numerous times. The movement's Scottish figurehead, James Stuart, presided over an exiled court in Rome. The aborted invasion of 1744 had dashed his hopes for a Stuart restoration, and the reticent Old Pretender sat comfortably in his make-believe kingdom. Core supporters within Great Britain included Roman Catholics, Non-juring Anglican Clergy, and the Scots Episcopalians. The movement's great external ally was England's archrival France. Opposing William and Mary in 1689 and the Hanoverians in 1715, French-sponsored invasions had nearly toppled the established government. By 1745 Jacobitism's political appeal waned both within and outside of Britain. The movement took on the characteristics of a social association. Its most ardent supporters were certain disgruntled Scottish Highland clans, patriotic and anti-Hanoverian. Moreover Jacobitism tended to be a patrician phenomenon, which partly explains its subsequent failure to attract a mass following. Militant domestic support diminished after the death of the most-German George I (r.1714–27) and the succession of George II. But exiled Stuart patriots retained a greater ideological commitment to the cause. They tended to be disenfranchised aristocrats and mercenaries for whom the struggle satisfied a desire for adventure or revenge. Henry Lloyd belonged to that Jacobite faction.[41]

The would-be Prince of Wales symbolized the romanticism that plagued the movement. Styled the Young Pretender, he and his close companions believed invading Scotland would force France to rally once more around his father's banner. Bonnie Prince Charlie as he was affectionately called journeyed to Nantes in late June 1745. Along the way he gathered a few hundred supporters from the Royal Écossais garrisoned at Tournai.[42] The expedition required skilled soldiers, and Charles commissioned many adventurers, two of whom were veterans of Fontenoy: Henry Lloyd and John Drummond. Lloyd became a third engineer with the rank of captain.[43] In lieu of official French support Charles received aid from sympathetic merchants in Nantes desirous of raiding English shipping in the Caribbean. The Jacobites departed on 3 July aboard the small 16-gun frigate *Doutelle*. At Belle-Isle they rendezvoused with the *Elisabeth,* a 64-gun ship with 100 marines, 3,000 muskets, and 600 broadswords.[44] The flotilla left for Scotland on 5 July with Lloyd and Drummond aboard this last vessel. Charles sent word of his designs to France, Spain, and his father in Rome.[45]

At sea the Jacobites encountered the H.M.S. *Lion,* a 58-gun frigate commanded by Captain Peircy Brett (1709–81). The *Doutelle*'s captain, Antoine Walsh, wanted to avoid a fight and so ordered the *Elisabeth* to remain on the defensive to no avail. After a brief cat-and-mouse chase on 9 July, Captain D'Eau of the *Elisabeth* seized the weather gauge and approached the *Lion*. He planned to capture it by firing broadsides and boarding with marines.[46] The gambit failed because the English crew's superior seamanship helped the *Lion* seize the weather gauge, and much to D'Eau's chagrin, close in on the *Elisabeth*. The ensuing fight lasted nearly six hours. The French ship, in its futile attempt to board the *Lion,* received several shots without returning fire. D'Eau settled for a firefight at close range and the ships poured shot after shot into one another's hull and masts. Lloyd behaved gallantly and received a wound in the right shoulder, probably from deadly splinters caused by the broadsides.[47] The clash ended at 9:00 P.M. when the *Lion* was obliged to withdraw like a "tub" upon the water.[48] The *Elisabeth* lost thirty to forty officers and men killed or wounded.[49] One Jacobite participant, James Johnstone, chevalier de Johnstone (1719–1800?), remarked it was so riddled with holes he was surprised it remained afloat.[50] The victory no doubt was due to the skill of their English foes. As the *Elisabeth* made her way back to Nantes for repairs, the *Doutelle* continued unescorted to Scotland. Charles launched his invasion, but he had failed to surprise the British government. To make matters worse, he also lost many good officers and soldiers in the short term, including Lloyd.

On 5 August Charles and seven companions landed at Loch-non-Uamh. After rallying several Highland clans during his inland march, he raised the Stuart standard at Glenfinnen on 30 August. By now nearly 1,600 men had flocked to his banner. From France Drummond and Lloyd soon joined him in Scotland.[51] The Young Pretender then began his march that has since made him a quasi-national hero. In fact it took little martial prowess to overrun the countryside. Charles "liberated" Scotland simply by walking from Glenfinnen to Edinburgh.[52] In September he took Blair-Athoil and then Perth where Lord John Drummond's brother James joined the crusade. On 26 September the Jacobites occupied Sterling just eight miles from Edinburgh without resistance. Emboldened by his success Charles set up headquarters at Holyrodhouse where he planned the invasion of England. John Cope (1673–1749), the general commanding Scotland's defense, entertained counter designs. With a small, rag-tag force of 2,300 men, he had shadowed Charles since his march inland. He reached Dunbar on 27 September and resolved to march north toward Edinburgh and force a battle with the rebels. On 30 September Cope learned that the Jacobites were actually south of his army, so he quickly occupied a strong position and allowed his enemy to seize the initiative. Prince Charles was eager for a battle that would rally the masses to his cause and persuade the French government to openly support the "liberation." He attacked Cope at Prestonpans on 2 October.

Cope arranged his army in a long line from west to east facing south toward the Jacobite forces. The gardens of the village of Preston anchored his right with his left flank protected by a marsh. In front of Cope's lines was an enclosure surrounded with a ditch three to four feet deep, and five or six feet wide."[53] To the rear was the sea. His position was strong indeed, and by twilight of 1 October Charles withdrew to Tranent leaving behind 500 men to guard the road from Preston to Edinburgh. Cope retained his position relative to Charles by rotating his entire line 45° counterclockwise. The trenches anchored his right flank and the sea his left with the morass directly in front of his troops. That night Charles discovered Cope's maneuver, marched his army once again toward Preston, and formed his order of battle east of the marsh.

At 3:00 A.M. Charles arrayed his 2,200 men in two lines directly in front of the marsh. Cope, later vilified for his ineptitude, was none the wiser.[54] On the right of the first line stood the Highland troops under James Drummond, while Lord George Murray commanded the clan Camerons and Macgregors on the left. The second line under the leadership of Lord William Murray of Nairn contained most of Perth's men and the remaining Highlanders. Several gentlemen on horseback and their servants formed a third line at the rear of the battle formation. Lloyd probably observed the engagement from this position. "Follow me, gentlemen," Charles urged as the battle commenced, "by the assistance of God, I will this day make you a free and happy people."[55] The Jacobites crossed the marsh under the cover of darkness, but they emerged disordered. It did not matter. They regrouped and attacked the English at an oblique angle. Apart from a handful of astute dragoons, Cope's troops failed to notice the approaching Highlanders, who ritually removed their caps, prayed, and charged. The English artillery rained down upon the Jacobites without effect because the marshy ground absorbed most of the cannon shot. The Highlanders overran the artillery and dispensed with Cope's dragoons. Sensing victory, they discarded their muskets, unsheathed their broadswords and in no time completed the rout that tactical surprise afforded them. "Terror," wrote Johnstone, "had taken entire possession of their [English] minds."[56] At the point of contact the clans broke through the extended lines of the infantry at several points and threw them into confusion. Within minutes the Highlanders routed both the English foot and horse and drove them from the field.[57] Prestonpans was a stunning Jacobite victory if not one of the more decisive eighteenth-century battles. Of Cope's 2,500 men, 500 lay dead, 400 wounded, and 1,400 taken prisoner. Jacobite losses numbered thirty-four killed and seventy-six wounded. In addition, Charles captured Cope's baggage and seized much-needed money and supplies.[58]

Charles wrote to his father and confided that had he possessed more cavalry they surely would have destroyed Cope's entire army.[59] Regardless of

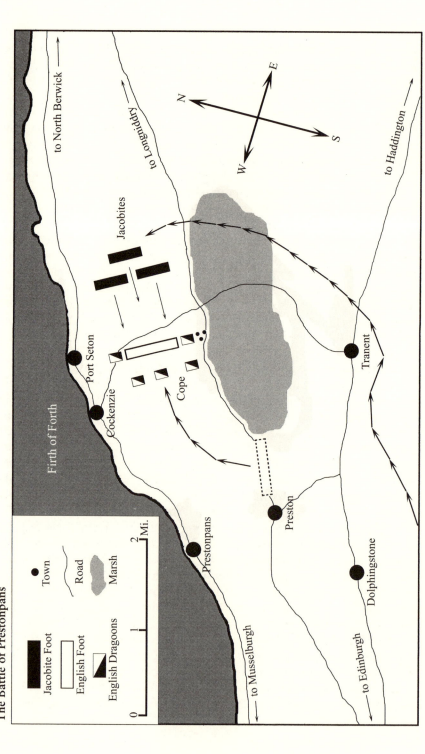

The Battle of Prestonpans

Jacobite Foot

English Foot

English Dragoons

Town

Road

Marsh

Firth of Forth

to North Berwick

to Longniddry

Jacobites

Port Seton

Cockenzie

Cope

Prestonpans

Preston

Tranent

Dolphingstone

to Musselburgh

to Edinburgh

to Haddington

N   E   S   W

0   1   2 Mi.

Charles' lamentations, Prestonpans solidified the Jacobite conquest of Scotland.[60] The battle also conceivably convinced Henry Lloyd of the necessity of hand-to-hand combat. In later writings, he openly disparaged the use of gunpowder weapons when attacking enemy formations and concluded that firearms suited the defense because they kept an enemy at a safe distance. Hand-held weapons like the pike, lance, or broadsword proved far more effective during close-quarter fighting. In his opinion European warfare lacked true decisiveness because armies used muskets for both defense and attack, thereby rarely achieving any significant results.[61] Modern armament offered the enemy too many opportunities to retreat and disengage. He expressed this sentiment succinctly: "The musket is the resource of prudence and weakness; hand-weapons are the arms of valor and vigor."[62] Taken out of context Lloyd could mistakenly be labeled as a reactionary mired in the classical tradition of the Greeks and Romans.[63] But the context of his experience suggests otherwise. One suspects the battle of Prestonpans provided impetus for Lloyd's ideas on the tactical attack and defense.

After Prestonpans Charles occupied Edinburgh and prepared for his invasion of England. On 28 October the French government paid Lord John Drummond and his Royal Écossais three months wages and ordered them to join the Young Pretender. Lord Drummond sent word to his brother James on 13 November that France now supported the invasion. He embarked with a thousand dedicated and zealous Jacobites who were eager to restore the defunct dynasty.[64] With Cope's army decimated there was much cause for concern in England as rumors of a French flotilla gathering at Dunkirk fired Jacobite hopes and imagination. On 19 November Charles's army of 5,000 men invaded England in two columns and converged on his first objective, Carlisle.[65] Mayor Thomas Pattinson refused to surrender, thus precipitating a siege two days later. Before a shot was fired the once bold magistrate capitulated and surrendered the castle as well as the town. In the meantime the English had rallied their forces and re-occupied Edinburgh. Undeterred, Charles garrisoned Carlisle with 200 men and resumed his march south into England. But the once strong Jacobite army became subject to desertion. The wear and tear of three months of campaigning began to demoralize the Highland clansmen, who wanted to return to their homes. If Charles retreated the French would surely call off their invasion. If he proceeded his troubled army faced defeat at the hands of Cumberland's army recently arrived from Flanders. Charles chose to resume his campaign, knowing that without French intervention his cause was doomed.

Lloyd avoided the Jacobite army's fate. He had left Carlisle for Wales where he hoped to foment an insurrection.[66] The Welsh Jacobites might have considered coming to the prince's aid even though a Jacobite move into Wales was seen as a remote possibility.[67] Lloyd carried letters from the Pretender to sympathizers, but no rebellion ensued. Wales' two Jacobite societies, the Sea Serjeants and the Cycle Club of the White Rose, supported the Stuart cause, but apart from their sentimental attachment they saw no reason to upset the status quo, especially without a French army on English soil.[68] The Welsh sideshow was in part a ruse by the Young Pretender to scare London and obfuscate his designs.[69] Lloyd surveyed the southern coast of England in the guise of a priest, anxiously awaiting a French invasion. On 15 December Charles entered Derby pursued by the Duke of Cumberland. France frantically organized for another invasion at Dunkirk, but they could not muster enough transports for a cross-channel expedition. Without French support Charles retreated into Scotland for want of provisions and men. Lloyd did not rejoin the Jacobite army. He traveled from Milford Haven to Barnstaple and Bridgewater Bay, and then to Plymouth and Devon. From there he ventured to the Downs, Margate, and finally London. The intelligence gathered on his clandestine mission prepared the groundwork for his later treatise on the invasion and defense of Great Britain published in 1779.[70] As John Drummond said of the fruits of this mission: "No man was ever more correct with his eye; he saw at once the advantages and disadvantages of ground, and his remarks were made with so much penetration and judgment, that all his observations were to be depended upon."[71]

On 26 December numerous ships left Dunkirk destined for Boulogne, two days ahead of Richelieu, who found no fleet. It did not matter. The French abandoned the invasion in February 1746 after news arrived that Charles had retreated into Scotland.[72] Undeterred the Jacobites besieged Stirling Castle in January and attacked an English army under Lieutenant-General Henry Hawley (1679–1759) at Falkirk. Once again Charles defeated the English, but his army increasingly suffered from desertion and lack of provisions. The British government thereafter issued General Warrants for the arrest of suspected Jacobites. Due to an unspecified misfortune agents apprehended Lloyd, transported him to London, and placed him under house arrest at the residence of Nathan Carrington, a King's Messenger, for the duration of the rebellion.[73] The incarceration saved him from the debacle in the coming months. Charles's campaign culminated in the devastating Jacobite defeat at Culloden on 27 April 1746 where Cumberland avenged his loss at Fontenoy and gained the sobriquet "The Butcher" for his ruthless extermination of Jacobite refugees. Charles escaped by going into hiding and the Forty-Five came to an abrupt end. One deft observer noted that France had shrewdly fomented civil war without sacrificing a single Frenchman.[74] For Charles and his fellow rebels French failure to invade was tantamount to betrayal.

Supporters of the Young Pretender faced legal and state retribution. Some hanged from the gallows, but most lost their estates and livelihoods. Agents arrested Lord Drummond's son John as a prisoner of war rather than a rebel because he was officially a French subject. His captors sent him to

London in the winter of 1746 where he was reunited with Lloyd, whose role in the rebellion was still unknown. In fact, Lloyd had entertained his captors and made himself an object of interest. They released him from custody due to the intervention of Drummond's relatives. John hired him as a tutor, all the time careful not to reveal their relationship. Lloyd's involvement in the Forty-Five signaled the high watermark of his early career. He probably lacked the religious conviction found in more zealous Jacobites, but like so many others he was attracted to the romanticism and adventure of the Forty-Five. During the next twenty years his convictions and predilections would change. He would abandon his fealty to Jacobitism and the House of Bourbon and embrace the basic tenets of the Enlightenment; essentially transforming his political rebellion into an intellectual one. However, the romantic nature of his character would remain with him throughout his life. He seemed to be driven by a quest for adventure. Accordingly, he and Drummond left England in 1747 and traveled to France where Marshal Saxe was in the throes of unleashing a final military campaign to end the war.[75]

Lloyd's romantic nature suggests an immaturity or perhaps a much deeper pathos exhibited in almost every era: the fascination for the unique and awful activity of war. Often regarded as a sport or game it more closely resembles a ritual, religious in its style and passionate in its substance. The keepers of its traditions acculturate participants with their norms and standards of behavior. For instance, humans do not form lines and unleash volleys of lead into one another by instinct, nor do they naturally wish to inflict such carnage on their fellow men. European warfare in the eighteenth century was highly ritualized, formalized, and codified. Battlefield rules and customs governed the conduct of soldiers and generals, which in turn helped restrict the arc of destruction that followed any army. As reasonable as this ritual seemed, passion lurked beneath its veneered surface ready to erupt with a fury. Nowhere was this innate tension more apparent than at the siege of Bergen-op-Zoom, which exposed Lloyd's romantic image of war as fiction.

Saxe designed the campaign of 1747 to end the long, drawn-out conflict. In 1746 the French army overran much of the Low Countries, capturing Brussels, Antwerp, Mons, St. Chislom, Huy, and Namur. In the process it also defeated the allies twice, humbling Prince Charles of Lorraine in August and rebuffing a combined allied army at Rocoux in October. Saxe believed Maastricht was the key to securing a favorable peace. Throughout May and June 1747 he danced a military minuet with Cumberland's army and gradually advanced toward Breda, a key point on the road to Maastricht. Materially and morally superior, Saxe's army slowly forced the allies backward toward the sea. On 2 July it defeated the allied army at Laffeld and forced it to retreat. The only obstacle between his forces and Maastricht was a strong allied army concentrated there. Unwilling to risk another battle Saxe searched for other means to obtain the objective when his chief subordinate Lowendal proferred a solution. He proposed to lead a detachment of 30,000 men into Dutch Brabant. Such a move, he argued, would compel the allies to send relief from Maastricht and thus expose that city to Saxe's army. The marshal was a prudent man and he deemed the plan unwise. Furthermore he did not want to risk a large part of his army on what was essentially an unnecessary operation. Lowendal wanted a marshal's baton and assured Saxe that if he encountered strong resistance, he would retire and rejoin the main army. Saxe relented and authorized the diversion.[76]

Lowendal's personal objective was the great fortress of Bergen-op-Zoom, or "hill upon the Zoom," situated on the left bank of the Scheldt River.[77] Emmo van Coehoorn had improved older structures and made it a formidable site "so strong by Nature as well as Art, that this, if any Place, may be look'd on as Impregnable."[78] Ten bastions covered with five hornworks adorned the walls that stretched nearly three miles in circumference. The partially deaf octogenarian Isaac Kock, Baron Cronström commanded the town's 3,000 soldiers.[79] Additionally, a fortified camp of twenty battalions and fourteen squadrons was connected to the fortress. Protecting this camp, Forts Moormont, Pinsen, and Rover guarded the region north and east of the citadel. To the west and adjacent to the river was a large marshy landscape that prevented any enemy advance. If this terrain was not enough to ward off would-be attackers, the town was fortunate in that the River Zoom flowed directly through the town's center, with access in and out controlled by the inner gates.[80] A besieging force could not stop water and food supplies shipped via the Scheldt or Zoom. On 12 July Lowendal's army appeared before its walls and opened the trenches two days later.[81] More significant was the fact that the allied army at Maastricht did not come to the fortress's aid. The gambit had failed.

Reports of Lowendal's advance into Dutch Brabant preceded his arrival, and the news was disconcerting. The tradition of military contributions demanded the formal request and delivery of supplies to an invading army by the inhabitants whose land it occupied.[82] Lowendal apparently did not follow these rules regulating plunder. With the French army ten miles east of the fortress, refugees began to trickle in with reports that the invaders were "ruining and depopulating all before them."[83] By the time Lowendal arrived at Bergen-op-Zoom the Dutch thoroughly hated and feared him. At that moment infused with passion the relatively humane rules of siege warfare faded into obscurity. Lowendal expected his terror campaign would convince the over-matched garrison to capitulate, but he misjudged the situation. Instead, he faced a full-blown siege he had to win at all costs. Marshal Saxe later wrote that at Bergen-op-Zoom, "pride overtook prudence, for we were ready to sacrifice our army for this place!"[84]

After rejoining the French army, Henry Lloyd and John Drummond accompanied Lowendal on his ill-conceived operation. As engineers they would play a significant role in the digging of trenches, mining, and sapping. They completed the first line of parallel trenches by 15 July, whereupon the French army assaulted the Dutch ramparts. For a week they repeatedly attacked the outworks with great loss of life.[85] Time was of the essence because Lowendal wanted to present the fortress to Louis XV on his birthday. After a few days he managed only to destroy St. Lambert's Church with incendiary bombs. In retaliation for his indiscriminate attack on their city, the Dutch garrison did not grant his request to suspend action in order to bury his dead. As an observer wrote: "Our batteries keep a continual firing to prevent the enemy's burying their dead, which, as they lie in heaps at the head of their trenches, are a constant nuisance to the workmen."[86] Throughout the siege the dead remained on the field and created a gruesome scene that sapped French morale and fueled their rage.

Lowendal settled in for a long siege. Short on supplies, he sent letters to surrounding areas demanding additional contributions.[87] Lloyd and fellow engineers began the second line of parallel trenches as the French artillery began to pound the Dutch hornworks and bastions. The garrison parried frequent and futile French assaults. In turn, Dutch sorties only escalated the slaughter and atrocities committed by both sides. Fort Rover and Fort Pilsen received the wrath of the French onslaught in early August, but again the Dutch successfully defended these areas. Battery fire also produced considerable havoc on the advancing French lines. By 4 August the Dutch expended nearly 55,000 pounds of shot every twenty-four hours. French casualties numbered above 8,000 as Lowendal's army inched ever so slowly toward the bastions. But a state of insurrection gripped part of his army largely because of the stench of the dead.[88] Nearly 2,000 men deserted, which compelled Lowendal to appeal to Saxe for more men and supplies. On 7 August the French launched their largest assault yet on the covered-way of the town. Again the Dutch repulsed them, this time killing 1,500 attackers.[89]

Engineers and sappers dominated the next phase, which eventually settled into a lengthy period of mining and counter-mining. Lloyd acquired a high reputation in directing these mining operations as well as choosing and mounting batteries.[90] He and others targeted the lunettes of Zealand and Utrecht as troops shouting, "Kill, kill!," assaulted those positions.[91] The slow French advance produced considerable slaughter by the time the engineers began the third line of parallel trenches. On 25 August, the king's birthday, Lowendal was mired in a bloody siege with an army whose morale decreased daily. Frustrated, the would-be marshal ordered red-hot balls and bombs lobbed into the city to terrify the remaining civilian population.[92] Dutch fears mounted as their powder supplies ran low, outworks

The Siege of Bergen-op-Zoom

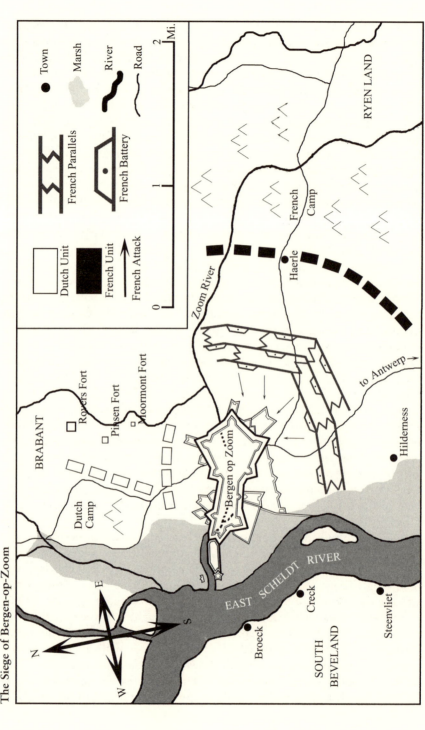

began to crumble, and Lowendal received 700 supply wagons. Vauban's idealistic vision of siege warfare had collapsed into a costly battle of attrition and slaughter.

The final stage of the siege began on 3 September when the Dutch celebrated the birthday of their Stadtholder with a prodigious artillery salvo that caused great misery in the French lines. Indeed, as an observer recalled the morale of the Dutch garrison was high and increased daily.[93] Theirs was a misplaced optimism. On 7 September the French moved their large guns to the nearly completed third line of trenches and began to demolish the counterscarp and punish the town with artillery fire. The next day the lunettes began to crumble and the Dutch army withdrew into the city. They prepared to open the sluices and flood the besiegers if they stormed the fortifications. On 12 September the Dutch faced a serious crisis after the French erected three new batteries in the third trench line. Without the aid of a relief army the storming of Bergen-op-Zoom was imminent. At 4:00 A.M. on 16 September Lowendal attacked with fifty grenadier companies and sixteen infantry battalions. They supposedly penetrated a breach and entered the town via its sally ports.[94] In no time they "drove all before them, notwithstanding the efforts made to oppose them, and forced the entrenchments which the enemy had made in the bastions."[95] Fighting in the city went from house to house and street to street. The Dutch soldiers put up a futile defense as French soldiers put the town's inhabitants to the sword.[96] "My heart bleeds," wrote an allied officer, "when I think of the inhumanities and cruelties committed after the assault upon the poor inhabitants of Bergen-op-Zoom."[97] It was an unremitting scene of horror and destruction. Plundering followed the storming, which one French soldier claimed was impossible to prevent. Lowendal wrote Saxe that he had lost control of his troops and they burned the city against his orders.[98] The marshal quipped that the king "must either hang him [Lowendal] or make him a marshal of France."[99] Louis XV gave Lowendal a marshal's baton.

Altogether these initial exploits and associations provided the genesis and groundwork for Lloyd's military thought. First, he learned the lessons of tactics and their interrelationships with topography. Knowledge of terrain was necessary in war. *Mes Rêveries* provided a model for military theory and an appreciation of those qualities a commander must possess to succeed. Saxe was methodical, cautious, and sophisticated in his techniques. Lloyd admired such prudence, and this admiration is nowhere more evident than in his later military theory based upon lines of operation. In addition to this Fabian-like mentality, Lloyd's experiences with the Young Pretender at Prestonpans and Lowendal at Bergen-op-Zoom provided models for audacious and sometimes reckless action. Prestonpans taught tactical lessons Lloyd incorporated into his New System, but the tragedy of the Jacobites reinforced his emphasis on wise, prudent action. The rash nature of the Young Pretender's invasion led to an army beset with desertion, unable to feed itself, and finally defeated and routed. Lowendal's siege of Bergen-op-Zoom offered another case against rash action. Only material superiority overcame his imprudence. The sacking and slaughter perpetrated by the French army also demonstrated the need for battlefield command and control. An army's strength and discipline rested in Lloyd's estimation on the general's authority and powers of persuasion, not on force or coercion.[100] Bergen-op-Zoom revealed the inherent tension within war between the forces of order, reason, and control and the passions of fear, hatred, and revenge. Henry Lloyd's theory of warfare sought to craft methods that would promote the forces of order and regulate the passions.

The Treaty of Aix-la-Chapelle concluded the War of the Austrian Succession in 1748. The conflict's end created new problems for soldiers faced with the prospect of unemployment. Henry Lloyd was not immune to the tenuous nature of the military profession. Lowendal promoted him to the rank of major during the siege, but with the peace Lloyd saw no future in French service.[101] Drummond traveled to Spain and Lloyd received an appointment in the Prussian service with the help of James Keith, a personal friend of Frederick II and a former Jacobite. He served Prussia from 1748–54 and traveled often, publishing in 1761 the fruits of his observations.[102] As a tutor, rebel, intelligence officer, and engineer Lloyd gained valuable experience, but had not reached his ultimate goal. He had not achieved any measure of fame and there seemed to be little opportunity for him to do so. But Europe's winds of war did not subside; they merely changed direction. Henry Lloyd soon found himself participating in the century's most destructive conflict, the Seven Years' War, which propelled him to the rank of military historian and philosopher.

Toward a Theory
of Principles

I did not draw my principles from my prejudices but from the nature of things.

—*Montesquieu,* The Spirit of the Laws

Lloyd gained valuable military experience in the ensuing decade, from which he developed the foundation of his military theory. He was fortunate to live at a time when European politics created ample employment for military adventurers. All the great powers viewed war as a means to protect and enhance their interests. Prussia retained Silesia, Austria coveted its lost province, and both Great Britain and France sought more influence in the extra-European world. In 1755 a colonial conflict erupted between Great Britain and France, followed by a new German war between Austria and Prussia the next year. The synthesis of these two conflicts, the Seven Years' War, was the formative military event in Henry Lloyd's life. He served both sides, first the Austrians and then the Prussians, and combined this experience with his education to devise the first elements of his military thought. First, Lloyd became a premier military historian and sought to use his writings as instructional tools for officers. Next, he distilled the "principles of war" from his experience and study of the war's campaigns. These elements formed the core of his early military thought and provided a basis for his later studies on man and society. Even with these accomplishments, he still faced societal barriers of the old European order. To advance his career, Lloyd still had to rely on his competence, intellect, and strength of character to elevate his esteem, notoriety, and social standing above that of the ordinary professional soldier.

Lloyd rejoined the French army in 1754 and obtained the rank of major with the daily pay of five *louis*. His previous French service and Jacobite experience attracted the attention of Marshal Belle-Isle, who envisioned yet another invasion of England.[1] The Diplomatic Revolution engineered by Wenzel Anton, Reichsgraf von Kaunitz-Rietburg (1711–97) of Austria recently aligned that country with France and Russia. Kaunitz's entente targeted Prussia; Belle-Isle wanted to use it against Great Britain. When the eve of war approached he ordered Lloyd to cross the English Channel, survey the English coast, and determine if and where an invasion was feasible. Disguised as a merchant, he fulfilled the clandestine mission and presented his report to Belle-Isle in 1756. Lloyd's analysis kept the minister from attacking England; he considered an invasion next to impossible.[2] Instead, the French government looked at the advantages of fighting a colonial war. But Frederick II of Prussia upset their strategy when he invaded Saxony on 29 August 1756, thereby precipitating a continental conflict.

France did not immediately join Austria and Russia in their crusade against Prussia, and Lloyd chaffed anxiously to experience war. He resigned his French commission and rejected offers to rejoin his Spanish friends. With the aid of the Marqués de la Mina he secured letters of introduction to *Feldmarschall* Joseph Wenzel Laurenz, Fürst von Liechtenstein (1696–1772) and Christoph Bartholomäus Anton, Graf Migazzi zu Wall und Sonnenthurn (1714–1803), the Archbishop of Vienna. He traveled to the Habsburg capital and impressed Migazzi, who recommended him to *Feldmarschall* Leopold Josef, Reichsgraf von Daun (1705–66). Lloyd thereafter departed to join *Feldmarschall-Leutenant* (Lieutenant-General) Franz Moritz, Graf von Lacy's (1718–1800) *Generalquartiermeister* corps in the winter 1758–59.[3] Like other notable Habsburg generals Lacy was an outsider from an Irish Jacobite family.[4] After entering the Austrian army in 1740, he had quickly advanced in rank due to his intelligence, organizational skills, and erudition in military theory. He acquired the rank of *General-Feldwachtmeister* (Major-General) in 1756 and *Feldmarschall-Leutenant* when he took over command of the staff corps in 1758. His *Generalquartiermeister* or staff corps, a product of the Empress-Queen's postwar reforms, handled the functions of chief of staff for the army, which initially included planning campsites and protecting baggage.[5] Lacy used it as the eyes and the *ad hoc* nervous system of the Austrian army. It planned and directed marching routes on campaign and gathered information on the Prussian foe. In this capacity his corps repeatedly frustrated the plans of Frederick the Great and his lieutenants during the Seven Years' War and was responsible for several Austrian victories.

An excellent organizer and planner, Lacy personally assembled and trained the personnel for the corps because he intended to make it the elite arm of the Austrian army. Under his leadership, the staff emerged as the most professional military institution in Maria Theresa's armed forces. It required of its members a high level of dedication, education, and scientific expertise. Each handpicked recruit required knowledge of cartography, the gift of *coup d'oeil,* and the ability to make quick decisions. He commanded two major generals and a coterie of *Titular-Obrists* (colonels), *Obrist-Leutenants* (lieutenant colonels), *Majors,* and *Hauptmänner* (captains) until the staff grew large enough to add intelligence gathering and operational planning.[6] Armed with letters of recommendation, Lloyd located the new *Generalquartiermeister* and introduced himself in November 1758. The details of the meeting below provide a glimpse into Lloyd's character and the dynamics of military society in general.

The cosmopolitan world of eighteenth-century military life revolved around patronage and reputation. Because of his plebeian birth, Lloyd struggled past these hurdles to entry and promotion. He always managed to secure the "protection" of a well-placed person as a prerequisite for office, not an uncommon *modus operandi* even for lesser nobles. For a military adventurer, outsider, and non-noble, the "protection" and recommendation of influential patrons was indispensable. Pietro Verri later remarked that Lloyd possessed a seductive, warm manner and spoke the language of generosity and nobility; a gift that may have helped him mingle in polite society.[7] The Marqués de la Mina, Lord John Drummond, Marshal Saxe, and Lowendal all served these ends, and they partially determined Lloyd's career advancement. Now, all patrons were dead except the Marqués, who opened the door to Austrian service for his protégé. Lacy interviewed the Welshman in the presence of his subordinates, and after reading Lloyd's papers explained he could provide only the subaltern commission of *Leutenant* in the army's baggage guard. Lloyd recognized the insult and responded that he had not traveled nearly nine hundred miles to guard the army's baggage. The exchange was as follows:

Lacy: What therefore have you come here to do?

Lloyd: To learn the profession of war.

Lacy: [with a mocking laughter] So you want to understand the profession of war?

Lloyd: I want to understand what I suppose Your Excellency knows.

Lacy: I do not have a position for a man with so much talent.

Lloyd: [pause] Sir, you do not know me; maybe I do not have the highest merit, but perhaps today I possess more of it than you.[8]

After turning his back to Lacy, Lloyd departed and applied for a return passport to Vienna. Lacy respected his straightforward manner and upon reflection changed his mind. He located the fiery Welshman and made him an aide-de-camp with the commission of *Ober-Leutenant* (first lieutenant).[9] In a larger context, Lloyd's interview symbolized the general tension within eighteenth-century elite society. Lloyd represented the world of merit and talent as opposed to the world of privilege and birth that dominated the military caste. Fortunately for Lloyd, the Habsburg military apparatus had yet to be monopolized by central authority, thereby allowing disproportionate numbers of military adventurers and foreigners to serve.[10] Aside from the institutional imperative, Lloyd succeeded because like-minded individuals, in this case Lacy, prized talent and merit more than status. Verri used the episode to comment on Lloyd's two personal shortcomings: impatience and a propensity to speak as an equal to his superiors. "They are defects that will jeopardize his future if they are not controlled," he wrote.[11]

Even after successfully entering an army, advancement and promotion remained an entirely different matter. This was especially true in the Austrian army, an illustrative example of the "state-commission" army.[12] The volunteer rank-and-file came predominantly from Habsburg domains, often augmented by foreign mercenaries when the army experienced recruiting shortfalls. The officer corps, like the soldiery, also exhibited a wide range of social diversity. Landowning Magnates reigned supreme at the highest levels of command. They often raised or maintained regiments from their own pocket, making them attractive to the monetarily anemic Habsburg government.[13] Selling officer commissions to these wealthy aristocrats provided much-needed revenue for state coffers and helped stratify the officer corps along lines of privilege. Lesser nobles and commoners struggled to purchase promotions and advance through the seniority-based promotion system. The financial imperative of this "state-commission" army outweighed the sense of inequity or inefficiency it created. As a subaltern officer, Lt. Lloyd faced a career barrier from the outset. Like many ambitious gentlemen adventurers, he seemed destined to languish in this so-called officer "proletariat" from which few escaped.[14] Lacy's patronage and favor helped further his career. When Lloyd resigned his commission in 1761, he had advanced rapidly in rank, rising from *Ober-Leutenant* to *Hauptmann.*

Three factors contributed to his quick promotion. First, he was highly intelligent and erudite in the theory of war and the specifics of planning; second, he impressed influential persons; and third, he exhibited relentless energy and zeal in his duties. Not the standard basis for promotion, Lloyd's abilities and capacity for work impressed Lacy and cleared traditional obstacles to advancement. Pietro Verri, whom Lloyd met in Saxony in 1759, claimed that his friend "knew incomparably more than anyone else in camp."[15] Unlike the typical Habsburg officer he understood the details of regimental life and he actually educated his Italian friend in the ways of the military. Verri often accompanied him on reconnaissance missions where

Lloyd explained the interaction and relationship between armies and topography. Noting Lloyd's gift of *coup d'œil*, Verri claimed: "I have learned more in the time with my friend Lloyd than I would have learned on my own in a year and a half with these officers."[16] The Welshman also exhibited a calm and at times humorous demeanor in the face of danger. On one reconnaissance mission he actually persuaded a Prussian outpost they stumbled upon not to attack. In another encounter Lloyd wildly mocked a party of Hussars caught on the wrong side of a ravine, prompting the astonished Verri to exclaim: "I assure you [Alessandro] he is the only man of his kind."[17] He also valued Lloyd's friendship in a less-than civilized environment. "Lloyd is my mentor, my consolation," he wrote, "the more I know of him, the more I esteem and admire him."[18] His praise bordered on veneration, but Verri's description offers the best insight into Lloyd's personality. "Lloyd has a passion for war which is untiring," he explained.[19] His military romanticism, intellect, and charitable nature struck Verri as profound. A high degree of intelligence and compassion differentiated him from the average mercenary. For instance, a poor officer himself, Lloyd was highly generous to friends and subordinates. When assigned a task such as the construction of field fortifications, he would labor alongside his men and refer to them as "brothers."[20]

Foreign observers valued Lloyd for his succinct and frank opinion of the war effort and his knowledge of military theory. Observers like the French general Antoine de Montazet, Dom João Carlos, duque de Bragança, and Ludwig, Fürst von Württemberg sought his opinion on Austria's campaigns.[21] Lacy also valued his energy and bravery, calling him *Souffre-douleurs* in reference to his ability to accomplish difficult or dangerous tasks. One day Lacy left on a reconnaissance mission and ordered no one to follow. Lloyd learned of this and shadowed Lacy to insure his safe return. After being admonished for his insubordination, Lloyd asked, "Do you believe, my General, that you are the only brave one?"[22] Touched by his flattery Lacy did not reprimand him and from that instance "employed him in every thing and in preference to all others."[23] Fellow officers, in part jealous of Lacy's favoritism, disliked Lloyd's behavior. Verri wrote his brother: "Lloyd is generally feared and hated because he does not know how to restrain himself from displaying the contempt he has for those he believes deserve it."[24] He was opinionated and habitually gave unsolicited advice to superiors and fellow officers. In November 1759 he urged the Austrian command to attack the Prussian army camped near Torgau by setting fire to the countryside and surprising the enemy through the smoke screen.[25] No one listened to a mere *Ober-Leutenant*. The anecdote in part reflected Lloyd's disillusionment with the slow, cautious methods of the Austrian army under Marshal Daun. "They [the Austrians] had not, it should seem, any fixed plan of operations," he later wrote, "they wandered from one place to the other, waiting events."[26] He told the observers that the Austrians could easily win the war if Daun would be more aggressive.[27] Insubordination only increased the contempt noble officers had for the poor, non-noble Welshman.

For a time Verri financially supported Lloyd, but in the winter of 1759–60 his situation was dire. Nearly destitute, he told his friend that without a promotion he would be forced to leave.[28] Lloyd approached Lacy and revealed that the Spanish army had offered him a commission with a salary of 100 florins. He confessed that poverty forced his hand and he could not long remain without a promotion. Impressed by his honesty, Lacy immediately appointed him *Hauptmann* (captain) in the *Feld-Jäger-Corps* (light infantry).[29] Fellow officers disliked this fast-track promotion, but respected his abilities and considered him a talented officer. Verri viewed the promotion as bittersweet because his friend soon departed to serve his new commission.[30] Captain Lloyd commanded a company of soldiers (approximately 125–75 men).[31] The *Jägers* excelled in reconnaissance missions, a role that emphasized speed and mobility, and provided a screen for the army's advance guard. These dangerous tasks were the chief means by which Austria collected intelligence on its Prussian enemy. The Prussians, however, failed to employ widespread reconnaissance, and Frederick often found himself blind as to what his enemy was doing. Only the lackluster leadership of the high command prevented the Austrian army from exploiting its advantage. Lloyd distinguished himself in his new role. Throughout the 1760 campaign he successfully commanded a large contingent of infantry and cavalry (200 chasseurs and 100 dragoons) to observe, shadow, and follow Frederick's army.[32] Career possibilities seemed endless at this point when Lloyd's tendency toward controversy led to his resignation.

The politics of the Austrian army involved a clash of personalities between Lacy (promoted to *Feldzeugmeister* or General in 1760) and *Feldmarschall* Gideon Ernst Loudon (1717–90), another Russian-trained commander.[33] Lloyd obviously favored Lacy, which exposed him to the wrath and intrigues of Loudon's supporters.[34] In particular, he quarreled with the new commander of the staff corps, Josef, Graf von Siškovíc apparently over promotion.[35] The travails did not end there. He also defended an officer unjustly charged of wrongdoing, and incurred the wrath of his superiors when he openly spoke in favor of the accused. Disgusted with his maltreatment, he resigned his commission at the end of February 1761.[36] Verri's prediction about Lloyd's character had come true. The Austrian high command feared that Lloyd, now intimately familiar with the inner-workings of the army and its methods of campaigning, marching, and reconnaissance, may join the Prussian army. They demanded a pledge from him that he would not offer his services to the King of Prussia. With characteristic pride he responded: "I am an Englishman; I am free; I shall give to whom I please my sword and my heart; however, I have no objection to promise that I will not offer my services to the King of Prussia."[37] Upon Liechtenstein's request, Lloyd joined the Court of Prince Xavier Auguste of Saxony (1730–1806) during the winter of 1761. Bored with courtly life he kept his promise not to offer his services to Prussia until Karl I, Herzog von Brunswick (1713–80) offered him employment. Under the aegis of Brunswick, an ally of Prussia, Lloyd served in the last two campaigns of the war (1761–62).[38]

Lloyd had joined the Austrian army to learn the military profession and had excelled in his duties while closely observing military operations and battles. He carefully studied battles, took notes, and compiled various accounts and reports, often observing a site from the foot of a hill or tree line.[39] His intense study and knowledge of war impressed his contemporaries. From personal experience and observation (empirical evidence was the bedrock of his theory) he developed a method of writing military history and analyzing campaigns. The fruit of his early intellectual labor embodied two volumes entitled *The History of the Late War in Germany,* one published anonymously in 1766 and the other posthumously in 1790. Interest in the war, especially its military operations, peaked in the post-war decade as soldiers studied Frederick the Great's battles in order to understand and copy his methods. In the long run the war had profound implications for the history of Europe and the future United States. Lloyd and other participants considered it different from previous wars because it had exhibited a "sense of movement and change restrained by an instinct for order and balance."[40] He had witnessed the occurrences of the war, which at times appeared to escape the control of both civilian and military masters. The Seven Years' War could provide lessons to the military elite that would advance their understanding of the military profession.[41]

Lloyd formulated what he called a "New Plan" for the study of military history. In order to understand the context and form of military operations, he thought it important to "give a clear, and exact account of the most essential transactions which have occurred, during the course of this important war."[42] Actually, his stated purpose was not new; it was ancient. Thucydides, over two thousand years earlier, proposed and justified his account of the Peloponnesian War (431–404 B.C.) using similar reasoning. Lloyd too justified his authorship by invoking his own participation in the war and method of collecting sources: written accounts of battles by participants.[43] He also spent much of his time traveling across Europe revisiting battle sites. Thus, the so-called scientific historical method of Thucydides resurfaced. But Lloyd did more than emulate Greco-Roman authors. His method related to his own understanding of the two forms of contemporary military writing: didactic and historical. The difference between the two types held a double meaning. Didactic works attempted to delineate rules and guidance for military officers, but they lacked historical basis or explanation. Rules, principles, and precepts were meaningless and forgettable without an empirical framework. Didactic writers also tended to be non-military figures. Lloyd aimed his critique and prejudice against writers, Niccolò Machiavelli for example, who analyzed war via fictional battles.[44]

Lloyd admired the historical writers encountered during his education. He invoked the Greek and Roman historians, Xenophon, Polybius, Caesar, and Arrian, and argued that narrative history was the ideal method of conveying the art of war. The "Battle of the Books" over the relative import of the ancients vis-à-vis modern writers during the late seventeenth and early eighteenth centuries informed him on this account.[45] Proponents of the ancients believed they had understood the world in a more comprehensive manner than modern writers did. Lloyd judged ancient histories to be more valuable than those of modern writers because the latter were "chiefly men of learning, and utterly unacquainted with the nature of military operations."[46] Historical writers surpassed didactic writers in so far as they too had military experience. In short, writing military history was best left to educated professional soldiers. Of course, his target audience consisted chiefly military men; he admitted as much.[47] Lloyd's dichotomy of the two groups of writers revealed his own prejudices against civilian historians and the tensions inherent to civil-military relations in general.

Lloyd's history acted as a conduit between the ancient historical heritage and modern analytical writing developed during the Enlightenment.[48] He venerated ancient writers, but he was not fettered to their outlook. His was a romantic and superficial adoration.[49] For instance, his "New Plan" included a methodology absent even in the works of the most celebrated ancient historians. He chastised modern and ancient writers for failing to understand the role geography played in military campaigns and to explain the numbers of troops engaged in war, as well as how they were armed and arrayed. Previous authors developed general explanations of wars and military campaigns, but they failed to understand war's interaction with geography. Without geographic knowledge Lloyd, an engineer by training, considered it impossible to understand the nature of war. His more detailed empirical method could achieve an accuracy of understanding unequaled by ancient historians.[50] The analytical tools illustrate the utility of this new plan. First, his history incorporated analyses of the political events that sparked the war as well as a geo-political survey of the belligerents. Lloyd's "War & Society" approach was embodied in the "Preliminary Discourse" of the first volume accompanied by the "seat of war," or an overview of the military geography of central Europe explained through hand-drawn maps.[51] The "seat of war" outlined the limitations imposed on operations by geography, while the "Preliminary Discourse" analyzed the goals of the various belligerents. Often critical of foreign governments and prominent individuals who might influence his career, Lloyd published the book anonymously, thereby diminishing any negative publicity he might receive.[52]

Lloyd's primary contribution to military history was his steadfast method for describing battles, campaigns, and entire operations. He was one of the first military writers to conceive of operations as a long sequence of interrelated events with their own beginning, process, and termination point. "All accounts of battles, from malice or ignorance," he asserted, "are generally imperfect, and very often false."[53] Too much superfluous material made historical examinations of war useless. His general rule for analyzing a campaign was "to leave out everything that is not connected with the operations of the troops, and to give an exact description of the ground.[54] He believed first-hand accounts, especially his own, were far more valuable than plans or secondary sources. Where he did not witness a battle, he visited the site and then used accounts from participants that seemed plausible.[55] The battles were central to his narrative, but not ends in themselves.

Lloyd's criticism of Frederick the Great sparked a controversy that survived long after the Welshman's death. In general he argued the king's pride and secretive nature led him to commit political and military mistakes that led to an avoidable European war. First, Frederick had discovered that his enemies planned to wage war against him, but he did not try to counterbalance Kaunitz's alliance with one of his own. Second, had Frederick attacked in 1755 or early in 1756 his enemies could not have defended themselves. Last, Frederick should have advanced rapidly into Bohemia rather than consolidating his hold on Saxony, because he could have opened the next campaign with a siege of Vienna.[56] The Prussian Georg Friedrich von Tempelhof (1737–1807) wrote his multi-volume history of the Seven Years' War primarily to refute Lloyd's criticisms.[57] The Prussian mainly attacked Lloyd's descriptions of battles using a wider array of source material. But it is shortsighted to condemn Lloyd for not having access to official Prussian documents. Tempelhof's attempt to make Frederick a peaceful king and flawless military genius is suspect. In fact, he seemed far more interested in attacking Lloyd for critiquing Frederick the Great, which perhaps began the century long hagiography the Prussian and German General Staff used with success against later critics, most notably Hans Delbrück.

Derived from the historical content of his work, Lloyd deduced the principles of war from his analysis of military operations. These principles governed war and existed in nature like Newton's laws of gravity and physics. Whereas the universe operated in vast space, the mechanics of war operated on a frictional geographic plane. Those officers who misunderstood or misapplied these principles suffered defeat; those who respected them achieved a higher measure of success. Because of his effort, critics warmly recommended *The History of the Late War in Germany* "to the perusal of all those who are engaged in the study of the art of war."[58] It went through numerous foreign editions and had a diverse readership included Henry Clinton, John Adams, Alexander Hamilton, Samuel Bentham, and Winfield

Scott.[59] As a modern Thucydides, Lloyd presented the history of war in the most accurate way possible; as the Newton of warfare he sought to delineate the principles and rules that guided its conduct.

The belief that underlying principles governed the technique and form of war did not arise with the Enlightenment. The genesis was seventeenth-century French Classicism, which interpreted art, painting, sculpture, literature, etc. using rational language in an effort to transform the sublime into a logical, coherent system.[60] Eighteenth-century theorists or Neo-Classicists inherited this outlook and sought to imitate and represent nature as a whole using the process of mimesis, borrowed from Aristotle, whom they considered the first western art theorist.[61] Military writers influenced by French Classicism and ancient authority interpreted war as an art and sought to distill its principles and rules.[62] With a mosaic-like intellectual heritage, Lloyd developed his own body of theory from various precedents. Lloyd argued the art of war was "founded on certain and fixed principles, which are by their nature invariable."[63] In a confusing dichotomy, the science of war, on the other hand, comprised two distinct parts. The first element involved all that prepared an army for war such as training, marching, and basic education for officers. A straightforward equation in Lloyd's estimation, this facet was obvious could be mastered by everyone. The second element Lloyd deemed not teachable: "it consists in the just application of the principles and precepts of war, in all the numberless circumstances, and situations, which occur, no rule, no study, and application, however assiduous, no experience, however long, can teach this part."[64] The skepticism implicit in this statement reveals a pervasive characteristic of his philosophical outlook. Within a complex world and its web of events, humans were limited in their ability to understand the meaning behind such complex phenomena as warfare.

The first element of the science of war comprised three general laws or principles, analogous to Newton's mechanical laws of motion. A comprehensive statement of organizing principles for training and doctrine, they are as follows:

1st Law, Principle: "That a soldier be cloathed [*sic*] and armed relative to the action he is to perform."

2nd Law, Principle: "That he be taught nothing, but what is of use to him, in the different situations which can occur, before the enemy."

3rd Law, Principle: "That he [an officer] be taught everything that is absolutely necessary for him to know, in every case that may happen."[65]

Lloyd used these principles to criticize contemporary military institutions. The Seven Years' War had exposed grave defects in the organization of European armies. As a reformer Lloyd proposed new clothing for troops because the current hat and woolen coat "exposed [the soldier] to the inclemency of the weather, and being tight, hindered the men from moving with ease and facility."[66] He calculated that illness during winter campaigning inflicted a 25 percent casualty rate because of this uniform. "I would therefore recommend it to those, who have it in their power," he suggested, "to invent some better form of dress as well out of humanity, as for the service of their country."[67] Attrition rates due to sickness were high in any season, but lighter more comfortable clothing would partially solve the manpower shortage that all European armies faced. Perhaps influenced by his experience with the Austrian army Lloyd feared that most officers knew little about the art of war and had reduced it to the science of adjusting hats and buttons. The adoption of Prussian training and dress by European armies met with his disapproval. Ignorant of these principles his contemporaries "with great care and diligence, even with a degree of madness, introduced the Prussian exercise into all the troops of Europe."[68] Drill alone did not translate into military effectiveness, that quality resulted from adherence to the general principles of war.

The Austrian and Russian use of artillery batteries during the war demonstrated the efficacy and firepower of gunpowder weapons in general. Lloyd, who considered the musket the best infantry weapon developed, observed drawbacks to its use because it was awkward to hold and slow to fire. First, he proposed increasing its length by two feet thereby moving the center of gravity toward the breech. Next, instead of the muzzle-loader, he called for the development of a breech-loading musket. These changes would make it easier to handle and increase the rate of fire. To complement the new ordnance, he called for the reintroduction of the lance or pike, not nearly as forward-looking as his other reforms. "I confess," he wrote, "I think it [the lance] a very useful arm on many occasion; and particularly in the attack and defence of retrenchments, and against cavalry."[69] He had witnessed and studied many modern battles like Fontenoy where frontal assaults using muskets proved ineffective and highly fatal. He believed the lance would solve this tactical problem. The soldier could rapidly advance without stopping to reload. Thus, it offered a chance for tactical decisiveness based upon hand-to-hand and close-quarter combat. In certain circumstances it might prove useful, but overall the breech-loading musket's increased accuracy and rate of fire would counterbalance any of the supposed advantages. Eighteenth-century technology could not solve the tactical dilemma caused by muskets and gunpowder weapons in general, but Lloyd's argument was a practical one within the context of the times.[70]

Lloyd also advocated a proto-*Auftragstaktik* approach to decentralized command decision-making. The manual of arms, he argued, needed simplification because it involved far too many steps. The technical efficiency of the Prussian army convinced him that reducing the firing drill to six to eight steps would increase the effectiveness of the soldier. Training reform would enable troops to be proficient "in all the different cases which occur before

the enemy"[71] and facilitated a higher level of independent action during battle. His concerns reflected the growing complexity and expansion of the
battlefield during the eighteenth century. The growth of armies made rigid
centralized decision-making in the heat of the battle difficult if not impossible. Once engaged, Lloyd believed low-level officers had to take the initiative and make quick, important decisions based upon training and their
overall education in the military profession.

Disgusted by the mediocre ability of his fellow officers, Lloyd emphati-
cally promoted "all that can be taught in the art of war:"[72] education,
marching, firing, maneuvering, fortifications, artillery, and geography. Officer incompetence resulted from the failure of military institutions to intel-
lectually study their own profession.[73] Lloyd believed all education and
training should focus on preparation for battle, "the key which leads to all
the sublime motions of an army."[74] For instance, he abridged marching to
three steps: slow, fast, and oblique. The latter should be used when forming columns in the face of an enemy, much like Frederick the Great's famous
oblique line of battle. Again, he stressed simplification. "That evolution is
best," he argued, "which with a given number of men, may be executed in
the least space, and consequently in the least time."[75] Converting battlefield
formations rapidly from line to column and vice versa was the hallmark of
an effective army and foreshadowed the basics of Napoleonic grand tactics.
Impressed by Frederick's success in the Seven Years' War, Lloyd concluded:
"[T]he army which marches the best must, if the rest is equal, in the end
prevail."[76]

The commander required knowledge of geometry and arithmetic in order
to develop proficiency in maneuvering.[77] For example, a soldier occupied
two feet from elbow to elbow and made a step every second, with each step
equaling twenty inches. An educated commander, he argued, could plan
and execute any type of maneuver using these simple facts. "A little experience," he claimed, "and a certain *coup d'œil,* ordered by this theory, will
enable a man to judge with great precision, of the time and space necessary
to execute any evolution whatever."[78] Battlefield maneuver was the most
difficult facet of command, and Lloyd considered the officer corps of
Europe deficient in the proper understanding of this topic. "The ignorance
of generals in this sublime and delicate part of war," he wrote, "is the reason why you see them quite suspended in time of action, incapable of
changing their plan, according as new circumstances arise."[79] Therefore, the
knowledge of principles meant little if the officer failed to learn the funda-
mentals of his profession.

Geography formed the link between the two elements of the study of war,
its organization and its practice. As a metaphor of physics, an army was a
body with impulse that traversed a topographic or frictional plane.[80] Various types of terrain such as rivers, forests, and mountains posed unique
obstacles and required specific operations. Lloyd emphasized the concept of

the geographic strong point, the key to all military operations. "The science of positions, camps, marches, and even the project of campaign or plan of operations," he wrote, "must be regulated by these points.[81] They reduced chance and uncertainty by providing reference points for campaign analysis and planning. He concluded: "[W]ise generals, will always choose to make them the foundation of their conduct.[82] Geography enabled the commander to formulate a campaign and define concrete objectives for the use of military force.[83]

The general principles of war followed the tradition of European military thought which concentrated primarily on the organization of armed forces. The second element of the science of war was more complex than the first; it involved the conduct of war and rules which governed warfare. Lloyd intertwined principles and rules to that effect within *The History of the Late War in Germany,* but never presented them in list form. Drawn from his experience and reflection, they are the ancestors of the "Principles of War" found in nearly every western military institution.[84]

The battles of Zorndorf (25 August 1758) and Paltzig (23 July 1759) shaped Lloyd's theoretical disposition toward the offensive and defensive. In the former battle, Frederick attempted to repeat his Leuthen victory, this time pitting his 37,000 Prussians against 43,000 Russians under Count William Fermor in East Prussia. The oblique attack failed to surprise the Russians, and Frederick's frontal assault ended in mutual exhaustion and stalemate. At Paltzig, out of desperation the Prussian Lieutenant-General Johann von Wedell with 23,000 soldiers attacked Russian General Peter Saltykov's 48,000 troops. Wedell's frontal assault ground to a halt and the Russians inflicted 8,000 casualties on his army.[85] These examples convinced Lloyd that to successfully attack troops with modern armament an army had to move quickly. Gaining the initiative was imperative to victory. The principle of the offensive, therefore, occupied the center of his operational concept. He warned against slow, cautious attacks and encouraged rapidity of motion and velocity. Once victorious an army had to pursue the defeated enemy and annihilate it.[86] Echoing a later tenet of Napoleonic warfare, Lloyd's concept of the offensive was aggressive, audacious, and decisive.

The study of such battles as Kolin (18 June 1757) and Leuthen (5 December 1757) tempered Lloyd's aggressive outlook. At Kolin Frederick suffered his first defeat, due to faulty intelligence and reckless generalship. An Austrian army of 55,000 men attempting to relieve Frederick's siege of Prague actually surprised and routed the entire Prussian army of 25,000 men as it made a blind frontal assault. At Leuthen the Prussian king advanced with 39,000 men against an Austrian army exceeding 66,000. Frederick maneuvered under cover of terrain and attacked the left wing of the Austrians at an oblique angle. He surprised them, routed the left wing, and defeated the entire army. The Austrians lost 3,000 dead, 7,000 wounded, and 12,000 prisoners.[87] In Lloyd's opinion risking a battle against a superior enemy was sheer folly, but he did not forsake the traditional clash of armies. Maneuvering against an enemy's communications or tactical flank (as at Leuthen) he thought more effective than opposing it head-on. Only for the sake of preserving an important city, fortress, or key geographic point should a commander on the defensive risk battle.[88] For prudence's sake an inferior army was obliged to retire and retreat, if need be in many small detachments.[89] Lloyd considered movement and action more important than battle, especially when disastrous results could occur from an ill-considered engagement. The defensive principle was similar to George Washington's basic strategy: keep an army in being and exhaust the enemy.

Lloyd's emphasis on the centrality of achieving an objective also tempered his more natural offensive impulse. "I am of the opinion," he argued, "that no operation whatever should be attempted, or post attacked, unless the possession of it be absolutely necessary to facilitate some capital enterprise."[90] The lackluster Austrian campaign of 1758 served as his model of lethargic leadership. Frederick's army was battered and bruised by the Russian army in East Prussia, but Daun could not decide upon a plan of action, relegating most activity to raiding supply lines. Lloyd accused Daun's headquarters of "waiting events . . . schemes, new projects were made and none executed; such a vague and undetermined mode of making war, renders it everlasting, and finally it ends in doing nothing at all."[91] Lloyd understood the aim of a military operation according to define an objective and pursue it without distraction.[92] Therefore it was imperative that the commander gather as much data and intelligence as possible.[93]

A more debatable principle was Lloyd's concept of mass and army size. He agreed with conventional wisdom that a field army should not exceed 50,000 men. In part, the difficulty of supplying and moving large numbers of soldiers without adequate roads and communications limited the number of men in a given army. Simplicity was essential. The more numbers, the greater the confusion and chaos. He concluded: "[T]he only advantage of a superior army, in a day of action, consists in this only, that the general can bring more men into action than the enemy; but if they do not move with facility and quickness, and are not all brought into action at the same time, that superiority of numbers will be of no use: on the contrary, will serve only to increase the confusion."[94] Lloyd reflected the standard opinion of his day. He continued by singling out a spectacular operation conducted by the Prussian General Wunsch against superior Austrian opponents in 1759. "By all this one sees," he quipped, "that a brave man, with a few troops, who have confidence in him, can do great things; and that numbers are nothing in the hands of an ignorant General."[95] With this example, he concluded too much from too little. Most future critics of Lloyd pointed to the efficacy of Napoleon's large armies; yet, the nature of Europe's military infrastructure in the mid-eighteenth century could not support armies on the Napoleonic scale. It should be noted that even with national conscription a Napoleonic corps never exceeded 50,000 men and usually numbered 30,000.[96]

Russian operations in East Prussia convinced Lloyd of the value of the principle of maneuver. After their victory at Kunersdorf (12 August 1759) the Russians failed to appreciate what he called the "lines of operation," or imaginary lines or zones of control stretching from an army, through its supply points, to its home base. "It is a certain rule, from which a General ought never depart," wrote Lloyd, "to shorten continually as he advances his line of operation, by forcing new depots behind him on *that very line,* and no where else, otherwise he cannot move at all."[97] The Russian lines of operation had extended too far, and the threat to their unprotected flanks caused them to withdraw.[98] Lloyd expanded this definition of lines of operation and developed the strategic benefit of interior lines. He proclaimed: "It is owing to this circumstance [interior lines] that the King [Frederick the Great] was enabled to support both countries [Saxony and Silesia] during the whole war, by marching from one to the other as occasion required."[99] Thus, Lloyd prefigured the Napoleonic concept of the strategy of the central position, in which an army interposed between two hostile forces attacks and defeats them in detail. Indeed, this was the key strategic reality the anti-Prussian coalition confronted during the war.

Lloyd also fashioned operational and tactical maneuvers from his study and experience in the battles of Leuthen, Hochkirch (14 October 1758), and Maxen (20 November 1759). Inspired by Frederick's use of terrain at the battle of Leuthen, he delineated perhaps the first statement of the principle of economy of force. Lloyd did not witness the battle but concluded: "That general, who, by the faculty of his motions, or by artifice can bring more men into action, at the same time, and at the same point, must if the troops are equally good, necessarily prevail."[100] Rather than making large, difficult frontal assaults, he believed that partial attacks were more successful, because "you can bring part of your line to act against particular points: whereas the other parts of the enemy's line must remain inactive."[101] Such reasoning applied equally to the operational or strategic level as to the tactical sphere.

From his analysis of the battle of Maxen, Lloyd outlined an operational *manœuvre sur les derrières.* Frederick sent a Prussian detachment of 15,000 men into Saxony under Friedrich August von Finck to block the road from Bohemia and threaten Marshal Daun's supply lines. Lacy persuaded Daun to make an aggressive move against the Prussian detachment. He concurred and the Austrians won an overwhelming victory by enveloping the Prussian position with three columns.[102] Lloyd fought at Maxen and provided shrewd insight into the Prussian debacle. He considered Finck's position hopeless: "Neither he [Finck] nor any general on earth, could have escaped the catastrophe which befell him."[103] Lacy's overall plan and the surprise

The Battle of Maxen

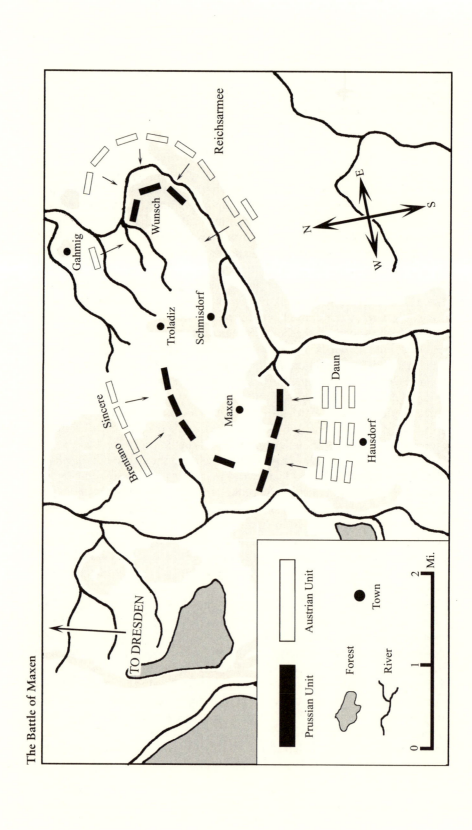

Reichsarmee

Gahmig

Wunsch

Troladiz

Schmisdorf

Sincere

Brentano

Maxen

Daun

Hausdorf

TO DRESDEN

N
E
S
W

Prussian Unit

Austrian Unit

Forest

Town

River

0   1   2 Mi.

the Austrians achieved proved decisive. Lloyd postulated: "[T]hat no army however strong, can keep its ground if you advance against it in front, and at the same time send a powerful corps to act on its flank and rear."[104] The Prussian king had attempted to repeat his success of Leuthen at every possible opportunity, but his oblique march rarely succeeded because his enemies knew he would execute that type of maneuver. After Maxen, Lloyd succinctly added: "it is possible in war, as in most other situations, to overdo a thing, and drive a nail further than it can go."[105]

In his analysis of the battle of Hochkirch, Lloyd emphasized the utility of converging attacks and the importance of surprise. That battle was the culmination of an Austrian strategic offensive into Saxony, which found Frederick's army at the village of Hochkirch. The king's 26,000 men fought against nearly 80,000 Austrians. Again Lacy provided the plan: an assault force of five columns would converge under cover of darkness and attack Frederick's position at Hochkirch while the remaining Austrian units advanced on the Prussian center and left wing. The move surprised Frederick. By 10:00 A.M. he ordered a retreat and left 9,000 casualties on the field.[106] Lloyd praised Lacy's plan and leadership on the field, but concluded victory improbable if the Prussians had been prepared. He warned that generals must be ready for any contingency so they are never surprised. "Whatever is possible, a general should think probable," he added, "that like old women he may not say; who would have thought it?"[107]

Lloyd did not present these principles in any list or quantitative format because he wanted officers to read the history from which he derived them.[108] His goal was to train their judgment and outlook. Principles ordered chaotic phenomenon and enabled analysis and reflection. They could be guidelines for action and fundamental constructs of military thought.[109] Yet, he understood the subjective nature of human passions and the ever-present elements of contingency and chance. His principles were only a means to demonstrate truths and common-sense observations behind the nature of things. To make everything subservient to these rules and proclaim them the only guide to follow was a mistake.[110] From his analysis of the Seven Years' War, Lloyd had derived a body of theory for the military profession.

Lloyd served Karl I of Brunswick from 1761–65 as a military officer and emissary. As an general adjutant, he helped organize and administer Brunswick's war effort against France and Austria in the Rhineland region under the command of Karl's brother Prince Ferdinand (1721–92) and the Hereditary Prince Karl Wilhelm Ferdinand (1735–1806). Prince Ferdinand commanded all allied forces in the region and was chiefly responsible for defending Prussia along the Rhine throughout the entire war.[111] The Hereditary Prince, known better for defeats at Valmy (20 September 1792) and Auerstädt (14 October 1806), became a significant military figure as well. During his tenure in Brunswick Lloyd also encountered and befriended

The Battle of Hochkirch

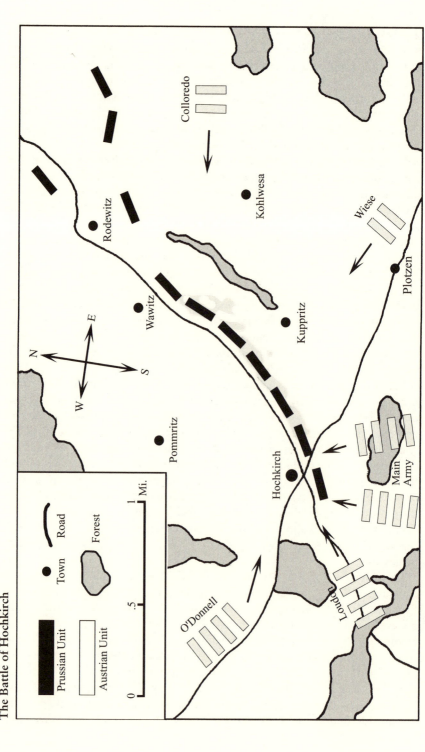

Colloredo

Kohlwesa

Wiese

Plotzen

Rodewitz

Wawitz

Kuppritz

N

E

W

S

Pommritz

Hochkirch

Main
Army

O'Donnell

Loudon

Prussian Unit

Austrian Unit

Town

Road

Forest

0   .5   1 Mi.

leading members of the British army stationed in Germany. But his role in Brunswick's 1761 campaign remains elusive, since *The History of the Late War in Germany* ends with 1759. He apparently did not receive a field command, and spent the remaining war years calculating and managing the supply system and raising troops. When the campaign ended, Karl sent him to England to negotiate a marriage treaty between the Hereditary Prince and King George III's (r.1760–1820) eldest sister, Princess Augusta. The union would bind England and Brunswick together by blood, and facilitate closer relations between England and Prussia. The plan made geopolitical sense. Brunswick was adjacent to Hanover, King George's patrimony and ancestral homeland.[112] Unfortunately, Lloyd's diplomatic mission failed. "I had a thousand difficulties," he wrote, "and was happy to leave."[113] For his efforts Karl promoted him to colonel with a monthly pension of 100 *ecus*.

In 1762 Lloyd resumed the role of general adjutant, and at the urging of several British officers attempted to raise a large corps of infantry from foreign deserters to remedy England's manpower shortfall. He believed it possible to raise nearly 30,000 men within three months.[114] Nothing came of the plan he forwarded to Lord John Ligonier, but it does shed some light on his thinking about society and warfare.[115] The first object of any nation, he wrote, was to conserve its subjects, and the second was to employ them usefully. England required foreign troops to garrison its empire and therefore free native manpower for home defense and the country's economy. Spain and Italy illustrated what happened to states when their subjects were not properly employed: poverty and decline ensued. German, Danish, Swedish, Prussian, and Austrian deserters could fulfill the requirements. In addition to garrisoning the colonies, these troops would be given land to sustain themselves and insure their loyalty. They would defend the colony because by default they would be defending their own property.[116] In short, loyalty or national sentiment could be ensured through proper planning. Lloyd urged Ligonier to adopt his measures. Nothing came of the proposal, but his attempt to gain influence within the British military establishment prefigured his quest for employment and advancement in the coming years.

After the Peace of Paris (1763) ended the Seven Years' War, Lloyd and fellow officers faced unemployment, the traditional peacetime dilemma for soldiers in early modern Europe. States typically trimmed defense spending after any war, and the physical and economic destruction of the Seven Years' War caused governments to slash budgets. Brunswick in particular was exhausted by military campaigns fought upon its soil, so Colonel Lloyd indeed had reason to fear being discharged of his duties and stripped of his pension. He sought patronage from Friedrich Wilhelm Ernst, Graf zu Schaumburg-Lippe (1724–77), an intellectual, artillerist, and sovereign of the small German principality of Bückeburg. Lippe served with distinction under Prince Ferdinand, and the Portuguese King Joseph I (r.1750–76) hired him to reorganize his military after he had successfully commanded the

Anglo-Portuguese army against Spain in the brief war of 1762.[117] Lloyd asked Lippe for employment in the newly reorganized Portuguese army and, hoping to impress him, sent an excerpt of his military history that covered the campaign of 1757.[118] Lippe secured Lloyd a commission in the Portuguese artillery corps, but he refused it after Karl promoted him to Inspector-General of the Brunswickian artillery with an annual pension of £250.[119]

Insecurity plagued the military profession. In 1765 Karl cut the budget and eliminated Lloyd's pension. He appealed to his friend British Colonel Henry Clinton (1738–95) to help obtain British employment from John Manners, marquis of Granby (1721–70), and confessed he would even accept a position in the artillery or engineer corps.[120] He sent a memoir on Portugal to Granby and traveled to Spain to gather freelance intelligence for the British government in July. Lloyd sent a similar memoir to Schaumburg-Lippe in August asking once more for help in securing a Portuguese commission.[121] Lippe contacted the Marquis de Pombal and related his knowledge of the Welshman, concluding that Portugal should give him a commission since he was a "man of an illuminated and assiduous mind."[122] His knowledge of the art of war and the Spanish court in Madrid would be useful Lippe argued, but he warned against giving Lloyd a pension since it was not clear for whom he worked. Lippe received no response from Pombal.[123] Lloyd remained adrift until Maximilian Friedrich von Königsegg-Rothenfels, Elector and Archbishop of Cologne (r.1761–84) conferred on him the honorary title of major-general. It came without financial compensation.[124] Undeterred, he again pressed Schaumburg-Lippe for employment, claiming that his attachment to Lippe was not based on motives of interest.[125] By then the Portuguese option seemed remote.[126] Lloyd turned again to Henry Clinton and sent him memoirs on France and England respectively. He asked for Clinton's help in securing an appointment in the Hanoverian army via England's Crown Prince Frederick. Lloyd wrote with no small sense of urgency that his only remaining resource was the protection and humanity of his Highness.[127] Once more he contacted Lippe, but to no avail.[128]

The memoirs on Portugal reveal Lloyd's emerging enlightened views and the important role that geography played in eighteenth-century society. Large sections of both memoirs contain detailed geographic and topographic information of the Portuguese and Spanish border provinces to aid Portuguese and English officials draw up a defensive war plan against Spain.[129] Lloyd also presented a detailed analysis of Portuguese society and inserted his opinion on how to reform and strengthen the kingdom. Enlightened reformers often envisioned a top-down process of change, or what later came to be known as enlightened despotism. Lloyd was no different in his approach to reform and economic development. First, he called for a decree to increase the value of Portuguese money in order to attract foreign buyers and investment. Although the country's commerce relied on such agricultural products as sugar instead of manufacturing, Lloyd argued that increased global trade of agriculture would also attract foreign investment upon which Portugal could establish industry.[130] The state had to promote the expansion of agriculture for its economic livelihood, else like France it would succumb to periodic famine and starvation.[131] His remedy was not the typical mercantilist prescription for wealth; rather, he advocated free trade and an end to monopolies within Portugal and its empire, both basic tenets of the liberal economic thought born of the Enlightenment.

A healthy, functioning economy provided the basis of state power via taxation. Lloyd argued against traditional taxation of grain and agricultural produce, which effected the largest and poorest segment of the population, and advocated the taxation of the land itself. The first only legitimate principle of political economy, he wrote, was to enrich the subject and tax him without destroying him.[132] Taxing land would provide incentive for owners to maximize agricultural production, create a national surplus of grain, and provide for the well-being of the entire population. The King should raise only enough revenues to pay for expenditures, and return any excess revenue to the economy to increase general prosperity. Lloyd wrote: people with wealth and who have something to lose fear revolutions.[133] Nor did he end there; he also advocated the more radical abolition of noble privilege, which inevitably channeled the expense of government on the poor. People should contribute, Lloyd argued, according to what they possessed.[134] Economic growth and just administration kept society stable and a dynasty on the throne.

Unlike the typical enlightened reformer, Lloyd viewed economic progress as a means to increase a state's military power. His first rule stated that any given country should employ 1/20 the number of men capable of bearing arms. To pass this proportion would ruin the country and reduce the population to unredeemable poverty.[135] For Portugal the ideal size amounted to 30,000 men, but due to its far-flung global empire this small army would be inadequate to defend state interests. Lloyd suggested introducing militia conscription similar to Prussia's canton system.[136] He argued that 100,000 men should be taken into a provincial militia, who would then assemble and train on Sundays and holidays. Each year a small portion of them would be discharged so long as they kept up their training. This system would insure that in a few years the entire nation would be militarized.[137] To augment the native force of regular troops and militia Lloyd emphasized the need and desirability of hiring foreign mercenaries, some 4–6,000 from Hesse or Brunswick. Foreign troops were loyal to the King who paid their wages, increased discipline in the army, and protected the government from revolts and popular uprisings.[138] Whether influential or not, the memoir on Portugal was Lloyd's first excursion into enlightened political, economic, and military reform.

By the time *The History of the Late War in Germany* appeared in print in 1766, Lloyd lacked income and patronage, and clung to a precarious financial situation. Fearing Clinton's help not forthcoming, he placed himself at the mercy of his friends for travel and lodging. In the autumn he went to Spain and tried in vain to contact the touring British Crown Prince Frederick. Lloyd sailed to Alicante and Cartagena, but had to travel overland to Cádiz. He did not find Prince Frederick, and returned to France destitute and hungry in December.[139] With few options left, he promptly sent a memoir on Spain to the Marquis of Granby in one final effort to secure his favor. Any position would suffice in Hanover or even Florida.[140] In a desperate letter to Clinton he candidly confessed that he traveled just to find bread and that without Lord Granby's patronage soon he would "fall to the ground."[141] In March he again wrote Clinton, this time demanding that he talk to Granby and settle the matter once and for all.[142] Lloyd's future appeared dim in an age of enlightenment. The situation demonstrates the difficulties that a military career and a public life in general presented to educated persons lacking wealth, status, or influential patrons.

The Seven Years' War served as the formative event in Henry Lloyd's career. From it he emerged as a formidable military personality. Although he published *The History of the Late War in Germany* anonymously, its authorship was known within Anglo-Portuguese circles. With that work he embarked on his literary career and framed a modern category of military analysis: the principles of war. These observations and maxims, in all their forms, provided the military profession with a set of guidelines for institutional development and operational theory. Both concepts he derived from precedents pre-dating the Enlightenment or part of its early stage. Limited in its scope and outlook and chained to past authority, his military thought had not advanced much further than his contemporaries. Lloyd's philosophy required a break from the past and a new way of understanding human society. He found such a break in the intellectual maelstrom of the Enlightenment.

Henry Lloyd's Enlightenment

The philosopher is no enthusiast; he does not set himself up for a prophet; he does not represent himself as inspired by the Gods.
—*Voltaire*, Philosophical Dictionary

The 1760s brought a transition in Lloyd's professional development. In July 1767, Lord Granby awarded him an annual pension of £500 on behalf of King George III apparently without Clinton's intervention.[1] He was still an outsider and opponent of illegitimate authority, but his youthful romantic rebellion turned to a mature intellectual one. This transformation corresponded with his absorption of enlightened philosophy and his subsequent writings and publications on man and society. In short, he became a *philosophe* who understood humanity within a secular context, void of all the mysteries and vagaries of the Christian past: the very mission of the Enlightenment. Lloyd envisioned man, society, and warfare from a psychological and physical context. Along with this new political and intellectual orientation, Lloyd secured an official passport and embarked upon his career as a British agent and spy.[2] His first assignment took him to an Italy immersed in the "Milanese Enlightenment." The journey was both intellectual and clandestine.[3]

Lloyd traveled to Milan in January 1768 and lodged with his friend Pietro Verri, a government official and reformer.[4] He arrived wearing the blue uniform of Cologne and easily maneuvered his way into noteworthy literary and philosophical circles. Verri and his brother Alessandro introduced him to such leading Italian intellectuals as Paolo Frisi, a mathematician, astronomer, and co-founder of the short-lived journal *Il Caffe* (1764–66). According to Pietro, Lloyd's history of the Seven Years' War was widely sought after by this community. But it was reform not war that dominated intellectual life in northern Italy, and the debate of the day concerned the Jesuits. Lloyd agreed that the Society of Jesus appeared universally discredited. They had already been expelled from Portugal and were in danger of being expelled from Spain.[5] It was popularly and erroneously believed the Jesuits, angered by attempts to limit their authority in Paraguay, orchestrated the revolts in Madrid that led to the resignation of Finance Minister Leopoldo di Gregorio, marchese di Squillacci.[6] A consensus endorsed barring religious organizations from influencing politics and government altogether. Henry Lloyd's enlightenment occurred within this anti-religious context.

The enlightened mind embraced three fundamental convictions: the rejection of the religious interpretation of humanity, the elevation of a secular or materialist interpretation in its stead, and the need for societal reform. The battle cry of the *philosophes,* "Crush the Infamy," signified a break with the past and embodied an overt attack on religious institutions and theology. Philosophers questioned original sin and the "Fall of Man," and concluded that the religious interpretation of the world was without empirical basis and anathema to human happiness.[7] The first and most popular assault came from John Locke (1632–1704), who founded the quasi-science of psychology in the late seventeenth century.[8] A wide, unquestioned acceptance of his proclamations against innate ideas supplied the germ for further doubt about existing beliefs and practices. Following Locke's rejection of innate ideas, David Hume (1711–76) argued in *The Natural History of Religion* (1757) that religion was not an instinct of man, and natural reasons caused its institutional development. Humanity's ignorance of nature and the meaning of contingency produced an anxious fear of future events. Imagining gods, demons, and natural spirits was the only way primitive humanity could reasonably explain the often calamitous and tragic events witnessed in daily life. As a society slowly emerged from its ignorance, it posited one supreme god as the creator of the universe and the first cause of all things.[9] Henry Lloyd inherited this outlook toward religion, and his "Essais philosophiques sur les gouvernements,"[10] written during his two-year sojourn in Italy, wrenched what was left of a divine spark from the human equation.[11]

Lloyd believed fear to be the origin of religion. In the distant past, thunder, lightning, and storms had frightened the archaic nomadic peoples. They eventually deduced that invisible forces controlled nature and inflicted pain upon humanity. Lloyd surmised that these people probably blamed the mysterious phases of the moon for their sufferings and eventually began to worship it as a deity to placate nature's destructive tendencies. Soon other natural phenomena were equated with different unseen forces, thus creating a polytheistic belief system. While unnatural to humanity, the construction of monotheism and the belief in a Supreme Being embodied all that was good and pleasurable in the world.[12] Monotheism might well mark the advancement of religious belief, but it remained equally grounded in ignorance and the hope of future reward. Yet neither the *philosophes* nor Lloyd condemned religion outright; after all it was natural. They assailed religious institutions' parasitic relationship with society. As mankind progressed, people's needs and fears increased, which promoted religious formality. Invoking a divine spirit gave rise to rituals controlled by a clerical class, which claimed a special knowledge of the god. The monopoly of power concentrated in their hands led to the corruption of religious values and control over the minds and bodies of people. Questioning their authority or, worse still, their religious beliefs met with violent opposition from the secular arm of government.[13] To spread religion, clerics developed doctrines that increased the moral duties of people, giving them more powerful positions in the community.[14] The rewards of Paradise, the immortality of the soul, and the punishment of Purgatory or Damnation rested with man's obedience to the clerical class.

Lloyd planned to curb religion's "Universal Despotism" by lifting the veil of ignorance and combating superstition and oppression. Secular education would undermine the Church's divine authority and cause the clerics' position to depend on the good will of society.[15] A fallen orthodox Christian, Lloyd also argued that numerous sects would undermine the influence of religion over the state: only one was necessary, but a thousand would be far better.[16] Like Voltaire he believed a diverse religious environment would promote tolerance and commerce as in England. It would also promote human happiness, the goal of the enlightened society.[17] The tool of enlightenment would be the science of reason, which would supercede religion. Scientific reason placed natural forces, not an otherworldly divinity, behind creation. After all, *philosophes* believed no infinitely just and perfect being could exist with all the suffering caused by harmful actions of mankind.[18] Lloyd, no idealist, qualified his optimism about the chances of such a society ever emerging. The imperfect nature of humanity posed a nearly insurmountable barrier to the free pagan society. To Pierre Bayle's rhetorical question on whether a society of atheists could exist, he answered in the negative. Most people would continue to believe in some form of religion and refuse to see the truth.[19]

More than an attempt to overcome and erase superstition, anticlerical thinkers believed they were engaged in a battle for human freedom. Lloyd concurred and saw the oppression of the people everywhere as the result of religious institutions. Supported by heavy-handed taxation of the poor, the clerical class continually waged a silent war for their minds, spirit, and goods.[20] For this reason Lloyd condemned the clergy as the most useless and dangerous to society.[21] The malignant influence of religious intolerance also extended to warfare. A society formed upon religious principles was destined to fight other people who worshipped different gods. Such foolishness inevitably ended with the extermination of one side for the sake of the divinity.[22] No doubt Lloyd's knowledge of Europe's turbulent religious wars of the sixteenth and seventeenth centuries reinforced his critical outlook. For these reasons he drafted a plan to reorganize Europe to curtail the pernicious influence of organized religion by military means if necessary. The Pope should be exiled to Elba and serve merely as a spiritual figurehead for Europe's Christians. Next, Lloyd proposed an alliance between Austria and Prussia to counter Bourbon France, the great enemy of peace and supporter of religious orthodoxy and oppression.[23]

Lloyd was an agnostic or theist, someone who believed only in the creation of the universe by an omnipotent power. Otherwise an unbeliever, he developed a utilitarian and materialist psychology of man utterly void of divine elements to explain ethics and morality. The most infamous materialist tract was Julian Offray de la Mettrie's (1709–51) *L'Homme Machine* published in 1748. In it La Mettrie argued that humans were merely machines.[24] There was no immaterial soul; the human brain, perfectly malleable, was the origin and end of all thoughts. Censored and proscribed throughout Europe, it presented man as a weak, passive creature without will and controlled by his immediate surroundings.[25] Lloyd instead followed the Epicurean views contained in *De l'Esprit,* written by the young and restless Claude Adrien Helvetius (1715–71). It proposed that the mind was merely the assemblage of all thoughts produced by physical sensations.[26] Helvetius deduced that morality was relative and that an individual's search for pleasure and the aversion to pain guided his or her actions.[27] Pleasure promoted happiness and pain produced sadness. If self-interest functioned unimpeded, then society would be full of happy people. The state, therefore, had an interest in promoting this Public Utility to the greatest extent possible without intervening in the natural process.[28] With wide-ranging implications for human morality and ethics, the idea of man guided by pleasure and pain became a staple of enlightened thought from Jeremy Bentham's (1742–1832) Utilitarianism to Cesare Beccaria's (1738–94) penal reform.[29]

Taken as a body of theory, the work of La Mettrie, Helvetius, and other eighteenth-century psychologists established the "sensationist" theory of knowledge.[30] Lloyd adopted sensationism and contrived a materialist outlook that denied the existence of the soul and traced all human thought to the physical environment. Life consisted solely of motion and death of total tranquility.[31] All movement was reaction to the environmental stimuli of heat and gravity, not the result of instinct or innate knowledge. They produced motives for human activity and sensations, which were then translated into ideas.[32] But human action (no doubt directly attributable to environmental stimuli) derived from the two aspects of the human being, "phys-ical man" and "moral man." From the first emerged wants and desires orig-inating from biological causes such as hunger. From the latter came the understanding of one's duties and obligations to other human beings. Lloyd believed the bulk of human misery and conflict resulted from the infinite variety and permutations of human society's sense of duty and obligation. The struggle over what was moral or right was the constant variable. Reli-gious institutions and religious belief offered no better answer to this prob-lem than any individual human inclination. Since moral duties arose from man, then morality should be determined by man's physical needs and not by his opinions. Lloyd's recipe for right and morality was purely utilitarian. All actions necessary for survival were just and any action interfering in self-preservation was unjust.[33] All other decisions on duties to others should be left to the discretion of the individual because they were relative to any situation and based purely on opinion.[34] Self-preservation, the fundamental objective element of "physical man," determined human action and should be the basis for an objective morality.[35]

Utilitarian morality seemingly offered a simple alternative to traditional morality and ethics. Lloyd, incorporating Helvetius' law of pleasure and pain, concluded that people are "claivoyant" about their own interests and would not willingly violate this general principle of human action.[36] More specifically, people used their sensory impressions to weigh the amount of pleasure and pain resulting from their behavior. Once the pleasure thresh-old was reached the body would naturally want to rest. When in pain the person naturally would want to remedy his or her displeasure.[37] But utili-tarianism is an overly optimistic creed because it assumes everyone ration-ally understands their own self-interest. What if a person derived pleasure from the pain of others? "Moral man" was Lloyd's explanation. Moral sen-sations apart from physical desires arose from society and the societal value systems based on the collective outlook of "moral man." Yet, these moral sensations forever changed, multiplied, and often led to severe disagree-ments.[38] Thus, Lloyd did not ignore the power of passions arising from the conflict of opinions. No rules could guide their conduct. Like Hume he believed they often usurped reason and confounded the attempt to under-stand and fulfill one's objective self-interest. This resulted in deprivations far worse than any found in the natural world. And in European society the quest for religious orthodoxy or conformity only exacerbated the problem of the passions.[39] Civil and religious institutions cannot prevent crime or evil acts exclusively through the fear of punishment. Society must encour-age people to substitute destructive passions with innocuous ones. It served its members best by refraining to do harm rather than by doing what opin-ion deemed good or just.[40] The only way to reduce the role of destructive passions in society was to limit the amount of pain and suffering.[41]

From this theory Lloyd deduced that human nature was neither inherently malicious nor righteous. If essentially malicious, then man's desire to follow the law of self-interest took on ominous overtones. If basically good, then how could one explain the vast amount of human misery in the world? In an almost modern fashion he concluded that the environment shaped and formed man's nature.[42] People naturally tended toward peace out of their desire for physical pleasure. Yet, they possessed free will to choose between pleasurable actions or even choose a more dangerous option. Lloyd explained a man would forever expose himself to war because the pain suffered by the absence of glory exceeded that of the inherent danger.[43] But free will involved the manner by which one acted. Because of self-preservation people are not free to choose inaction. Until science can understand the inner workings of the brain, in Lloyd's opinion the attempts of theologians and philosophers to uncover the mysterious nature of man were folly. Nothing short of radical, he concluded reason alone does not make humanity distinguishable from the animal kingdom as all animals possess a degree of rational thought. All beings have their limitations and any attempt to understand the meaning of life exceeded the natural rational functions of man. Such matters were best left to the "Sovereign of the Universe."[44]

Lloyd adapted his utilitarian theory to war and crafted the first example of military sociology. He borrowed from Montesquieu and posited climate, geography, and political institutions formed human psychology. He began with the assumed dichotomy of northern and southern peoples to illustrate his point.[45] He believed people from northern regions (which included most European countries) tended to be more vigorous, active, and industrious because cold weather conditioned them to work in order to survive. The difficulties involved with growing food in cooler climates infused its inhabitants with strength. Southern peoples (those who lived near or below the equator) did not exhibit the same hardy physical constitution because the hot and humid climate enervated their bodies.[46] Such conditions encouraged lethargy, slowness, and weakness in physical activity, the result being that when stimulated they quickly reacted, but then returned to a docile state—all characteristics conducive to despotic government. Lloyd elevated the influence of geography and government institutions over climate. They contoured the general characteristics of soldiers, which if understood would allow for their proper training and discipline. Geography produced good and bad characteristics in soldiers. People living in plains and cities, who often owned property, engaged in commerce and in the latter case bought rather than produced their food, were weakened by the vice and comforts of easy living. This situation resulted in disobedient, weak and effeminate soldiers. On the contrary, people from poorer, mountainous regions tended to be stronger and more active. Protected from outside threats by their landscape, they cherished their freedom and valued it over life itself. Thus, they did not succumb to the deleterious effects of physical luxuries. These people made the best soldiers, because they would undertake great hardships without complaint. He singled out the Scottish Highlanders and Croatian light troops as notable examples.[47]

A society's political structure or government acted as the most significant influence on human psychology. Loosely following Montesquieu's political theory, Lloyd used two fundamental categories: a government of one (despotism and monarchies) and of many (aristocracies and democracies).[48] Subjects in despotic states made fine soldiers. Since birth they had been taught obedience, highly desirable for military discipline. Unfortunately, the guiding principle of despotism was fear, and if that principle totally alienated and oppressed the population only religion could make them effective soldiers.[49] Monarchies produced subjects most fit for military service because they were shaped by the principle of honor, which encouraged the love of glory and riches: natural passions he believed were "ingrafted in the human heart."[50] Their fealty to King or Queen also conditioned them to be subordinate to authority. Aristocratic and democratic republics possessed the potential for both superior and inferior soldiers. Guided by the principle of equality, people in democracies tended to be unruly and hold great pretensions to liberty, a trait incompatible with subordination. Yet, they could be made effective soldiers if disciplined and manipulated by the "fire of liberty."[51] In that event a republican army would become invincible. How these determinants contoured psychology formed the core of Lloyd's military sociology he termed National Character.

Lloyd applied National Character to gauge the organic military potential and capacity of the peoples of Europe.[52] For instance, he regarded the French as poor soldiers because they came from fertile plains and cities. They appeared to him "gay, light, and lively, governed by an immediate and transitory impulse."[53] During military operations one only needed to attack and keep them in retreat in order to break their spirit and undermine their discipline. But climate and geography counted less than political organization. English soldiers, for example, lived in a cooler climate, but they also faced institutions that conditioned them in a way not unlike the French. They lacked any coherent system of discipline and suffered from an inequitable distribution of favors stemming from the purchase and selling of commissions.[54] Germanic soldiers offered an interesting contrast. Because Austria recruited its soldiers from laborers and vassals of the Magnates, they tended to be hard working, loyal, and steadfast, though void of religious motivation. He considered them superior to any army not inspired by some form of enthusiasm.[55] Prussian armies suffered from a lack of native soldiers. Recruits often hailed from non-Prussian lands and reflected various backgrounds and religious proclivities. Only strong military discipline cemented the army, "a vast regular machine."[56] Without the genius of

Frederick the Great, Lloyd predicted it "would probably fall to pieces, and leave nothing but the traces of its ancient glory behind."[57] Thus, two German powers varied significantly in their National Character, primarily because of institutional factors. The best European soldiers, the Russians, reflected the three environmental determinants. First, they lived in a cool climate, which made them vigorous, and were recruited from a hardy peasant population. Their veneration of the Czar (or Czarina) and their enthusiasm for the Russian Orthodox Church made them superior to all other soldiers. "Courage alone," he confessed, "has rendered them victorious."[58]

Based upon sketchy empirical data, his military sociology, however crude, was the first of its kind. Its importance rested in the training and discipline of armies. After the Seven Years' War military reformers such as Claude Louis, comte de Saint-Germain (1707–78) promoted the use of Prussian discipline throughout Europe.[59] Lloyd warned that transplanting Frederick's discipline onto a foreign National Character endangered the moral integrity and effectiveness of an army.[60] Each nation possessed a National Character connected to its history, political structure, and geography; therefore each nation had to develop a system of military discipline conducive to the strengthening of that National Character. Armies in Lloyd's opinion truly reflected (or should reflect) the societies in which they operated.

Lloyd's enlightened philosophy incorporated more than military applications. His utilitarian analysis launched his theory on the development of human society in which war played an essential role. He rejected fashionable notions about humanity's state of nature including Jean-Jacques Rousseau's (1712–78) contention that man was born free from society yet consciously created it to his misfortune.[61] Lloyd cleverly attacked the assumption by invalidating the question. Humans could not be born out of society; they were born in society. They were attached to it by habit, by physical wants and by others in society itself.[62] Society existed for no other reason than because humanity existed. Nor was man by nature inclined toward a social contract based upon equality. Inequality of conditions and property emerged from the inequality of physical strength. Social and economic classes arose from the natural environment in which some were more powerful then others.[63] Inclined to seek individual advantages, human ambition required government to protect the weak from the strong. But a social contract which made men equal also made government obsolete. That was impossible.[64] Lloyd understood Rousseau's critique of society as a well-crafted but misguided attack on humanity itself.

Of all of Rousseau's contentions, his argument that war ensued from the creation of private property vexed Lloyd more than any other. Lloyd believed war had nothing to do with property rights, private or communal.[65] Humanity was by nature peaceful, and so war was not innate to society (unlike property). War resulted from the stress and hardships of the physical environment and disagreements in opinion: in other words politics. Only if humanity could overcome the restraints and challenges of nature could war be eradicated.[66] Within the modern context, warfare had been codified and regulated in hope of limiting its destructive tendencies. Ideally, a state could wage war only to redress a grievance or to defend its borders.[67] But the law of war upon which these rules depended justified the use of violence. He admitted that a state had the right to use force because no universal tribunal or world court existed to restrain it.[68] Civil society eliminated anarchy within its boundaries, but Lloyd was skeptical whether the international anarchy of the European state system could ever be regulated by a higher authority, especially since the power of the supranational Christian Church had fragmented beyond repair. War was a controllable, but permanent social activity.

From these observations Lloyd constructed a wide-ranging sociological model that outlined the historical development of human society. His hypothesis, now called the four-stage theory, was an extension of "sensationist" principles. It argued that human society had progressed over time through four more or less distinct and consecutive stages in relation to their physical environment.[69] Societies could suffer a reverse or remain static depending on their physical circumstances. Born of seventeenth- and eighteenth-century travel literature from the extra-European world, the theory attempted to explain the different customs, languages, and governments among human societies. Lloyd presented his own explanation of how the process operated, paying special attention to the military context. He divided humanity into two basic groups: traditional societies of either hunter-gatherers *(peuple chasseur)* or pastoralists *(peuple pasteur)* and civil societies incorporating agricultural *(peuple agricole)* and commercial states *(peuple commercante).*

The first state of any people was the hunter-gatherer. They lived together in small bands gathering fruit, hunting animals, and possessing no real property apart from what they could carry. All rules and customs of the tribe conformed to the preservation of hunting as the sacred activity. Conflict generally arose between tribes from competition over food supplies. Plagued by an uncertain life, these perfectly free societies wandered about a region in search of nourishment, not tied to any one locale. Offensive to Europeans, cannibalism came naturally to these people living in desolate regions or on islands lacking food.[70] A scattered population, difficult communications and rugged geography perpetuated humanity's simple way of life. Chance, however, played a significant role in historical change. Where communication between tribes occurred easily and water and food became abundant, the hunter-gatherers gradually transformed over eons into pastoral peoples, who domesticated animals, particularly horses, and practiced simple agriculture. These societies developed a more stable way of life. Divided into tribes, the changing seasons forced them to migrate periodically in search of food for their flocks. Natural cavalrymen, pastoral tribes developed a high degree of mobility in all types of geography thereby promoting a penchant for war. Lloyd viewed pastoral peoples as historically powerful conquerors. The Mongol and Tartar conquest of China illustrated his point. Their military weakness stemmed from a lack of technology and the fluid nature of their society; they could not consolidate their conquests. Often their expeditions involved raiding and pillaging, acts viewed by Europeans in the eighteenth century as little more than robbery and murder.[71]

Lloyd did not write to deprecate non-European societies, rather to warn that European methods were not universally applicable. For instance, he condemned as barbaric and unjust England's attempt to subdue and pacify Native Americans in their colonies. The natives fought on foot and were easily killed, but not easily controlled.[72] The answer was assimilation, not extermination. The mother country would benefit more by encouraging their settlement of land and gradually incorporating their tribes into colonial society: an idea too progressive for the eighteenth century.[73] In addition, he cautioned modern commercial states against war with traditional societies. European wars with pastoral societies in particular were misguided because they were too poor and difficult to control. They were often dispersed over large isolated areas and could not be permanently subdued by contemporary European means.[74] The historic threat posed by the Mongols no longer existed in Lloyd's time. Their descendants could not conduct sieges nor form supply systems to effectively combat European institutions.[75] He used the example of Russia during the Seven Years' War. Its armies had occupied most of East Prussia, but they could not keep their conquest because of a lack of depots and supply lines. Lloyd believed their Tatar heritage condemned them forever to raid and retire in a never-ending pattern of pillaging.[76]

Pasquale Paoli's Corsican revolt of 1768–69 reinforced Lloyd's conviction that the various stages of society produced fundamentally different and incompatible militarily systems. In May 1768 Genoa sparked a nationalist uprising in Corsica when it ceded the island to France.[77] Lloyd observed the conflict as a secret emissary between Britain and Paoli's national government. He traveled often to Genoa, Turin, and Corsica prior to the hostilities, even going so far as to stop at Gibraltar in this capacity.[78] By September a French army had consolidated its hold over Cap Corse, the most northern tip of Corsica, and planned to march south. Public opinion considered Paoli's uprising doomed. But the Nebbia campaign did not go well for François-Claude, marquis of Chauvelin's troops.[79] By October, Paoli had driven the French from the Nebbia, prompting English merchants in Florence to send arms and money. From Leghorn Lloyd supported this clandestine operation.[80] Under an assumed name he crossed over to Corsica in a Danish ship, only to be apprehended by French officials and sent back to Tuscany.[81] He too believed the patriot cause was in danger of collapsing.

Notwithstanding the early victories, Paoli's poorly trained forces tended to act in small bands with little coordination. Lloyd believed the clan-like nature of their society undermined its effectiveness. To defeat the French army the Corsicans had to attack its flanks, force it to divide, and annihilate it piecemeal. This Paoli could not do. In December Lloyd returned to Milan as the war continued.[82] On 8 May 1769 the patriots lost the battle of Ponte-Nuovo to the French army under Noël Jourde, comte de Vaux. Paoli and his closest supporters fled the island on 13 June aboard English ships.[83] The Corsicans could not match French firepower, organization, and leadership.

For Lloyd, Paoli's tragic defeat symbolized the military anomalies between a more traditional society like Corsica and a modern civil society like France. Civil society, represented first by agricultural and then commercial peoples, conferred a more complex way of life and enabled a more effective use of military resources. With the introduction and gradual dominance of an agricultural way of life, the freedom of traditional societies was lost. People became tied to land and property in specific villages and towns. Because property in the form of land became more private, people's needs, desires, and wants increased in proportion to their wealth. The simple physical desires of traditional peoples gave way to a more complex web of human relations further complicated by a significant population increase. This situation required the formation of laws that regulated the actions of people and subordinated them to a higher authority, often under the rubric of religion or a Supreme Being.[84] The mechanical process followed the Newtonian frame of reference that dominated the Enlightenment. Lloyd posited that agriculture, the "Mother" that feeds humanity,[85] allowed all art, industry, and trade to flourish. As agricultural production increased, so did population. Agricultural surplus promoted trade between societies tempered only by geography. Mountainous regions curtailed trade and kept even advanced agricultural societies relatively poor and dispersed. Such was the case with the Swiss cantons and Spain.[86]

Whereas the power of traditional societies depended on the number of horses they possessed, the absolute strength of an agricultural society was determined by the number of men it could arm and the quantity of food it could produce to feed them. In Europe's case agricultural society first gave rise to a feudal system centered on the mounted knight, and then as trade increased between states, to larger armies composed chiefly of infantry. Lloyd romanticized the simple agricultural society of Europe's past. But Europe in Lloyd's day was leaving behind a pure agricultural society and embarking upon commercial expansion and industrial change. The transformation to a society based on trade, commerce, and civil law came about through unintended consequences. A decentralized feudal political network had dominated Europe for hundreds of years, but the European discovery of the Americas and Far East changed the entire balance. With it came a vast quantity of riches resulting in a commercial system based on coined money that undermined and gradually destroyed the feudal system. In its place European states emerged with centralized monarchies and large standing armies based on gunpowder weapons. The lifeblood of commercial society centered around trade within a monetary system and its wars reflected this commercial context.[87] Military conflict had progressed from simple disagreements over food resources to encompass the complex web of human interaction in a modern commercial state.

Lloyd later presented his economic theories in published form. His *Essay on the Theory of Money* (1771) promised to reveal money's effect on industry, manners, and government in a civil society. He called money the Universal Merchandise because it could be exchanged for any other commodity, and he defined its basic properties: it needed to be rare and uncommon, easily carried, durable, equally divisible, and small in relation to goods it could purchase.[88] The definition, similar to Pietro Verri's in *Meditazioni sulla economia politica* (1771), caused a controversy over who first invented it that vexed the Italian count for the rest of his life.[89] Unlike the reform-minded Milanese bureaucrat, Lloyd endeavored to understand the nature of money as well as its role in modern commercial society. But Lloyd's most original and lasting contribution to economic thought stemmed from his observation of the relationship between the quantity of money and the prices of goods. He expressed it thus: the price of a commodity was in a compound ratio related directly to quantity of circulation and inversely to the amount of that commodity.[90] In other words, when the quantity of circulation increased so did the price of goods, and vice versa. When the quantity of goods fell, the price increased, and so forth.[91] He became a pioneer of modern economics and framed the Quantity Theory of Money, more forcefully developed and conveyed by Adam Smith, David Ricardo, and James Mill in the nineteenth century.[92]

Lloyd conceptualized a commercial economy much as eighteenth-century physicians, informed by William Harvey (1578–1657), conceived the human circulatory system. Money acted as the life-blood of a state, and banks were the pumps that regulated its supply and circulation.[93] For instance, they provided loans to individuals and the state, thereby negating the effects of taxation on the subjects. As such, banks created national wealth and ameliorated the negative impact of taxation and warfare on society. Lloyd moved beyond mercantilist economics and criticized large public debts and government spending because he believed those policies forced governments to raise taxes, which in turn led to high interest rates.[94] Heavy-handed intervention and manipulation only decreased a nation's money supply or circulation, which together with foreign trade was the chief indicator of prosperity.[95] The greater the circulation meant the greater the prosperity. Lloyd linked population directly to this fiscal cycle. The food supply and the quantity of money in circulation supported a growing population.[96] The increased demand for food spurred its production, which in turn increased internal trade and the income of the food producers. As such, the standard of living increased and internalized the process in an endless (or seemingly endless) loop. Therefore, population indicated the quantity of money in circulation; an iron law of monetary economics Lloyd believed applicable to Britain's dynamic society.[97]

Monetary circulation and population set the constraints of industrial productivity. The more money in circulation the larger the output of manufactured goods. Yet, the physical configuration of a nation tempered this linear relationship. If a population lay scattered across a large territory, the difficulties of circulation, transportation, and communication retarded the larger process.[98] Such was the case of Russia. Britain's concentrated population facilitated this development while Russia's dispersed population hindered this development. Therefore the system on which a commercial economy relied was absent, or at least underdeveloped in the land of the Tsars. Industry, while a significant ingredient for national wealth, also created problems for a commercial state. Poverty spurred industrial development as a means to eradicate subsistence living with profit; but it also produced a greater of financial inequality.[99] Lloyd argued that England's "vast circulation has produced a great inequality of fortunes and with it a general corruption of manners."[100] With the country ruled by the wealthy, who satisfied their vanity with luxuries to the detriment of the poor, the corruption of morals inevitably would result in general poverty and political despotism.[101] The two conditions were inseparable.

A state's political configuration, therefore, reflected its general prosperity and quantity of circulation. For instance, in a despotic state the quantity of money in circulation remained in only a few hands, leaving the majority of the population in poverty. Lloyd criticized the French government, for example, because it placed too many restrictions on work and industry. He compared it unfavorably with China, where despotism kept trade and industry at bay. Turkey lacked commerce and a monetary system, which explained its despotic nature of government as well. Thus, Lloyd concluded that the liberty or individual freedom of a political system was in proportion to the equality of circulation: "for where all are equally rich or equally poor, they must be equally powerful."[102] Yet, prosperity did not necessarily signify political liberty. As such he reversed his earlier belief in climatic determinism. Climate, he now suggested, did little to form the differences observed in the manners, customs, and governments of various nations. Rather, the quantity and equality of monetary circulation determined the life of a nation. The inequality of wealth, for example, could corrupt a people's sense of duty and obligation. But a complete equality of wealth would undermine the basis of commercial society by eliminating surpluses, trade, and consumers, and would return to a traditional society. He concluded that for England to maintain a free government, it was necessary to insure a general equality of circulation among all subjects. Merely increasing the quantity of money without ensuring its circulation throughout the body of the nation (as done in England and Holland) caused high prices, undermined the equality of circulation, and led to economic stagnation.[103] Thus, a commercial society's economy revolved in a circular pattern that took it from a state of idleness through successive movements that peaked and returned to a primitive inertia in the pursuit of such equality.[104] Lloyd had articulated in a simple mechanical formula the basic description of the economic cycle of boom and bust.

Like the circulation of money Lloyd's Italian odyssey kept him in perpetual motion. He left Milan in December 1768, traveled to Parma and Genoa and back again to Milan in February 1769.[105] Granby, the British minister of war, recalled Lloyd in March, probably for his report on Paoli's revolt.[106] In the interim the Verri brothers uncovered information about their friend. Alessandro met Vincent-Louis Dutens (1730–1812), who had recently encountered Lloyd in Florence and cast doubt on Lloyd's veracity and reasons for visiting Italy.[107] Even though Count and Countess Ragnini spoke highly of Lloyd, Baron de Ruys revealed he and Lloyd recently traveled to Constantinople, possibly in a vain attempt to join Russian forces in the Mediterranean.[108] Lloyd's sojourn was no pleasure trip after all. More unsettling to Pietro was that Lloyd had been involved in several altercations during his travels. In Parma, he quarreled with excise collectors and appealed to the finance minister, Guillaume-Léon du Tillot, for help. Lloyd's conduct embarrassed Verri, especially when he insulted an abbot by the name of Costelli in the house of Count Firmian. Perplexed by this behavior, Verri concluded Lloyd was a violent man of genius,[109] who nevertheless possessed a great knowledge of politics, war, mathematics, and languages.[110] His erudition in finance and government finances astounded Pietro, but his ethics were unclear. When Lloyd informed Verri that he was returning to Milan, the count was not enthused. "He [Lloyd] is a man of great talent and ambition," he wrote, "but a good deal annoying."[111] By September 1769, Verri had also uncovered Lloyd's secret relationship with Granby. He had lied to Pietro not only about his pension but also about the debt incurred during his Italian travels. Their friendship ended even though he saw a marked difference in Lloyd's conduct due to the fact he now traveled with a young woman, who "tamed his natural ferocity."[112] The unidentified woman was Mary Garnett, niece of the Reverend John Garnett, Bishop of Clogher. She and Lloyd married in Milan, making this second trip an unofficial visit.[113] The Lloyds departed for England in February 1770 upon hearing of Granby's resignation.

They arrived in London to find the capital in a state of political upheaval over the case of John Wilkes (1727–97). Wilkes was a founder of *The North Briton,* a pro-Scot, anti-Hanoverian political journal. Arrest warrants for libel were issued for its authors, printers and publishers after the journal lampooned King George III and his Court in April 1763. Guilty by association, Wilkes was targeted for arrest, even though the warrants had no jurisdiction and did not state his name. After a brief incarceration in the Tower of London the court ruled that Wilkes, an MP from Aylesbury, was protected by privilege from any charge except felony or the breech of the peace. George Grenville passed three resolutions in Parliament that condemned the seditious libel, lifted the privilege, and expelled Wilkes. He fled to France and was convicted in absentia of blasphemy and libel. In February 1768 he returned to London (General Warrants were deemed illegal in 1766) and was elected to Parliament for Middlesex. His arrest for the past offenses sparked popular protest at St. George's Fields in London. The mob was dispersed by force, but Wilkes's second conviction was overturned (though not his first). He thereafter petitioned and waged a pamphlet war against the government resulting in his final expulsion from the House of Commons (February 1769).[114] His popular movement, called "Wilkes and Liberty," resonated throughout England and prompted Lloyd to predict imminent civil war and to condemn Parliament as an organ of the King against the English people.[115] In 1770 Lloyd anonymously published *An Essay on the English Constitution* as a critique of the government.[116] The essay took Wilkes, colonial policy, and the military power of England as its major themes. Lloyd, now an enlightened *philosophe,* decided to apply his principles in order "to confirm the rights of the subjects, so lately and so wantonly violated."[117] Philosophical inquiry became a platform for social and political reform.

Lloyd's tract espoused the enlightened belief, heavily influenced by Montesquieu, in the superiority of mixed governments. In this case the best government for England balanced power equally among King, Commons, and Lords. Without this equilibrium one part of the machine would dominate the others and extend despotism over the people. The predominance of Parliament had deprived John Wilkes of his rights without a trial.[118] The abuse of privilege by the House of Commons implied that it existed above the law, exempt from the consent of the people. Lloyd wrote: "For if any body of men can do what they please without being responsible to any other power, it is plain, they are despotic."[119] Parliament, Commons and Lords possessed the powers to formulate laws, not to punish someone it believed violated the laws.[120] Parliament's actions effectively usurped the British constitution. Lloyd demanded the King and Lords return Wilkes's seat to him because Parliament could not elect itself.[121]

Lloyd also advanced a reform agenda for England's constitutional system. First, MPs should reside in the counties they represented, and their number should be based upon how much a county paid in yearly land taxes. All heads of households, regardless of class, should receive the franchise as long as they met a property requirement. Next, a secret ballot in both the Commons and Lords would augment each member's freedom to vote in the best interests of the nation. Lloyd added that no member should be expelled unless he refused to submit to the rules of the body, which in any event could not try a man for crimes committed outside that body. Nor could Parliament hinder a man from sitting if he was properly and legally elected. Last, Lloyd decried voting by proxy and suggested MPs be forced to sit unless ill.[122] The adoption of these measures would ensure the liberty of the people and balance of the government. Many years would elapse before significant reform became reality.

Lloyd's critique of Parliament served as a launching pad for his attack on British colonial policy, especially in North America. He warned that Spain had established colonies and lost a significant portion of its population to them, which resulted in poverty and misery for the home country. No doubt influenced by the ill-conceived Stamp Act of 1765 and the colonial reaction to it, he believed the American colonies would ruin England. Modern colonies required only small naval centers and trading posts, not the large commercial or populated continental lands found in North America.[123] England's American colonies required too much military protection and expenditure; they could not be defended or properly controlled. "They will soon be alienated from the mother country," he warned. When they acquired enough military and commercial strength they would necessarily form an independent government and become the enemies of England.[124] In that event England should grant their freedom, because a war would be disastrous. Lloyd warned: "[N]o force whatever, can subdue three millions of inhabitants dispersed over an immense continent . . . you cannot follow and conquer them."[125] If the colonies refused to pay taxes to support the mother country, Lloyd reasoned, Britain should simply withdraw military protection. When their defenses began to falter against the Indians and other Europeans, they would ask for British help and agree to pay taxes for their defense. Still, the Stamp Act was folly, and subsequent measures to make the colonies pay Lloyd proclaimed "absurd, inadequate, and unjust."[126] If nothing came of his proposals for Parliamentary reform, his pronouncements on British colonial policy in North America in hindsight appear prophetic.

Lloyd concluded with a discussion on the relative military strength of England and France. In particular he responded to a pamphlet war between William Knox, an ardent supporter of George Grenville, and Edmund Burke.[127] Knox proposed that England suffered from internal weakness due to the large debt incurred from the Seven Years' War. England, he argued, had emerged victorious but weak; France emerged without colonies, but with its power enhanced. Burke attacked the pamphlet and argued the contrary. Possibly trying to reassure a ruling establishment rocked by colonial and domestic unrest, he declared England was strong and France weak. Lloyd took the middle course and claimed that France was indeed weakened, but it did not follow that England was strong.[128] He feared that

Burke's analysis might convince the government to rest on its laurels and allow France to recover and once again threaten its security. In addition, England was plagued by real poverty (third only to Spain and Italy) masked by the opulence of London. If not checked, Lloyd warned, this moral corruption would sap the nation's strength in much the same way that Athenian power declined after the Peloponnesian War.[129]

Both pamphlets posited British strength indirectly proportional to the national debt and directly proportional to overseas trade. Lloyd believed this analysis too simplistic, so he offered his own mechanistic method for a comparative analysis of national power. The first indicator of national power Lloyd termed the "absolute force" of a nation. Expressed mathematically, absolute force equaled the sum of the number of inhabitants and the quantity of their industry.[130] With this formula Britain's absolute force equaled eighteen while France's totaled thirty-eight.[131] In a purely quantitative analysis France was twice as powerful as England: a troubling conclusion indeed, especially with France's efforts to build a large navy underway.[132] In qualitative terms England's situation, even if dire, was correctable. Lloyd juxtaposed "absolute force" with the "relative force" of a nation that depended on the nature of the government, geography, domestic production, and the genius of the inhabitants.[133] The English government leaned toward industry and commercial enterprise, while the French government relied on an agrarian economy. But the Bourbons had remedied that deficiency with an effective foreign policy in which Spain and to a lesser extent Austria acted as potential enemies of England. France could easily threaten the coast of England with Spain on its side. In fact, the loss of Canada actually strengthened French sea power because it could now concentrate its efforts in the English Channel. Lloyd warned that England's victory in the Seven Years' War resulted as much from good fortune and the ineptitude of its enemies as from effective leadership and wise foreign policy.[134] Internal discord, such as the present political condition could lead to military defeat, especially since no other nation would come to Britain's aid.[135]

Lloyd's basic remedy for the situation would later be called the "blue water" strategy associated foremost with the defense policies of the Tory Party. He assigned a modest force to home defense, amounting to 32,000 infantry, 12,000 cavalry, and militia.[136] The army in England would be stationed centrally between Dover and Portsmouth. In order to invade England, France would have to land and capture one of those two ports in order to ferry troops and supplies. The English army could quickly attack and defeat any French landing near those areas. The Royal Navy, Britain's main line of defense, would make a land battle unlikely. Lloyd believed forty ships-of-the-line stationed in the Bay of Biscay would defeat any invasion launched by France. "If these do their duty," he claimed, "we have nothing to fear at home or abroad."[137] Albeit skeptical of France's weakness and worried about political unrest in England, Lloyd's analysis of the quantitative and qualitative factors of sea-borne and naval warfare led him to believe that a "blue water" naval strategy unfettered by continental entanglements the best course of action.[138] Lloyd had predicted the three basic national issues that Great Britain would wrestle with over the course of the next decade. England would have to wait nine years, however, to see whether his pronouncements were accurate when it faced imminent invasion from a combined Franco-Spanish fleet.

Henry Lloyd's enlightenment incorporated various strains of thought, from Lockean sensationism to Voltaire's anticlericalism to Helvetius' utilitarianism. His grand intellectual product attempted to explain and analyze society within a secular context and offer practical social and political reform. In the process he placed warfare within the realm of social science. How he would incorporate this enlightened thought, especially the role of the passions, into military theory would require ten more years of reflection. But the pull of military glory was strong. He had in effect lived two lives: an official one marked by his quest for military command, and a radical one characterized by his materialistic philosophy and attempts at reform. After the Wilkes controversy subsided the clandestine radical gave way to the military man. For the rest of his life he would serve his master, Mars.

Servant of Mars

When he may enjoy peace without dishonor or harm, he chooses war; when he may live in idleness, he prefers toil, provided it be the toil of war; when he may keep his money without risk, he elects to diminish it by carrying on war.

—*Xenophon*, Anabasis

The tumultuous decade of the 1770s marked the twilight of the Age of the Enlightenment and of Lloyd's mercenary career as he transformed himself into a patriotic Englishman. The path was circuitous. No stranger to the inherent inequity of eighteenth-century society, Lloyd continued to cultivate patrons and manipulate powerful individuals as a means to advance his career in the British establishment. In 1772 he joined the Russian army, tried to facilitate the much sought-after Anglo-Russian alliance, and fought in the final campaign of the Russo-Turkish War (1768–74). Afterward he retired to the Austrian Netherlands and concentrated on his military writings, interrupted only by the Franco-Spanish invasion scare of 1779 and his futile attempts to acquire a command in Britain's war with its American colonies. General Lloyd, the outsider, had become "English," but he received little compensation for his patriotic duty. His experiences and frustrations appeared in his developing philosophy of war.

By 1772 Great Britain had entered an era of commercial expansion and political stability. The turmoil of the past decade receded. Even colonial unrest in North America abated somewhat. Regardless of the wished-for

tranquility, however, currents of change ran deep. The early Industrial Revolution accelerated society's transformation and the colonial repose masked
divergent, if not incompatible, interests between the colonists and Parliament. But the desire for stability was strong in British political institutions.
The archaic borough voting system had long outlived its logic, but not its
utility: it kept specific interests in power. King George III's government
added to this conservative attitude. The patronage system allowed the most
powerful aristocratic families to regulate entry into the government bureaucracy. A complex web of interlocking, mutually dependent, and often hostile networks resulted that provided a good deal of stability if not efficiency
to government institutions. Family connections, history of service, and to a
lesser extent wealth determined how far a man could rise in political power.
The barrier seemed insurmountable for ex-Jacobites, poor commoners, or
would-be military adventurers.

Nowhere is the inequity and irony of the patronage system better illus-
trated than in the trajectory of Frederick North's (1732–92) career. Becom-
ing First Minister in 1770, Lord North was the son of Francis North, the
Earl of Guilford, whose ancestors had served Henry VIII, Charles II, and
James II. His pedigree included an education at Eton and Oxford. Like his
Welsh counterpart, North excelled in his studies, especially in Greco-
Roman classics and modern languages. The similarities ended there.
Whereas Lloyd voluntarily exiled himself, North experienced little trouble
advancing his political career. Elected MP of Banbury in 1754, he rose to
junior Lord of the Treasury in 1759, Paymaster-Master General in 1766,
and Chancellor of the Exchequer and First Lord of the Treasury in 1770.
The inertia of patronage had moved him beyond his own aspirations. North
exhibited little ambition for office apart from his sense of familial obligation. He enjoyed the House of Commons and was considered an amiable,
easy-going fellow. Reluctantly he led the first charge against John Wilkes
and supported George Grenville's Stamp Act of 1764; policies Lloyd
opposed. Perpetually plagued by personal debt, his contemporaries nevertheless considered him an effective and adroit treasury official. Always
under the shadow of his father (who lived until 1790), North, a Whig with
Tory tendencies, sincerely supported the establishment. Nonetheless at the
height of the American War of Independence he repeatedly asked for
George III to relieve him from office.[1] North contrasted sharply with Lloyd,
who held ambitions for military office but was compelled to flee Britain as
a young man. An outsider and rebel, he abandoned fealty to established
authority and embraced the Enlightenment, often its more radical tenets.
But he likewise entered the patronage system and received a pension for his
service to the crown. His lack of family connections and possibly his association with ex-Jacobites all but precluded advancement. With Granby's
death in 1770 his door to the upper echelons of the military establishment
abruptly closed.

Lloyd directly appealed to Lord North, a man uncomfortable with exercising the patronage that had furthered his own career. Using a familiar method of deference, Lloyd dedicated his latest publication, *An essay on the theory of money,* to the First Minister and confessed: "The good opinion I have of your Lordship's ability and integrity is my only motive for inscribing the following Essay to you."[2] With his wife Mary and newborn son Hannibal to support, General Lloyd required more than his annual pension.[3] There is no indication however that it helped Lloyd's position or that North even read the book. But patronage in eighteenth-century society could come from a variety of directions. Lloyd married into the Garnett family, which had connections with the Bank of England and the upper hierarchy of the Church of England. That family also brought with it Jacobite ties, with which Lloyd naturally identified. Actually, he constructed a kinship network from two sub-sections of British society. First, through the Garnetts he befriended such former Jacobites as the Johnstone family and others of Scottish, Irish, or Welsh heritage. His relationship with the Fitzwilliam family of Merionethshire may have predated this time, but it was an important component in this Celtic coterie. Second, ties to the British armed forces, especially officers he met while in Brunswick's service, augmented his circle of friends and displayed a wide range of political proclivities and social affiliations. Chief members of this military cabal included Major General Henry Clinton, Major General Robert Boyd, Lieutenant General Edward Harvey, and Lieutenant General Robert Clerk. The network generally operated on the fringe of British elite society, but in the case of Clinton, who was groom of the bedchamber to the Duke of Gloucester,[4] it also penetrated more powerful circles of the realm. Henry Lloyd's prospects were not nearly as hopeless as one might think.

Since 1768 war had ravaged the Balkans. For three years Russia and Turkey grappled in a war of attrition over Polish sovereignty, the Russians supporting Orthodox and Protestant dissidents and Turkey (in an ironic twist) defending the interests of the Roman Catholic establishment.[5] Lloyd once intimated to Pietro Verri his desire to join the Russian army. In early 1772 with the protection of his wife's relative William Pulteney, 2d Earl of Bath (1729–1805), and the support of the outgoing British ambassador to Russia, Charles Schaw, 4th Baron Cathcart (1721–76), he procured an audience with Catherine II (r.1762–96) and her ministers.[6] Impressed by his polished demeanor and knowledge of military affairs, the empress offered him the commission of major general, which he accepted after first securing the liberty to travel to England at his convenience.[7] Lloyd's long sought-after military command was at last a reality. Foreign dignitaries, in particular the Austrian ambassador, reported his presence.[8]

Lloyd joined an officer corps comprised of a large number of foreigners during the eighteenth century. By 1770, nearly 40 percent of all officers were foreign-born, and some of them, largely ex-Jacobites, came from

Great Britain.[9] Most however were German and Swedish. Although recruited on merit, they did not attain high office, because they lacked family connections with the political cliques that governed the Russian court.[10] Lloyd's entry into the upper echelon of the army establishment, apart from the obvious military utility, must also be viewed through the prism of both domestic and foreign politics. First, Catherine, who obtained power through a coup, feared retaliation against her regime, not universally considered legitimate. After a brilliant 1770 campaign, her armies failed to win a breakthrough and succeeded only in inadvertently spreading the plague from the Balkans to Kiev and even as far north as Moscow.[11] The ensuing peasant unrest (culminating in the Pugachev Revolt of 1773–74) and rumors of a court conspiracy prompted a shift of power from the Orlov clique to the Panin party headed by her foreign minister, Nikita Ivanovich Panin (1718–83).[12] As a subject of the pro-Russian King George III, Lloyd provided unquestionable loyalty to Catherine unlike the officers associated more closely with internal opposition. But it was in foreign affairs that he initially made his mark.

Throughout the 1760s Britain attempted to solidify an Anglo-Russian alliance to counterbalance French predominance on the continent. Blame for its failure rested mostly with the British, who refused to concede to Russian demands of undermining royal authority in Sweden and forming a mutual defense pact against the Ottoman Empire.[13] Yet Panin coveted a British alliance; it was a key component of his diplomatic Northern System.[14] Throughout the first years of the Russo-Turkish War Britain used Lord Cathcart's embassy in Petersburg and its support of the Russian navy's voyage into the Mediterranean as means to mediate a peace and revive diplomatic talks. Because his involvement in the Russian service could be interpreted as a possible conflict of interest, Lloyd feared that King George III would cancel his pension. He wrote Clinton offering to quit Catherine's service if His Majesty disapproved, and to reassure him that the Empress and her court were sincerely pro-English.[15] But the British government viewed his dual loyalty as a benefit. With the arrival in June 1772 of the new minister plenipotentiary and envoy extraordinary Robert Gunning (1731–1816), the stage was set for the last attempt at an Anglo-Russian alliance.[16]

Russia and Turkey signed a truce in May 1772, which Britain hoped would lead to peace negotiations and an end to the war. Successful British mediation coupled with Russian flexibility over the Swedish problem appeared to make the alliance a definite possibility at this time. During the summer Panin attempted to reopen treaty negotiations through Count Ivan Chernyshev and Lloyd, with the latter serving as an intermediary between the foreign minister and Robert Gunning.[17] Lloyd wrote Clinton that he could secure for Great Britain 30,000 Russian troops, 10–12 ships of the line plus 10,000 sailors without a peacetime subsidy, and a mutual guarantee of European and American territory without a British war against Turkey.[18] Contingency upset these designs when Gustavus III (r.1771–92) of Sweden staged a coup in August and became an absolute ruler. The unexpected turn of events frightened the Russian court. Panin now demanded an Anglo-Russian war against Sweden, which the British rejected. Lloyd approached the Prussian ambassador, Victor Friedrich, Graf von Solms, to sound out Frederick's interest in an Anglo-Prussian-Russian entente. Frederick, an Anglophobe, rejected any such accommodation.[19] British influence declined and the truce between Russia and Turkey endured until 1773.

By the end of 1772, Russia suffered from the plague, peasant unrest, and a stalled war in the Balkans. The Polish Partition in August had averted Austrian intervention on Turkey's side, therefore keeping the conflict from expanding into a general European war. Lloyd, who had yet to receive a field command, began pressing for a Siberian military expedition against Manchu (Ch'ing) China. Border excursions south of Lake Baikal near Kyakhta almost triggered a Sino-Russian war in the 1760s. If not for the eruption of war with Turkey, failed trade talks and perceived Chinese insults may have pushed Catherine into war. By 1772 Russia had added seven dragoon regiments to its border forces, bringing the total to 15,000 troops.[20] Lloyd boasted if given command of 20,000 soldiers he could invade Mongolia, ransom Chinese cities beyond the Great Wall, and return with enough booty to assuage Russia's financial difficulties and solve its lingering border problem with China.[21] Expecting peace with Turkey in early 1773, Catherine gave Lloyd nominal command of 24,000 men for the proposed Chinese campaign, which she viewed in the larger context of continued Russian expansion and settlement of her Siberian territories.[22] When the Russo-Turkish truce collapsed in May 1773 hostilities recommenced and the Chinese war was shelved. Field-Marshal Count Petr Aleksandrovich Rumiantsev (1725–96) led Russian forces in the Balkans on a disastrous campaign.[23] Lloyd, no doubt frustrated, exercised his liberty and returned to London: a move first mistaken for resignation or outright dismissal by foreign officials.[24] By year's end, Anglo-Russian relations cooled over Britain's refusal to subsidize Denmark and support Prussian claims in Danzig.[25] The chance for an alliance was over.

During the winter of 1773–74 Catherine recalled Lloyd from his self-imposed vacation.[26] He took this opportunity to forward his own plan for the next campaign. It called for crossing the Danube and fighting a decisive battle or two against the Grand Vizier's forces.[27] With peace negotiations again stalled, the Russian army under Rumiantsev began mobilizing along the Danube River in Wallachia and Bulgaria.[28] Lloyd, with four Russian servants, returned to England but intended to join the army in the Balkans by June. He persuaded several English "observers" to accompany him on this 2,500-mile adventure. The group included Major General Henry Clinton; his cousin and next Duke of Newcastle, Thomas Pelham Clinton

(1752–95); Richard Fitzwilliam (1745–1816) the future 7th Viscount Fitzwilliam; and Major Thomas Carleton of the 20th Regiment of Foot (Lancashire Fusiliers).[29] Clinton's party joined Lloyd (who wore a green great coat and donned a bearskin cap) and his staff at Chatham on 27 April.[30] From Dover they crossed the English Channel, a most unpleasant passage.[31] They landed at Ostend the next day and were greeted by an Austrian major, an Abby named Ignatius O'Hagarty, and several merchants, who acted as guides during part of the journey. They moved to Bruges later that night after a noisy altercation between Lloyd and their coachman. Clinton remarked this incident revealed yet another "specimen of his wrath."[32] From Bruges they traveled to Ghent, Brussels, Laffeld (where they examined the famous battlefield), then to Aix-la-Chapelle, Cologne, Coblentz, and Frankfurt am Maine without incident.[33] After arriving at Frankfurt on 1 May, they surveyed the battlefield of Bergen east of the city where Clinton had fallen wounded on 13 April 1759. They departed the next day and traveled first to Hanau (where they saw the Dettingen battlefield), Wittenburg, Göttingen, Nuremburg and then to Ratisbon, where they embarked on the Danube River.[34] Clinton incorrectly predicted they would be at Bianza by 7 May in time to visit Emperor Joseph II (r.1765–90).[35] They reached Vienna on 12 May where they remained for over a week until procuring an audience with both Prince Kaunitz and Emperor Joseph.[36]

During their stay in Vienna word arrived through the Russian Count Dmitry Aleksandrovich Golitsyn that Catherine now forbade foreign volunteers from joining the Russian army for fear of espionage. Several French observers, one a close acquaintance of the Empress, had recently been discovered as spies.[37] After much discussion with the Russian envoy, Lloyd and his party obtained "a kind of permission" to proceed to the Russian camp.[38] In late May they ventured overland into Transylvania. From Belsburg the party traveled by horse to Temesvar and then Hermanstadt where they arrived on 6 June. From there they traveled to Kronstadt and embarked on the Danube toward the Russian camp in Wallachia.[39] After witnessing a clash between Turks and Cossacks along the Danube on 19 June they arrived the next day and were received by Marshal Rumiantsev, who showed them great hospitality.[40] But the Marshal's attention quickly returned to the war, which was going well for the Russians.[41]

Rumiantsev's campaign had begun in April as his army, organized in four corps, prepared to cross the Danube and proceed south between it and the Black Sea coast in Bulgaria.[42] His goal was Shumla (ninety miles southeast of Bucharest), the Grand Vizier Muhsinzade Mehmed Pasha's (1706–74) headquarters and main Turkish camp. The advance guard under General Mikhail Kamenskii and General Aleksandr Vasilevich Suvorov's (1750–1800) 8,000 troops attacked and inflicted a devastating defeat on a large Turkish army (40,000) under Reis Effende at Kozludzhi (twenty miles

northeast of Shumla) on 20 June.[43] Ivan Saltykov's corps then advanced and
blockaded Rushchuk (fifty miles northwest of Shumla), which effectively
cut it off from the main Turkish army. Only the fortress of Silistria (thirty
miles north of Shumla) on the Danube River hindered a general advance on
the Grand Vizier's camp. It was at this point in the operations General
Lloyd and his party of observers joined the Russian camp near Silistria.[44]

Lloyd took command of the First Division and covered the advance of
Rumiantsev's main army toward Silistria on 23–25 June.[45] In fact, Rumiantsev did not intend to capture Silistria, but rather he wanted to blockade the
stronghold so he could move on Shumla unmolested.[46] The Turkish garrison
commander realized the ploy and led sorties against Lloyd's positions
(mostly artillery-laden redoubts) across the Danube only to be turned back
by gunboats and Russian troops now across the river.[47] On 2 July the Turks
opened an artillery barrage that forced the gunboats out of range. Four days
later, under cover of these guns, a large relief force of 6,000 Turks attacked
Lloyd's island redoubt northeast of the fortress. Several Turkish boats full of
Janissaries landed, but were driven from the beachhead by furious bayonet
charges and two squadrons of light cavalry led by Major Welianow.[48] Having repulsed the attack, Lloyd continued the holding siege and successfully
bottled up Silistria until Rumiantsev drove south to Shumla.[49] The stage was
set for a great artillery barrage (of 300 guns) against Silistria by General
Lloyd's forces.[50] But peace negotiations cut short the siege and the war ended
on 16 July when the Turks signed the Treaty of Kutchuk-Kainardji.[51]

Lloyd's participation in this operation significantly influenced his military
theory; a short analysis of the Russian and Ottoman ways of war will shed
light on his later ideas. The Balkan geography and environment demanded
methods of war different from those of Western Europe. A virtual land
ocean existed over the entire theater of war, devoid of urban areas or large
population bases. Such a military ecosystem hindered the mobility and supply of large armies. Religious hostility and the periodic ravaging of diseases
like the plague made campaigning extremely difficult and precarious.[52]
Ottoman defensive strategy allowed the Turks to operate close to their supply bases. In fact, their supply system was far superior to Russia's and for
that matter nearly every European army. The Russians, on the other hand,
operated far from home and faced the dilemma of diminishing returns with
every advance.[53] In contrast to the Turks, however, the Russian army possessed superior leadership, which in the end accounted for its spectacular
victories over superior enemy forces.[54]

A major reason for this superiority was Rumiantsev's flexible and innovative approach to tactics and operations. Dispensing with the large unitary
armies once used by Peter the Great and Field-Marshal Burkhard
Christoph, Graf von Münnich (1683–1767), he developed formations
called "divisional squares" to combat the Turks. Comprising between two
and six battalions, each square was actually a hollow, oblong formation

The Siege of Silistria

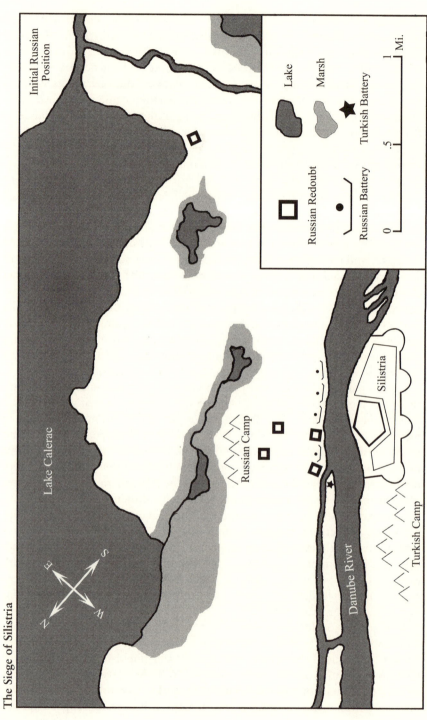

Initial Russian Position

Lake Calerac

Russian Camp

Silistria

Danube River

Turkish Camp

Russian Redoubt

Russian Battery

Lake

Marsh

Turkish Battery

0   .5   1   Mi.

with infantry, usually in two or three ranks, forming its perimeter. When grouped together with mobile artillery and connected by formations of light infantry and cavalry, the squares permitted operational and tactical flexibility. They were relatively easy to supply in the desolate Balkan theater and they could maneuver over large expanses, but still quickly converge on an enemy army, often enveloping it and attacking on several fronts. Rumiantsev's great victories in the 1770 campaign at Ryabaya Mogila (28 June), Larga (18 July), and Kagul (1 August) testified to the efficacy of his novel approach to Balkan warfare. At Kagul with five squares he enveloped a Turkish army of 150,000 soldiers and won a decisive victory, leaving nearly 20,000 Turks dead on the battlefield. The squares proved they could defend against irregular Turkish units like the Tartar cavalry, attack with massed firepower, and rapidly change direction of maneuver in sight of the enemy.[55]

The Turkish order of battle encouraged Russian mobility. On campaign the Turkish forces entrenched in two infantry lines, each flanked by large numbers of cavalry, and a third line of reserve cavalry. The elite Janissaries formed the center of the second line and anchored the entire battle formation. The system's immobility proved fatal when fighting Rumiantsev's squares, which could surround and attack the lines with ease. Also, the lack of central control over the irregular cavalry forces and feudal infantry caused considerable confusion on the battlefield and did nothing to enhance Turkish effectiveness. Rumiantsev's use of light forces weakened the feudal host and relayed Turkish positions back toward the Russian square formations. Furthermore, his charismatic style of leadership and unorthodox methods like night attacks, bayonet charges, and a general disdain for the defensive did much to invigorate the Russian army with enthusiasm and fighting spirit.[56] Lloyd, who advocated light troops, mobile formations, and the use of enthusiasm, admired Rumiantsev and Suvorov's military acumen.[57] The experience offered a stirring alternative to the methods of war practiced in Western Europe.

Immediately after the conclusion of the Russo-Turkish War, Lloyd retired to Warsaw to recuperate from a severe illness contracted during the campaign.[58] He remained in Russian service and Catherine promised him command of an army of 30,000 soldiers poised to invade Finland in the projected war with Gustavus III of Sweden.[59] But tensions decreased, the military campaign was canceled, and later in 1777 the King gained Catherine's goodwill during a personal visit to St. Petersburg.[60] Resuming his emissary role, Lloyd may have been involved in Britain's unsuccessful entreaty in 1775 to secure 20,000 Russian mercenaries to fight in North America.[61] With the decline of Panin's influence and pro-British policy, Lloyd realized his position was precarious. When he asked for leave to go to London on important business, Catherine at first refused, but then sent Count Panin to accept any of the general's conditions. Knowing that enemies in the court influenced her first refusal, an agitated Lloyd responded: "Tell her Majesty that I am satisfied; she is under great obligations to me; I am under none to her."[62] His pride wounded, he departed, forsaking a pension as well as the expected Order of St. George.[63] Once again the prejudices of aristocratic society had thwarted his aspirations. He remained in London from 1776 until Mary's death in 1778.[64] Afterward he traveled extensively, residing in France (Brest) and the Austrian Netherlands (Huy) away from official life until the unforeseen events of the American Revolution pulled him back into the stream of events.[65]

The war, which began at Lexington on 19 April 1775, initially appeared manageable to the British government. With George Washington's retreat from Long Island and New York City in August and September 1776, the rebel cause seemed doomed. Defeats at Trenton and Princeton in early 1777 did not undermine British confidence, and General Sir William Howe's (1729–1814) occupation of Philadelphia in September only strengthened imperial resolve. However, Major General John Burgoyne's (1722–92) surrender at Saratoga in October 1777 and the ensuing Franco-American alliance of February 1778 changed the character of the war from a colonial to a European struggle. In June 1779 war erupted between France and Britain; Spain, bound by the Third Family Compact, declared war as well. Immediately France planned yet another invasion of England, one of the true continuities of its eighteenth-century military policy.

A sea-borne invasion was not France's initial choice; rather, Spain required the invasion as well as assaults on Gibraltar and Minorca as conditions for its continued support.[66] The Treaty of Aranjuez (12 April 1779) called for the defeat of the Royal Navy by combined Franco-Spanish forces in the English Channel followed by an attack on Portsmouth with 25,000 men under the victor of Corsica, Noël Jourde, comte de Vaux, and a Spanish siege of Gibraltar. Britain lacked allies and with its navy in poor condition, an invasion seemed probable. Lord North ministry's crisis of confidence trickled down to the general populace.[67] In June reports from British agents abroad reached London, and a general panic ensued. North soon received more specific details regarding the French plan to descend on Portsmouth and Plymouth in July. Acting on his own initiative, Lloyd passed detailed information of the Franco-Spanish combined fleet to North's ministry throughout the summer as well as warning the Portsmouth governor of French intentions.[68] Thereafter, he traveled from Boulogne to Brest, where the invasion force concentrated, supplying London with important intelligence.[69]

French plans went awry from the start. In July smallpox ravaged the fleet and expeditionary force, killing the favorite son of its commander Louis Guillouet, comte d'Orvilliers (1708–92). He never recovered from his grief. The Spanish fleet arrived a month late from Cádiz and nearly caused considerable consternation in the French army and government. The combined fleet, now sixty-six ships of the line (Lloyd's exact figure), met stiff winds in the Channel, and came in sight of Plymouth on 16 August. The smaller British fleet (thirty ships of the line) under Admiral Charles Hardy (1716–80) spotted D'Orvilliers, but within three days the fleet had vanished from sight. Fog continued to keep the fleets apart and in October the invasion was canceled. The failed invasion did not inhibit Spain from launching a siege of Gibraltar that lasted nearly four years with no effect.[70] Of course, Lloyd had visited the place beforehand and instructed Lieutenant General George Augustus Eliott (1717–90) as to the best methods for its defense.[71]

Lloyd gained renown during the summer of 1779, less from his clandestine activities than by his publication of a pamphlet titled, *A Rhapsody on the Present System of French Politics; on the Projected Invasion, and the Means to Defeat It*. It was the culmination of a lifetime of study on British home defense (often from the perspective of its enemies); few people outside of France knew more about French capability to invade England than the ex-Jacobite. North's government, fearful that its contents might reveal information otherwise unknown, immediately paid Lloyd a handsome sum for its suppression.[72] The general attached little weight to the contents (he circulated copies among his friends). Rather, he intended the publication to rally the nation around King George III and "inspire the government, as well as the nation in general, with that confidence which the situation of our affairs require."[73] He reassured the nation that the British Isles were safe so long as the Royal Navy did not fight a general engagement. Only a naval defeat would allow the transport of a French army and supplies across the English Channel. If they landed troops without first defeating the Royal Navy, then the invasion was doomed.[74] In this opinion, he agreed with the official policy of the Royal Navy, which prohibited any confrontation with the combined fleet. He disagreed, however, with the government's preparations, and these controversial statements, more than a desire for secrecy, probably prompted Lord North to suppress the pamphlet.

First, Lloyd's overall strategic analysis coincided with that of the government: the French would try to invade England with secondary efforts against Gibraltar and perhaps Ireland as well. He differed in his belief that Plymouth and Portsmouth should be fortified and secured before the interior or even London. Both General Sir Jeffery Amherst, Baron Amherst (1717–97), commander of British land forces and member of North's cabinet, and Deputy Quartermaster General Colonel William Roy (1726–90), an engineer and defense specialist, initially discounted the notion of a Plymouth or Portsmouth landing. Instead, they concentrated on garrisoning and fortifying London, perhaps more for political than military reasons. Lord North did not overrule Amherst even though he learned that the French had targeted Portsmouth and Plymouth. Had the invasion actually occurred in July without defending Plymouth or Portsmouth, Lloyd believed England would have been forced to sue for peace.[75]

The governor of Portsmouth, Lieutenant General Robert Monckton (1726–82), was an able tactician, and upon receiving Lloyd's intelligence prepared the place for the expected French landing and siege. Plymouth, under the command of Lieutenant General David Lindsay, suffered from malaise. Not until the arrival of Master-General of Ordnance George Townshend (1724–1807) did order emerge from the confused and unorganized preparations.[76] Lloyd believed each position, if well defended, capable of halting a French assault. Any attack on Portsmouth required occupation of the Isle of Wight, a place he considered too difficult for the French to control for any length of time.[77] Monckton's vigorous and competent preparations mollified Lloyd's concerns. The half-hearted attempts to secure Plymouth did not. Lloyd feared it would be the primary target of France's sea-borne assault (it was actually the secondary target after Portsmouth). If captured it would mean certain ruin: British forces were far too scattered in a cordon-like system for them to concentrate rapidly, bottle up the French army, and halt its advance on London.[78]

In August, at the height of the invasion scare, British home forces totaled about 20,000 regular troops and 30,000 English and Welsh militia. They were positioned accordingly: 10,000 in Kent (Coxheath); 6,300 in Essex (Warley); 3,200 in Salisbury; the Guards and Household Cavalry in London; two regular and two militia battalions in Plymouth, three militia regiments at Portsmouth, two militia corps in Chatham, and one militia corps each in Dover, Southampton, and Winchester.[79] With defenses spread thinly across the countryside, Lloyd believed that if a French assault captured Portsmouth or Plymouth, London would lie open to attack. He proposed bolstering the line extending from Plymouth to Dover, which would keep the French army from marching inland or east toward London. Portsdown, the central point on that line, required one-third of the army, as did Haldon Hill just beyond Exeter and the position between Sussex and Kent. A more concentrated array of forces would allow them to mutually support one another if attacked and block a French advance if forced to operate on their own.[80]

Lloyd analyzed several scenarios to demonstrate the difficulties that would befall a French landing. If they successfully landed and besieged Plymouth, the forces at Haldon Hill could quickly come to its aid and inflict a "total overthrow of the enemy."[81] Even with the fall of Plymouth, French difficulties would not abate. They could not remain for long due to a lack of supplies, and the combined fleet could not remain forever in the English Channel as a supply chain. As long as British troops held nearby Mount Edgecombe, the French army could not leave Plymouth and eventually would be forced to evacuate. Their only recourse was to march toward Haldon Hill and advance into the interior. A French capture of the hill would mean disaster for Britain, but Lloyd was confident that it could be easily defended with 10,000 troops.[82]

Yet, Lloyd did not consider Britain's defense of a sea-borne invasion easy or simple. He believed the French army possessed several advantages over the British army. With an experienced high command and well-trained regiments, the French could defeat the British army in an open battle. Therefore, the British army had to avoid battle and use the closed nature of the English countryside to remedy these deficiencies. From Plymouth or Portsmouth to London, the French army faced only a few roads wide enough for columns; for the most part this terrain was hilly and full of defiles or hedges. Such topography would force the French army to march in one column, leave behind its heavy artillery, and rely only on the supplies it could carry to London. Because it had to remain in one large formation, it would be unwieldy and easily hemmed in by geography.[83] Its line of communications would weaken as it advanced, opening it to rapid counterattacks on its flanks and sure destruction. "I am persuaded," Lloyd boasted, "that no army, however numerous, will ever be able to penetrate forty miles into the country, if proper [his] methods are taken to oppose it."[84]

No other British military figure had as much knowledge about French invasion plans and the English countryside as did Lloyd. No doubt his critique of home defense planning rankled Amherst, but the pamphlet gained notoriety both in and out of England. In 1780, Edmund Jennings asked John Adams to procure a copy, which in any case he failed to do.[85] Both Lord Townshend and Colonel James Branham afterwards studied and circulated its contents within the military establishment.[86] After Lloyd's death the British government purchased the remaining manuscript copies, but his agent (who possessed the original plates) reprinted the book five times during the 1790s and in 1803 as propaganda to assure the British populace that a French invasion was wholly improbable.[87] Napoleonic France responded in kind with a French translation with editorial commentary arguing the contrary.[88] Ironically, Lloyd received a measure of fame posthumously with an anonymous book suppressed before its general sale to the public. For the next twenty years copies were much sought after, especially by military men.[89]

Lloyd's treatise was highly critical of British foreign policy in general and North's ministry in particular, which further angered the British government. As a partisan of Wilkes and a critic of Britain's colonial policy, Lloyd lamented the current state of affairs and the war against the North American colonies. He placed the conflict's cause on the undo influence the merchant class held over Parliament. Due to their interests Britain had chosen its conquests (Canada) in the Seven Years' War unwisely. "We act upon too narrow a scale," he declared, "like our traders, and seldom as a powerful nation."[90] Colonial unrest stemmed from that unfortunate acquisition and an unwise taxation policy. In addition, without continental allies or a significant presence at foreign courts, Britain had allowed French influence to grow. Coupling this difficulty with the disastrous neglect of the Royal Navy, he predicted the end of England's overseas predominance.[91]

Lloyd also regretted the management of the American rebellion. Burgoyne's defeat at Saratoga and Clinton's southern operation into the Carolinas seemed absurd. The only way to defeat the Americans was to persist and erode support for the rebellion, not conquer each colony in succession. To do this British forces must hold New York, Long Island, Rhode Island, and Philadelphia, and "cease those fruitless and unmeaning excursions in the American woods."[92] Lloyd believed colonial political resolve would collapse and a peaceful accommodation, perhaps a renewed union between the two, could be reached, if the British army ceased offensive military operations and occupied the major seaboard cities. Offensive operations were to be relegated to the West Indies in order to divert French and Spanish material support of the American cause. Therefore, the problem facing North's government was political, not military. British forces could simply outlast the Continental Army and erode public support of the war via economic hardships. By 1780 reconciliation seemed implausible, but at the war's end it was clear that the American cause was teetering on the verge of collapse, preceded only by the disintegration of Britain's will to endure another campaign.[93] Yet, it is difficult to believe, as many British statesmen did as late as 1782, that the colonies could be restored *status quo antebellum*.

Lloyd's criticism betrayed his desire to join the fight against the American colonies. He first made his opinions known in 1777 after Burgoyne boasted of easy victory before departing to take charge of British forces in Canada. "I am sure this fine flourishing fellow," Lloyd jested, "will come home with his arms tied behind his back."[94] Saratoga fulfilled that prophecy, but he found it impossible to gain a command, any command, in North America, most likely due to his aforemetioned criticism of Lord George Germain's (1716–85) and Amherst's war effort.[95] In 1780, Clinton tried to appoint Lloyd commander of the Provincial (royalist) Troops with the rank of lieutenant general, but Amherst objected.[96] Denied a military post he continued his unofficial clandestine activities. His presence in Paris evoked the concern of Edmund Jennings, who warned John Adams to be aware of Lloyd, "a very bad man."[97] Between visits, he resided in Huy in the Bishopric of Liège and continued his military writing and criticism of the British war effort.[98] In 1782 the new ministry headed by William Fitzmaurice Petty, 2d Earl of Shelburne (1737–1805), sent word that Lloyd would be named commander-in-chief of the British Army in North America if treaty negotiations in Paris collapsed.[99] Excited by his prospects, Lloyd returned to London, but the Treaty of Paris (30 November 1782) ended his last chance for military glory. He retired to Huy.

During the many upheavals that shook the British Empire, Henry Lloyd, an archetype of the eighteenth-century mercenary soldier, remained a servant of Mars. He defended Great Britain against invasion in 1779 and tried in vain to persuade it to change its strategy in America. Despite the sincerity of his patriotism, he never procured a commission in the British military establishment. Another irony in a lifetime of ironies was his employment in the Russian army in the last campaign of Catherine's Turkish War. This last taste of war altered, or at least modified Lloyd's conception of military organization and operations. No longer exclusively the student of western European warfare, his experience in Moldavia and Bulgaria proved pivotal to his final work on the art of war. The classical heritage of his education, the wisdom of his thirty-year military career, and the intellectual fermentation of his own enlightenment combined and coalesced to form a statement of tactics, operational doctrine, and military philosophy intended to shake the Western European military establishment at its core.

Philosopher of War

Custom is a tyrant, who governs mankind with more despotic sway
than an Eastern monarch.

—*Henry Lloyd*, CHLWG

Henry Lloyd published his philosophy of war in 1781 to challenge the traditions of European military establishments. The general tenor was critical
and iconoclastic. He argued blind obedience to practices born in the age of
Louis XIV had produced the indecisive warfare that plagued the eighteenth
century. Military theorists should discredit those "truths" in the same manner that modern philosophers dismissed the "dreams and visions" of Plato
and Aristotle. Four general themes permeate the *Continuation of the History of the Late War in Germany*.[1] The first examined the role of moral
forces. Blending enlightened psychology with the study of human nature
and personality, Lloyd presented one dimension of war as a complex interaction of human will and imagination. As a corollary, he depicted war's
political nature, and the effect political and governmental institutions had
on its conduct. Obviously an extension of politics and diplomacy, a given
society's socio-economic structure influenced the nature of warfare. The last
general theme concentrated on the material and physical causes of Europe's
indecisive warfare. Lloyd unveiled his own plan for army reform and articulated the beginnings of operational and strategic thought to remedy the
shortcomings of modern military practice. He not only questioned the organization of armies and the conduct of war, but also inveighed against the

social inequities of European society. Europe's political and social structure prohibited a meritocracy of military talent in favor of the nobility and landed aristocracy, who viewed military office as a privilege of birth.[2] Lloyd's final publication attacked military traditions and social inequality offering instead an enlightened philosophy of war.

Lloyd began the examination of moral forces with an analysis of military leadership. A critic of European society, he concluded that competent military officers did not result from birth, status, or other accidents of circumstance conferred upon the nobility. High birth did not insure success, and because nobles viewed service as a right, their monopoly of military offices retarded the military profession.[3] Lloyd considered the man of merit, regardless of social class, the ideal candidate for military office—he exemplified the true military professional. A society based on egalitarianism rather than hierarchy would insure the creation of a meritocracy. Reforms of that magnitude implied significant change in the European social order. Not until Napoleon Bonaparte seized the remains of the French Revolution in 1799 would the meritocratic spirit pervade a European military institution.[4] Nonetheless genius was the preeminent example of military talent that transcended social barriers. The man of genius, more than the man of merit, was naturally endowed for war. Enlightened thinkers wrestled with the problem of genius and concluded it was a gift of nature, not society.[5] Denis Diderot advanced an organic definition, comparing the genius for war to divine inspiration in that it could perceive the whole and understand the entirety of things.[6] Alexander III the Great (356–323 B.C.) personified the classic archetype, with the modern version embodied by Frederick the Great of Prussia. Lloyd developed his understanding of genius from such English empiricists as William Gerard, who viewed it as an "enthusiastic fire" and "divine impulse," and William Duff, who termed it a "divine fury."[7] A rare commodity, genius intuitively understood how to apply military principles through direct action. But Lloyd explained that ordinary European officers stumbled "for want of that enthusiastick [sic] and divine fire."[8] Comparing warfare to the art of poetry, Lloyd confessed that the vast majority of military officers were not poets and therefore required intense study of their profession. An important product of the German *Aufklärung* and object of interest to Carl von Clausewitz, Lloyd first grafted the concept of genius on military theory.[9]

In the absence of genius, officers could master the art of military leadership, which required the proper understanding of human nature and the adoption of specific personality traits. Like a music conductor who directed the actions of the numerous instruments in an orchestra, the military leader persuaded and directed the actions of an army. He could not force an army to act, because it was not a simple machine like a clock that could be wound up and set into motion. The moral forces and passions of the soldiers created a reciprocal relationship between them and the commander. Remembering Bergen-op-Zoom, Lloyd used the metaphor of the sea to explain the actions of armies: they could be calm or furious. The art of command resided in harnessing the power of these moral forces and directing them toward an assigned objective or purpose. Success reinforced discipline and élan, defeat or idleness engendered corruption and revolt. Once a commander lost moral control, no amount of persuasion, reasoning, or argument would restrain the common soldier, who on the whole was a "rude, ignorant, intractable being."[10] A proper personality induced authority and enabled a leader to direct the motions of an army.

Lloyd's experience within the noble-led armies of Europe convinced him that personality was the key to effective leadership. Noble pride, avarice, envy, and intemperate behavior instilled a general dislike and disdain for the military leader. For instance, jealous superiors often intrigued against gifted subordinates and resorted to open cruelty. The Austrian army had been riddled with competing cliques revolving around eminent commanders. Lloyd's quarrel with Siškovíc during the Seven Years' War resulted from a like clash of personalities and mutual enmity. Such incidents alienated the leader from his men and caused morale to collapse throughout the army, resulting in its defeat on the battlefield. Lloyd warned that soldiers did not follow officers because they held noble title or owned large estates, nor did they respect or love officers out of force or fear. Integrity weighed more than status. The Prussian attitude towards soldiers, that they should fear their officers more than their enemies, was inimical to his idea of enlightened leadership. Gallant conduct and professional merit, traits rare in the nobility, furthered the acquisition of personal authority and leadership. Exemplary behavior included avoiding favoritism, remaining confident in all situations, and most important sharing all the toils and dangers of war with one's men. Lloyd identified with the common soldier, perhaps because of his common origins, and encouraged leniency in punishment except in cases of capital crimes.[11] "No man is infallible," he wrote, "[and] it is the duty and the interest of the general to be just, humane, and kind to those he commands, and particularly to those of the lower class."[12] Respect and compassion, not fear and hatred, defined the character of the ideal military leader. Such authority, once established, provided the means to motivate and encourage an army to accomplish great deeds.

Soldier motivation required a complete understanding of human passions. Lloyd applied his sensationist psychology and claimed all action stemmed from the desire for pleasure and the avoidance of pain. All animals possessed sensual passions to some degree, but only man experienced what Lloyd called the social passions. Based on the desire for pre-eminence and distinction, these passions caused all social action, and thus were the keys to unleashing the enthusiasm of soldiers. Men satisfied their social desires by attaining glory and renown on the battlefield. But little room for advancement existed for the common soldier in Europe's hierarchical society, since he typically came from the lower classes. The artificial barriers against non-nobles effectively undermined natural motivation.[13] Too often fear filled the vacuum, thus negating the military virtues of courage and heroism. If unchecked, fear of a dangerous situation, the enemy, or an uncertain future would debase the common soldier and reduce him to what Lloyd termed his animal state. "What can be expected from an ordinary soldier in the ranks," he wrote, "agitated by the cries of the dying, and by the terror of death floating before his eyes."[14] Paralysis, panic, and defeat inevitably ensued. The effective leader had to ingrain in his soldiers the concepts of honor, awarded for brave conduct, and shame, bestowed for cowardice, to counter the influence of fear. Lloyd was convinced that "when the principle of honour and a sense of shame are firmly established in the human heart, they . . . are the source of all great and heroic actions."[15] An *esprit de corps,* or regimental glory, could fill the void and reinvigorate the soldiers. The experienced commander manipulated the enthusiasm created by honor and shame, thus motivating his soldiers to accomplish great feats.

Several social factors fanned the flames of enthusiasm according to Lloyd's analysis. The common soldier desired monetary reward and promises of plunder. Lloyd predicted the men would exert much energy in acquiring riches of the corrupt condition of European society. He lamented the lack of virtue, but confessed "we cannot form men to our wishes, and must take them as they are."[16] Monetary rewards could be substituted in lieu of social honors, so long as they were commensurate with the achievements and not excessive. Historical precedents convinced him of the efficacy of monetary honors. The Greeks and Romans fought for riches, and the present-day Turks acted primarily from the desire for plunder. But fighting solely for money was unseemly and did not unleash the true potential of the soldier. "The coin may make a tolerable slave," Lloyd confessed, "but can never form a hero."[17] Religion and patriotism, or the love of liberty, also motivated soldiers, but in eighteenth-century Europe neither element appeared useful. Lloyd rebuked Christianity because its theology emphasized submission and pacifism rather than military virtues. Islam, on the other hand, promised divine rewards for the killing of infidels. Lloyd became convinced that religion's marginal military utility could not justify the great threat it posed to society. The clergy, a dangerous group of people, used religious passion to promote discord and obtain political power. Europe's past religious wars, excessively cruel and destructive, strengthened Lloyd's enlightened conviction against religious motivation because it only increased the power of the clergy and therefore was not worth promoting in any great degree.[18]

All animals (including man) loved liberty and freedom and existed with some measure of each. The motivating potential of each was endless, but the European monarchical states effectively suppressed liberty with artificial class constraints. Even Great Britain, considered a "free" country, had offended the liberties of its American colonists and fomented a civil war. The conflict revealed the proclivity of political liberty to undermine other loyalties and forms of motivation. Monarchies and aristocratic republics actively discouraged patriotism and formed armies loyal only to the sovereign. Lloyd warned that armies inspired by the "enthusiastic fire of liberty" were far superior to ones fighting for riches or the honor of their masters.[19] Lloyd did not live to see the social factors of liberty and patriotism utilized by European armies, but prophetically cautioned: "[T]remble, ye mighty monarchs, and beware, the effects of despair are terrible."[20] It is not clear whether Lloyd would have supported the French Revolution.

In an age of coalition, conflict and diplomatic realignment politics greatly influenced warfare. Lloyd extended his analysis of moral forces and social criticism to an examination of the connections among politics, government, and war. The despotic, monarchical, and republican forms of government affected the character of war and the nature of military establishment in distinct ways. For instance, the corrupt nature of despotic states (in Lloyd's experience personified by the Ottoman Turks) damaged military effectiveness. These empires stretched across the Asian land mass and subjugated many diverse peoples. The army existed to suppress its unwilling subjects, impose order, collect tribute, and perpetuate the despotic system. A lack of energy or purpose characterized despotic wars, especially in the initial campaigns. Garrisoned throughout the empire, troops took too long to assemble and concentrate for military action. Peacetime dispersion also eroded the army's moral qualities. Failing to undergo routine training, discipline, and subordination, it lacked the necessary unit cohesion. As a result of its political role, Lloyd argued the Ottoman army resembled no more than a provincial militia. Led by fearful Grand Viziers (who faced execution if defeated) it never possessed a fixed plan or strategy and engaged in no more than skirmishing if the enemy failed to act aggressively. When victorious the army disintegrated into plundering hordes; when defeated it fled cutting short the entire campaign.[21] An expression of contemporary European prejudices against the East, Lloyd's derision of despotic war reflected his own experience and study of modern Turkish conflicts.

European monarchies and republics did not practice the despotic way of war. The polity differed from a despotic state in the relationship with its subjects. In despotism, the people submitted to the power of the sovereign with no recourse to civil law or tribunals; it was a simple aggregate of individuals. Western powers historically developed the "nation" expressed in various political combinations. A nation unlike a despotic state united a number of provinces under a sovereign power (king or Parliament) and bound them together with general laws and mutual obligations.[22] The structure of a civil society or nation could exercise a positive influence on the conduct of warfare.

In a monarchy (similar to a despotism) one person wielded power, but that power was circumscribed by intermediary bodies and property-owning subjects. Initially these lords had controlled the king, but over time the pendulum swung against them. Lloyd believed the absolute monarchies of his day dangerously approached despotism buttressed by an inequitable social order. The once proud nobles, dependent on state employment in the army and bureaucracy, contributed to this inequity by zealously defending their privileges. Therefore, European armies composed of mercenaries did not reflect the nation, and their aristocratic officer corps actually opposed the nation's interests. Thus, monarchs typically desired short wars, not to lessen the effects of war on their subjects, but because the longer the war the greater the discomfort for the aristocracy. Rapid and energetic opening campaigns characterized their wars, which were subsequently followed by subsequent long, drawn-out operations.[23] Lloyd condemned prior European wars (referring to Louis XV's France) as products of royal caprice and the influence of court favorites.[24] This political-military cycle contributed to indecisive wars of mutual exhaustion and bankruptcy.

Democracies and republics displayed unique forms of war. Unlike monarchies, democratic states feared standing armies controlled by centralized political power and relied instead on citizen militias. Due to this social consideration, warfare tended to be defensive, because a militia sought only to safeguard the nation's borders. But democratic wars could drag on indefinitely as the Peloponnesian War clearly demonstrated. Unable to defeat one another decisively, Sparta and Athens resorted to years of pillaging and small-scale incursions against enemy territory. Therefore, political structure did not determine the relative success of warfare; but armies in a democracy did reflect the societies they served and contoured the kind of war a society could conduct.[25]

Republics, whether democratic or not, were well suited to fight defensive wars for two reasons. First, citizenship tied an individual to the state. Second, liberty and patriotism motivated him to defend the homeland at any cost. The Swiss Confederation's wars against Austrian and French invaders in the Middle Ages typified the defensive strength of republics.[26] An aristocratic republic, however, faced more difficulty in rallying the nation to its defense. It tended to employ mercenaries loyal to the ruling class or to specific interests. Britain's war against its American colonies illustrated the inherent weaknesses of aristocratic warfare. Internal political upheaval and poor military leadership undermined the effort, which then lapsed into a war of exhaustion.[27] Rome represented Lloyd's ideal military republic. Over the centuries it had wedded the concept of the citizen with the virtues of the soldier and conquered much of the known world. Only after succumbing to the corruption of aristocracy and mercenary armies did its glory fade and its walled cities crumble.[28]

Lloyd linked the political nature of war to military theory. In despotic states where the oppressed people had no voice; logistics, leadership, and discipline suffered. Where people had obtained some measure of political liberty, as in monarchies and republics, military effectiveness increased in proportion to that liberty. The study of moral forces implicitly criticized the social and political structure of European society. Social inequality and political corruption hindered the development of the military as an effective instrument. This argument intrigued Gerhard Johann David von Scharnhorst (1755–1813), a Hanoverian officer who published an extended review of the book in his military periodical *Die Militair-Bibliothek*.[29] Lloyd also emphasized the relationship between people, state and society. Writing in an "era of democratic revolution" marked by increasing political tensions, it is not surprising to see that the political nature of warfare occupied the center-stage of Lloyd's analysis of moral forces. In essence he introduced the idea of war as a function of the relationship among people, army, and government; that "paradoxical trinity" later identified by Carl von Clausewitz.[30]

The centerpiece of Lloyd's military theory addressed the army reform necessary to revive decisive warfare. Europe's three great wars of the eighteenth century failed to resolve the political issues that sparked them, and each dragged on for several years, exhausting all parties, bankrupting the states, and ruining the populations. "Wars are not now as formerly terminated by battles, and complete victories," he argued, "[h]ence, in our days, no kingdoms are overturned, no nation is enslaved.[31] The reason for this indecisiveness lay not in politics or even the inequitable military organizations that perpetuated professional mediocrity.[32] War remained indecisive primarily because the organization and tactics of armies made battlefield victory less than complete. European armies equipped with the flintlock musket and bayonet could never reach a tactical decision; and that deadlock reverberated upward into operations, strategy, and diplomacy.[33] Arrayed in two long, thin lines of infantry, opposing armies never closed with one another to decide a battle. One side or the other exhausted themselves and withdrew before the moment of decision, thereby prolonging a war.[34] Military tradition and custom thwarted any reform. In an era when criticism was viewed as a form of treason or rebellion, Lloyd challenged orthodoxy in the guise of an enlightened military *philosophe*.[35]

Lloyd believed an army required three essential properties: strength, agility, and universality. Strength arose from the manner in which troops were arranged and armed; agility defined the celerity of movement acquired through extensive drill and training; and universality embodied the ideal arrangement in which troops could act on any type of ground against any kind of troops. Lloyd posited that all weapons and tactical evolutions must be analogous to these three principles, which alone made an army victorious. The current fashion of imitating the methods of Frederick the Great countered this theory; the king's success had depended on his own genius and the incompetence of his enemies.[36] That did not mean Lloyd romanticized the ancients and wished to revive their military formations. He analyzed the Greek phalanx and Roman legion and found both wanting: the phalanx lacked agility and universality, while the legion lacked sufficient strength to act independent of cavalry.[37] All European armies, ancient and modern, exhibited fatal flaws.

In particular the reliance on firearms made modern European armies ineffective. As they approached one another from a distance, gunfire gradually weakened the soldiers' resolve to continue forward to the decisive clash of close-quarter combat. Much of the future criticism of Lloyd's theory would be animated by this assertion. But Lloyd never suggested that battles waged with muskets would not be destructive and murderous. Even a bloodied army, weary of the decisive clash, had time to disengage and withdraw because the enemy approached slowly and in proportion to their rate of gunfire.[38] Without gunpowder weapons, Greek and Roman wars exhibited a level of decisiveness unseen in modern times.[39] Lloyd did not advocate, however, abandoning firearms. He believed soldiers armed with muskets proved highly effective in broken terrain or behind entrenchments, where linear formations could not operate. Therefore muskets suited defensive operations.[40] Firearms were not universal weapons; and the attempt to transform them into offensive weapons with linear formations that maximized firepower countered the principles of agility, strength, and universality.

The modern order of battle consisted of two long lines (often several miles each), with three ranks of musket-wielding infantry. Lloyd saw several problems with this arrangement which contributed to indecisive battle. First, the long thin lines could not protect any one segment from cavalry charges. Only three men deep, the formation lacked the requisite strength required of Lloyd's ideal army formula. The smoothbore musket in line formation could not defend against cavalry. Dependent on weather, the quality of gunpowder, the skill of the soldier, the inaccuracy of the gun, and the effect of moral forces; these weapons could not be trusted to deliver the volume of fire required to stop enemy cavalry from advancing.[41] Next, once deployed the long lines could not maneuver. They could only move forward and backward (with great difficulty), and in broken terrain not at all. The long linear formation was ideally suited for large flat plains, but lacked agility and universality on other terrain.[42] A more mobile enemy could outmaneuver it, attack its flanks, and rout it without much of a fight (much like the battle of Leuthen). But Lloyd's own experience in the Austrian army (at Maxen and Hochkirch) demonstrated that traditional tactical formations could be adapted to unusual circumstances. The three-rank line was more flexible than Lloyd was prepared to admit. Succumbing to the nature of enlightened polemic, Lloyd simply overstated his case and inadvertently cultivated a stereotype of eighteenth-century warfare that persisted long after his death.

Lloyd posited that the current use of heavy cavalry (cuirassiers) added to the ineffectiveness of gunpowder armies. Because of feudal tradition, large masses of cavalry were stationed on the flanks of the long lines, ostensibly to protect the infantry from enemy cavalry assaults. Arranged in three ranks like the infantry, but with much more depth, cavalry squadrons theoretically provided the "shock" power of an army against enemy infantry and cavalry. Lloyd considered cavalry "shock power" an absurd concept. Cavalry's real power existed in its ability to infiltrate and destabilize the cohesion and order of enemy formations. Based on speed and velocity, the proper role of cavalry did not require mass formations. Light cavalry acting individually like Hussars were far more effective in disrupting enemy formations. Traditional methods of placing cavalry in tightly-packed formations resulted in cavalry remaining inactive during a battle. Infiltration required open-order tactics. More important, cavalry placed on the army's flanks did not have an opportunity to support the infantry. An army was ideally an integrated weapons system. Each part of an army had to be mutually supported in Lloyd's opinion, and placing cavalry on the flanks prohibited them from supporting the bulk of the infantry and also prohibited the infantry from protecting the cavalry. Infantry could provide its own flank support by forming squares against a cavalry charge, but Lloyd did not believe stationary cavalry could defend itself against enemy cavalry or an infantry charge without either retreating or suffering defeat.[43] Heavy cavalry also slowed the operations of armies, because it required extensive logistical support in the form of forage.

The European tools of war, therefore, were blunt and unable to accomplish the task required of them. Later writers and observers concurred with Lloyd's general conclusion. The conduct of operations suffered from these deficiencies so much that modern historians have discovered a "crisis of strategy" in the eighteenth century.[44] Marching (even in column) was slow and elaborate due to a lack of good roads. Therefore commanders maneuvered cautiously, fearful of discovering the enemy by chance and compromising their position as did the French army at Rossbach (5 November 1757). For this reason they used reconnaissance in mass (large battalions of light troops) to search for the enemy and keep headquarters informed of its movement. Lloyd believed large advanced forces betrayed one's position and gave the enemy time to adjust his positions and react to one's movement. This caused a reciprocal cycle in which each side constantly changed and rearranged its units to avoid being caught unprepared. Each plan of attack rapidly became obsolete as the enemy reacted to one's movement and deployments. Thus, battles rarely occurred, and when they did neither side enjoyed any advantage of position or surprise. The Austrian defeat at

Liegnitz (15 August 1760) illustrated Lloyd's point. *Quartiermeistergeneral* Siškovíc had changed the main army's positioning the night before battle, which caused a considerable delay in its advance. By the time it arrived on the battlefield, Laudon's advance corps had been defeated and the victorious Prussian army already withdrawn.[45]

Rather than conduct reconnaissance in force, Lloyd advocated the use of small groups to shadow an enemy, keeping themselves concealed, much as he had done in the 1760 campaign. This method would allow the long lines of infantry to deploy closer to the enemy and at a tactical advantage. But other obstacles hindered an army's mobility, especially the slow approach necessitated by the logistical requirements of a large artillery train. Furthermore, officers too often fought for ground rather than making war against enemy soldiers. Fatigued from attacking fortified posts, an army failed to pursue a defeated enemy.[46] Therefore, battlefield victory only lengthened a war destined to exhaust all sides mutually. "Indeed our battles . . . are commonly nothing more than great skirmishes," he railed, "an army, though much inferior in number to the enemy . . . when commanded by an able leader, will occupy some advantageous post, stop the progress of the mighty and victorious for years, till victor and vanquished are almost equally exhausted and ruined."[47] Avoiding these useless battles was as important as winning a battle. Modern historians have also identified the general problem of indecisive warfare, a phenomenon not confined to the eighteenth century.[48]

Lloyd's angst over European armies and warfare must be viewed in a wider perspective and with circumspection. Warfare often appeared indecisive because of the factors he detailed, and gunpowder weapons did pose challenges to effective warfare because of their awesome defensive firepower and their general tendency of bleeding armies to the point where they could not operate effectively for long periods of time. But this reality does not prove Lloyd's somewhat biased and stereotyped vision of eighteenth-century combat. Being an enlightened *philosophe* contoured his military thought in entirely new directions, but it also pushed him into the role of propagandist. To affect change and popularize one's ideas, the *philosophe* necessarily argued in the extreme. Similar to his political writings, Lloyd lost touch of objectivity when he attacked the military status quo. Within the context of his experience he forwarded the most pernicious characteristics of the Austrian military establishment as the general character of all European armies.

With the limitations of Lloyd's agenda in clear view, it is important to note that contemporary military writers believed serious problems did limit military effectiveness. Lloyd was no Don Quixote. The call for tactical reform did not begin with him; it appeared as a constant feature of the military literature of the era, especially French writers like Feuquiéres and Jacques-François Maximo de Chastenet, marquis de Puységur (1656–1743), who reflected on warfare in the flintlock musket era.[49] The Cheva-

lier de Folard put forth the first program of reform in his *Nouvelles Décou-
vertes sur la Guerre* and *Histoire de Polybe* by calling for a return to the
massed infantry phalanxes of the Greeks and Macedonians to enhance
the offensive shock value of musket-wielding soldiers. Partisans of the column or *ordre profond* argued that only infantry shock action would return
tactical decisiveness to the battlefield. Folard's most prominent disciple
was François-Jean de Graindorge Dorgeville, baron de Mésnil-Durand
(1729–99), who called for a *plésion* of 768 soldiers to attack through shock
action alone without recourse to firearms.[50] Supporters of the flintlock musket and bayonet tactical system, or the *ordre mince,* also forwarded plans
for tactical reform to enhance firepower and achieve tactical decision.
Jacque Antoine Hippolyte, comte de Guibert (1743–90) tried to reconcile
the two schools by emphasizing drill, aimed fire, and rapid mobility.[51]
Guibert ranked shock action as a desirable tactic, but superiority of fire
ranked higher. Battalions should approach an enemy in column formation
to enhance movement, but then rapidly form lines to unleash volleys. The
army that could perfect the rapid change from column to line would have
a great advantage in mobility over the enemy who deployed in line formation from the outset. The future belonged to firepower.[52]

Consensus seekers like Paul Gédéon Joly, comte de Maizeroy (1719–80)[53]
called for additional ranks to reinforce the line. Others simply attacked
Guibert's suggestions. Mésnil-Durand created a new system for his column
in which masses of skirmishers screened the approaching *plésions.*[54] In 1778
at the camp of Vaussieux, the French army (awaiting transport for the invasion of England) tested the column formations advocated by Mésnil-
Durand and his supporters. The results revealed the defects of the column.
It worked well when maneuvering toward an enemy, but once engaged it
became bogged down by its mass, lacked firepower, and had no defense
against artillery.[55] The two schools of thought converged when Guibert
developed the *ordre mixte,* a combination of column for maneuver and linear tactics for actual fighting.[56] The French Revolutionary Ordinance of
1791 codified his basic system.[57]

Lloyd's "New System," or theory of tactics, originated within this general
framework of military reform, but it did not conform to either school of
thought.[58] Rather, he reflected on years of experience, in particular his Russian experience, and produced a unique if not innovative form of grand tactics. In organization, armament, and use of each military arm, he broke from
tradition and emphasized the utility of tactical and operational mobility over
the reliance on firepower. He believed his methods would make battle decisive once again and in turn ensure short wars (and in essence limit the effect
of war on society) to the benefit of Europe. Without knowledge of his career
and intellectual scope, the system appears strange, odd, and somewhat
reactionary—the basic conclusion reached by modern interpreters of
Lloyd.[59] In reality, as in all other spheres of his writings, he put forth a progressive if not prophetic vision of war (not intended to be a universal theory)

later employed by Napoleon Bonaparte in spirit if not in actual form. Lloyd simply endeavored to bring mobility to battle formations at both the operational and tactical levels. Therefore, he proposed a broken line of musket-wielding infantrymen, three ranks deep, with a fourth rank composed of pikemen. Each division of the line would operate quasi-independently when approaching the enemy, who Lloyd assumed still used the long unbroken three-rank line. Within the intervals between each "divisional line" (author's terminology) he placed light cavalry and light infantry. On the flanks he placed small-caliber artillery to support the infantry and defend it from enemy attacks.[60] The creation of divisions within the order of battle was not new. The French army under Broglie experimented with broken lines at the close of the Seven Years' War in an attempt to outflank and envelop enemy linear formations.[61] Lacy had used broken formations at Maxen and Hochkirch. But Lloyd advocated a version of Rumiantsev's order of battle successfully used during the Russo-Turkish War of 1768–74. An analysis of the details of this formation will reveal that he was not simply imitating the Russian method.

The first three ranks of infantry carried flintlock muskets with barrels shortened by nearly twelve inches. This adaptation would reduce the range and accuracy of the weapon, but allow the soldier to place a short lance, about four feet in length with a six-inch steel tip, on the end of the gun creating a pole-arm for close-quarter combat. The fourth infantry rank would be armed with twelve-foot pikes, sabers, and pistols. Lloyd thought all infantry should wear cotton uniforms with wide-brimmed leather caps and thick leather cuirasses or breastplates that ran from neck to waist. On the cap several small chains attached to the cuirass, providing additional protection to the neck and face. The formation was designed for shock action, not firepower. Its function was to approach an enemy, perhaps fire a pre-loaded shot, and charge *en masse* with lances fixed and pikemen close behind. The leather armor and face protection could shield the soldier from bayonets, swords, and musket balls fired at a distance, or when up close at an angle. Once engaged with an enemy using traditional techniques (and after suffering many casualties from short range musket fire) Lloyd believed his divisional lines would easily defeat and turn an enemy to flight. The cavalry, wielding seven-foot long lances, four-foot sabers, and two pistols apiece, also played a crucial role.[62] Unlike traditional European heavy cavalry placed in deep formation to charge enemy lines, Lloyd dispersed his cavalry among the divisional lines as well as on their flanks to offer some protection to the infantry. More importantly, they acted as the chief engines of pursuit once an enemy began to flee the battlefield. Then acting individually like Hussars or Turkish *spahis,* the cavalry would annihilate the beaten foe and swiftly run down the remnants of that army pell-mell.[63] The light cavalry and Hussars, while assisting in this battlefield role, primarily acted as reconnaissance, and therefore used only muskets.

Llyod's New System

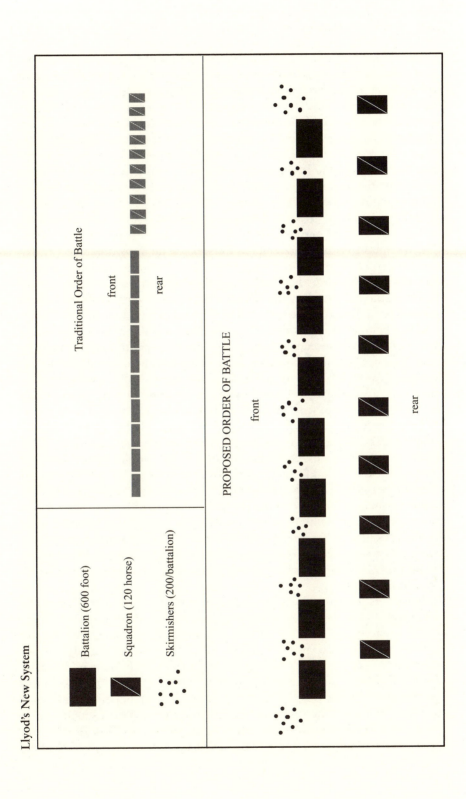

Traditional Order of Battle

front

rear

Battalion (600 foot)

Squadron (120 horse)

Skirmishers (200/battalion)

PROPOSED ORDER OF BATTLE

front

rear

Lloyd's light infantry played an integral part within this tactical system, and constituted his most profound contribution to the military theory of his time. These troops, armed with the musket-lance, could act in an individual capacity or in open-order formation.[64] At the beginning of battle they screened the advance of the divisional lines, thus shielding the infantry from musket fire as long as possible. Next, instead of fleeing the field and moving to the rear, they would fill the intervals between lines and protect the extreme flanks of the larger army formation. Enemy penetration between lines or on the flanks would be met with a combined counterattack by light infantry, light cavalry, regular cavalry, and artillery placed on the flanks of each divisional line.[65] During defensive operations light troops assisted the advance of the army and threatened the enemy's rear areas and supply lines. Lloyd's innovative vision attempted to integrate all arms (infantry, cavalry, and artillery) so that each could support the other during combat. However the divisional line army had both strengths and weaknesses.

The battalion served as the primary tactical and organizational unit of the divisional line army. It consisted of five companies (four heavy infantry and one light infantry) totaling 712 men. Once arrayed in the four-line system each company occupied a thirty-two-man front with the light infantry (200 men per battalion) on either flank of the battalion. The battalion formation measured 100 yards in length allowing for small breaks in the line between each company.[66] Lloyd envisioned an army of sixty infantry battalions (42,000 men) with intervals of as much as 150 yards between battalions. The potential for flexibility and its disregard of long linear formations gave the formation great strength. The front could expand from 6,000 yards to 14,700 yards depending on the length of the enemy line and envelop the flanks of an equal number of troops placed in traditional linear formations, which Lloyd assumed could not exceed 12,000 yards. The intervals enabled an army to maneuver in all types of terrain, since it was not necessary to maintain cohesion along its entire front. Lloyd's ideal maneuver called for a pinning force of forty battalions to engage the enemy while a "hammer" comprising twenty battalions attacked its flank or rear.[67] What the old system viewed as a vice (a break in the line) had been transformed into virtue.

Despite its strengths, the implementation of the battalion formation posed several problems. How would these dislocated lines defend against enemy cavalry charging at the intervals? The divisional light troops, cavalry, and artillery offered some protection, but Lloyd instilled an organic defense mechanism. On being attacked by enemy cavalry, each infantry company formed divisional squares reminiscent of Rumiantsev's army. A square measured eight men across and sixteen men deep. The combination of pikemen and close-range gunfire supported by crossfire from adjacent squares made them if not impervious to enemy cavalry charges, at least difficult to break. In the event of large, massed charges against an entire portion of the line, entire battalions could form oblong squares and be reinforced on their wings by the light infantry, cavalry, and artillery in the intervals between battalions.[68] The cavalry stood poised for that support role. Consisting of forty squadrons (6,500 men), it formed behind the divisional lines, each squadron arranged in loose four-rank formations with an eight-man front. In this manner the flexible squadrons could maneuver easily through and between the intervals and support the infantry as well as pursue a defeated enemy.[69]

Highly flexible, Lloyd's system nevertheless lacked both infantry and artillery-based firepower. With one 3- or 4-pound cannon and one 7- or 8-inch howitzer per battalion, the army wielded sixty of each, all of which were dispersed along the line for infantry support. Lloyd regarded large, massed artillery formations as unwieldy (yet powerful) and lacking the speed and mobility that his formation required to succeed.[70] The logistical requirements of artillery created a strategic and operational paralysis inimical to his overall vision of battle. The short infantry muskets and fourth rank of pikemen also reduced firepower. After considerable debate, the consensus rejected reviving the pike, notwithstanding its brief use by French revolutionary armies.[71] Again, Lloyd should not be vilified for failing to predict the evolution of technology like the rifle and machine gun, which made infantry shock action relatively obsolete.[72] Lloyd's use of cavalry flew in the face of the chivalric traditions of that combat arm, resulting in censure from such notable personalities as Napoleon Bonaparte. Bonaparte's reputation was enough to diminish the "New System" in the eyes of contemporaries and future scholars.[73] Finally, Lloyd did not consider the possibility of a battle between two divisional line armies. He remarked only that the outcome of such combat would be decided by the skill of the opposing generals. But the paradox remained that the wholesale adoption of these armies would negate the benefits of innovation Lloyd described in convincing detail. The utility of these armies had but a small window of opportunity until once again battle would become indecisive, as each opponent deployed the same formations on the battlefield.

Lloyd's divisional line army was a harbinger of future developments. If understood in the context of his times and overall operational theory, they resemble in spirit, if not actual form, the organizational innovations and operational methods of the French Revolutionary and Napoleonic armies. The use of large numbers of light troops before and during a battle foreshadowed the changes made by European armies over the next thirty years.[74] The system also required a high level of decentralized decision-making (and therefore skilled officers), with the result being that no European army adopted it. Apart from the potential problems and benefits of the divisional line army, it revealed Lloyd's enlightened approach to warfare. He believed Vauban's scientific methods had debilitated field warfare and contributed to indecisive battle and wars of mutual exhaustion. His depreciation of artillery on campaign reflected this bias and in part revealed

his own ideology against scientific warfare in favor of close order combat.[75] His aversion to gunpowder-dominated armies countered such
authorities as Puységur who argued in favor of firearms as superior
weapons. The divisional lines existed to fight offensive-minded battles and
annihilate an enemy army. They did not exist to besiege fortresses; that he
left to engineers, artillerymen, and logistics experts (though he did believe
they could attack fortified camps and positions).[76] All too often battle
resembled siege warfare; its pace was slowed by artillery trains and cavalry,
which required a tremendous amount of logistical support on campaign.
Lloyd's system foreshadowed Napoleonic warfare and paralleled the writings of Guibert in seeking to liberate field armies from excessive logistical
constraints, restore mobility to field warfare, and make possible the annihilation of an enemy army.[77] An integral part of Lloyd's military theory, the
moral and physical destruction of the enemy army was the quintessential
goal of western warfare.

Lloyd's theory did not end with his New System, nor did he leave to fate
the execution of the military campaign that would bring about the decisive
clash of arms. Warfare possessed a higher level of organization and planning above tactics or grand tactics. This operational level, which he
described in his narrative of the Seven Years' War, was symbolized by what
he termed "lines of operation." These imaginary lines connected supply
depots, cities, and fortresses via roads, waterways, and passable topography and represented the channels of communication and movement along
which entire armies moved and maneuvered.[78] The basic premise of his
defense of Great Britain from a French invasion rested on the ability of the
British army to control the lines of operation from the enemy army's landing zone to the interior of the country and London. In essence, lines of operation reflected the increasing use and reliance upon detailed and highly
accurate maps for military campaigns.

The understanding of lines of operation, or operational movement, could
aid in the planning of campaigns in order to force an enemy to battle on
favorable terms. Lloyd offered a few rules of thumb for operational planning and maneuver: the shortest and least difficult line of operation was
preferable to all others when possible or feasible; the direction of the line
should be such that an enemy army cannot threaten the flanks and cut the
supply and communication; and the line of operation must lead to some
decisive object or activity.[79] Shorter lines improved the position of an army
relative to an enemy, and longer lines weakened the army's position and
exposed it to being cut off by the enemy.[80] But his principles were not simply a geometric theory that tried to reduce operational movement to an
exact science using a protractor. They heralded the beginning of operational
and strategic thinking contoured by the geographic realities of eighteenth-
century Europe.

The empirical basis for Lloyd's operational concepts was geography. Lloyd advocated the development of permanent frontier quarters for the army to expedite the operational methods based on lines of operation. Permanent frontier garrisons would serve as the first base on a line of invasion (thus shortening that line) and protect the nation from an enemy invasion. Each garrison town would then connect with others and serve as a link in a chain of fortified areas that could serve as depots, hospitals, and mobilization centers. Such towns also served as recruiting centers and the backbone of re-supply and reinforcement. Lloyd proposed that all soldiers and their families reside in the towns based around regiments. In peacetime the soldiers would farm allotted lands, whose produce would be stored for military campaigns. At the age of ten, the sons of soldiers would become cadets and be allotted farmland. The chief aim was to create widespread military colonies (perhaps influenced by the Austrian Military Border) in which every soldier would believe himself tied to the state. In this way the training and morale of the regiment would be maintained year-long and the loyalty of the soldiers ensured.[81] To wage war a state had to prepare for war during periods of peace.[82]

The operational theory that emerged with lines of operation did not represent idealism or abstract concepts. It was based upon years of reflection, mostly from Lloyd's experience and study of the Seven Years' War. At a more fundamental level it was based on the appreciation of the relationship of space and time resulting from the predominance of geography and topography in the course of military operations. Revealing the steadfast empirical spirit of Lloyd's philosophy of war (and his enlightened philosophy in general), the role of geography in tactics, operations, and strategy dwarfed all other considerations in the formation of war plans.[83] He inserted an analysis of Europe's geography as related to military operations and gauged the strength of each state's frontier.

For instance, he divided France's frontier into three segments each with its own choke points or geographic strong points that could impede an enemy invasion and serve as a force multiplier for the defending army. Strasbourg protected the first line from Basel to Landau along the Rhine River, and 30,000–40,000 troops stationed there could prevent an enemy's crossing of the Rhine, which guarded the French frontier. The second line, from Landau to Sedan, was strong because of geography and a sophisticated fortress system. Lloyd deduced that an army encamped at Landau and one at Sedan could prevent an enemy from crossing the Rhine or from advancing into Lorrain or Champagne. The last line from Sedan to Dunkirk was the weakest segment, which explained its historic role as the most common European battle region. An army of 40,000 placed on the Sambre River and one stationed near Condé would block an invasion and be poised for an advantageous invasion of Flanders.[84] Overall Lloyd considered the

French frontier superior to all others and predicted that only Austria had the geographic capability to invade the Bourbon kingdom. With the Austrian Netherlands exposed to a French invasion, he counseled Austria to exchange it for Bavaria in order to bring geographic continuity to its possessions.[85]

His military advice for Austria was to concentrate its efforts on Eastern Europe and Turkey. Because of advantageous geography it could overrun Moldavia and Wallachia before the Turks could act. In the case of an Austro-Turkish war it should send an army from the Danube up the Save River and detach another composed of light troops into Croatia to advance into Bosnia. Those lines of operations would force Turkey to fight a battle or retreat and flee the region entirely.[86] As for Russia, Lloyd noted its problems in the second volume of his history of the Seven Years' War. It needed to occupy Poland and establish depots and supply lines in order for it to conduct a European war successfully.[87] The weak spot in Russian military geography was the line of operation between Smolensk, a poorly fortified city, and Moscow. Lloyd cautioned that Russia needed to defend this line at all costs, because "by occupying Moscow, the empire is overturned."[88] Perhaps Napoleon's familiarity with Lloyd's strategic concepts was deeper than the sources warrant. His route of invasion followed that line of operation, but to his misfortune and surprise the empire was not overturned by his occupation of Moscow. Seemingly proved wrong in his geopolitical conclusion, Lloyd did add the caveat that the vast expanse of Russia precluded its conquest and that a "conquering" army could not long stay in Moscow. Napoleon's 1812 campaign proved the verity of these theoretical suppositions.

Lloyd recognized the existence of both offensive and defensive war, each with its own nature and set of criteria for the conduct of operations. An offensive war required quick, decisive action whether it aimed to extort contributions, destroy enemy supply bases, or conquer an entire province. The basic rule called for a strategic penetration of one line of operation to capture a fortified place or construct a fortified camp from which to base further operations in an enemy country. Battle with the enemy inevitably resulted, but the goal was to fight with the shortest line of operation possible. Lloyd considered any one line exceeding 40 miles dangerous to the army; any line exceeding 100 miles meant certain defeat. The defensive was a much more flexible and stronger type of war, and if the defender acted on multiple lines of operation and managed to envelop the enemy army and cut its line, then disaster would ensue, such as John Burgoyne's defeat in America.[89] The Russian army in the Seven Years' War also demonstrated the debilitating nature of long lines of operation: it could not re-supply itself effectively and therefore lacked the ability to maneuver and fight vigorously.

Lloyd offered a test case for his operational and geopolitical military theory in his plan for the conquest of Britain's American colonies. He singled out the meddling of politicians in military operations as a significant reason for stalemate in North America. The larger reason for failure was the unsound military strategy used by the British army, which did not take into account the geopolitical realities of the situation. The thinly populated and expansive colonial landscape inhibited rapid, decisive military operations because it was far too difficult to supply and reinforce armies in the interior of the country. The fact that Great Britain supplied its war effort over a 3,000-mile oceanic line of operation explained many of the difficulties as far as Lloyd was concerned.[90] Logistics and geography in the case of America could not be overcome; therefore a military strategy had to be formed with those constraints in mind.

The winning military strategy also needed to conform with a political solution to the American rebellion. All the diversions and campaigns into the wilderness and Southern colonies meant nothing because they had no real purpose and could not be supported by the British fleet. Lloyd wanted to return to the early strategy of severing New England from the rest of the colonies. "The head, the heart, and support of the rebellion, revolt, insurrection," he claimed, "are the four provinces included between Hudson's River and Boston: if we could or can subdue these four provinces, the war is at an end."[91] He called for the occupation of Boston by 20,000 troops, the capture of Albany by 6,000–8,000 men sent from Canada, and the occupation of Rhode Island and Newport by 6,000–8,000 light troops supported by the Royal Navy. Once this was accomplished the lines of operation drawn between each place formed an iron barrier which would cut off those colonies from the rest of America and prevent the Continental Army or any rebel force from crossing without fear of annihilation from the mutually-supported bases.[92] Lloyd predicted the collapse of the political will of the rebellion and some form of reconciliation between the colonies and Britain. Whether or not the British army could have executed the capture of Albany and exhausted the American political will was possible but improbable. Britain's will to fight the war had eroded past the point from which it could be revived, especially with most of Europe armed against it. With Cornwallis's defeat at Yorktown and the loss of another army, British will collapsed and Lloyd's opportunity to enact his strategy disappeared. Britain made peace before he could assume the command purportedly promised by Lord Shelburne.

Lloyd's conception of defensive war contained revolutionary ideas about military operations and maneuver warfare. The reverse of the offensive, a defender's goals were to avoid battle if inferior to the invader and exhaust the enemy army by attacking or threatening its flank and line of operation. But Lloyd realized that victory was not purchased at a discount. "No army conquers merely by resisting," he warned, "you may repel an enemy, but victory is the result of action."[93] Unlike the invader, a defender had several options available. He could simply maneuver and slip away from the enemy or aggressively threaten a flank, forcing the enemy to shorten its line of operation, and thereby compelling him backward from where he came.[94] Lloyd's operational ideas take on a larger significance with his ideas on defending against multiple armies or a far superior enemy. When confronted by multiple armies Lloyd urged a defender to use the lines of operation to keep them separated. That is, he suggested interposing one's army between the converging forces and rapidly attacking and defeating each in detail.[95] Thus was born the Napoleonic concept of the strategy of the central position.[96] When confronted by a single superior enemy the defender could use lines of operation and maneuver to put him at an operational and therefore tactical disadvantage. Once the enemy penetrated thirty to forty miles, an army was to leave one-fifth its forces to oppose his advance and act as a pinning force. Next, three-fifths of the army (the main body) should be sent to act on the enemy army's flank, with the remaining forces (mostly light troops) cutting off its line of operations. The enemy, facing envelopment, could neither flee nor fight a battle at an advantage. Lloyd believed the result would be a decisive victory if one adhered to the lines of operation necessary to entrap the enemy.[97] Thus was born the Napoleonic concept of *les manœuvre sur les derrières*.[98]

The suggestion that Lloyd influenced the strategic and operational thinking of Napoleon Bonaparte is not just speculation. Notwithstanding Napoleon's criticism of the New System, Jean Colin and David G. Chandler argue the Emperor digested both Guibert's and Lloyd's writings prior to the French Revolution.[99] His offensive-minded approach to war reflected in the two strategies outlined above did resemble Lloyd's basic approach to the operational level of war. The Emperor's continual use of the terms "lines of operations" or "lines of communication" also reveals his exposure to Lloyd's concepts. Further circumstantial evidence suggests the proliferation of Lloyd's ideas in the armies of the French Revolution. During the Reign of Terror a manuscript copy of a French translation in the possession of the Germain Hyacinthe, marquis de Romance de Mesmon, fell into the hands of authorities. The Committee of Public Safety had the portions dealing with operations and strategy published and sent to all generals of the Republic.[100] It took Napoleon as Emperor of the French however to merge the ideas of offensive and defensive operations into a coherent system for bringing an enemy to battle and winning the decisive battle.

The final testament of an experienced military life and intellectual adventure, Lloyd's philosophy of war provided the seeds of the "Revolution in Military Thought" produced by the French Revolutionary and Napoleonic wars. His concern with moral forces, military leadership and the psychology behind soldier motivation predated the Clausewitzian synthesis, as did his unique concern with the political nature of warfare. Neither the product of the so-called Counter-Enlightenment nor the reflection of the Napoleonic era, the emphasis on the preeminence of the human element in war resulted from the combination of standard enlightened precepts and military theory. Similar enlightened principles animated his spirited critique of European society and provided genesis for his attack on military tradition. That assault resulted in his New System and the first theory of military operations, both harbingers of the warfare that ravaged Europe a few decades after his death and the advent of the science of strategy in the nineteenth century. Translated into several French and German editions, his final treatise occupies the apex of his philosophic thought, military or otherwise.[101] Perhaps the most insightful evaluation came from Lloyd himself: "In military affairs my errors can do no harm; they will be treated with contempt and vanish."[102]

Conclusion: The Death of General Lloyd

On 19 June 1783, Henry Humphrey Evans Lloyd died suddenly, cause unknown. He had completed his second volume on the Seven Years' War and was in the process of planning a larger history of European warfare since 1600. Not long thereafter British agents appeared in Huy and seized his papers under the pretext of debt collection. Buried at the end of the Grand Chemin (as were all non-Catholics) in death as in life Lloyd found no rest. A group of Roman Catholic fanatics disinterred and mutilated his body, thereby beginning the posthumous attack on Lloyd, the enlightened *philosophe*.[1] That desecration was symbolic for non-religious reasons as well. As a *philosophe* he attacked established traditions of the church and state, among them military traditions and practices. Enemies accumulated over the years because of his polemical rhetoric now sought retribution. For instance, in 1784 Tempelhof commenced his attack of Lloyd's critique of Frederick the Great. Over the succeeding decades, the details and context of Lloyd's military and political thought faded into obscurity.

Lloyd's accomplishments, because of their enduring value, stand out among the military writers of the eighteenth century. His study of military history and its relationship with theory, and his creation of a doctrine and call for professional institutions prefigured developments in the nineteenth century. His methodology of operational analysis and the delineation of principles of war derived from modern experience became a mainstay in military establishments. As the father of military sociology, Lloyd enriched military thought with his "National Character" concept by introducing into the literature the importance of studying and understanding the role of moral forces and human passions in warfare. His break from military tradition and the iconoclastic nature of his final writings make him one of the first true military critics. Alongside these notable achievements, Lloyd outlined the vocabulary and early conceptual models for operational planning and strategic thinking that dominated European military thought long after his death. But General Lloyd suffered two deaths, one physical and the other philosophical. Later interpreters and military writers misconstrued his inheritance. The military positivists of the nineteenth and twentieth centuries saw him as the inspiration for creating an exact and predictable science of strategy. Others who followed the historicist tradition set forth by Carl von Clausewitz saw in Lloyd the embodiment of eighteenth-century warfare; a lethargic and ineffective system which the Napoleonic era had exposed as inept and outdated.

Adam Heinrich Dietrich, Freiherr von Bülow (1757–1807) commenced the positivist science of strategy. A former Prussian officer, Bülow wrote *The Spirit of the Modern System of War* as the first interpretation of warfare during the French Revolution.[2] Seizing the language, but not the spirit, of Lloyd's writings, he posited that modern war was an exact science that could be reduced to a geometric analysis of the base of operations, the line of operations, and the military objective. He analyzed several scenarios using various combinations of lines of operations (concentric, eccentric and diverging lines) in relation to the angles between their base, line, and object.[3] This triangular theory was just that, an exercise in geometry using a protractor as the tool of military science. Most of his theorems concluded with the basic observation that victorious armies maintained short lines of communication and protected their flanks from enemy attacks.[4]

Contrary to Lloyd, Bülow believed that modern war rested more on numbers than on training and morale of soldiers.[5] Even stranger, he insisted on the obsolescence of defensive war while at the same time rejecting battle with an enemy army.[6] Although determined by superior numbers, modern warfare could not be won by actual fighting. Lloyd would have disagreed with these ideas, especially the suggestion that strategy was essentially geometric and existed apart from the actual physical realities of war. Bülow's idealism place him more a part of the nineteenth century than the eighteenth. His prophetic voice added that Europe one day would be dominated by several great powers, which after obtaining their natural limits would inaugurate a perpetual peace and extinguish war and the desire for military glory.[7] He mentioned Lloyd, but did not digress to reveal his influence, though he mistakenly credited Tempelhof with creating the idea of lines of communication.[8] In marked contrast to the Welshman, Bülow disregarded the entire empirical apparatus of his enlightened theory of war (especially geography) in favor of abstractions and geometric certainty. To Lloyd's misfortune, future theorists linked him and Bülow as the progenitors of the "Geometric School of War." As a result he became, like his *Doppelgänger* Bülow, a marginal if not discarded figure.[9]

The long and remarkable career of Antoine Henri, baron de Jomini (1779–1869), hastened Lloyd's descent into obscurity. Considered the nineteenth century's chief interpreter of Napoleonic warfare, the one-time staff officer under Napoleon and a deserter to the Russian army had far less military experience compared to Lloyd's colorful career. But Jomini ranks alongside Carl von Clausewitz as the greatest philosopher of modern warfare because of his voluminous writings on Napoleon and military strategy, aided by his penchant for self-promotion, and because he outlived his critics.[10] He acquired lasting fame for *The Art of War* and *Traité des grandes opérations militaires*.[11] The former was a theoretical treatise on military policy and strategy, borrowed heavily from Bülow's various combinations of lines of operations and strategic positivism.[12] The latter, a translation of Lloyd and Tempelhof's history of the Seven Years' War, Jomini proffered as his own in order to receive a staff position under Marshal Michel Ney (1769–1815).[13]

Yet because of Jomini's prolific publications, Lloyd's concepts reached a wide audience in the nineteenth century. Dennis Hart Mahan (1802–1871) first introduced French military literature to the fledgling United States officer corps attending the U.S. Military Academy at West Point, New York. Other such figures as John Michael O'Connor (fl.1812–1824) and Henry Wager Halleck (1815–1872), Mahan's protégé, specifically introduced Jomini's writings and theories into the growing body of America's professional military literature by the mid-century.[14] The latter's *Elements of Military Art and Science* dealt extensively with the concept of lines of operations and the importance of geography.[15] But the spirit and substance of Lloyd had been altered during this transmission. Gone was his skepticism concerning a complete knowledge of the art of war and opposition to reducing it to a few simple, scientific rules. His strategic inheritance lost much of its enlightened luster and with the help of Jomini had been distilled into a textbook and prescriptive manual. The age of positivism in military thought had arrived.

Military theorists and writers outside France and the United States did not suffer from an over-reliance on Jomini, but still they used Lloyd to validate their quest for an exact science of military strategy. In Russia, the General Staff officer Genrikh Antonovich Leer (1829–1904) followed Lloyd's insistence that the study of history and geography formed the backbone of strategy, and he trained an entire generation of officers to that effect, outlining modern principles of war from Lloyd's historically derived eighteenth-century corpus.[16] Leer's efforts echoed well into the twentieth century. In particular Lloyd's concept of military operations informed the Russian military theoretician Alexandr Andreevich Svechin (1878–1938), a founder of the Soviet operational art.[17]

In Great Britain, Lloyd's legacy fell to John Frederick Charles Fuller (1878–1964). Aghast at the carnage and destruction of World War I (1914–1918), Fuller discovered Lloyd's principles of war, which he used as the basis of his largely unsuccessful science of war.[18] Fuller believed Lloyd had attempted to reduce war to a science, and that he was the heir to this tradition in military thought. However, Fuller's interpretation, especially attacking any attempt to view war as an art, reveal a questionable and selective reading of Lloyd.[19] A mystic entranced by the number three and the idea of the Trinity, Fuller adopted Lloyd's three elements required of an army (strength, agility, and universality) and applauded his notion of balance between weapons, soldiers, and military formations.[20] Contrary to his stated goal, however, Fuller admitted only military genius "can produce original combinations out of the forces of war."[21] Fuller's effort floundered due to its own inconsistencies, but the idea that Lloyd represented the first attempt at a science of war became accepted belief, if not dogma.

The second intellectual trend to distort the military tradition of Lloyd and the Enlightenment in general was nineteenth-century historicism, exemplified by the writings of Carl von Clausewitz. In *On War* Clausewitz outlined a simplified sketch of the progress of military theory from the preceding era through his present day. To set himself apart from the pre-French Revolutionary writers, and to make himself stand out as original, Clausewitz chastised all predecessors for being preoccupied with the preparation for war rather than the conduct of war.[22] Previous theorists had moved from siege warfare to the examination of tactics not because of any creative intellectual activity, but to design a military instrument able to discharge its activity like the gears in a clock. Disregarding the limitless complexities of war, they continued to form a positive theory based upon rules and principles, resulting in operational concepts such as material factors and lines of supply. Clausewitz accused his predecessors of removing the moral factors of human psychology and violence from the military equation and ignoring the workings of genius "which rises above rules."[23] Obviously ignorant of Lloyd's final writings, Clausewitz yearned to create a philosophy of war remedying those defects, a philosophy that included the effects of danger, emotion, psychology, and opposition of human will.[24] The result was a mass of abstract reasoning combining the same objective and prescriptive elements of military thought he so despised. In the end he could not escape the more utilitarian theory of the pre-Napoleonic period, and as such should be considered one of the last enlightened military *philosophes*.[25]

The misconceptions and intellectual presuppositions of Clausewitz defined the Prusso-German reception of military theory in the nineteenth century. As a result of Clausewitz's influence, military writers such as Rudolf von Caemmerer (1845–1911) rejected eighteenth-century writers as offering nothing of value because they came from a period of warfare considered flawed and contrary to the dictates of nineteenth-century war.[26] Bülow became the symbol of the dynastic warfare of the eighteenth-century (even though he had tried to explain the new warfare of the French Revolution), and all those who continued to rely on such antiquated doctrines of Archduke Karl of Austria (1771–1847) were bound to suffer defeat.[27] With no small degree of irony, Lloyd himself had helped perpetuate this stereotyped view of eighteenth-century war with his zealous attack on military traditions and institutions.

The military historian and iconoclast, Hans Delbrück (1848–1929), in his attempt to revise the German General Staff's official view of the history of Prusso-German warfare, contributed unwittingly to the historicist attack on eighteenth-century military literature. In emphasizing the discontinuities between Frederick the Great and Napoleon's strategies (the origin of the war of attrition vs. annihilation debate), he pushed his case too far; not unlike Lloyd. He concluded that eighteenth-century theorists, Lloyd chief among them, had "established at that time the proposition that one could undertake military operations with geometrical strictness and wage war continuously without ever arriving at the necessity of fighting."[28] Lloyd had become the standard-bearer of military orthodoxy and a purveyor of the limited warfare of the *Ancien Régime*.[29] Delbrück's reputation as the first modern military historian and the depth and strength of his scholarship helped legitimize the distorted understanding of Lloyd's thought.

Lloyd himself added to the confusion over his work. The philosophy of the Enlightenment combined an ambiguous mix of polemics, authentic scientific investigation, and inquiry. In any single writing, one could discover what one wanted to find. Lloyd's isolated pronouncement that the correct use of geographic strong points could make battle unnecessary certainly appears to support nineteenth-century strategic positivism. His stereotyped analysis of contemporary warfare appears to support the historicist interpretation of eighteenth-century war. But his role as an enlightened *philosophe* tempers these limitations, which should be taken as a whole and not piecemeal. He offered no universal theory of war; he embroiled himself in the concerns of his day by combining philosophy and polemics, whose unifying thread was the interdependence of all the disparate parts.

Lloyd is unique in that he combined the military writer with the *philosophe*. Following the growth of his philosophy in relation to his experience reveals the important role of the Enlightenment. He had absorbed the canon of Greco-Roman literature, which he used as a model for his historical method. But the corrosive nature of enlightened discourse, in particular its anti-religious impulse, transformed him into an intellectual rebel, who applied the Enlightenment's critical spirit to military history and theory. By viewing warfare as a product of society, Lloyd shaped military thought for a secular age. Warfare could now be examined and reforms enacted to enhance military effectiveness and its ability to serve the state. The legacy of Henry Lloyd and the military inheritance of the Enlightenment was the conception of human conflict as an interrelated web of military, social, and human factors.

Lloyd's Principles of War

I. THE LAWS, OR PRINCIPLES OF WAR

1st Law, Principle: "That a soldier be cloathed [*sic*] and armed relative to the action he is to perform."

2nd Law, Principle: "That he be taught nothing, but what is of use to him, in the different situations which can occur, before the enemy."

3rd Law, Principle: "That he be taught everything that is absolutely necessary for him to know, in every case that may happen." This principle includes marching, firing, maneuvering, choosing camps, fortifications, artillery, geography, natural history, and national characters. *HLWG* 7[unnumbered].

II. PRINCIPLES, RULES, AND MAXIMS OF WARFARE

Rules of Marching, Maneuver, and the Exercise of Arms

General Rule of Marching: "That evolution is best, which with a given number of men, may be executed in the least space, and consequently in the least time possible." *HLWG* 13[unnumbered].

Security Axiom: "That no manœuvre [*sic*], whatever be executed, especially when near the enemy, unless it be protected by some division of the troops." *HLWG* 13[unnumbered].

Rule for Maneuver/Evolutions: "As all kinds of evolutions is founded on calculation, being a combination of space and time, it is morally impossible for a man to compute these two objects, without some knowledge of geometry and arithmetick [*sic*]." *HLWG* 16[unnumbered].

Maxim of the March of Armies: "that the army which marches best must, if the rest is equal, in the end prevail." *HLWG* 15[unnumbered].

Miscellaneous Principle of Maneuver: "cannot be calculated with any degree of precision, without the help of mathematicks [*sic*]: because whatever is not reduced to space and time, will in practice, turn out very uncertain." *HLWG* 19[unnumbered].

Rules of Firing: 1. "The utmost silence must be observed; and therefore the commanding officer of the batallion [*sic*] shall alone command the different firings; 2. That a batallion [*sic*], or regiment, in advancing to the enemy, must never be broke, unless forced thereto by the nature of the ground; 3. That the first rank must never kneel, under pretence of giving the third an opportunity to fire, with safety, because it is very dangerous, if near the enemy; and moreover, fatigues the soldier in such a manner, that he is soon useless." *HLWG* 16[unnumbered].

Positional and Irregular Warfare

Principles of Choosing Camp: 1. Geometrical: "calculating the distance relative, to the number and species of troops which compose an army; 2. Genius: "seeing all the different combinations, that may be formed on a given piece of ground, with a given army, and in the choice of that precise combination." *HLWG* 19 [unnumbered].

Principles of Strong Points: 1. "The science of positions, camps, marches, and even the project of campaign or plan of operation, must be regulated by these points: it is on this knowledge only, you can determine the number and species of troops that must compose the army; and consequently the quantity and quality of your magazines; 2. If you possess these points, you may reduce military operations to geometrical precision, and may for ever make war without error or being obliged to fight." *HLWG* 29[unnumbered].

Principles of Key Points: 1. "There is in every camp a certain point, which may very properly be called, the key of it, and on which depends the success of an action; while you keep this, the enemy has nothing; and when you lose it, all is lost." *HLWG, 54*; 2. "no rule can be given as to the manner of occupying properly a piece of ground; genius alone can do it, and precepts are in vain." *HLWG, 58.*

Rules of Fortification: 1. "It is with the ground, as with the features of men: there are not, perhaps, in the whole world, two features perfectly alike, nor two pieces of ground, of a given extent, perfectly similar; and consequently where the same species of works, or the same order of battle, would be equally proper for both," *HLWG, 20*[unnumbered]; 2. "to find such a construction, and such a formation of the troops, as may with the greatest simplicity, and consequently velocity, be adapted to those numberless circumstances which occur." *HLWG, 21*[unnumbered].

Rules of Siege Warfare: 1. "Sieges are attended with so great expence, and so much loss of time, and men, that they ought never to be undertaken without the utmost necessity," *HLWG, 75*; 2. "If therefore the enemy has any force at all in the field, a siege cannot be carried on unless the place is surrounded by good lines," *HLWG2, 68*; 3. "People grow tired in a long siege, grow impatient, right or wrong will advance, this brings on heavy calamities, because you cannot advance with safety, but step by step, and in proportion as your fire increases; and that of the place diminishes." *HLWG2*, 70. Both 2 and 3 based on the siege of Olmütz.

Two Capital Points of Siegecraft: subsistence and safety. *HLWG2*, 66.

Rules for Determining a Siege: 1. "When the fortresses are placed on the passes which lead into the enemy's country;" 2. "When they are near your communications;" 3. "When they are necessary;" 4. "When they contain considerable magazines of the enemy;" 5. "When the conquest of them is necessarily followed by that of some considerable district." *HLWG*, 75. Based on Prussian defeat at Kolin (1757).

Rules of Mountain Warfare: 1. "The knowledge of all of this [terrain, roads, and defiles], when improved by superior Talents, will enable a small army to make a successful war against one infinitely superior;" 2. "never to let an enemy send a patrol near your army: on the contrary, you must always send yours on his flanks," *HLWG*, 27 unnumbered; 3. "No corps whatever must be placed in a valley, unless you are Masters of the mountains which form it; and, if you cannot occupy both sides, you must at least, one." *HLWG*, 36–37. 1 and 2 are based on the Duke of Brunswick's Hessian campaign, while 3 is based on Austrian mistakes made in the 1757 campaign.

Offensive War

Principles of Prudence: 1. " 'Tis, in general, very imprudent to attack an army near a fortress; because, in case of success, 'tis impossible to proceed with cavalry, which alone can destroy a defeated army," *HLWG*, 57; 2. "It is always a great fault to fight, when nothing can be got by it." *HLWG*, 34. 1 is based on Prussian siege of Prague, while 2 is based on the battle of Reichenberg (1757).

Principles of Initiative: 1. "When you act offensively you must fight, and force those who oppose your march to give way, that you may proceed on your journey," *HLWG2*, 94; 2. "In general it is highly necessary to oppose an enemy beyond your frontiers, and advance as far as possible to meet him, because many advantages arise from this method." *HLWG2*, 137. 1 is based on the battle of Zorndorf, while 2 is based on Prussian defeat at Paltzig.

Rule of Pursuit: "For my part, I should upon such an occasion pursue the enemy with my whole army, and attack one or other of his columns with my principal force, while the remainder should be employed in harassing the others." *HLWG2*, 73. Based on criticism of Daun to pursue Prussians after Olmultz.

Principle of Velocity: "Velocity is every thing in war, particularly if the country be open and fruitful like Poland." *HLWG2*, 94. Based on Zorndorf campaign.

Principle of Time: "Time is every thing in war, and nothing makes you lose it so much as delays, in receiving the necessary supplies." *HLWG2*, 89. Based on Russian ineptitude after Zorndorf.

Defensive War

Rules of Prudence: 1. "When a general has the misfortune to command an army that is much inferior to that of the enemy, he must certainly retire before them," *HLWG* 90; 2. "When on the defensive never run the hazard of a battle, because if the enemy acts on a long line, you may undoubtedly, by placing yourself on his flanks, force him to retire," *HLWG2*, 94, 167; 3. "A general should scarce ever fight when on the defensive, but to preserve some important place, and hinder the enemy from taking winter quarters in his country, or force him to abandon it, if he is in possession." *HLWG2*, 113. 1 is based on Kolin, 2 on Zorndorf, 3 on Leuthen.

Principle of Defensive War: "An enemy so superior as the Russians were must not be opposed in front unless some uncommonly strong camp offers, which he cannot by an attack in front, or manœuvres [*sic*] on your flanks force you to abandon." *HLWG2*, 131. Based on Paltzig.

Rule of Retreat: "That an army retreating must be divided into as many strong corps as the nature of the country will admit of; because, in this case, the enemy can do you no very essential damage." *HLWG*, 89. Based on Prussian escape after Kolin.

Objective

- "I am of the opinion, that no operation whatever should be attempted, or post attacked, unless the possession of it be absolutely necessary to facilitate some capital enterprise." *HLWG2*, 2.

- "they had not, it should seem, any fixed plan of operations; they wandered from one place to another, waiting events; and when these turned out even more favourable [*sic*] then could reasonably have been expected, they were at a loss how to avail themselves of them; new schemes, new projects were made and none executed; such a vague and undetermined mode of making war, renders it everlasting, and finally it ends in doing nothing at all." *HLWG2*, 122.

- "In war all data are clearly given and known, the respective forces are easily calculated, from whence a probable opinion may be formed, and some certain object fixed and determined on, which must be invariably pursued without any the least deviation." *HLWG2*, 122. These three principles are based on criticisms of Austrian campaign of 1758.

Mass

- "the only advantage of a superior army, in a day of action, consists in this only, that the general can bring more men into action than the enemy; but if they do not move with facility and quickness, and are not all brought into action at the same time, that superiority of numbers will be of no use: on the contrary, will serve only to increase the confusion." *HLWG*, 139. Leuthen.

- "By all this one sees, that a brave man, with few troops, who have confidence in him, can do great things; and that numbers are nothing in the hands of an ignorant General." *HLWG2*, 169. General Wunsch's operations.

- "It matters not how numerous an army is, unless, by superior activity and disposition, you can and do bring more men into action against the different points you attack, than the enemy can oppose to you." *CHLWG*, 22.

- "Number, beyond a certain point, can add nothing to the force of an army, unless they can be made to act together; they increase its activity, and render it altogether unmanageable." *CHLWG*, 28.

Economy of Force (Leuthen Principle)

- "Though his [Frederick the Great's] army was much inferior to that of the enemy, yet by dint of superior manœuvres [*sic*], he brought more men into action, at the point attacked, then they; which must be decisive when the troops are nearly equal in goodness." *HLWG,* 139.

- "Wherefore, generals must make it their study to establish, in time of peace, such evolutions as facilitate the manœuvres of armies; and, in time of war, choose such a field of battle, if possible, as enables them to hide part of their motions, and so bring more men into action than the enemy." *HLWG2,* 139.

- "That general, who, by the faculty of his motions, or by artifice, can bring more men into action, at the same time, and at the same point, must, if the troops are equally good, necessarily prevail; and, therefore, all evolutions, which do not tend to this object, must be exploded." *HLWG,* 139.

- "partial attacks are more vigorous, and if properly supported, generally succeed: you can bring the main part of your line to act against particular points: whereas the other parts of the enemy's line must remain inactive." *HLWG2,* 139. Based on Paltzig.

- "It is an axiom, that you ought to bring as many men into action at once as possible." *CHLWG,* 47.

Lines of Operations

- "the final success of a war must chiefly depend on the length and nature of the line of operation; if this is well chosen and directed to some capital object, success will in general attend it; but if ill chosen, victory itself will lead to nothing." *HLWG2,* 87. Based on Zorndorf.

- "It is a certain rule, from which a General ought never to depart, to shorten continually as he advances his line of operation, by forcing new depots behind him on *that very line,* and no where else, otherwise he cannot move at all, for if he does form such depots, if they are not placed on his line, the enemy will destroy them, and put an end to his operations." *HLWG2,* 89.

- "it proved, that an army whose line of operation is considerably too long can execute no solid enterprize [*sic*], though it be ever so powerful: and that a handful of men well conducted . . . infallibly stop their program, and finally force them to retire, without doing any thing." *HLWG2,* 157–58. Based on Russian operations in Kunersdorf campaign.

Principle of Interior Lines (Central Position): "It is owning to this circumstance [interior lines] that the King [Frederick the Great] was enabled to support both countries [Saxony and Silesia] during the whole war, by marching from the one to the other as occasion required." *HLWG2,* 121.

Maxen Axioms *(La manoeuvre sur les derrières)*

- "that no army however strong, can keep its ground if you advance against it in front, and at the same time send a powerful corps to act on its flank and rear."

- "that if you do not keep up the communications, between the army and such a corps, they will be lost, if the enemy is at all an able officer." *HLWG2*, 185.

Surprise and the Fog of War

Hochkirch Maxim: "Whatever is possible, a general should think probable, and take his measures accordingly, that like old women he may not say; who would have thought it?" *HLWG2*, 110. Based on battle of Hochkirch.

Principle of Surprise: "it is possible in war, as in most other situations, to over-do a thing, and drive the nail further than it can go." *HLWG2*, 186. Criticism of Frederick's repeated flank attacks, especially at Maxen.

Publishing History of Lloyd's Works

(Original editions are numbered.)

1. *Lists of the Forces of the Sovereigns of Europe &c. viz. Ranks, Uniforms, Numbers of Officers, Private Men &c. of each Nation.* Methodized by J. Millan & Engraved by the best hands. London: Printed for J. Millan, 1761.
2. *History of the Late War in Germany, Between the King of Prussia, and the Empress of Germany and her Allies.* London: Printed for the Author, and Sold by R. Horsfield, L. Hawes and Co., J. Dodsley, J. Walter, T. Davies, W. Shropshire, and E. Easton, 1766.
3. *An essay on the English constitution.* London: Published for the Author, and Sold by J. Almon, in Piccadilly, 1770.
4. *An essay on the theory of money.* London: Printed for J. Almon, 1771.

Geschichte des letzten Kriegs in Teutschland; zwischen den Könige von Preussen und der Kayserin Königin und ihren Alliirten in den Feldzögen in den Jahren 1756 und 1757. Frankfurt und Leipzig: [s.n.], 1777. (Translation of no. 2)

5. *A rhapsody on the present system of French politics; on the projected invasion, and the means to defeat I, by a Chelsea pensionert.* Illustrated with a Chart of the Opposite Coasts of England and France. London: W. Faden and T. Jeffreys, 1779.

History of the Late War in Germany, between the King of Prussia, and the Empress of Germany and her Allies. London: Printed for S. Hooper, 1781. (Reprint of no. 2)

6. *Continuation of the History of the Late War in Germany.* Part II. London: Printed for the Author, and Sold by S. Hooper, 1781.

Abhandlung ueber die allgemeinen Grundsaetze der Kriegkunst. Tr. Hermann Flensberg. Frankfurt: Ph.H. Perrenon, 1783. (Translation of no. 6)

Histoire de la guerre d'Allemagne en 1756; entre le roi de Prusse et l'impératrice d'Allemagne et ses alliés. Traduite par le C. Roux Fazillac. Lausanne: [s.n.], 1784. (Translation of nos. 2 & 6)

Introduction à l'histoire de la guerre en Allemagne, en MDCCLVI entre le roi de Prusse, et l'impératrice reine avec ses alliés, Ou, Mémoires militaires et politiques du général Lloyd. Traduit et augmenté de notes et d'un précis la vie & la caractere de ce général. Londres, 1784. (Translation of nos. 2 & 6)

Geschichte des siebenjährigen Krieges in Deutschland zwischen dem Könige von Preussen und der Kaiserin Königin mit ihren Alliirten, vom General Lloyd. 2 Volumes. Berlin: Johann Friedrich Unger, 1785–94. (Translation of nos. 6 & 7)

De la guerre de campagne á l'usage d'un officier général Henry Lloyd. Maestrict: [s.n.], 1786. (Translated selections of nos. 2 & 6)

7. *History of the Late War in Germany, Between the King of Prussia, and the Empress of Germany and her Allies: Containing the Campaigns of 1758, and 1759, with a correct Military Map of the Seat of War; and Plans of the Siege of Olmütz, and the Battles of Zorndsorf, Hochkirchen, Paltzig, Cunnersdorf, or Frankfurt, and Maxen.* Volume 2. Published from the General's Manuscripts, under the Inspection of an English Officer, and Illustrated with Notes Critical, Historical, and Explanatory. London: Printed for T. and J. Egerton, 1790.

A political and military rhapsody on the invasion and defence of Great Britain and Ireland. Illustrated with three Copper-plates. To which is annexed an Introduction, and a short Account of the Author's Life. London: Sold by T. and J. Egerton, and J. Sewell, 1790. (New edition of no. 5)

A political and military rhapsody, on the invasion and defence of Great Britain and Ireland. 2d ed. Illustrated with three Copper-plates. To which is annexed, a short Account of the Author, and a Supplement by the Editor. With additions and improvements. London: Sold by Debret; Sewell; Clark; and Mayler, Bath, 1792. (New edition of no. 5)

A rhapsody on the present system of French politics; on the projected invasion, and the means to defeat it. London: Printed for John Stockdale, 1793. (New edition of no. 5)

A political and military rhapsody, on the invasion and defence of Great Britain and Ireland. 3d ed. To which is annexed, a short Account of the Author, and a Supplement by the Editor. London: Sold by J. Debrett; J. Egerton; and J. Mottley, Portsmouth, 1794. (New edition of no. 5)

A political and military rhapsody, on the invasion and defence of Great Britain and Ireland. 4th ed. To which is annexed, a short Account of the Author, and a Supplement by the Editor. London: Sold by Debrett; Egerton, 1795. (New edition of no. 5)

Mémoires politiques et militaires du Général Lloyd, ou, Extrait de l'introduction a l'histoire de la guerre en Allemagne en 1756 entre le roi de Prusse et l'impératrice-reine et ses alliés. Basle: J. Decker, 1798. (Translation of nos. 2 & 6)

A political and military rhapsody, on the invasion and defence of Great Britain and Ireland. Illustrated with three copper plates. To which is annexed, a short account of the author, and a supplement by the editor. 5th ed. With additions and improvements. London: Sold by Egerton, Debrett and by the principal booksellers in Great Britain, 1798. (New edition of no. 5)

Mémoires militaires et politiques du Général Lloyd: servant d'introduction à l'histoire de la guerre en Allemagne en 1756, entre le roi de Prusse et l'impératrice reine avec ses alliés. 2 vols. Traduits et augmentes de notes et d'un precis sur la vie et le caractere de ce general, par un officier francais. Paris: Magimel, 1801. (Translation of nos. 2 & 6)

Mémoire politique et militaire sur l'invasion et la défénse de la Grand Bretagne. Limoges: Barrois l'aîné, An IX [1801]. (Translation of no. 5)

Histoire de la guerre d'Allemagne, pendant les annees 1756 et suivantes, entre le Roi de Prusse et l'Imperatrice d'Allemagne et ses allies. 3 vols. Traduite en partie de l'anglais de Lloyd, et en partie redigee sur la correspondance originale de plusieurs officers francais et principalement sur celle de M. de Montazet, par le C. Roux Fazillac. Paris: Magimel, an XI [1803]. (Translation of nos. 2, 6 & 7)

A political and military rhapsody, on the invasion and defence of Great Britain and Ireland. 6th ed. To which is added a supplement by the editor and in this edition, the sketch of an original plan for the fortification and defence of London. With improvements and corrections. London: Printed by W. Bulmer and Co., 1803. (New edition of no. 5)

Memoria politica e militare spora l'invasione e la difesa della Gran-Brettagna, e riflessioni su l'invasione di Francia, del Generale Lloyd. Tr. Sulla 6th ed, ed. Accresciuta di note politico-statistiche da Lorenzo Manini. Milano: Presso Pirotta e Maspero, 1804. (Translation of no. 5)

The History of the Seven Years' War in Germany, by Generals Lloyd and Tempelhoff; with observations and maxims extracted from the Treatise of great Military Operations of General Jomini. Translated from the German and French by Captain Hamilton Smith of the Quarter-Master-General's office and published under the authority of His Royal Highness the Commander in Chief. London: Printed by R. G. Clarke, 1808. (Excerpts from no. 2)

Mémoires militaires et politiques du Général Lloyd. Bibliothèque historique et militaire, tome V. Paris, 1851. (Translation of 2 & 6)

An essay on the theory of money. Ristampa anastatica della prima edizione del 1771 con introduzione di Oscar Nuccio. Roma: Bizzarri, 1968. (Facsimile reprint of no. 4)

Notes

INTRODUCTION

1. Germain Hyacinthe, marquis de Romance de Mesmon, "Précis sur la Vie et le Caractère de Henri Lloyd," foreword to *Mémoires militaire et politiques du* Général *Lloyd, servant d'introduction à l'histoire de la guerre en Allemagne en 1756, entre le Roi de Prusse et l'Imperatrice reine avec ses allies,* by Henry Lloyd, traduits et augmentés de notes et d'un précis sur la vie et le caractère de ce Général par un Officer Français (Paris: Magimel, An IX [1801]), xxxviii.

2. Michael Howard, "Jomini and the Classical Tradition in Military Thought," in *The Theory and Practice of War: Essays Presented to Captain B. H. Liddel Hart,* edited by Michael Howard (London: Cassell & Company LTD, 1965), 5; Tim Travers, "The Development of British Military Historical Writing and Thought from the Eighteenth Century to the Present," in *Military History and the Military Profession,* eds. David A. Charters, Marc Milner, and J. Brent Wilson, foreword by Anne N. Foreman (Westport, CT: Praeger, 1992), 24–25.

3. Representative works include Eric Robson, "The Armed Forces and the Art of War," in *The Old Regime,* vol. 7 of *The New Cambridge Modern History,* ed. J. O. Lindsay (Cambridge: At the University Press, 1963), 163–89; Theodore Ropp, *War in the Modern World,* rev. ed. (New York: Collier Books, 1962), 46–51; and Robert R. Palmer, "Frederick the Great, Guibert, Bülow: From Dynastic to National War," in *Makers of Modern Strategy: Military Thought from Machiavelli to Hitler,* edited by Edward Meade Earle (Princeton, NJ: Princeton University Press, 1943), 49–74; reprint, *Makers of Modern Strategy from Machiavelli to the Nuclear Age,* edited by Peter Paret with the Collaboration of Gordon A. Craig and Felix Gilbert (Princeton, NJ: Princeton University Press, 1986), 91–119.

4. John Shy, "Jomini," in *Makers of Modern Strategy from Machiavelli to the Nuclear Age,* 149; Wolfgang Petter, "Zur Kriegskunst im Zeitalter Friedrichs Großen," in *Europa in Zeitalter Friedrichs des Großen: Wirtschaft, Gesellschaft, Kriege,* edited by Bernhard R. Kroener (München: R. Oldenburg Verlag, 1989), 250; Piero Pieri, *Guerra e Politica negli Scrittori Italiana* (Milan e Napoli: Riccardo Ricciardi Editore, 1955), 167–68; and Alfred Vagts, *A History of Militarism,* rev. ed. (New York: Meridian Books, 1959), 80–82.

5. Azar Gat, *The Origins of Military Thought from the Enlightenment to Clausewitz* (Oxford: Clarendon Press, 1989).

6. Chief among them are Matthew Smith Anderson, *War and Society in Europe of the Old Regime, 1618–1789* (New York: St. Martin's Press, 1988), and Russell F. Weigley, *The Age of Battles: The Quest for Decisive Warfare from Breitenfeld to Waterloo* (Bloomington: Indiana University Press, 1991). For the limitations imposed on war-making see, Geza Perjés, "Army Provisioning, Logistics and Strategy in the Second Half of the Seventeenth Century," *Acta Historica Academiae Scientiarum Hungaricae* XVI (1970): 1–52. Claims of an eighteenth-century military revolution are found in Jeremy Black, "Eighteenth-Century Warfare Reconsidered," *War in History* 1, no. 2 (July 1994): 215–32; idem, *European Warfare, 1600–1815* (New Haven, CT: Yale University Press, 1994).

7. For the history and outcome of this debate see Robert S. Quimby, *The Background of Napoleonic Warfare: The Theory of Military Tactics in Eighteenth Century France* (New York: Columbia University Press, 1957).

8. See Robert Nicklaus, "The Pursuit of Peace in the French Enlightenment," in *Essays on Diderot and the Enlightenment in Honor of Otis Fellows,* edited by John Pappas (Geneva: Éditions Droz, 1974), 231–45; Adrienne D. Hytier, "Les Philosophes et le problème de la guerre," in *Studies on Voltaire and the Eighteenth Century,* ed. Theodore Bestermann, vol. 127 (Banbury: The Voltaire Foundation, 1974), 243–58; and Pierre Aubery, "The Encyclopédie on War and Peace," in vol. 3 of *Transactions of the Eighth International Congress on the Enlightenment, Bristol, 21–27 July 1991,* Studies on Voltaire and the Eighteenth Century, ed. Theodore Bestermann, no. 305, 1827–29 (Oxford: The Voltaire Foundation at the Taylor Institution, 1992).

9. Examples include Peter Gay, *The Enlightenment: An Interpretation,* 2 vols. (New York: Alfred A. Knopf, 1966–69); Paul Hazard, *European Thought in the Eighteenth Century: From Montesquieu to Lessing* (New Haven, CT: Yale University Press, 1954; originally published as *La pensée europeene au 18e siècle de Montesquieu à Lessing,* Paris: Boivin & Cie, 1946); and Ernst Cassirer, *The Philosophy of the Enlightenment,* trans. Fritz C. A. Koelln and James P. Pettegrove (Princeton, NJ: Princeton University Press, 1951; originally published as *Die Philosophie der Aufklärung,* Tübingen: Mohr, 1932).

10. Voltaire to Catherine II, Ferney, 26 February 1769, D15487, vol. XXXIV of *Correspondence and Related Documents,* ed. Theodore Bestermann, vol. 118 of *The Complete Works of Voltaire,* ed. Theodore Bestermann (Banbury: The Voltaire Foundation, 1974), 303.

11. John A. Lynn, "The Treament of Military Subjects in Diderot's *Encyclopédie,*" *The Journal of Military History* 65, no. 1 (January 2001): 133.

12. Walter Emil Kaegi, Jr., "The Crisis of Military Historiography," *Armed Forces and Society* 7, no. 2 (Winter 1981): 311. Peter H. Wilson, "War in German Thought

from the Peace of Westphalia to Napoleon," *European History Quarterly* 28, no. 1 (January 1998): 5–50, and David D. Bien, "The Army and the French Enlightenment: Reform, Reaction, and Revolution," *Past & Present: A Journal of Historical Studies* 84 (August 1979): 68–98, are two exceptions. David Kaiser, *Politics and War: European Conflict from Philip II to Hitler* (Cambridge, MA: Harvard University Press, 1990), limits his discussion to enlightened despotism.

13. I am indebted to the pioneering work of Franco Venturi and Azar Gat. See Venturi, *Le Vite incrociate di Henry Lloyd e Pietro Verri* (Torino: Editrice-Stampatori, 1977); idem, "Le Avventure del Generale Lloyd," *Rivista Storica Italiana* 91, no. 2–3 (April–September 1979): 369–433; and Gat, "Lloyd: His Career, Intellectual Scope, and the Campaigns of the Seven Years' War," in *The Origins of Military Thought from the Enlightenment to Clausewitz,* 67–78.

CHAPTER 1

1. Geraint H. Jenkins, *The Foundations of Modern Wales, 1642–1870* (Oxford: Clarendon Press; University of Wales Press, 1987), 88; Frank Emery, "Wales," chap. 12 in *1640–1750: Regional Farming Systems,* vol. 5, pt. 1 of *The Agrarian History of England and Wales,* ed. Joan Thirsk (Cambridge: Cambridge University Press, 1984), 393–428.

2. Legend claims Cunedda originally settled north Wales in 420. He gave his son Meirion the territory of Cantrev Meirionydd, or "the Hundred of Meirion," later named Merioneth. A. Morris, *Merionethshire,* Cambridge County Geographies, ed. Francis H. H. Guillemard (Cambridge: At the University Press, 1913), 2–4. Merioneth was one of the original eight counties created by Edward I with the Statute of Rhuddlan (1284). The 1974 county reorganization divided it between Gwynned and Clwyd.

3. Richard Douglas Lloyd, *Pride Prejudice and Politics: A History of the Lloyd Family in Wales, Pennsylvania, and Ontario,* part 1-A (Toronto: Genealogical Pub. Co., 1992), xi, 12. The ancestry is corroborated by Hannibal Evans Lloyd, *Memoir of General Lloyd, Author of the History of the Seven Years'War, etc. etc.* (London: Printed for Private Circulation, 1842), 1. The Lloyd Family's coat of arms is the Cadogan Lion. See Thomas F. Tout, "Cadwaladr (d.1172)," *The Dictionary of National Biography: From the Earliest Times to 1900,* ed. Leslie Stephen (London: Oxford University Press; Henry Milford, 1937), 3:642–43.

4. His actual date of birth is unknown. Henry Manners Chichester, "Lloyd, Henry, or Henry Humphrey Evans (1720?–1783)," *The Dictionary of National Biography: From the Earliest Times to 1900,* eds. Leslie Stephen and Sidney Lee (London: Oxford University Press; Humphrey Milford, 1937), 9:1301, denotes the year 1720. Franco Venturi claimed he was born in 1718, citing the plate on the Nathaniel Hone painting, *General Lloyd (1773),* stored in the Fitzwilliam Museum, Cambridge. See Franco Venturi, *Le Vite incrociate di Henry Lloyd e Pietro Verri,* 4; idem, "Le Avventure del Generale Lloyd:" 369n. Venturi was mistaken. The plate that reads (1718–1784) denotes the inclusive dates of Nathaniel Hone's life. See Jack W. Goodison, ed., *The British School,* vol. 3 of *Catalogue of Paintings* (Cambridge: Cambridge University Press, 1977), 118. Both Pietro Verri (1728–97) and Germain Hyacinthe, marquis de Romance de Mesmon (1745–1831) believed Lloyd was born around 1729. See Pietro Verri to Alessandro Verri, Bautzen, 13 settembre 1759,

Lettere e scritti inediti di Pietro e di Alessandro Verri, ed. Carlo Casati (Milan: Giuseppe Galli, 1879), 1:49; and Romance de Mesmon, "Précis sur la Vie et le Caractère de Henri Lloyd," vii. Since parishes kept no birth records prior to the 1740s, the exact date of his birth will remain a mystery. One of Henry's close companions during his Jacobite period, John Drummond, concluded that he was between twenty and thirty years of age when he first met him in 1744. See John Drummond, "Mr. Drummond's Letter to the Editor," foreword to *A Political and Military Rhapsody, on the Invasion and Defence of Great Britain and Ireland,* by Henry Lloyd, 2d ed., to which is annexed a short account of the author and a supplement by the editor (London: Sold by Debret; Sewell; Clark; and Mayler, 1792), xi.

5. This term in general pertains to one's ability to see things clearly and understand their interrelationships, or intuition. In particular it pertains to one's ability to picture mentally the lay of the land and understand how troops could be best utilized on such ground. See Christopher Duffy, *The Military Experience in the Age of Reason* (New York: Atheneum, 1988), 140–41.

6. In Wales pedigree rather than property made one a member of the gentry. See David W. Howell, "Landlords and Estate Management in Wales," chap. 15 in *1640–1750: Agrarian Change,* vol. 5, pt. 2 of *The Agrarian History of England and Wales,* ed. Joan Thirsk (Cambridge: Cambridge University Press, 1985), 252–97.

7. Thomas Nicholas, *Annals and Antiquities of the Counties and Country Families of Wales,* 2d ed., rev. and enlarged, 2 vols. (London: Longmans, Green, Reader, 1875; reprint, 2 vols. in 1, Baltimore: Genealogical Publishing Co., Inc., 1991), 662; Hugh J. Owen, *Echoes of Old Merioneth* (Dolgelley: Printed and Published by Hughes Brothers, "Y Dydd" Office, 1946), 2.

8. Peter R. Roberts, "The Social History of the Merioneth Gentry," *Journal of the Merioneth Historical and Records Society* 4 (1961–64): 216; idem, "The Gentry and the Land in Eighteenth Century Merioneth," *Journal of the Merioneth Historical and Records Society* 4 (1961–64): 324–39; idem, "The Merioneth Gentry and Local Government," *Journal of the Merioneth Historical and Records Society* 5 (1965–68): 21–38; and Howell, "Landlords and Estate Management in Wales," 252.

9. Thomas Pennant, *Tours in Wales* (London: Printed for Wilkie and Robinson; J. Nunn; White & Co., 1810), 2:277.

10. Roberts, "The Social History of the Merioneth Gentry," 221. Welsh parishes were the least lucrative in the kingdom. Most curates subsidized their incomes by working the land and raising livestock. Over the course of the eighteenth century these middle-rank and lesser gentry slowly disappeared from the social stratum as large landowners bought up their estates. Hannibal Lloyd, *Memoir of General Lloyd,* 1.

11. Lucy S. Sutherland, *The University of Oxford in the Eighteenth Century: A Reconsideration* (Oxford: Oxford University Press, 1973), 13. Tory sentiment was especially strong in Jesus College. See Peter Langford, "Tories and Jacobites, 1714–1751," chap. 4 in *The Eighteenth Century,* eds. Lucy S. Sutherland and Leslie G. Mitchell, vol. 5 of *The History of the University of Oxford,* ed. Trevor H. Ashton (Oxford: Clarendon Press, 1986), 99–127. Horace Walpole remarked as late as 1760 that Jacobite sympathies brought privileges at Oxford; Horace Walpole to George Montagu, 19 July 1760, pt.1 of *Horace Walpole's Correspondence with George Montagu,* eds. Wilmarth Sheldon Lewis and Ralph S. Brown, Jr., vol. 9 of

The Yale Edition of Horace Walpole's Correspondence, ed. Wilmarth Sheldon Lewis (New Haven, CT: Yale University Press; London: Humphrey Milford, Oxford University Press, 1941), 288–90.

12. George Birkbeck Hill, ed., *The Life (1776–1780)*, vol. 3 of *Boswell's Life of Johnson; Together with Boswell's Journal of a Tour to the Hebrides and Johnson's Diary of a Journey into North Wales*, rev. and enlarged ed. by Lawrence F. Powell (Oxford: At the Clarendon Press, 1934), 14. John Murray, ed., *The Autobiographies of Edward Gibbon*, 2d ed., with an introduction by John Holroyd, Earl of Sheffield (London: John Murray, 1897), 67.

13. Oxford was one of three European universities to which Catherine II of Russia sent a dozen young Russians in 1767. John S. Bromsley, "Britain and Europe in the Eighteenth Century," *History: The Journal of the Historical Association* 66 (1981): 403.

14. Elizabeth I, "Patent of 27 June 1571," quoted in John N. L. Baker, *Jesus College, Oxford: 1571–1971* (Oxford: Oxonian Press Ltd., 1971), 1.

15. Joseph Foster, ed., *Alumni Oxonienses: The Members of the University of Oxford, 1715–1886: Their Parentage, Birthplace, and Year of Birth, with a Record of their Degrees* (Oxford: Parker and Co., 1888), 3:861. Romance de Mesmon, "Précis sur la Vie et le Caractère de Henri Lloyd," viii.

16. William Norman Hargreaves-Mawdsley, *A History of Academical Dress in Europe until the End of the Eighteenth Century* (Oxford: At the Clarendon Press, 1963), 98–99; Graham Midgley, *University Life in Eighteenth-Century Oxford* (New Haven, CT: Yale University Press, 1996), 1–13.

17. Lucy S. Sutherland, "The Curriculum," chap. 15 in *The Eighteenth Century*, eds. Lucy S. Sutherland and Leslie G. Mitchell, vol. 5 of *The History of the University of Oxford*, 470. The Laudian Statutes governed every facet of the students' life. For an English translation of the original Latin text, see George R. M. Ward and James Heywood, trans., *The Caroline Code, or Laudian Statutes*, vol. 1 of *Oxford University Statutes* (London: William Pickering, 1845).

18. Romance de Mesmon, "Précis sur la Vie et le Caractère de Henri Lloyd," viii.

19. Martin L. Clarke, "Classical Studies," chap. 17 in *The Eighteenth Century*, eds. Lucy S. Sutherland and Leslie G. Mitchell, vol. 5 of *The History of the University of Oxford*, 513.

20. Lloyd, *The History of the Late War in Germany; Between the King of Prussia, and the Empress of Germany and Her Allies* (London: Printed for the Author, and Sold by R. Horsfield, L. Hawes and Co., J. Dodsley, J. Walter, T. Davies, W. Shropshire, and E. Easton, 1766), 1[unnumbered] (hereafter cited as *HLWG*); idem, *Continuation of the History of the Late War in Germany; Between the King of Prussia, and the Empress of Germany and Her Allies*, part ii (London: Printed for the Author, and Sold by S. Hooper, 1781), i (hereafter cited as *CHLWG*).

21. Lloyd, *HLWG*, 1[unnumbered]. Gaius Julius Caesar, *The Civil Wars*, trans. Arthur G. Peskett, Loeb Classical Library, ed. George P. Goold, no. 39 (1914; reprint, Cambridge, MA: Cambridge University Press, 1990); idem, *The Gallic War*, trans. Henry J. Edwards, Loeb Classical Library, ed. George P. Goold, no. 72 (1917; reprint, Cambridge, MA: Harvard University Press; London: William Heinemann LTD, 1986).

22. Xenophon, *Anabasis*, trans. Carlton L. Brownson, Loeb Classical Library, ed. George P. Goold, no. 90 (1922; reprint, Cambridge, MA: Harvard University Press;

London: William Heinemann LTD, 1980); idem, *Hellenica,* trans. Carleton L. Brownson, Loeb Classical Library, ed. George P. Goold, no. 88 (1918; reprint, London: William Heinemann LTD; Cambridge, MA: Harvard University Press, 1980); idem, *Cyropaedia,* 2 vols., trans. Walter Miller, Loeb Classical Library, ed. George P. Goold, nos. 51–25 (1914; reprint, Cambridge, MA: Harvard University Press; London: William Heinemann LTD, 1979); idem, "Lessons of Generalship," Book III of *Memorabilia* in *Memorabilia;Oeconomicus;Symposium;Apology,* trans. Edgar C. Marchant, Loeb Classical Library, ed. George P. Goold, no. 168 (1923; reprint, Cambridge, MA: Harvard University Press; London: William Heinemann LTD, 1979), 169–261.

23. Xenophon, "On the Cavalry Commander," in *Scripta Minora,* trans. Edgar C. Marchant and Glen W. Bowersock, Loeb Classical Library, ed. George P. Goold, no. 183 (1925; reprint, Cambridge, MA: Harvard University Press; London: William Heinemann LTD, 1971), 233–93; Onasander, "The General," in *Aeneas Tacticus, Asclepiodotus, Onasander,* trans. Illinois Greek Club, Loeb Classical Library, ed. George P. Goold, no. 156 (1928; reprint, Cambridge, MA: Harvard University Press; London: William Heinemann LTD, 1986), 342–527; Sextus Iulius Frontinus, *The Stratagems/The Aqueducts of Rome,* trans. Charles E. Bennett, Loeb Classical Library, ed. George P. Goold, no. 174 (1925; reprint, Cambridge, MA and London: Harvard University Press, 1997).

24. Henry Lloyd, *HLWG,* 1[unnumbered]; idem, *CHLWG,* i.

25. Historians have yet to analyze deeply the relationship between classical and modern military thought. See Donald A. Neill, "Ancestral Voices: The Influence of the Ancients on the Military Thought of the Seventeenth and Eighteenth Centuries," *The Journal of Military History* 62, no. 3 (July 1998): 487–520. His general conclusion is that modern military thinkers, particularly in the early modern period, paid heed to the classical authorities only when relevant to their particular circumstances and that they were not shackled by an outdated, inapplicable body of thought as is often perceived.

26. John Drummond, "Mr. Drummond's Letter to the Editor," xi; Romance de Mesmon, "Précis sur la Vie et le Caractère de Henri Lloyd," xviii–xx. For the venal officer system see Arvel B. Erickson, "Abolition of Purchase in the British Army," *Military Affairs* 23, no. 2 (Summer 1959): 65–76.

27. Pietro Verri to Alessandro Verri, Bautzen, 13 settembre 1759, *Lettere e scritti inediti,* 1:49–50.

28. William Duff, *An Essay on Original Genius; and its Various Modes of Exertion in Philosophy and the Fine Arts, Particularly in Poetry* (London: Printed for Edward and Charles Dilly, 1767; reprint, Gainesville, Florida: Scholars Facsimiles & Reprints, 1964), 76–77. Duff called genius "the sovereign decree of Nature."

29. Biologists now speculate that "genius" is an inborn manifestation (or emergenesis) of particular combination of genetic traits. This theory was developed from the studies of monozygotic twins (those with identical genetic configurations) reared apart in different environments. Regardless of circumstances a large number of these twins exhibited traits, tastes, and proclivities remarkably similar to their siblings. It is not a large leap in logic to suggest, as the authors of these studies themselves suggest, that more general human characteristics like musical aptitude and even a penchant for war may arise from these non-hereditary constellations of genetic traits. For a more scientific explanation of emergenesis, see David T. Lykken, "Genes and

the Mind," *The Harvard Medical School Mental Health Letter* 4, no. 2 (August 1987): 4–6; David T. Lykken, M. McGue, A. Tellegen, and T. J. Bouchard, Jr., "Emergenesis: Genetic Traits that may not Run in Families," *American Psychologist* 47, no. 12 (December 1992): 1565–77.

30. Pietro Verri to Alessandro Verri, Bautzen, 13 settembre 1759, *Lettere e scritti inediti*, 1:55.

31. Hannibal Lloyd, *Memoir of General Lloyd*, 1–2; Pietro Verri to Alessandro Verri, Bautzen, 13 settembre 1759, *Lettere e scritti inediti*, 1:49–50. Verri did not mention the loss of an estate, but he suggested that it had not been a pleasant time in Henry's life, and that he was compelled to leave Britain; Romance de Mesmon, "Précis sur la Vie et le Caractère de Henri Lloyd," xxv.

32. Christopher Stoors and Hamish M. Scott, "The Military Revolution and the European Nobility, c.1600–1800," *War in History* 3, no. 1 (January 1996): 13–22.

33. Hannsjoachim W. Koch, *A History of Prussia* (New York: Longman Group Limited, 1978; reprint, New York: Dorset Press, 1987), 100–01.

34. The best analysis of the Prussian military under Frederick II is Christopher Duffy, *The Army of Frederick the Great*, 2d ed. (Chicago, IL: Emperor's Press, 1996).

35. William Edward Mead, *The Grand Tour in the Eighteenth Century* (New York: Benjamin Blom, Inc., Publishers, 1972), 291–94.

36. Pietro Verri to Alessandro Verri, Bautzen, 13 settembre 1759, *Lettere e scritti inediti*, 1:50. The Welsh gentry were noted for their love of gambling. Like activities may have contributed to Lloyd's misfortunes.

37. William V. Bangert, *A History of the Society of Jesus* (St. Louis: The Institute of Jesuit Sources, 1972), 215.

38. Pietro Verri to Alessandro Verri, Bautzen, 13 settembre 1759, *Lettere e scritti inediti*, 1:50; Bangert, *A History of the Society of Jesus*, 27.

39. Bangert, *A History of the Society of Jesus*, 288; Michel Ulysse Maynard, *The Studies and Teaching of the Society of Jesus, at the Time of its Suppression, 1750–1773*, trans. from the French (Baltimore, MD: John Murphy & Co.; London: C. Dolmon; Pittsburgh, PA: George Quigley, 1855, 200–02); originally published as *Des études et de l'enseignement des Jésuites á l'époque de leur suppression (1750–1773)* (Paris: V. Paoussielgue-Rusand, 1853). Boškovíc taught at the Roman College from 1740–60.

40. Josef W. Konvitz, *Cartography in France, 1660–1848: Science, Engineering, and Statecraft*, with a foreword by Emmanuel Le Roy Ladurie (Chicago, IL: The University of Chicago Press, 1987), 92. Jesuit schools served as noble finishing schools prior to military service. Noble families often distrusted military schools and academies in favor of the traditional Jesuit religious curriculum. Storrs and Scott, "The Military Revolution and the European Nobility, c.1600–1800," 25.

41. François-Marie Arouet de Voltaire to Charles Augustin Feriol, comte d'Argental and Jeanne Grâce Bosc du Bouchet, comtesse d'Argental, 17–18, 20 April 1762 (9622), in *January–May 1762*, vol. XLVIII of *Voltaire's Correspondence*, ed. Theodore Bestermann (Genève: Institut et Musée Voltaire, 1959), 209–12; Pietro Verri to Alessandro Verri, Milan, 27 gennaio 1762, CXCI(83), vol. 1, pt. II of *Carteggio di Pietro e di Alessandro Verri dal 1766 al 1797*, eds. Emanuele Greppi and Alessandro Giulini (Milano: Editrice L. F. Cogliato, 1923), 148.

42. Robert R. Palmer, "The French Jesuits in the Age of Enlightenment: A Statistical Study of the *Journal de Trévoux*," *The American Historical Review* 45, no. 1

(October 1939): 44–58; idem, *Catholics and Unbelievers in Eighteenth-Century France* (Princeton, NJ: Princeton University Press, 1939).

43. Catherine M. Northeast, *The Parisian Jesuits and the Enlightenment, 1700–1762,* Studies on Voltaire and the Eighteenth Century, ed. Haydn T. Mason, vol. 288 (Oxford: The Voltaire Foundation at the Taylor Institution, 1991), 55.

44. Pietro Verri to Alessandro Verri, Bautzen, 13 settembre 1759, *Lettere e scritti inediti,* 1:50. For the Marqués de la Mina, see Jerónimo Bécker, "La Embajada del Marqués de la Mina, 1736–1740," *Boletin de la Real Academia de la Historia* 83, no. 6 (December 1923): 364–78; 84, no. 2 (February 1924): 184–96; no. 4 (April 1924): 393–402; 85, no. 1 (July 1924): 5–14; 86, no. 1 (January–March 1925): 42–115; William Norman Hargreaves-Mawdsley, *Eighteenth-Century Spain, 1700–1788* (Totowa, NJ: Rowman and Littlefield, 1979), 78.

45. See Hargreaves-Mawdsley, *Eighteenth-Century Spain, 1700–1788,* and John Lynch, *Bourbon Spain, 1700–1808* (Oxford: Basil Blackwell, 1989).

46. See Reed Browning, *The War of the Austrian Succession* (New York: St. Martin's Press, 1993), and Matthew Smith Anderson, *The War of the Austrian Succession, 1740–1748* (London: Longman, 1995).

47. Pietro Verri to Alessandro Verri, Bautzen, 13 settembre 1759, *Lettere e scritti inediti,* 1:50; Venturi, "Le Avventure del Generale Lloyd," 371–72.

48. Storrs and Scott, "The Military Revolution and the European Nobility, c.1600–1800, 23–27. Training schools and academies developed before cadet companies. The first were expensive and served the high aristocracy. The latter attracted nobles regardless of rank and proved more successful.

49. Ibid., 28–34. Nobles joined the military in increasing numbers for advancement, income, and adventure. Monarchs considered nobles the only group who could contribute effectively to the monetary upkeep of regiments. The incentives helped engrave on military institutions the corresponding societal hierarchy. For instance the bulk of enlisted men came from the unprivileged third estate while lesser nobles became sub-altern officers and their social superiors became regimental commanders and members of the high command.

50. The classic work on the Prussian army's political activities is Gordon A. Craig, *The Politics of the Prussian Army, 1640–1945* (New York: Oxford University Press, 1956). For Frederick's analysis of his army and the value of military education see Jay Luvaas, ed. and trans., *Frederick the Great on the Art of War* (New York: The Free Press; London: Collier-Macmillan Limited, 1966), 53–76.

51. Walter H. G. Armytage, *A Social History of Engineering* (Cambridge, MA: The M.I.T. Press, 1961), 99.

52. See André Corvisier, *Armies and Societies in Europe, 1494–1789,* trans. Abigail T. Siddall (Bloomington, IN: Indiana University Press, 1979), 105–08; originally published as *Armées et Sociétés en Europe de 1494 à 1789* (Paris: Presses Universitaires de France, 1976).

53. For a concise overview see John R. Western, "War on a New Scale: Professionalism in Armies, Navies and Diplomacy," chap. 6 in *The Eighteenth Century: Europe in the Age of Enlightenment,* edited by Alfred Cobban (New York: McGraw Hill Book Company, 1969), 182–216.

54. Established in 1751, the École Militaire provided a basic technical education to poor, uneducated rural nobles and instilled a sense of subordination. David B. Bien, "Military Education in Eighteenth-Century France: Technical and Non-Technical

Determinants," in *Science, Technology and Warfare: Proceedings of the Third Military History Symposium, United States Air Force Academy, 8–9 May 1969*, eds. Monte D. Wright and Lawrence J. Paszik (Washington DC: Office of Air Force History, United States Air Force Academy, 1971), 51–9.

55. Storrs and Scott, "The Military Revolution and the European Nobility, c.1600–1800," 14, 23–24. A virtual parity existed between non-noble and noble officers in the technical branches. The explanation is social. States found it difficult to attract nobles to the technical branches. Nobles for reasons of tradition and prestige served in the line regiments, or those units which actually fought during wartime, thereby preserving the medieval *raison d'être* for the second estate.

56. Engineering schools predated the first artillery academy established at Segovia in 1764. Pere Molas Ribalta, "The Early Bourbons and the Military," chap. 2 in *Armed Forces and Society in Spain, Past and Present*, edited by Rafael Bañón Martínez and Thomas M. Barker (Boulder, CO: Social Science Monographs; New York: Distributed by Columbia University Press, 1988), 51–80.

57. For Vauban's career see, Reginald Blomfield, *Sebastien Le Prestre de Vauban, 1633–1707* (London: Methuen & Company Limited, 1938); and Anne Blanchard, *Vauban* (Paris: Fayard, 1996). For his contribution to military theory see Henry Guerlac, "Vauban: The Impact of Science on War," chap. 4 in *Makers of Modern Strategy from Machiavelli to the Nuclear Age*, edited by Peter Paret with the collaboration of Gordon A. Craig and Felix Gilbert (Princeton, NJ: Princeton University Press, 1986), 64–90. His most famous work was *De l'attaque et de la défense des places*, 2 vols. (La Haye: Pierre de Hondt, 1737–42). An early English translation that went through subsequent editions was, *The new method of fortification as practised by Monsieur de Vauban, Engineer-General of France: with an explanation of all the terms appertaining to the art*, trans. A. Swall (London: Printed for Abel Swall, 1691). See the recent edition entitled *A manual of siegecraft and fortification*, trans. George A. Rothrock (Ann Arbor, MI: University of Michigan Press, 1968).

58. His basic methods are contained in, *Nieuwe vesting vouw, op een natte of loge horisont* (Leewarden: Hendrik Rintjes, 1685). An early French edition is *Nouvelle fortification*, trans. Hendrik van Bulderen (La Haye: Hendrik van Bulderen, 1706); while the first English edition is *The New Method of Fortification*, trans. Thomas Savory (London: D. Midwinter, 1705). For an analysis see David Chandler, *The Art of Warfare in the Age of Marlborough* (London: Batsford, Ltd., 1976; reprint, New York: Sarpedon, 1994), 278–81; and W. H. Schukking, "Menno van Coehoorn (1641–1704) et la 'Fondation' qui porte son nom," *Revue Internationale d'Histoire Militaire* no. 19 (1957): 332–43.

59. Montecuccoli was the "Clausewitz" of the eighteenth century. See Thomas Mack Barker, *The Military Intellectual and Battle: Raimondo Montecuccoli and the Thirty Years' War* (Albany, NY: State University of New York Press, 1975); and John Ashley Mears, "Count Raimondo Montecuccoli: Practical Soldier and Military Theoretician," (Ph.D. diss., University of Chicago, 1964). His basic writings are *Memorie del general principe de Montecuccoli* (Colonia: Compagnia de I librari, 1704); *Arte universal de la guerra, de principe Raymundo Montecucoli*, traducido de italiano en español par don Bartolomé Chaffrion (Lisboa: M. Marescal, 1708); and *Memoires de Montecucoli, généralissime des troupes de l'empereur; ou, Principes de l'art militaire en général*, traduits d'italien en français par Jacque Adam (Paris: Jean Musier, 1712). A modern edition is *Le opere di Raimondo Montecuccoli*, 2 vols., ed.

Raimondo Luraghi (Rome: Stato maggiore dell'Esercito, Ufficio storico, 1988). For modern analyses see, Gunther E. Rothenberg, "Maurice of Nassau, Gustavus Adolphus, Raimondo Montecuccoli, and the "Military Revolution" of the Seventeenth Century," chap. 2 in *Makers of Modern Strategy from Machiavelli to the Nuclear Age*, 32–63; and Azar Gat, "Montecuccoli: The Impact of Proto-Science on Military Theory," chap. 1 in *The Origins of Military Thought from the Enlightenment to Clausewitz* (Oxford: Clarendon Press, 1989), 13–24.

60. See Henry Lloyd, "Reflections on the general principles of war; and on the composition and characters of the different armies of Europe," *The Annual Register, or a View of the History, Politics, and Literature, for the Year 1766*, 7th ed. (London: C. Baldwin, 1816): 169–77. These early notions were reproduced as the preface for both *The History of the Late War in Germany* and *Continuation of the History of the Late War in Germany*.

61. Standard editions in Lloyd's day were, *Memoires sur la guerre; ou, l'on a rassemblé les maximes les plus necessaires dans les operations de l'art militaire* (Amsterdam: François Channguion, 1731); and *Memoirs Historical and Military: Containing a Distinct View of all the Considerable States of Europe*, 2 vols., trans. from the French (London: Printed for T. Woodward and C. Davis, 1735–36; reprint, New York: Greenwood Press, 1968).

62. Feuquières, *Memoirs Historical and Military*, 2:200.

63. Jay Luvaas, "Frederick the Great: The Education of a Great Captain," in *The John Biggs Cincinnati Lectures in Military Leadership and Command, 1986*, edited by Henry S. Bausum (Lexington, VA: The VMI Foundation, Inc., 1986), 31.

64. Lloyd, *CHLWG*, 1.

65. For his career see Miguel Corrasco-Labadia, *El Marqués de Santa Cruz de Marcenado; noticias historicas de su vida, sus excritas y la celebración de su centenario en 1884*, 2d ed. (Madrid: Impr. y litografía de Depósito de la Guerra, 1889); and Manuel Sánchez de Arco, *El marqués de Santa Cruz de Marcenado* (Madrid: Editora Nacional, 1945).

66. Duffy, *The Military Experience in the Age of Reason*, 54. Standard editions of his writings in Lloyd's time included, *Reflexiones militares*, 11 vols. (Turin: Juan Francisco Moriesse, 1724–30); *Reflexiones militares* (Paris: Simon Langlois, 1730); and *Réflexions militaires et politiques*, 11 vols. (Paris: J. Rollin, 1738). A facsimile reprint of a later French edition of the 1730 abridgment is *Reflexiones Militares* (Madrid: Imprenta de Enrique Rubiños, 1893; reprint, Oviedo: Principado de Asturias, Instituto de Estudios Austurianes, 1984). For Lloyd's discussion of soldier motivation see Lloyd, *CHLWG*, 80–87.

67. Jaime Miguel Guzman, marqués de la Mina, *Maximas para la guerre*, sacadas de las obras del excelentisimo Sr. marqués de la Mina con un epitome de su vida (Vich: Pedro Mosera, 1767).

68. Folard's basic works include *Nouvelles decouvertes sur la guerre, dans une dissertation sur Polybe*, 2d rev. ed. (Brussells: F. Foppens, 1724); and *Histoire de Polybe; avec un commentaire au un corps de science militaire enrichi de notes critiques et historiques*, 6 vols. (Paris: P. Gondouin, 1727–30). For Folard's life and ideas see Jean Chagniot, *Le Chevalier de Folard: la Stratégie de l'incertitude* (Manaco: Éd. de Rocher, 1997).

69. Lloyd, *CHLWG*, 7.

70. Pietro Verri to Alessandro Verri, Bautzen, 13 settembre 1759, *Lettere e scritti inediti*, 1:49–50.

CHAPTER 2

1. The chief minister Pierre Guérin, cardinal de Tencin (1679–1758) enlarged France's war with the Treaty of Fountainebleau (Second Family Compact) of 25 October 1743, in which it and Spain agreed to declare war on Great Britain at an unspecified date. By placing the Stuart, James Francis Edward, on the throne as James III they believed France could secure a favorable peace.

2. Francisque Michel, *Les Écossais en France, les Français en Écosse* (London: Trübner and Co., 1862), 2:433 no. 2.

3. Hermann Maurice, comte de Saxe to Marc Pierre de Voyer de Paulmy, comte d'Argenson, Dunkerque, 9 March 1744, and same to same, 11 March 1744, *Deux Prétendants au XVIIIe siècle: Maurice de Saxe et Le Prince Charles-Edouard*, ed. Maurice Charles Marc René de Voyer de Paulmy, marquis d'Argenson (Paris: Albert Messein, Éditeur, 1928), 125, 132. Reed Browning, *The War of the Austrian Succession*, 158. Frank J. McLynn, *France and the Jacobite Rising of 1745* (Edinburgh: Edinburgh University Press, 1981), 24.

4. Drummond, "Mr. Drummond's Letter to the Editor," xi; Hannibal Lloyd, *Memoir of General Lloyd*, 2; Bruce Lenman, *The Jacobite Risings in Britain, 1689–1746* (London: Methuen, 1980), 238.

5. Drummond, "Mr. Drummond's Letter to the Editor," xii; Hannibal Lloyd, *Memoir of General Lloyd*, 2.

6. Dutch troops had been garrisoning the forts since the Barrier Treaty of 1715. According to Alice Carter the Dutch barrier was less an effective defensive barrier than a "sop" to uninstructed public opinion in the Northern Netherlands. Alice C. Carter, "The Dutch Barrier Fortresses in the Eighteenth Century, as shewn in the de Ferraris map," in *La Cartographie au XVIIIe Siecle et l'Œuvre du Comte de Ferraris (1726–1814)*, International Colloquium, Spa, 8–11 September, 1976 (Brussells: Crédit communal de Belgique, 1978), 270.

7. They formalized this agreement in the Quadruple Alliance of 8 January 1745. There already was a sizable British force in the Netherlands at this time. It had been an auxiliary of the Pragmatic Army that defeated the French at Dettingen (27 June 1743).

8. Francis Henry Skrine, *Fontenoy and Great Britain's Share in the War of the Austrian Succession, 1741–48*, with an introduction by Frederick Sleigh Roberts, Earl of Kandahar and Waterford (Edinburgh: William Blackwood and Sons, 1906), 56. For Lowendal see André Louis Woldeman Alphée, marquis de Sinety, *Vie du maréchal Lowendal*, 2 vols. (Paris: Librairie Bochelin-Deflorenne, 1867–68).

9. Allied intelligence failed to discover Saxe's move until the first week of May. John W. Fortescue, *A History of the British Army*, 2d ed. (London: Macmillan and Co., Limited, 1910), 2:109.

10. Drummond, "Mr. Drummond's Letter to the Editor," xii; Hannibal Lloyd, *Memoir of General Lloyd*, 2.

11. Hermann Maurice, comte de Saxe, *Reveries on the Art of War*, trans. and ed. by Thomas R. Phillips (Harrisburg, PA: The Military Service Publishing Company, 1944), 114, originally published as *Mes rêveries; ou Mémoires sur l'art de la guerre* (La Haye: Pierre Gosse, 1756). Saxe completed the manuscript in 1732, but it was not published until after his death.

12. Edward Cust, *Annals of the Wars of the Eighteenth Century, Compiled from the Most Authentic Histories of the Period*, 3d ed. (London: John Murray, 1869), 2:61.

13. Saxe, *Reveries on the Art of War*, 98.

14. Fortescue, *A History of the British Army*, 2:111. Marshal Saxe to Comte d'Argenson, Tournai, 13 May 1745, "Two Despatches Relative to the Battle of Fontenoy,"ed. Ernest M. Lloyd, *The English Historical Review* 12, no. 312 (April 1897), 524.

15. Saxe, *Reveries on the Art of War*, 81.

16. Henry Lloyd, *HLWG*, 18 [unnumbered].

17. In general the British public blamed the defeat on the Dutch inability to capture Fontenoy. Waldeck's defenders noted "that Fontenoi, which they attacked, was too strongly against them." See George Townshend, marquis of Townshend, *A Brief Narrative of the Late Campaigns in Germany and Flanders, in a Letter to a Member of Parliament* (London: Printed for J. Lion, 1751), 26.

18. "Account of the action between the allied Army and that of France, near Tournay, the 11th of May, N.S. 1745, with the names of the general and other Officers, and number of private men, and horses, that were killed, wounded and missing in each Regiment," *The Gentleman's Magazine* 15 (May 1745): 247; Skrine, *Fontenoy and Great Britain's Share in the War of the Austrian Succession*, 163.

19. Saxe was ill and for some reason known only to eighteenth-century medicine resorted to sucking on lead bullets to quench his thirst. Fortescue, *A History of the British Army*, 2:116.

20. A French observer remarked the formation became "extremely deep." "Account of the action between the allied Army and that of France, near Tournay," 250.

21. "Farther relation of the battle of Fontenoy, dated Paris, May 24," *The Gentleman's Magazine* 15 (June 1745): 315–16; Henry Seymour Conway to Horace Walpole, Ath, 14 May 1745, pt. 1 of *Horace Walpole's Correspondence with Henry Seymour Conway, Lord and Lady Hertford, Mrs. Harris*, eds. Wilmarth Sheldon Lewis, Lors E. Troide, Edwine M. Martz and Robert A. Smith, vol. 37 of *The Yale Edition of Horace Walpole's* Correspondence, ed. Wilmarth Sheldon Lewis (New Haven, CT: Yale University Press; London: Oxford University Press, 1974), 191.

22. "Farther relation of the battle of Fontenoy," 316–17. Ingoldsby publicly criticized Cumberland, but he failed to win much sympathy. Cumberland's subordinates generally supported him. See Henry Seymour Conway to Horace Walpole, Ath, 14 May 1745, pt. 1 of *Horace Walpole's Correspondence with Henry Seymour Conway, Lord and Lady Hertford, Mrs. Harris*, 191. Ingoldsby was court-martialed and found guilty on the lesser charge of "error in judgement." Rex Whitworth, *William Augustus, Duke of Cumberland: A Life* (London: Leo Cooper, 1992), 49.

23. Horace Walpole to Horatio Walpole, London, 7 May 1745 (Old Style), *Horace Walpole's Correspondence with the Walpole Family*, eds. Wilmarth Sheldon Lewis and Joseph Reed, Jr., with the assistance of Edwine M. Martz, vol. 36 of *The Yale Edition of Horace Walpole's* Correspondence, ed. Wilmarth Sheldon Lewis (New Haven, CT: Yale University Press; London: Oxford University Press, 1973), 11.

24. "Account of the action between the allied Army and that of France, near Tournay," 252. See Cust, *Annals of the Wars of the Eighteenth Century*, 2:65. A more recent study is Jean-Pierre Bois, *Fontenoy, 1745: Louis XV, arbiter de l'Europe* (Paris: Economica, 1996). For a short analysis of the Dutch army see H. L. Zwitzer, "The Dutch Army during the Ancien Régime," *Revue Internationale d'Histoire Militaire* no. 58 (1984): 15–36.

25. He argued that attacking dislocated parts of an enemy's line allowed him to react to those attacks and concentrate his forces. Lloyd, *CHLWG*, 21.

26. Lloyd, *HLWG*, 12–13 [unnumbered]; idem, *CHLWG*, xxiv–v. Lloyd was considered an able geographer/cartographer. In 1772, Henry Seymour Conway referred him to Horace Walpole to no avail since he was out of country. Horace Walpole to Horace Mann, Strawberry Hill, 23 July 1772, vol. 8 of *Horace Walpole's Correspondence with Sir Horace Mann,* eds. Wilmarth Sheldon Lewis, Warren Hunting Smith, and George L. Lam, vol. 23 of *The Yale Edition of Horace Walpole's* Correspondence, ed. Wilmarth Sheldon Lewis (New Haven, CT: Yale University Press; London: Oxford University Press, 1967), 421–22.

27. Lloyd, *HLWG*, 28[unnumbered]; idem, *CHLWG*, xxx.

28. Lloyd, *HLWG*, 29[unnumbered]; idem, *CHLWG*, xxxi.

29. Lloyd, "Reflections on the General Principles of War," 172; idem, *HLWG*, 12[unnumbered]; idem, *CHLWG*, xiv.

30. Lloyd, "Reflections on the General Principles of War," 172; idem, *HLWG*, 12[unnumbered]; idem, *CHLWG*, xiii.

31. He later wrote: "A battle is a changeable scene, in which every circumstance is instantaneous and transitory, without activity, those favourable opportunities, which always occur in days of action escape, and perhaps do not return in twenty campaigns. Lloyd, *CHLWG*, 2.

32. For Saxe's military career see Jon Manchip White, *Marshal of France: The Life and Times of Maurice, Comte de Saxe [1696–1750]* (Chicago, IL: Rand McNally & Company, 1962).

33. Saxe, *Reveries on the Art of War,* 18.

34. Ibid., 20.

35. Lloyd, "Reflections on the General Principles of War," 175; idem, *HLWG*, 33[unnumbered]; idem, *CHLWG*, xxxvi. See chapter 4 for Lloyd's psychological theory and his concept of 'National Character.'

36. See Saxe, "Clothing Troops," chap. 2 of *Reveries on the Art of War,* 22–24; Lloyd, "Reflections on the General Principles of War," 170–71; idem, *HLWG*, 9[unnumbered]; idem, *CHLWG*, ix–x, 37–9. For the breech-loading gun see Saxe, *Reveries on the Art of War,* 40; Lloyd, "Reflections on the General Principles of War," 171; idem, *HLWG*, 10[unnumbered]; idem, *CHLWG*, xi. For the ideas pertaining to the pike and lance see Saxe, *Reveries on the Art of War,* 45; Lloyd, *HLWG*, 10[unnumbered]; idem, "Of Defensive Arms and Armour," chap. 12 of Part the First in *CHLWG*, 39–43.

37. See Saxe, "Formation of the Legion," chap. 7 of *Reveries on the Art of War,* 36–38; Lloyd, "A New System," chap. 10 of Part the First of *CHLWG*, 35–37.

38. See Saxe, "The General Commanding," chap. 31 of *Reveries on the Art of War,* 117–20; Lloyd, "Of the General," chap. 1 of Part the Second in *CHLWG*, 69–80.

39. Saxe, *Reveries on the Art of War,* 121.

40. Lloyd, *HLWG*, 29[unnumbered]; idem, *CHLWG*, xxxi. After Fontenoy, Saxe is said to have looked with horror upon the battlefield strewn with mangled corpses and exclaimed: "You see what a battle means!" Quoted in Skrine, *Fontenoy and Great Britain's Share in the War of the Austrian Succession,* 188.

41. See Frank J. McLynn, "Issues and Motives in the Jacobite Rising of 1745," *The Eighteenth Century: Theory and Interpretation* 23, no. 2 (Spring 1982): 97–133; Paul Kleber Monod, *Jacobitism and the English People, 1688–1788* (Cambridge, MA: Cambridge University Press, 1989); and Edward Gregg, "Monarchs without a Crown," in *Royal and Republican Sovereignty in Early Modern Europe: Essays in Memory of Ragnhild Hatton,* edited by Robert Oresko, G. C. Gibbs and H. M. Scott

(Cambridge, MA: Cambridge University Press, 1997), 382–422; Daniel Szechi, *The Jacobites: Britain and Europe, 1688–1788* (Manchester: Manchester University Press, 1994), 126.

42. Robert Forbes, "Journal of the Prince's imbarkation and arrival, etc., the greatest part of which was taken from Duncan Cameron at several different conversations I had with him," *The Lyon in Mourning, or a Collection of Speeches, Letters, Journals, etc. Relative to the Affairs of Prince Charles Edward Stuart*, ed. Henry Paton (Edinburgh: Printed at the University Press by T. and A. Constable for the Scottish History Society, 1895; reprint, Edinburgh: Scottish Academic Press, 1975), 1:201.

43. Drummond, "Mr. Drummond's Letter to the Editor," xiii; Hannibal Lloyd, *Memoir of General Lloyd*, 2.

44. McLynn, *France and the Jacobite Rising of 1745*, 31.

45. Forbes, "Journal of the Prince's imbarkation and arrival, etc.," *The Lyon in Mourning*, 1:202.

46. John Burton, "Journal of Prince's imbarkation and arrival, etc., taken from the mouth of Æneas MacDonald (a banker in Paris, and a brother of Kinlochmoidart) when he was in a messenger's custody in London," *The Lyon in Mourning*, 1:285. The battle occurred thirty-nine leagues west of Lizard Point at the latitude of 47° 57'. James Johnstone, chevalier de Johnstone, *A Memoir of the Forty-Five*, ed. Brian Rawson (London: Folio Society, 1958), 24; originally published as *Memoirs of the rebellion of 1745 and 1746* (London: Printed for Longman, Hurst, Rees, Orme, and Browne, 1820).

47. Drummond, "Mr. Drummond's Letter to the Editor," xiii; Hannibal Lloyd, *Memoir of General Lloyd*, 2.

48. Forbes, "Journal of the Prince's imbarkation and arrival, etc.," *The Lyon in Mourning*, 1:203.

49. George Lockhart, ed., "Journals and Memoirs of the Young Pretender's Expedition in 1745," *The Lockhart Papers: Containing Memoirs and Contemporaries upon the Affairs of Scotland from 1702 to 1715, by George Lockhart, Esq. of Carnwarth, His Secret Correspondence with the Son of King James the Second from 1718 to 1728, and his other political Writings; Also, Journals and Memoirs of the young Pretender's Expedition of 1745, by Highland Officers in his Army*, published from the original manuscripts in the possession of Anthony Aufrere, Esq. (London: Printed by Richard and Arthur Taylor for William Anderson, 1817), 2:439.

50. Johnstone, *A Memoir of the Forty-Five*, 25.

51. Drummond, "Mr. Drummond's Letter to the Editor," xiii; Hannibal Lloyd, *Memoir of General Lloyd*, 2.

52. Lenman, *The Jacobite Risings in Britain*, 250.

53. Walter Bigger Blaikie, ed., "A Short Account of the Battles of Preston, Falkirk, and Culloden; by a Gentleman who was in these Actions," *Origins of the Forty-Five and Other Papers Relating to that Rising* (1916; reprint, Edinburgh: Scottish Academic Press, 1975), 406.

54. For a spirited defense of Cope see Robert Cadell, *Sir John Cope and the Rebellion of 1745* (Edinburgh: William Blackwood and Sons, 1898).

55. Blaikie, ed., "A Short Account of the Battles of Preston, Falkirk, and Culloden," 407.

56. Johnstone, *A Memoir of the Forty-Five*, 40.

57. Cust, *Annals of the Wars of the Eighteenth Century,* 2:88; Blaikie, ed., "A Short Account of the Battles of Preston, Falkirk, and Culloden," 408.

58. Lockhart, ed., "Journals and Memoirs of the Young Pretender's Expedition in 1745," *The Lockhart Papers,* 2:450; John Heneage Jesse, *Memoirs of the Chevalier, Prince Charles Edward, and their Adherents,* 2d ed. (London: Richard Bentley, 1846), 1:275.

59. Charles Stuart to James Stuart, Pinkay House near Edinburgh, 21 September 1745 (Old Style), *The Lyon in Mourning,* 2:211.

60. The Jacobite threat was probably more serious than traditionally believed. Indeed, overthrowing a dynasty was the most radical political objective possible during the eighteenth century. The romantic nostalgia associated with Jacobite studies overshadows the benefit it brings to both British international and domestic history. Jeremy Black, *Culloden and the '45* (London: Grange Books, 1997), xiii.

61. Lloyd, *CHLWG,* 13–16. The battle of Prestonpans was a small-scale engagement, but it did lead to significant political results. Charles's smashing victory convinced France to prepare for another invasion this time commanded by the ambitious Cardinal Louis François Armand du Plessis, duc de Richelieu (1696–1788).

62. Ibid., 17.

63. See John Shy, "Jomini," in *Makers of Modern Strategy from Machiavelli to the Nuclear Age,* 143–85.

64. Lord John Drummond to the James Stuart, Dunkirque, 13 November 1745, *Memorials of John Murray of Broughton Sometime Secretary to Prince Charles Edward, 1740–1747,* ed. Robert Fitzroy Bell (Edinburgh: Printed at the University Press by T. and A. Constable for the Scottish Historical Society, 1898), 398.

65. Fortescue, *A History of the British Army,* 2:135. For Charles's Scottish army see Alastair Livingstone, Christian W. H. Aikman, and Betty Stuart Hart, eds., *Muster Roll of Prince Charles Edward Stuart's Army, 1745–46,* foreword by Donald Cameron of Lochiel and introduction by Bruce P. Lenman (Aberdeen, Scotland: Aberdeen University Press, 1984).

66. Drummond, "Mr. Drummond's Letter to the Editor," xiii; Hannibal Lloyd, *Memoir of General Lloyd,* 2.

67. Henry Seymour Conway to Horace Walpole, Litchfield, 30 November 1745 (Old Style), pt. 1 of *Horace Walpole's Correspondence with Henry Seymour Conway, Lord and Lady Hertford, Mrs. Harris,* 211.

68. Arnold G. Goyder, "Welsh Jacobite Societies," *The Stewarts* 11 (1960): 16–21. Richard H. Owen, "Jacobitism and the Church in Wales," *Journal of the Historical Society of the Church in Wales* 2 (1953): 112, observed it was strictly High Church in religion and Tory in politics. Herbert M. Vaughn, "Welsh Jacobitism," *The Transactions of the Honourable Society of Cymmrodorian* (1920–21): 32, argues that it was not strong in Wales, Jacobitism being a personal connection not a political one. See also Donald Nicholas, "The Welsh Jacobites," *The Transactions of the Honourable Society of Cymmrodorian* (1948): 467–74, Peter D. G. Thomas, "Jacobitism in Wales," *The Welsh History Review* 1, no. 3 (1962): 279–300, and Arnold G. Goyder, "David Morgan and the Welsh Jacobites," *The Stewarts* 10 (1955–58): 286.

69. Peter D. G. Thomas, *Politics in Eighteenth-Century Wales* (Cardiff: University of Wales Press, 1998), 144. But Charles sincerely believed a Welsh rebellion viable. Years later a cynical Charles commented: "I will do as much for my Welsh friends as they have done for me; I will drink their health;" quoted in E.L.B., "Jacobite

Relics, Denbighshire," *Archæologia Cambrensis: The Journal of the Cambrian Archæological Association,* 3d ser., 2, no. 6 (April 1856): 181.

70. Drummond, "Mr. Drummond's Letter to the Editor," xiii; Hannibal Lloyd, *Memoir of General Lloyd,* 2–3. It was published anonymously as *A rhapsody on the present system of French politics; on the projected invasion and the means to defeat it,* by a Chelsea pensioner, illustrated with a chart of the opposite coasts of England and France (London: W. Faden and T. Jeffreys, 1779).

71. Drummond, "Mr. Drummond's Letter to the Editor," xv.

72. Jacobite sympathizers accused France of duplicity. Apologists suggested the task was too difficult for Louis XV to undertake at that time. The French government could have supported Charles if it had been united in its strategy, but three cabals jockeyed for resources. One wished to wage war in the Caribbean, the other, headed by Saxe, wanted war in Flanders. The third interest group led by Richelieu supported the Jacobites, but with resources divided among the three campaigns, nothing significant was done on any front. McLynn, *France and the Jacobite Rising of 1745,* 163.

73. Drummond, "Mr. Drummond's Letter to the Editor," xiv.

74. Frederick II, "History of My Own Times," vol. 1, part II of *Posthumous Works of Frederic II, King of Prussia,* trans. Thomas Holcroft (London: Printed for G. G. J. and J. Robinson, 1789), 245.

75. Drummond, "Mr. Drummond's Letter to the Editor," xiv.

76. Hermann Maurice, comte de Saxe, "Memoir of M. of Saxony," *Lettres et mémoires choisis parmi les papiers du maréchal de Saxe* (Paris: J. J. Smits et Compagnie, 1794): 4:161. Lowendal had been clamoring for a chance at independent command since May; see Comte de Lowendal to Marshal Saxe, Anvers, 13 May 1747, *Lettres et mémoires,* 4:110. Cust, *Annals of the Wars of the Eighteenth Century,* 2:120.

77. "Description of Bergen-op-Zoom," *The Gentleman's Magazine* 17 (July 1747): 328.

78. English Volunteer, *An Authentic Journal of the Remarkable and Bloody Siege of Bergen-op-Zoom, by the French, under M. de Lowendahl: begun July 14, and ended Sept. 16, N.S. 1747: when the place was taken by storm, after a brave defence and desperate an attack, of two months and two days, as ever was known* (London: Printed for the Proprietors; and Sold by R. Griffiths, Publisher, 1747), v.

79. "Extract of a letter from a burgomaster of Bergen-op-Zoom, Jan. 31," *The Gentleman's Magazine* 17 (July 1747): 346.

80. English Volunteer, *An Authentic Journal of the Remarkable and Bloody Siege of Bergen-op-Zoom,* v–viii; "Description of Bergen-op-Zoom," 328–29.

81. For a brief description of the siege see Christopher Duffy, *The Fortress in the Age of Vauban and Frederick the Great, 1660–1789: Siege Warfare Volume II* (London: Routledge & Kegan Paul, 1984), 107–10; Browning, *The War of the Austrian Succession,* 319–21.

82. See John W. Wright, "Military Contributions during the Eighteenth Century," *The Journal of the American Military Institute* 3, no. 1 (Spring 1939): 3–13.

83. English Volunteer, *An Authentic Journal of the Remarkable and Bloody Siege of Bergen-op-Zoom,* 10.

84. Saxe "Memoir of M. of Saxony," 4:161.

85. "Progress of the Siege of Bergen-op-Zoom," *The Gentleman's Magazine* 17 (August 1747): 401.

86. "Extract of a letter from a burgomaster of Bergen-op-Zoom, Jan. 31," 346.

87. Lowendal demanded 40,000 rations of hay, 40,000 rations of oats, 100 wagons of straw, and 400 timber beams. If these demands were not met he promised that: "their towns, houses, hamlets, villages will be burned." The French colonel of the Regiment of Breton Volunteers, Olivier de Kermelle Penholt, added: "I would advise you to make a good use of the kindness which our general [Lowendal] has still for you; for otherwise I shall come and see you with a torch in my hand." "Some of the Severe Orders from the French Army before Bergen-op-Zoom," *The Gentleman's Magazine* 17 (August 1747): 378.

88. "Extract of a letter from a burgomaster of Bergen-op-Zoom," 346.

89. English Volunteer, *An Authentic Journal of the Remarkable and Bloody Siege of Bergen-op-Zoom*, 23.

90. Drummond, "Mr. Drummond's Letter to the Editor," xv; Hannibal Lloyd, *Memoir of General Lloyd*, 3.

91. "A Journal of the Works and the Trenches, during the Siege of Bergen-op-Zoom," *Remarks on the Military Operations of the English and French Armies, commanded by His Royal Highness the Duke of Cumberland, and Marshal Saxe, during the Campaign of 1747; to which are added, I. Military Principles and Maxims drawn from the Remarks; II. The Siege of Bergen-op-Zoom* (London: Printed for T. Becket, 1760), 119.

92. English Volunteer, *An Authentic Journal of the Remarkable and Bloody Siege of Bergen-op-Zoom*, 33.

93. "Progress of the Siege of Bergen-op-Zoom," 402.

94. Rumors spread that someone inside the fort purposely left open the sally ports. "Letter from an Officer in Bergen-op-Zoom, when it was taken," *The Gentleman's Magazine* 17 (September 1747): 411. See Horace Mann to Horace Walpole, Florence, 10 October 1747; Horace Walpole to Horace Mann, London, 2 October 1747 (Old Style); and Horace Mann to Horace Walpole, Florence, 7 November 1747, pt. 3 of *Horace Walpole's Correspondence with Horace Mann*, eds. Wilmarth Sheldon Lewis, Warren Heinty Smith, and George L. Lam, vol. 19 of *The Yale Edition of Horace Walpole's* Correspondence, ed. Wilmarth Sheldon Lewis, 440, 442, 444. Others blamed old Baron Cronström for incompetence. "Series of Proofs that Bergen-op-Zoom was surprised," *The Gentleman's Magazine* 17 (September 1747): 412; Elka Schrijver, "Bergen op Zoom: Stronghold on the Scheldt," *History Today* 26, no. 11 (November 1976): 751.

95. "Select Relations concerning the loss of Bergen-op-Zoom," *The Gentleman's Magazine* 17 (September 1747): 410.

96. English Volunteer, *An Authentic Journal of the Remarkable and Bloody Siege of Bergen-op-Zoom*, 48–53; "End of the Siege of Bergen-op-Zoom," *The Gentleman's Magazine* 17 (September 1747): 50.

97. "Letter from an Officer in Bergen-op-Zoom, when it was taken," 410.

98. Ulric Fréderic Waldemar, comte de Lowendal, "Letter from Count Lowendahl to Marshal Saxe, from the camp under Bergen-op-Zoom, Sept. 17," *The Gentleman's Magazine* 17 (September 1747): 439. Revenge and retribution, rather than honor or valor, motivated and justified the atrocities. "An army, like the sea," Lloyd wrote later, "is sometimes calm and slothful, at others, furious and outrageous, wholly ungovernable." Lloyd, *CHLWG*, 70. His experience at Bergen-op-Zoom no doubt reinforced this observation, if it did not provide its genesis.

99. Quoted in Skrine, *Fontenoy and Great Britain's Share in the War of the Austrian Succession*, 337.

100. Ibid., 69.

101. Drummond, "Mr. Drummond's Letter to the Editor," xv.

102. Hannibal Lloyd, *Memoir of General Lloyd*, 3. See Henry Lloyd, *Lists of the Forces of the Sovereigns of Europe &c. viz. Ranks, Uniforms, Numbers of Officers, Private Men &c. of each Nation*, methodized by J. Millan & engraved by the best hands (London: Printed for J. Millan, 1761). His survey included the armies of Britain, France, Hese, Prussia, Russia, Sweden, Bavaria, the Electors of Metz, Trier and Cologne, the Landgrave of Hesse-Cassel, and Saxony.

CHAPTER 3

1. Drummond, "Mr. Drummond's Letter to the Editor," xvi; Hannibal Lloyd, *Memoir of General Lloyd*, 3. For Belle-Isle see André Dusage, *Études sur la Guerre de Sept Ans: Le Ministère de Belle-Isle* (Paris: L. Fournier, 1914) and Jean Bérenger, "Le Marechal de Belle-Isle, General et Homme d'Etat a l'Epoque des Lumieres (1684–1761)," in *Soldier-Statesmen of the Age of the Enlightenment: Records of the 7th International Colloquy on Military History, Washington, D.C., 25–30 July 1982,* edited by Abigail T. Siddall (Manhattan, KS: Sunflower University Press, 1984), 181–210.

2. Drummond, "Mr. Drummond's Letter to the Editor," xvii; Hannibal Lloyd, *Memoir of General Lloyd,* 3. Hannibal claimed that his father's report influenced France's invasion of Minorca.

3. Hannibal Lloyd, *Memoir of General Lloyd,* 3; Pietro Verri to Alessandro Verri, Bautzen, 13 settembre 1759, *Lettere e scritti inediti,* 1:51; Romance de Mesmon, "Précis sur la Vie et le Caractère de Henri Lloyd," xxxii; Migazzi to Daun, 29 September 1758, Fond Pálfi-Daun: Stray Correspondence of the Field-Marshal, XXXIX, Státny Ústredeny Archív, Bratislava, Slovakia, cited in Christopher Duffy, *Instrument of War,* vol. 1 of *The Austrian Army in the Seven Years' War,* with the support of the Austrian Army Museum (Heeresgeschichtliches Museum), Vienna (Rosemont, IL: The Emperor's Press, 2000), 379.

4. His father, Peter, was an exiled Irish Jacobite who served with distinction in the Russian army. Franz Moritz had been a protégé of the highly regarded Russian Field Marshal Burkhard Christoph, Graf von Münnich (1683–1767). See Edith Kotasek, *Feldmarschall Graf Lacy: Ein Leben für Österreichs Heer* (Horn: F. Berger, 1956).

5. The diverse Austrian army embodied the Imperial ideal as it contained regiments of Germans, Italians, Poles, Hungarians, Croats, as well as Slovene, Czech, and Wallachian troops. Poor leadership and organization plagued its wartime effectiveness. Maria Theresa (r.1740–80) had begun a series of reforms in 1748 that standardized regiments, ranks, and regulations in order to combat the efficiency of the Prussian foe. A key reform in 1752 created the *Theresianische Militärakademie* at Wiener Neustadt to produce a competent officer corps from the sons of impoverished nobles and other faithful devotees of the Habsburgs. See Joseph Christoph Allmayer-Beck, "The Establishment of the Theresan Military Academy in Wiener Neustadt," in *East Central European Society and War in the Pre-Revolutionary Eighteenth Century,* eds. Gunther E. Rothenberg, Béla K. Király, and Peter F. Sugar, War and Society in East Central Europe, vol. 2, East European Monographs, no. 122 (Boulder, CO: Social Science Monographs, 1982), 115–21.

6. The corps consisted of two infantry regiments, one dragoon regiment and a pioneer battalion, which allowed it to fight as well. Christopher Duffy, *The Army of*

Maria Theresa: The Armed Forces of Imperial Austria, 1740–1780 (New York: Hippocrene Books, 1977), 135–36. The staff's advance guard comprised the first battalion of the staff infantry and dragoon regiments. Johann Gottlieb Tielke, *A Description of the Affair of Maxen, with Remarks on the Poisition; and a Treatise on the Attack and Defense of Unfortified Heights, on the Profiles of Positions, and the Placing of Batteries in Hilly Situations, with Plans, vol. 1 of An Account of Some of the Most Remarkable Events of the War between the Prussians, Austrians, and Russians, from 1756 to 1763: and a Treatise on several Branches of the Military Art,* with Plans and Maps, trans. Charles and Robert Crauford (London: Printed for the Translators; and Sold by J. Walter, 1787), 8n; originally published as *Beyträge zur Kriegs-Kunst und Geschichte des Krieges von 1756 bis 1763: mit Plans und Charten.* 6 vols. (Freyberg: Gedrunckt mit Barthelischen Schriften, 1775–86); Alphons Freiherrn von Wrede, *Geschichte K. und K. Wehrmacht: Die Regimenter, Corps, Branchen und Anstalten von 1618 bis Ende des XIX. Jahrhunderts* (Wien: L. W. Seidel & Sohn, 1898), 2:585; and Lars-Holger Thümmler, *Die Österreichische Armee im Siebenjährigen Krieg: Die Bautzener Bilderhandschrift aus dem Jahre 1762* (Berlin: Brandenburgisches Verlagshaus, 1993), 54.

7. Pietro Verri to Alessandro Verri, Milano, 13 settembre 1769, XXIII(237), in vol. 3 of *Carteggio di Pietro e di Alessandro Verri dal 1766 al 1797,* eds. Francesco Novati and Emanuele Greppi (Milano: Casa Editrice L. F. Cogliati, 1911), 55.

8. Pietro Verri to Alessandro Verri, Bautzen, 13 settembre 1759, *Lettere e scritti inediti,* 1:52–53. Verri heard three different accounts, but he believed this one best-illustrated Lloyd's character. The interview also appears in the narratives of Hannibal Lloyd and the Marquis de Romance de Mesmon.

9. Österreichisches Staatsarchiv, Wien, Kriegsarchiv, Personalevidenzen, Musterlisten und Standestabellen (1740–1820), Stabs-Infanterie-Regiment (1759), "Hauptmann Johann Jacob Edler von Fleischmann-Compagnie," Karton Nr. 11.264. He is listed as Ober-Leutenant Ignate de Loyde, 30 years old, born in England, Catholic, single.

10. Storrs and Scott, "The Military Revolution and the European Nobility, c. 1600–1800," 19–20.

11. Pietro Verri to Alessandro Verri, Bautzen, 13 settembre 1759, *Lettere e scritti inediti,* 1:53.

12. John A. Lynn, "The Evolution of Army Style in the Modern West, 800–2000," *The International History Review* 18, no. 3 (August 1996): 518–9.

13. See Arthur N. Gilbert, "Military Recruitment and Career Advancement in the Eighteenth Century: Two Case Studies," *Journal of the Society for Army Historical Research* 57, no. 229 (Spring 1979): 34–44.

14. Duffy, *The Army of Maria Theresa,* 30–31. To receive favor and promotion, subalterns were expected to give presents to regimental commanders. Lacy was noted and disliked for promoting subordinates without reference to their seniority. For an analysis of the nobility's role in the Habsburg armed forces see Thomas M. Barker, *Army, Aristocracy, Monarchy: Essays on War, Society, and Government in Austria, 1618–1780,* War and Society in East Central Europe, vol. 7 (Boulder, CO: Social Science Monographs, 1982), 37–60.

15. Pietro Verri to Alessandro Verri, Bautzen, 13 settembre 1759, *Lettere e scritti inediti,* 1:54. For the intellectual affinity between the two men see Franco Venturi, *Le Vite incrociate di Henry Lloyd e Pietro Verri.* Verri (1728–97) was an Italian count who served in the Habsburg army during the war. He later became a key

figure in the Milanese Enlightenment and was an important contributor to the short-lived journal *Il Caffè*. His standard biography is Nino Valeri, *Pietro Verri* (Firenze: Felice le Monnier, 1969).

16. Ibid., 55.

17. Ibid., 58; Pietro Verri to Alessandro Verri, Dresden, 20 dicembre 1759, *Lettere e scritti inediti*, 1:92–93.

18. Pietro Verri to Alessandro Verri, Hosterwitz in Sassonia, 8 ottobre, 1759, *Lettere e scritti inediti*, 1:70.

19. Pietro Verri to Alessandro Verri, Bautzen, 13 settembre, 1759, *Lettere e scritti inediti*, 1:55.

20. Pietro Verri to Alessandro Verri, Hosterwitz in Sassonia, 8 ottobre, 1759, *Lettere e scritti inediti*, 1:70.

21. Pietro Verri to Alessandro Verri, Bautzen, 13 settembre, 1759, *Lettere e scritti inediti*, 1:55. These "Volunteers" held no formal military rank or command and wore a blue uniform similar to the Prussians. Duffy, *The Army of Maria Theresa,* 28. Montazet was the French plenipotentiary in the Austrian headquarters.

22. Hannibal Lloyd, *Memoir of General Lloyd*, 4; Romance de Mesmon, "Précis sur la Vie et le Caractère de Henri Lloyd," xxxiii.

23. Lacy often said, "Send me Souffre-douleurs!," when faced with a dangerous assignment. Hannibal Lloyd, *Memoir of General Lloyd*, 4.

24. Pietro Verri to Alessandro Verri, Schilda, 1 novembre, 1759, *Lettere e scritti inediti*, 1:78.

25. Ibid.

26. Lloyd, *HLWG2*, 122. For Daun's career see Franz-Lorenz von Thadden, *Feldmarschall Daun: Maria Theresias grössten Feldherr* (Wien und Müchen: Herold, 1967).

27. Pietro Verri to Alessandro Verri, Bautzen, 13 settembre, 1759, *Lettere e scritti inediti*, 1:57.

28. Pietro Verri to Alessandro Verri, Dresden, 2 gennaio, 1760, *Lettere e scritti inediti*, 1:106.

29. Österreichisches Staatsarchiv, Wien, Kriegsarchiv, Personalevidenzen, Musterlisten und Standestabellen (1740–1820), Deutschen Feld-Jäger-Corps (1760), "Hauptmann Ignatz von Loyde-Compagnie," Karton Nr. 11.031. He is listed as 40 years old, born in Ireland. He was promoted on 1 February 1760. The Feld-Jäger-Corps was an elite unit of forest gamekeepers armed with rifles adept at reconnaissance and providing an advance screen for the army. It was under the authority of the Pionier-Corps, which in turn answered to the staff corps. By 1760 the Feld-Jäger-Corps comprised 1,000 soldiers. It was disbanded in 1763. Duffy, *The Army of Maria Theresa*, 67, 136; Wrede, *Geschichte der K. und K. Wehrmacht*, 2:505; and Thümmler, ed., *Die Österreichische Armee im Siebenjährigen Krieg,* 55.

30. Pietro Verri to Alessandro Verri, Dresden, 2 gennaio, 1760, *Lettere e scritti inediti*, 1:106–7. Pietro Verri to Alessandro Verri, Dresden, 23 novembre, 1759, *Lettere e scritti inediti*, 1:88. Verri considered uncommon Lloyd's rapid promotion.

31. Duffy, *The Army of Maria Theresa*, 63. Lloyd's salary and ration allotment also increased with his rank. He considered the light infantry indispensable even though it had "no influence on the success of a war." Lloyd, *HLWG*, 27.

32. He claimed his small force kept within a day's march of Frederick's army and skirmished often, losing less than twenty men (one do to drunkenness). Lloyd,

CHLWG, 53. Henry Lloyd to Friedrich Wilhelm Ernst, graf zu Schaumburg-Lippe (hereafter simply Lippe), 13 Juni 1764, A XXXV 18.177, Schaumburg-Lippe Family Papers, Niedersächsisches Staatsarchiv, Bückeburg, Germany (hereafter called *NSB*); Lloyd, *HLWG*, 4[unnumbered]; Hannibal Lloyd, *Memoir of General Lloyd*, 4; Romance de Mesmon, "Précis sur la Vie et le Caractère de Henri Lloyd," xxxiv. He was not promoted to Lieutenant-Colonel while in the Austrian army as Romance de Mesmon asserts.

33. Duffy, *The Army of Maria Theresa*, 193.

34. Hannibal Lloyd, *Memoir of General Lloyd*, 4.

35. Lippe to Sebastião José de Carvalho e Mello, conde de Oeyras, 19 Juillet 1765, (303), in *Wilhelm Graf zu Schaumburg-Lippe: Schriften und Briefe*, ed. Curd Ochwadt (Frankfurt am Main: Vittorio Klostermann, 1983), 3:251. Siskovocs informed Lacy of Lloyd's displeasure and his new threat to join the Spanish army. See Österreichisches Staatsarchiv, Wien, Kriegsarchiv, Alte Feldakten, Hauptarmee, "Joseph, Graf von Siskovics to Franz Moritz, Graf von Lacy, Dresden, 1 Decembre 1760," Karton Nr. 712.

36. Romance de Mesmon, "Précis sur la Vie et le Caractère de Henri Lloyd," xxxv; Österreichisches Staatsarchiv, Wien, Kriegsarchiv, Personalevidenzen, Musterlisten und Standestabellen (1740–1820), "Deutschen Feld-Jäger-Corps (1761)."

37. Hannibal Lloyd, *Memoir of General Lloyd*, 5; Romance de Mesmon, "Précis sur la Vie et le Caractère de Henri Lloyd," xxxv.

38. Lloyd did not find the Saxon Court congenial to his interests and left after two weeks. Henry Lloyd to Lippe, 13 Juni 1764, A XXXV 18.177, *NSB;* Lippe to Sebastião José de Carvalho e Mello, conde de Oeyras, 19 juillet 1765, (303), in *Wilhelm Graf zu Schaumburg-Lippe,* ed. Curd Ochwadt, 3:251; Hannibal Lloyd, *Memoir of General Lloyd,* 5; Romance de Mesmon, "Précis sur la Vie et le Caractère de Henri Lloyd," xxxvi.

39. Romance de Mesmon, "Précis sur la Vie et le Caractère de Henri Lloyd," xxxiii. Similar to modern staff rides, Lloyd preferred revisiting battle sites in order to reconstruct the action.

40. Christopher Duffy, "The Seven Years' War as a Limited War," in *East Central European Society and War in the Pre-Revolutionary Eighteenth Century,* 70.

41. The French army learned from their defeat and began to create the institutional structure and army organization that Napoleon would adopt and use with great success. See Robert S. Quimby, *The Background of Napoleonic Warfare.*

42. Lloyd, *HLWG*, 3[unnumbered].

43. Lloyd, *HLWG*, 4[unnumbered]. Thucydides emphasized the importance of factual source material. Thucydides, *History of the Peloponnesian War,* trans. Charles F. Smith, Loeb Classical Library, ed. George P. Goold, no. 108 (1919; reprint, Cambridge, MA: Harvard University Press; London: William Heinemann LTD, 1980), 1:3. Thucydides believed his conflict was "great and noteworthy" compared to all previous wars and that his narrative continued would have "a clear view both of the events which have happened."

44. Lloyd, *HLWG*, 1–2[unnumbered]. Traces of Lloyd's epistemological categories and his distinction between military and civilian writers are apparent in John Keegan, *The Face of Battle* (New York: The Viking Press, 1976), 22–27. Michael Howard went as far to claim that Lloyd ushered in "a new age in the history of military thought." Michael Howard, "Jomini and the Classical Tradition of Military Thought," 5.

45. Lloyd, *HLWG,* 1[unnumbered]. The debate of the "Ancients vs. Moderns" centered on the authority of the ancients concerning politics and religion. Lloyd expanded the debate to include military history, which in his opinion the ancients perfected.

46. Lloyd, *HLWG,* 1[unnumbered].

47. Ibid., xxxix.

48. Travers, "The Development of British Military Historical Writing and Thought from the Eighteenth Century to the Present," 24.

49. Lloyd wrote: "There is besides in every elevated mind, an emulation, which encourages and animates us to tread the footsteps of those great men [i.e. the ancients], whose actions and characters, are justly the object of love and veneration." Lloyd, *HLWG,* 2[unnumbered].

50. Ibid., 2–3 [unnumbered]. He prefigured Hans Delbrück with his emphasis on critical evaluation of source material and exactness of numbers and quantitative figures.

51. Ibid., i–xii; xiii–xxxix.

52. Henry Lloyd to Lippe, 13 Juni 1764, A XXXV 18.177, *NSB.* Lloyd did not want to offend anyone [i.e. Frederick the Great] who could damage his career.

53. Henry Lloyd, *The History of the Late War in Germany; Between the King of Prussia, and the Empress of Germany and Her Allies: Containing the Campaigns of 1758, and 1759, with a correct Military Map of the Seat of War; and Plans of the Siege of Olmütz, and the Battles of Zornsdorf, Hochkirchen, Paltzig, Cunnersdorf, or Frankfurt, and Maxen,* vol. 2, published from the General's manuscripts, under the inspection of an English officer, and illustrated with notes critical, historical, and explanatory (London: Printed for T. and J. Egorton, 1790), 108 (hereafter cited as *HLWG2*).

54. Ibid.

55. Otto Herrmann in his analysis of Georg Friedrich von Tempelhof's history of the Seven Years' War argued Lloyd's sources were insufficient and uncritically examined. Tempelhof used a vast array of published and unpublished primary sources, which were not available when Lloyd published his history. See Otto Herrmann, *Über die Quellen Geschichte des siebenjährigen Krieges von Tempelhoff: Inaugural-Dissertation zur erlangung der Doctor-würde von der philosophischen Facultät der Friedrich-Wilhelms-Universität zu Berlin genehmigt nebst den beigefügten Thesen öffentlich zu vertheidigen am 6 November 1885* (Berlin: Buchdruckerei von Gustav Schade (Otto Francke), 1885), 6–8, 27.

56. Lloyd, *HLWG,* 16–18.

57. Georg Friedrich von Tempelhof, *Geschichte des Siebenjährigen Krieges in Deutschland zwischen dem Könige von Preussen und der Kaiserin Königen mit ihren Alliirten, vom General Lloyd,* 6 vols., aus dem Englischen neue übersetzt mit verbesserten Planen und Anmerkungen (Berlin: J. F. Unger, 1783–1801). His criticism of Lloyd was translated and published as Colin Lindsay, *Extracts from Colonel Tempelhoffe's History of the Seven Years' War; His Remarks on General Lloyd; On the Subsistence of Armies; and on the March of Convoys,* 2 vols. (London: Printed for T. Cadell, 1793). See also *The History of the Seven Years' War in Germany, by Generals Lloyd and Tempelhoff, with observations from the Treatise of Great Military Operations by General Jomini,* vol. 1, trans. from the French and German by Captain Charles Hamilton Smith (London: Printed by R. G. Clarke, [n.d.]). This compilation underscores Tempelhof's agenda and defends Lloyd analysis.

58. John Berkenhout, "Review of *The History of the Late War in Germany,*" *The Monthly Review; or, Literary Journal* 35 (August 1766): 87. He remarked that the book reflected an author "highly skilful [*sic*] in his profession." Pietro Verri considered it an extraordinary work and first original history by a soldier. Pietro Verri to Alessandro Verri, Milano, 10 febbraio 1768, CC(87), in vol. 1, part II of *Carteggio di Pietro e di Alessandro Verri dal 1766 al 1797,* 165.

59. Lloyd and Clinton met one another during the Seven Years' War. The former often sent the latter books on military subjects. See Ira D. Gruber, "The Education of Sir Henry Clinton," *Bulletin of the John Rylands University Library of Manchester* 72, no. 1 (Spring 1990): 135. For instance, he later gave Clinton a manuscript copy of the 1758 campaign, which was not included in the 1766 publication. Henry Lloyd to Henry Clinton, 29 September 1770, vol. 7:26, Henry S. Clinton Papers, William L. Clements Library. John Adams requested Lloyd's history among other works to educate the young American military officers. John Adams to William Tudor, 12 October 1775, vol. 3 of *The Papers of John Adams,* eds. Robert J. Taylor, Gregg L. Lint, and Celeste Walter (Cambridge, MA: The Belknap Press of Harvard University Press, 1979), 194–95. James Wilkinson sent copies of Lloyd's history and Colin Lindsay's extracts to Alexander Hamilton upon his becoming a Major-General. James Wilkinson to Alexander Hamilton, New York, 16 August 1799, vol. XXIII of *The Papers of Alexander Hamilton,* ed. Harold C. Syrett (New York: Columbia University Press, 1976), 324. Jeremy Bentham's brother, Samuel, asked for Lloyd's history while serving in Russia. Samuel Bentham to Jeremy Bentham, Bender, 18/29 September 1790, no. 723, vol. 4 of *The Correspondence of Jeremy Bentham,* ed. Alexander Taylor Milne (London: The Athlone Press, 1981), 204. Winfield Scott's copy is now located in the Library of the United States Military Academy, West Point, New York.

60. Martin Weyl, *Passion for Reason and Reason for Passion: Seventeenth Century Art and Theory in France, 1648–1683,* Hermeneutics of Art, ed. Moshe Barasch, vol. 2 (New York; Bern; Frankfurt am Main; Paris: Peter Lang, 1989), 175–77. Classicists posited that an artist could discover and understand the rules that constituted his art. They invoked the Renaissance Mannerists and Greco-Roman writers on style—(Aristotle, Horace, Longinus, and Demetrius—(as their theoretical models. See Charles H. C. Wright, *French Classicism,* Harvard Studies in Romance Languages, vol. IV (Cambridge MA: Harvard University Press; London: Humphrey Milford, Oxford University Press, 1920), 22.

61. René Wellek, *The Later Eighteenth Century,* vol. 1 of *A History of Modern Criticism: 1750–1950* (New Haven CT: Yale University Press, 1955), 12–14. The belief that Aristotle first composed the principles of art arose during the Renaissance, but had little to do with his actual thoughts on the subject. See Aristotle, *Poetics,* ed. and trans. Stephen Halliwell, in *Aristotle; Longinus; Demetrius,* 2d ed., Loeb Classical Library, ed. George P. Goold, no. 199 (Cambridge, MA: Harvard University Press, 1995), 28–141.

62. Azar Gat, *The Origins of Military Thought from the Enlightenment to Clausewitz,* 28–29.

63. Lloyd, "Reflections on the general principles of war," 169; idem, *HLWG,* 6[unnumbered]. Lloyd's engineering and mathematics background also influenced his general quest for principles and rules. For the methodology of the early engineering profession, see Antoine Picon, *French Architects and Engineers in the Age of Enlightenment,* trans. Martin Thom, Cambridge Studies in the History of

Architecture, eds. Robin Middleton, Joseph Rykwert, and David Watkin (Cambridge, MA: Cambridge University Press, 1988), 106–8.

64. Lloyd, "Reflections," 169; idem, *HLWG*, 6[unnumbered]. Lloyd confessed, "[i]n this art, as in poetry and eloquence, there are many who can trace, the rules, by which, a poem or oration, should be composed, . . . But for want of that enthusiastick [sic] and divine fire, their productions are languid and insipid." Lloyd, "Reflections," 169; idem, *HLWG*, 6[unnumbered]. By "fire" he meant genius. Conceptualizing war as an art had classical precedents. See Xenophon "On the Cavalry Commander," *Scripta Minora*, 271. He also likened the art of war to music with the general as composer; idem, *Cyropaedia*, 1:121.

65. Lloyd, *HLWG*, 7–8[unnumbered].

66. Lloyd, "Reflections," 170; idem, *HLWG*, 9[unnumbered].

67. Lloyd, "Reflections," 171; idem, *HLWG*, 9[unnumbered]. His call for cotton uniforms reflected the development of the textile industry, particularly in Great Britain.

68. Lloyd, "Reflections," 170; idem, *HLWG*, 8[unnumbered].

69. Lloyd, "Reflections," 171; idem, *HLWG*, 10[unnumbered].

70. On this issue Lloyd foreshadowed attempts by military theorists prior to World War I to overcome the problem of firepower of modern armaments like machine guns and artillery. For example, Ferdinand Foch and others relied on the bayonet charge to solve the technological dilemma. For a discussion on the nature of "invention" and military developments, see Martin van Creveld, *Technology and War from 2000 B.C. to the Present* (New York: The Free Press, A Division of Macmillan, Inc.; London: Collier Macmillan Publishers, 1989), 217–32.

71. Lloyd, "Reflections," 171; idem, *HLWG*, 11[unnumbered]. The Classical precedent was Xenophon, who believed shock tactics superior to missile tactics. Xenophon, *Anabasis*, 77.

72. Lloyd, "Reflections," 171; idem, *HLWG*, 11[unnumbered].

73. Lloyd, "Reflections," 169; idem, *HLWG*, 5[unnumbered].

74. Lloyd, "Reflections," 171; idem, *HLWG*, 11[unnumbered].

75. Lloyd, "Reflections," 172; idem, *HLWG*, 13[unnumbered].

76. Lloyd, "Reflections," 173; idem, *HLWG*, 15[unnumbered].

77. Lloyd, *HLWG*, 16[unnumbered].

78. Ibid., 17[unnumbered].

79. Ibid.

80. Ibid., 23[unnumbered].

81. Ibid., 28[unnumbered].

82. Ibid., 29[unnumbered].

83. Precedents exist in classical literature. Both Onasander and Xenophon stressed the knowledge of terrain and topography. See Onasander, "The General," in *Aeneas Tacticus, Asclepiodotus Onasander*, 431–35; and Xenophon, "On the Cavalry Commander," in *Scripta Minora*, 259.

84. The standard Anglo-American "Principles of War" are Offensive, Objective, Security, Unity of Command, Mass, Maneuver, Economy of Force, Simplicity, and Surprise.

85. See Dennis Showalter, *The Wars of Frederick the Great*, 212–21(Zorndorf), 240–42(Paltzig).

86. Lloyd, *HLWG2*, 73, 94, 137; idem, *HLWG*, 89. Lloyd criticized Marshal Daun's failure to pursue the Prussian army after the siege of Olmütz.

87. See Showalter, *The Wars of Frederick the Great*, 158–67(Kolin), 192–206 (Leuthen). For Leuthen see Curt Jany, *Die Armee Friedrichs des Großen*, 1740–1763, vol. 2 of *Geschichte der Preußischen Armee vom 15. Jahrhundert bis 1914*, 2d ed. (Osnabrück: Biblio Verlag, 1967), 453–58; originally published as *Geschichte der königlich Preussischen Armee bis zum Jahre 1807*, 4 vols. (Berlin: K. Siegismund, 1928–33).

88. Lloyd, *HLWG2*, 94, 113, 167.

89. Floyd, *HLWG*, 89–92. Frederick's disastrous battle of Kolin was a model of imprudence that strengthened Lloyd's argument. Xenophon cautioned that a prudent general never made unnecessary attacks and should strike where the enemy is weak. Xenophon, "On the Cavalry Commander," *Scripta Minora*, 263.

90. Lloyd, *HLWG2*, 2.

91. Ibid. He added: "In war a general must think he has done nothing, while something remains unfinished; he ought to consider all his successes as means only that lead to something greater." Ibid., 88.

92. Ibid., 122.

93. Related to the objective is the essential unity of command. Lloyd lamented the Austrian army's lack of coherent and unified leadership, especially during the 1757 campaign. Marshal Brown was a fine general, but he did not want to subordinate himself to Prince Charles of Lorraine out of jealousy. The Austrian army suffered from internal friction because Brown performed without vigilance. "This shews [sic]," Lloyd commented, "how imprudent it is to employ, together, men whose private views of ambition can scarce ever coincide." Lloyd, *HLWG*, 55.

94. Lloyd, *HLWG*, 139. Organizational simplicity was more important than numbers. He wrote: "The perfection of our art would be . . . to find a construction, or an order of battle, equally proper for all kinds of ground," he wrote, "but this being impossible, the only thing remaining for them to do is to find . . . such a formation of the troops, as may with the greatest simplicity . . . be adapted to those numberless circumstances which occur." Lloyd, *HLWG*, 21[unnumbered].

95. Lloyd, *HLWG2*, 169. Xenophon argued that numerical superiority could not stand against superior morale or methods. See Xenophon, *Anabasis*, 195; idem, *Cyropaedia*, 1:137–41.

96. The basic difference between Lloyd's time and Napoleon's was that the latter had numerous reserves to replenish his corps and divisions, while the former constantly worried about manpower shortfalls and failed recruiting. In this matter the difference was political rather than military. The centralized French Revolutionary/Napoleonic authoritarian state more easily exploited the natural resources of its populace.

97. Lloyd, *HLWG2*, 89.

98. Security was a natural corollary to this concept. See Lloyd, *HLWG*, 13[unnumbered].

99. loyd, *HLWG2*, 121.

100. Lloyd, *HLWG*, 139. Xenophon argued that an army should be divided and maneuvered separately to converge on the enemy as economically as possible. See Xenophon, *Cyropaedia*, 2:403.

101. Lloyd, *HLWG2*, 139. Carl von Clausewitz incorporated this idea in the "principles of war" he used to train the Prussian Crown Prince Friedrich Wilhelm. He gave credit to Lloyd for discovering it. Carl von Clausewitz, "Einleitung in das Studium der Schalchten und Gefechte; Für den Kronprinzen," vol. 1 of *Schriften-*

Aufsätze-Studien-Briefe: Dokumente aus dem Clausewitz-, Scharnhorst- und Gneisenau-Nachlaß sowie aud öffentlichen und privaten Sammlungen, ed. Werner Hahlweg (Göttingen: Vandenhoeck & Ruprecht, 1990), 110.

102. Showalter, *The Wars of Frederick the Great,* 255–56. See also Georg Winter, *Die Kriegsgeschichtliche Überlieferung über Friedrich den Großen: Kritisch geprüßt an dem Beispiel der Kapitulation von Maxen,* Historische Untersuchungen, ed. J. Jastrow, vol. VII (Berlin: R. Gaertners Verlagsbuchhandlung; Hermann Heyfelder, 1888).

103. Lloyd, *HLWG2,* 184.

104. Ibid., 185.

105. Ibid., 186.

106. Showalter, *The Wars of Frederick the Great,* 221–27; Curt Jany, *Die Armee Friedrichs des Großen, 1740–1763,* 500–9. For a complete analysis see Norbert Robitschek, *Hochkirch: Eine Studie* (Wien: C. Teupen, 1905).

107. Lloyd, *HLWG2,* 110.

108. John I. Alger, *The Quest for Victory: The History of the Principles of War,* Contributions in Military History, no. 30, foreword by Frederick J. Kroesen (Westport, CT: Greenwood Press, 1982), 13, takes Lloyd to task: "[H]e left much doubt concerning the differences among principles, rules, maxims, and axioms, and he failed to state which of his lists, if any, represented the most important principles of war, and he did not try to specify the number of principles in existence."

109. Zvi Lanir, "The 'Principles of War' and Military Thinking," *The Journal of Strategic Studies* 16, no. 1 (March 1993): 7–15.

110. Lloyd, *HLWG,* 7[unnumbered].

111. The standard work in English on Ferdinand's campaigns is Reginald A. Savory, *His Britannic Majesty's Army in Germany during the Seven Years' War* (Oxford: At the Clarendon Press, 1966). John W. Fortescue, *First Part—To the Close of the Seven Years' War,* vol. 2 of *A History of the British Army* provides an excellent account of the campaigns from the perspective of the British expeditionary force. See also, Officer who served in the British Force, *The operations of the allied army, under the command of His Serene Highness Prince Ferdinand, Duke of Brunswick and Luneberg, during the greatest part of six campaigns, beginning in the year 1757, and ending in the year 1762* (London: Printed for T. Jeffrys, geographer to the King, 1764). The sole work in English on the Hereditary Prince, Edmond Fitzmaurice, *Charles William Ferdinand, Duke of Brunswick: An Historical Study, 1735–1806* (London: Longmans, Green, & Co., 1901), deals almost exclusively with his experience during the French Revolutionary and Napoleonic wars.

112. See David Bayne Horn, *Great Britain and Europe in the Eighteenth Century* (Oxford: Clarendon Press, 1967), 193–94, for the historic ties between the two states.

113. Henry Lloyd to Lippe, 13 juin 1764, A XXXV 18.177, *NSB.* The marriage took place in 1764 after another intensive round of talks in 1763. Lloyd's presence in Brunswick was no doubt helpful to the final outcome. See George III to John Stuart, 3d Earl of Bute, End of February 1763, (272), in *Letters from George III to Lord Bute, 1756–1766,* edited by Romney Sedgwick (London: Macmillan and Co. LTD., 1939), 192–93. Sedgwick refers to a letter from Brunswick concerning an interview between Lord Bute and Lloyd.

114. Henry Lloyd to Henry Clinton, Münster, 9 January 1762, vol. 1:32, Henry S. Clinton Papers, William L. Clements Library.

115. Henry Lloyd to John Ligonier, "Memorial (1760?)," A/24, Donoughmore Family Papers, Trinity College Library, Dublin, Ireland.

116. Ibid. Rex Whitworth, *Field Marshal Lord Ligonier: A Story of the British Army, 1702–1770* (Oxford: The Clarendon Press, 1958), 316–17, mentions Lloyd's memorial (listed in the Historical Manuscripts Commission).

117. For Lippe's Portuguese career see Christa Banaschik-Ehl, *Scharnhorsts Lehrer, Graf Wilhelm von Schaumburg-Lippe, in Portugal: Die Heeresreform, 1761–1777,* Studieren zur Militärgeschichte, Militärwissenschaft und Konflickts-forschung, ed. Werner Halweg, Band 3 (Osnabrück: Biblio Verlag, 1974); and Ernesto Augusto Pereira Sales, *O conde de Lippe em Portugal* (Vila Nova de Famalicão: G. Pinto de Sousa & Irmao, 1986). Ludwig Keller, *Graf Wilhelm von Schaumburg-Lippe: Ein Zeitgenosse und Freund Friedrichs des Grossen* (Berlin: Wiedmann, 1907), and Hans Klein, *Wilhelm zu Schaumburg-Lippe: Klassiker Abschreckungstheorie und Lehrer Scharnhorsts* (Osnabrück: Biblio Verlag, 1982) provide excellent overviews. Lippe was a significant military theorist and his contributions demand a modern biography. He and Lloyd often discussed ancient military history. Karl August Varnhagen von Ense, *Biographische Denkmale* (Berlin: G. Reimer, 1845), 3:85–86.

118. Henry Lloyd to Lippe, 13 juin 1764, A XXXV 18.177, *NSB*.

119. Henry Lloyd to Lippe, 18 juin 1764; Same to Same, 5 juillet 1764; Same to Same, Lisbon, 11 juillet 1764; and Same to Same, 14 juillet 1764, A XXXV 18.177, *NSB*. The cash amount comes from Hannibal Lloyd, *Memoir of General Lloyd,* 5.

120. Henry Lloyd to Henry Clinton, Hanau, 20 April 1765, vol. 2:13; Same to Same, Paris, 30 June 1765, vol. 2:25, *CPC*. Clinton had been aide-de-camp to Karl Wilhelm Ferdinand during the war. See William B. Willcox, *Portrait of a General: Sir Henry Clinton in the War of Independence* (New York: Alfred A. Knopf, 1964). Granby became the Commander-in-Chief of British Forces in Germany after the Battle of Minden (1759) and Commander-in-Chief of British Forces in 1766. See George P. R. James, "John Manners, Marquis of Granby," in *Memoirs of the Great Commanders* (Philadelphia: E. L. Carey & A. Hart; Boston: W. D. Ticknor, 1835), 2:195–220; and Walter E. Manners, *Some account of the military, political, and social life of the Right Hon. John Manners, marquis of Granby* (London: Macmillan and Co., Limited, 1899).

121. Henry Lloyd, "Extracts from a memoir on the present state of Portugal, addressed to His Serene Highness the Count Shaumburg-Lippe, Maréchal General and Commander in Chief of the Troops of that Kingdom," British Library, Addit. MSS 39201, ff. 53–81, is probably Granby's copy. For Lippe's copy see Arquivo Histórico Militar, Lisbon, Portugal, Arquivo do Conde de Lippe, "Memoirs on the present state of Portugal addressed to His Serene Highness the Count Schaumburg-Lippe, Maréchal-General and Commander-in-Chief of the Troops of that kingdom, etc. (1765)," Cauxa 7, No. 2: Documentos Lloyd. A Portuguese translation is found in A. Faria de Morais, "O Documento Lloyd (1765)," *Separata do Boletim do Arquivo Histórico Militar,* no. 21 (1951).

122. Lippe to Sebastião José de Carvalho e Mello, conde de Oeyras, 19 juillet 1765, (303), in *Wilhelm Graf zu Schaumburg-Lippe,* ed. Curd Ochwadt, 3:251.

123. Arquivo Histórico Militar, Arquivo do Conde Lippe, "Lippe to Henry Lloyd, Hagenburg, 14 August 1765," Cauxa 7, no. 2: Documentos Lloyd; and (308), in *Wilhelm Graf zu Schaumburg-Lippe,* ed. Curd Ochwadt, 3:255–56.

124. Henry Lloyd to Lippe, Munster, 18 September 1765, A XXXV 18.108, *NSB*. Pietro Verri to Alessandro Verri, Milano, 23 gennaio 1768, CXC(82), in vol. 1, part II of *Carteggio di Pietro e di Alessandro Verri dal 1766 al 1797*, 145.

125. Henry Lloyd to Lippe, London, 15 October 1765, A XXXV 18.108, *NSB*.

126. Lippe to Henry Lloyd, Hagenburg, 30 October 1765, (314), in *Wilhelm Graf zu Schaumburg-Lippe*, ed. Curd Ochwadt, 3:260–61.

127. Henry Lloyd to Henry Clinton, Salisbury, 23 November 1765, vol. 2:19, *CPC*.

128. Henry Lloyd to Lippe, London, 13 February 1766, A XXXV 18.108, *NSB*; Lippe to Martinho de Mello e Castro, 3 März 1766, (325), in *Wilhelm Graf zu Schaumburg-Lippe*, ed. Curd Ochwadt, 3:266–67.

129. Lloyd, "Memoirs on the present state of Portugal," 43–78; idem, "Extracts from a memoir on the present state of Portugal," ff. 65–81. He also added that Britain should ally with Portugal. Lloyd, "Memoirs on the present state of Portugal," 86–89; idem, "Extracts from a memoir on the present state of Portugal," ff. 53–54.

130. Lloyd, "Memoirs on the present state of Portugal," 12–15.

131. Lloyd, "Memoirs on the present state of Portugal," 29; idem, "Extracts from a memoir on the present state of Portugal," ff. 60–61.

132. Lloyd, "Memoirs on the present state of Portugal," 21; idem, "Extracts from a memoir on the present state of Portugal," f. 59.

133. Lloyd, "Memoirs on the present state of Portugal," 24; idem, "Extracts from a memoir on the present state of Portugal," f. 58.

134. Lloyd, "Memoirs on the present state of Portugal," 84.

135. Lloyd, "Memoirs on the present state of Portugal," 39; idem, "Extracts from a memoir on the present state of Portugal," f. 62.

136. The Canton System created by King Frederick William I was intended to balance the needs of the economy and the army. It replaced the somewhat arbitrary "furlough and enrollment" recruiting that so terrified the peasantry and damaged the rural agrarian economy. For a detailed analysis of its socio-economic ramifications see Otto Büsch, *Military System and Social Life in Old Regime Prussia, 1713–1807: The Beginnings of the Social Militarization of Prusso-German Society*, trans. John G. Gagliardo (Atlantic Highlands, New Jersey: Humanities Press, 1997); originally published as *Militärsystem und Socialleben im alter Preussen, 1713–1807: die Anfänge der Socialen Militarisierung der preussisch-deutschen Gesellschaft* (Berlin: De Guyter, 1962).

137. Lloyd, "Memoirs on the present state of Portugal," 40; idem, "Extracts from a memoir on the present state of Portugal," f. 61.

138. Lloyd, "Memoirs on the present state of Portugal," 41–2; idem, "Extracts from a memoir on the present state of Portugal," ff. 61.

139. Henry Lloyd to Henry Clinton, Cadiz, 10 September 1766, vol. 2:28; Same to Same, Bordeaux, 18 December 1766, vol. 2:33, *CPC*. Lloyd's letter from Cadiz contains a colorful description of southern Spain. For instance, on his trek to Cadiz he carried two muskets with bayonets fixed to frighten would-be marauders.

140. The British had begun to settle veterans in West Florida following the Seven Years' War in order to create a buffer zone against Spanish encroachments in the region. See Robin F. A. Fabel, "Born of War, Killed by War: The Company of Military Adventurers in West Florida," in *Adapting to Conditions: War and Society in the Eighteenth Century*, edited by Maarten Ultee (Tuscaloosa, AL: The University of Alabama Press, 1986): 104–16.

141. Henry Lloyd to Henry Clinton, 24 February 1767, vol. 3:8, *CPC.*
142. Henry Lloyd to Henry Clinton, Windsor, 29 March 1767, vol. 3:23; Same to Same, 10 June 1767, vol. 3:45; Same to Same, 8 July 1767, vol. 3:51, *CPC.* He also solicited Clinton to rent a house from his friend Richard Fitzwilliam, who owed him money. Fitzwilliam had already allowed Lloyd to sell the home's furniture to make good on these debts.

CHAPTER 4

1. Henry Lloyd to Henry Clinton, 25 July 1767, vol. 3:56, *CPC;* Hannibal Lloyd, *Memoir of General Lloyd,* 5. The pension was drawn from the Ordnance department and probably was awarded for his role in the marriage of Augusta and the Hereditary Prince of Brunswick.
2. It stated: "We pray and we require, in the name of His Majesty, that all Admirals, Generals, Governors, Commanding Magistrates, and other civil and military Officers, and Princes of friendly and allied states of His Majesty, not only to let Mr. Lloyd (Major General), a Subject of His Majesty, pass freely without giving him any obstacle, but also to lend him all the help which he needs during his travels." Henry Seymour Conway, "Le Sieur Lloyd, Passporte," 30 juillet 1767, Public Record Office, Kew, England, SP 44/413, fol. 61.
3. Lloyd promised to translate into English Alessandro Verri's history of Milan, and in return his Italian friends purchased and discussed *The History of the Late War in Germany.* See Pietro Verri to Alessandro Verri, Milano, 10 febbraio 1768, CC(87), vol. 1, pt. 2 of *Carteggio di Pietro e di Alessandro Verri dal 1766 al 1797,* 165; Alessandro to Pietro, Roma, 10 febbraio 1768, CCIV(114), vol. 1, pt. 2 of *Carteggio,* 174; same to same, Roma, 17 febbraio 1768, CCIX(116), vol. 1, pt. 2 of *Carteggio,* 183; same to same, Roma, 12 marzo 1768, CCXXII(123), vol. 1, pt. 2 of *Carteggio,* 212; Pietro to Alessandro, Milano, 9 aprile 1768, CCXXXV(104), vol. 1, pt. 2 of *Carteggio,* 232; and same to same, Milano, 16 aprile 1768, CCXXXIX(106), vol. 1, pt. 2 of *Carteggio,* 243.
4. Pietro Verri to Alessandro Verri, Milan, 20 gennaio 1768, CLXXXVIII(81), vol. 1, pt. 2 of *Carteggio,* 142; same to same, Milan, 23 gennaio 1768, CXC(82), vol. 1, pt. 2 of *Carteggio,* 144–46. Alessandro to Pietro, Rome, 26 gennaio 1768, CXCVI(110), vol. 1, pt. 2 of *Carteggio,* 157. Lloyd told Pietro he served of the Elector of Cologne. He had traveled the past two years (to England, the Baltic, Germany, France, Spain, and Portugal) and was seeking rest and relaxation.
5. Pietro Verri to Alessandro Verri, Milan, 23 gennaio 1768, CXC(82), vol. 1, pt. 2 of *Carteggio,* 144–45. Lloyd said the Portuguese government under the Marquis Pombal had overreacted because the Jesuits there were not that powerful.
6. Same to same, Milan, 27 gennaio 1768, CXCI(83), vol. 1, pt. 2 of *Carteggio,* 147–48. Verri informed Alessandro that Lloyd had received Jesuit aid in times of trouble and reciprocated during the last war by protecting their property from looting. Yet, both men agreed that the Jesuits had to leave for enlightened reform to take place. For the Squillacci Revolts of 1766 see Charles Petrie, *King Charles III of Spain: An Enlightened Despot* (New York: The John Day Company, 1971), 118–22.
7. Frank E. Manuel, *The Eighteenth Century Confronts the Gods* (Cambridge, MA: Harvard University Press, 1959); and Paul Hazard, *European Thought in the Eighteenth Century: From Montesquieu to Lessing,* provide the best overviews of this topic.

8. John Locke, *An Essay Concerning Human Understanding,* edited with an introduction, critical apparatus and glossary by Peter H. Nidditch (Oxford: At the Clarendon Press, 1975); originally published as *An essay concerning human understanding,* 4th ed. (London: A. and J. Churchil, and S. Manship, 1700). See especially Book I, chapter 2 "No innate speculative principles," 48–65, and chapter 3 "No innate practical principles," 65–84; Book II, chapter 1 "Of ideas in general and their origin," 104–18; and Book IV "Of reason," 668–88.

9. David Hume, "The Natural History of Religion," vol. 1 of *Essays, Moral, Political, and Literary,* eds. T.H. Green and T.H. Grose (New York: Longmans, Green, and Co., 1912), 309–30; originally published as *Four Dissertations* (London: Printed for A. Millar, 1757).

10. The work has survived in three manuscripts deposited in the Henry Lloyd papers at the Fitzwilliam Museum, Cambridge. The oldest version, titled "Essais sur l'homme," consists of twenty-six notebooks. He circulated the manuscript among his friends and acquaintances, the wear noticeable and marginalia faded. A revised manuscript consisting of thirteen notebooks, "Essais philosophiques sur les gouvernements," forms the basis of this chapter. The second half of this manuscript was published in 1770 and 1771 with Lloyd's essays on the English constitution and the theory of money. The third manuscript, "Philosophical Essay on the Different Species of Government," is an English translation of the first two notebooks of the revised manuscript. When citing these manuscripts I shall indicate both the notebook and the page number, since each is numbered non-sequentially. In July 1768, Pietro Verri reported that Lloyd was writing on the principles of Helvetius and Montesquieu. Pietro Verri to Alessandro Verri, Milano, 29 giugno 1768, CCLXXXI(127), vol. 1, pt. 2 of *Carteggio,* 182.

11. Lloyd may well have been a Freemason or at least associated with the "secret religion." See Alessandro Verri to Pietro Verri, Roma, 13 febbraio 1768, CCVIII(115), vol. 1, pt. 2 of *Carteggio,* 182. His clandestine career and radical philosophy place him within the milieu of the so-called "Radical Enlightenment." See Margaret C. Jacob, *The Radical Enlightenment: Pantheists, Freemasons, and Republicans* (London: George Allen & Unwin, 1981).

12. Henry Lloyd, "Essais philosophiques sur les gouvernements," Henry Lloyd Papers, The Fitzwilliam Museum, Cambridge, notebook 7:9–11. He later wrote "fear" is the true origin of religion and idolatry, notebook 8:7.

13. Ibid., notebook 7:11–4.

14. Ibid., notebook 7:15.

15. Ibid., notebook 7:21.

16. Ibid., notebook 8:4. His was not the typical view of a person with an Oxford and Jesuit education.

17. Ibid., notebook 8:6. He had urged the Portuguese government to subordinate the clerical class to the state and tax their land. See "Memoirs on the present state of Portugal addressed to His Serene Highness the Count Schaumburg-Lippe, Maréchal-General and Commander-in-Chief of the Troops of that kingdom, etc. (1765)," 85.

18. Lloyd, "Essais philosophiques sur les gouvernements," notebook 8:7–8.

19. Ibid., notebook, 8:6.

20. Ibid., notebook 7:25–8:1.

21. Lloyd, "Memoirs on the present state of Portugal addressed to His Serene Highness the Count Schaumburg-Lippe, Maréchal-General and Commander-in-Chief of the Troops of that kingdom, etc. (1765)," 84.

22. Lloyd, "Essais philosophiques sur les gouvernements," notebook 7:19. Enlightened writers exploited people's understanding of the Thirty Years' War (1618–48) and the English Civil War to make their point.

23. Pietro Verri to Alessandro Verri, Milano, 6 febbraio 1768, CXCVIII(86), in vol. 1, pt. 2 of *Carteggio,* 161. Other reforms advocated the conquest of Italy and the Ottoman Europe by Austria; the domination of northern Germany by Prussia; and the strengthening of Poland to serve as a buffer between Europe and Russia. He wanted to present the plan to Joseph I of Austria, but there is no indication that he did so. The project for peace was accompanied by several drafts of war plans to put it into effect.

24. Julian Offray de La Mettrie, "L'Homme Machine," in *Machine Man and Other Writings,* trans. and edited by Ann Thomson, Cambridge Texts in the History of Philosophy, eds. Karl Ameriks and Desmond M. Clarke (Cambridge: Cambridge University Press, 1996), 7; orignally published as *L'Homme Machine* (Leyde: Elie Luzac, 1748).

25. He developed this passive interpretation of man in "L'Homme-plante," in *Machine Man and Other Writings,* 77–88; originally publsihed as *L'Homme-plante* (Potsdam: Chretien Frederic Voss, 1748). The implications in La Mettrie's work were more important for nineteenth-century positivism than to eighteenth-century materialists. Paul Henri Thiry, baron d'Holbach (1723–89) furthered La Mettrie's line of reasoning with *Système de la nature, ou, Des loix du monde physique & du monde moral,* 2 vols. (Londres, 1770). He offered a pessimistic vision of man determined by his biology and environment, totally devoid of free will.

26. Claude Adrien Helvetius, *De l'Esprit, or Essays on the Mind and Its Several Faculties,* new ed. translated from the French (1810; reprint, New York: Burt Franklin, 1970), 1–7; originally published as *De l'Esprit* (Paris: Durand, 1758). His basic sensory explanation of knowledge is close to Hume's. See David Hume, "An Enquiry Concerning Human Understanding," in *Essays Moral, Political, and Literary,* 1:3–135; originally published as *Philosophical essays concerning human understanding* (London: Printed for A. Millar, 1748).

27. Helvetius, *De l'Esprit,* 283.

28. Ibid., 63.

29. Jeremy Bentham, *Introduction to the principles of morals and legislation* (London: Printed for T. Payne and Son, 1789); and Cesare Beccaria, *Dei delitti e delle pene* (Livorno: Coltelleni, 1764).

30. For its history, development, and relationship with materialism see John C. O'Neal, *The Authority of Experience: Sensationist Theory in the French Enlightenment,* Literature & Philosophy, ed. A. J. Cascardi (University Park, PA: The Pennsylvania State University Press, 1996). The school had its origins in Locke as well as the famed French philosopher étienne Bonnot de Condillac (1714–80) who articulated the theory metaphorically with his description of a statue awakening and discovering the world solely through its senses. See étienne Bonnot de Condillac, "A Treatise on the Sensations," in *Philosophical Writings of étienne Bonnot, Abbé de Condillac,* trans. Franklin Philip with the collaboration of Harlan Lane (Hillsdale, NJ; London: Lawrence Erlbaum Associates, Publishers, 1982), 175–344; originally

published as *Oeuvres Philosophiques de Condillac,* edited by Georges Le Roy (Paris: Universitaires de France, 1948). The essay was first published as *Traité des sensations,* 2 vols. (Londres, 1754). His role in the Enlightenment is well-defined in Isabel F. Knight, *The Geometric Spirit: The Abbé de Condillac and the French Enlightenment* (New Haven, CT: Yale University Press, 1968).

31. Henry Lloyd, "Philosophical Essay on the Different Species of Government," Henry Lloyd Papers, The Fitzwilliam Museum, 3.

32. Ibid., 1–5. Montesquieu had argued that climate formed outlook and general characteristics of a given society. See Montesquieu, *The Spirit of the Laws,* 231–35.

33. Lloyd, "Philosophical Essay," 11.

34. Ibid., 12.

35. Ibid., 52-4. What about people who might derive pleasure from the pain of others? Utilitarian theory suggests it is purely an effect of environmental perversion, which can be corrected.

36. Lloyd, "Essais philosophiques sur les gouvernements," notebook 4:6.

37. Lloyd, "Philosophical Essay," 14.

38. Ibid., 15–16.

39. Ibid., 19.

40. Ibid., 22.

41. Ibid., 25.

42. Ibid., 40.

43. Ibid., 42. Perhaps Lloyd's personal confession.

44. Lloyd, "Philosophical Essay," 6. His materialism never surfaced in the published excerpts of this manuscript even though his authorship was anonymous. He probably feared tainting his reputation and losing his pension, since materialists who publicly endorsed atheism like d'Holbach were not well-received in polite society.

45. Ibid., 13.

46. Lloyd, "Essais philosophiques sur les gouvernements," notebook 6:16–8. Montesquieu developed this theory and inserted a medical explanation to make it plausible for the time by simply arguing that cold weather contracted the extremities of the body's surface fibers, or nerve endings, while hot weather expanded them. See Montesquieu, *The Spirit of the Laws,* 231–35. He borrowed the ideas of Jean-Baptiste Dubos, one of the more influential pre-Enlightenment philosophers of art and culture. See Jean-Baptiste Dubos, *Reflexions critiques sur la poesie et sur la peinture,* 2 vols. (Paris: P.J. Moriette, 1719). Travel literature, especially Sir John Chardin's works describing the East, was an integral ingredient in the development of sociology in general. Hume was skeptical about climate's effect on National Character, but he concurred with the general dichotomy between the northern and southern peoples, going as far as to conclude that white Europeans were superior to all other peoples. See Hume, "Of National Characters," in *Essays Moral, Political, and Literary,* 1:246–50.

47. Lloyd, "Reflections on the general principles of war," 173–4; idem, *HLWG,* 29–30 [unnumbered]; idem, *CHLWG,* xxxi–ii.

48. Lloyd, "Essais philosophiques sur les gouvernements," notebook 8:8–10.

49. Ibid., notebook 8:10, 20; idem, "Reflections," 174; idem, *HLWG,* 30 [unnumbered]; idem, *CHLWG,* xxxiii; Charles Louis de Secondat, baron de La Brède et de Montesquieu, *The Spirit of the Laws,* trans. and edited by Anne M. Cohler, Basia

Carolyn Miller, and Harold Samuel Stone (Cambridge, MA: Cambridge University Press, 1989), 28. Notice both despotism and religion are founded on the principle of fear.

50. Lloyd, "Reflections," 174; idem, *HLWG*, 31 [unnumbered]; idem, *CHLWG*, xxxiii.

51. Lloyd, "Essais philosophiques sur les gouvernements," notebook 8:24; idem, "Reflections," 174; idem, *HLWG*, 30 [unnumbered]; idem, *CHLWG*, xxxiii.

52. Lloyd included 'National Character' in the preface to *The History of the Late War in Germany*, 29–26 [unnumbered]. David Hume first coined the term in 1748. See David Hume, "Of National Characters," in *Essays Moral, Political, and Literary*, 1:244–58. Sociology, a philosophical inquiry transformed into a positivist science in the nineteenth century, was the product of Montesquieu's writings. See Peter Gay, *The Science of Freedom*, vol. 2 of *The Enlightenment: An Interpretation* (New York: Alfred A. Knopf, 1969), 323–27.

53. Lloyd, "Reflections," 175; idem, *HLWG*, 32 [unnumbered]; idem, *CHLWG*, xxxiv; Hume, "Of National Characters," 1:252.

54. He concluded "they would surpass, [or] at least equal, any troops in the world" if these inequities were remedied. Lloyd, "Reflections," 176; idem, *HLWG*, 35 [unnumbered]; idem, *CHLWG*, xxxviii. Hume, who delineated National Character in quantitative rather than qualitative terms, argued that the English had the least possible degree of national character because they embraced "great liberty and independency." See Hume, "Of National Characters," 1:252.

55. Lloyd, "Reflections," 175; idem, *HLWG*, 34 [unnumbered]; idem, *CHLWG*, xxxvi.

56. Lloyd, "Reflections," 176; idem, *HLWG*, 34 [unnumbered]; idem, *CHLWG*, xxxvii.

57. Lloyd, "Reflections," 176; idem, *HLWG*, 35 [unnumbered]; idem, *CHLWG*, xxxvii. He did not mention the multi-ethnic character of the Austrian army, perhaps because regiments were segregated along linguistic lines and therefore did not pose a threat to each unit's "National Character."

58. Lloyd, "Reflections," 175; idem, *HLWG*, 34 [unnumbered]; idem, *CHLWG*, xxxvi. He added in his analysis of the battle of Gross-Jägersdorf (30 August 1757) that "[t]hey cannot be defeated; they must be killed" Lloyd, *HLWG*, 146.

59. See Knud J. V. Jespersen, "Claude Louis, Comte de Saint-Germain (1707–1778): Professional Soldier, Danish Military Reformer, and French War Minister," in *Soldier-Statesmen of the Enlightenment*, 305–21.

60. Lloyd, "Reflections," 175; idem, *HLWG*, 33 [unnumbered]; idem, *CHLWG*, xxxvi.

61. See Jean-Jacques Rousseau, *Discours sur l'origine et les fondemens de l'inégalité parmi les hommes* (Amsterdam: Marc Michel Rey, 1755).

62. Lloyd, "Philosophical Essay," 28–29; idem, "Essais philosophiques sur les gouvernements," notebook 8:16–21. He concluded that it was foolish to suppose that men were born apart like plants and that the misery of mankind was due to the creation of society. Lloyd also took issue with Rousseau's claim that the arts and sciences caused inequality and claimed that they were merely the effects of inequality.

63. Lloyd, "Essais philosophiques sur les gouvernements," notebook 8:19.

64. Lloyd, "Philosophical Essay," 37. Lloyd's manuscript is primarily a commentary on Rousseau and strengthens Ernst Cassirer's basic claim that the Enlightenment

sought to develop a philosophy that was not separated from science, government, and law.

65. Ibid., 36.

66. Lloyd, "Essais philosophiques sur les gouvernements," notebook 8:13–16.

67. Ibid., notebook 12:17, 13:10–12.

68. Ibid., notebook 12:15.

69. Ronald L. Meek, *Social Science and the Ignoble Savage* (Cambridge: Cambridge University Press, 1976), 2. The stages are generally defined as hunting, pastoral, agricultural, and commercial.

70. Lloyd, "Essais philosophiques sur les gouvernements," notebook 2:18.

71. Ibid., notebook 3:27b–3:42.

72. Ibid., notebook 3:41.

73. Ibid., notebook 2:17–3:27a.

74. Ibid., notebook 3:39–40.

75. Ibid., notebook 3:32–33.

76. Ibid., notebook 3:27b–37. For Russia's supply difficulties see, John Keep, "Feeding the Troops: Russian Army Supply Policies during the Seven Years' War," *Canadian Slavonic Papers* XXIX, no. 1 (March 1987): 24–44.

77. France did not initially seek to annex Corsica; it wanted only use of certain walled coastal towns. Fearing Paoli's patriotic movement would prohibit French occupation, Corsica's cession was the only alternative in 1768. The move was strategic and aimed at keeping the British out of the western Mediterranean Sea. See Thadd E. Hall, *France and the Eighteenth-Century Corsican Question* (New York: New York University Press, 1971). For the Italian viewpoint see Franco Venturi, *L'Italia dei Lumi (1764–1790),* vol. 5, pt. 1 of *Settecento riformatore* (Turin: Giulio Einaudi editore, 1987).

78. Lloyd's footsteps can be traced in Verri's correspondence. He went to Turin and Genoa in February 1768 to contact Paoli. Pietro Verri to Alessandro Verri, Milano, 10 febbraio 1768, CC(87), vol. 1, pt. 2 of *Carteggio,* 165. He returned but again planned to travel to Genoa, Corsica, and Tuscany in March, an itinerary that prompted the exasperated Verri to write, "Lloyd is in perpetual motion!" Pietro to Alessandro, Milano, 17 febbraio 1768, CCIV(114), vol. 1, pt. 2 of *Carteggio,* 177; same to same, Milano, 24 febbraio 1768, CCVII(91), vol. 1, pt. 2 of *Carteggio,* 181. Lloyd remained in Genoa throughout March and returned to Milan in April. Pietro to Alessandro, Milano, 16 marzo 1768, CCXXI(97), vol. 1, pt. 2 of *Carteggio,* 210; and same to same, Milano, 6 aprile 1768, CCXXXIII(103), vol. 1, pt. 2 of *Carteggio,* 233. In August Lloyd traveled to Leghorn (Livorno), an English commercial entrepôt in the western Mediterranean. Verri reported Lloyd had been surveying Corsica. Pietro to Alessandro, Milano, 24 agosto 1768, III(45), vol. 2 of *Carteggio,* eds. Francesco Novati and Emanuele Greppi (Milano: Casa Editrice L. F. Cogliati, 1910), 9. For Lloyd's Gibraltar trip see Commodore Richard Spry to John Manners, Marquis of Granby, Jersey in Gibraltar Bay, 17 September 1768, vol. II of *The Manuscripts of His Grace the Duke of Rutland, K.G., Preserved at Belvoir Castle,* Historical Manuscripts Commission, 12th Report, Appendix, pt. V (London: Eyre and Spottiswoode, 1889).

79. Verri suspected Lloyd more involved than he let on because he sent him detailed reports of the campaign. Lloyd too was pessimistic about Paoli's chances of success and believed that the French would win by October. Pietro Verri to Alessandro

Verri, Milano, 7 settembre, XI(149), vol. 2 of *Carteggio, 23*; Alessandro to Pietro, Roma, 14 settembre 1768, XVIII(149), vol. 2 of *Carteggio, 37*; Pietro to Alessandro, Milano, 17 settembre 1768, XVII(152), vol. 2 of *Carteggio, 36.*

80. Hannibal Lloyd, *Memoir of General Lloyd, 5.*

81. Pietro Verri to Alessandro Verri, Milano, 13 settembre 1769, XXIII(237), vol. 3 of *Carteggio,* eds. Francesco Novati and Emanuele Greppi (Milano: Casa Editrice L. F. Cogliati, 1911), 54. He did not learn these details from Lloyd. See Francis Beretti, *Pascal Paoli et l'image de la Corse au dix-huitième siècle le témoignage des voyageurs britanniques,* Studies on Voltaire and the Eighteenth Century, no. 253 (Oxford: The Voltaire Foundation at the Taylor Institution, 1988), 103–4.

82. See Pietro Verri to Alessandro Verri, Milano, 21 settembre 1768, XIX(153), vol. 2 of *Carteggio, 38–39*; same to same, Milano, 12 ottobre 1768, XXX(158), vol. 2 of *Carteggio, 59*; and same to same, Milano, 24 dicembre 1768, LIV(162), vol. 2 of *Carteggio, 97.*

83. Hall, *France and the Eighteenth-Century Corsican Question,* 200–6. French sovereignty converted the Corsican people into French subjects. On 15 August 1769, Napoleone Buonaparte was born in Ajaccio.

84. Lloyd, "Essais philosophiques sur les gouvernements," notebook 3:43–45.

85. Ibid., notebook 4:13.

86. Ibid., notebook 3:43–4:13.

87. Ibid., notebook 4:23–5:12.

88. Henry Lloyd, *An essay on the theory of money* (London: J. Almon, 1771), viii–ix.

89. Verri's definition of money was essentially the same as Lloyd's. See Pietro Verri, *Reflections on Political Economy,* trans. Barbara McGilvray (Fairfield, N.J.: A. M. Kelley, 1993), 8; originally published as *Meditazioni sulla economia politica* (Venizia, 1771). Verri maintained he did not know who first conceived the definition, because he and Lloyd had talked often about society and economics. Pietro Verri to Alessandro Verri, Milano, 16 novembre 1771, CLXXXIX(412), vol. 4 of *Carteggio di Pietro e di Alessandro Verri,* eds. Francesco Novati, Emanuele Greppi, and Alessandro Giulini (Milano: Casa Editrice L. F. Cogliati, 1919), 286; Same to Same, Milan, 27 May 1772, LXXX(465), vol. 5 of *Carteggio di Pietro e di Alessandro Verri,* eds. Emanuele Greppi and Alessandro Giulini (Milano: Casa Editrice L. F. Cogliati, 1926), 93. An extract of Lloyd's essay convinced him that neither person stole the other's ideas even though they did make similar conclusions. Pietro Verri to Alessandro Verri, Milan, 14 octobre 1772, CLV(451), vol 5. of *Carteggio,* 190. The extract was published as an appendix to the Livorno edition of Verri's treatise. See Paolo Frisi, "Estratto del Libro Intitolato *An Essay on the Theory of Money,*" appendix to *Meditazione sulla Economia Politica,* 6th ed. (Livorno: Nell Stamperia dell'Enciclopedia, 1772): 237–52. As late as 1781 Verri still answered questions as to the authenticity of the definition of money. He admitted that he believed it was his, but since Lloyd was a "high talent" and seeker of truth he was not averse to giving him credit. Pietro Verri to Alessandro, Milan, 11 aprile 1781, CCXII(1179), vol. 11 of *Carteggio di Pietro Verri e di Alessandro Verri,* ed. Giovanni Seregni (Milano: Dott. A. Giuffrè, Editore, 1940), 304. For the relationship between Lloyd's and Verri's economic theory see Franco Venturi, "Le '*Meditazioni sulla economia politica*' di Pietro Verri: Edizioni, echi e discussioni," *Rivista Storica Italiana* 90, no. 3 (October 1978): 530–93; Oscar Nuccio, "Introduction," *An*

Essay on the Theory of Money, by Henry Lloyd, Ristampe Anastatiche di Opere e Rare XCIV (Rome: Edizioni Bizzarri, 1968), i–xiv. Lloyd generally is given credit for influencing Verri and introducing him to the enlightened view of society. Nino Valeri, *Pietro Verri,* 73, 168, also credits Lloyd and helps place him within the larger context of Italian intellectual history.

90. Lloyd, *An essay on the theory of money,* 83. One of the first economists to use formulas, he expressed the relationship as: P = C/M, where P = price, C = circulation, and M = quantity of merchandise. He provided no term for the velocity of exchange or the speed of circulation, a limitation to the his original equation corrected by subsequent economists. See Hugo Hegeland, *The Quantity Theory of Money: A Critical Study of its Historical Development and Interpretation and a Restatement* (Göteborg: Elanders Boktryckeri Aktiebolag, 1951), 86.

91. He expressed the changes in either C or M as Y in the following formulas: C/MY = P/Y and C//M/Y = PY. Ibid., 86. These were the basic building blocks of the theory of supply and demand later attributed to Adam Smith and his followers. Lloyd also was the first to postulate the mathematical formula for the relative price of silver and gold, S/G = P (in the same manner as price of goods), and interest. Ibid., 103, 129. Hegeland, *The Quantity Theory of Money,* 86.

92. Terence Hutchison, *Before Adam Smith: The Emergence of Political Economy, 1662–1776* (Oxford: Basil Blackwell, 1988), 306.

93. Lloyd continued the line of historical development presented in "Essais philosophiques sur les gouvernements." The birth of money was due largely to chance or curiosity. At first based on precious stones or shiny metals, the use of a medium of exchange in turn led to trade (and often warfare) between societies. As prosperity increased, more food was available, which in turn increased population. The cycle repeated itself if not interrupted by some calamity, and agricultural society emerged into a commercial economy. To explain how a society used a money economy to increase the general welfare and prosperity of its inhabitants was the underlying purpose of his book. Lloyd, *An essay on the theory of money,* i–viii.

94. Lloyd, *An essay on the theory of money,* 2–10.

95. Ibid., 17. Countering the mercantilist perception that foreign trade depleted a nation's supply of precious metals, Lloyd posited that "foreign and active commerce and particular are in proportion to the quantity of paper circulation." "It is with nations as with individuals," he continued, "the more money a man has the greater will be the extent of trade." Ibid., 19.

96. Ibid., 29.

97. Ibid., 33. A reviewer, Abraham Rees, took the anonymous author to task for his insistence that population was in direct proportion to circulation. Rees called it a groundless principle and uttered the contemporary belief that British population was actually declining. Overall, he endorsed Lloyd's theory: "it must be acknowledged, that the Author of this essay is an "ingenius" and able writer, and that he has thrown out several observations, which merit the public attention." Abraham Rees, "Review of *An essay on the theory of money,*" *The Monthly Review; or, Literary Journal* 46 (January 1772): 75–76. Evidence does not support Rees' criticism. English population grew at the rate of 6.5 percent during the 1760s and 4.9 percent during the 1770s. Population in 1771 was 6.4 million, nearly 300,000 more people than in 1761. The belief in population decline was due probably to the poor harvests and grain riots of the 1760s and the political distress caused by the 'Wilkes and Liberty' episode. For population figures see

Edward A. Wrigley, R. S. Davies, James E. Oeppen, and Roger S. Schofield, *English Population History from family reconstruction, 1580–1837* (Cambridge: Cambridge University Press, 1997), 614–15.

98. Lloyd, *An essay on the theory of money,* 35.

99. Ibid., 56.

100. Ibid., 58.

101. Lloyd articulated an early theory of the "leisure class" claiming that the rich naturally sought luxury items and used them as external signs to distinguish themselves from the common person. Ibid., 75–78.

102. Ibid., 61.

103. Ibid., 67–72.

104. Lloyd, "Essais philosophiques sur les gouvernements," 7:7. Lloyd outlined a parallel political cycle in which all democracies ended in aristocracy, oligarchy, and last in despotism. Ibid., notebook 8:26.

105. Pietro Verri to Alessandro Verri, Milano, 28 dicembre 1768, LVIII(163), vol. 2 of *Carteggio,* 103; Alessandro to Pietro, Roma, 11 gennaio 1769, LXVIII(165), vol. 2 of *Carteggio,* 126; and Pietro to Alessandro, 22 febbraio 1769, LXXXIX(179), vol. 2 of *Carteggio,* 171.

106. Pietro to Alessandro Verri, Milano, 1 marzo 1769, XCIII(181), vol. 2 of *Carteggio,* 178; same to same, Milano, 8 marzo 1769, XCVII(183), vol. 2 of *Carteggio,* 186; and same to same, Milano, 15 marzo 1769, CI(185), vol. 2 of *Carteggio,* 195.

107. Dutens was a French-born Protestant minister employed as *chargé d'affaires* in England's Turin embassy. What was disconcerting to Verri was the fact that he was an opponent of the Enlightenment. Alessandro Verri to Pietro Verri, Roma, 17 dicembre 1768, LV(163), vol. 2 of *Carteggio,* 99; and same to same, Roma, 21 gennaio 1769, LXXV(168), vol. 2 of *Carteggio,* 145.

108. The Marchesse Ragnini especially adored Lloyd and jokingly referred to him as "Your Roundness," because of his "large belly and wig." Alessandro Verri to Pietro Verri, Roma, 25 gennaio 1769, LXXVII(169), vol. 2 of *Carteggio,* 148–49. A Russo-Turkish War began in 1768 ostensibly because of Russia's intervention in Poland and its violation of Turkish boundaries. The Russians in 1770 sent the fleet from Archangel into the Mediterranean to foment rebellion in Greece and seek out and destroy the Turkish navy. See Mathew Smith Anderson, "Great Britain and the Russian Fleet, 1769–70," *The Slavonic and East European Review* XXXI, no. 76 (December 1952): 148–63; and Isabel de Madariaga, *Russia in the Age of Catherine the Great* (New Haven and London: Yale University Press, 1981).

109. Pietro Verri to Alessandro Verri, Milano, 13 settembre 1769, XXIII(237), vol. 3 of *Carteggio,* 54–56.

110. The Verri brothers uncovered more unsettling news. For instance, they heard that Lloyd was in Italy in order to track the Russian fleet bound for Turkey. Pietro Verri to Alessandro Verri, Milano, 30 settembre 1769, XXXIII(242), vol. 3 of *Carteggio,* 82. From Dom João Carlos, duque de Bragança, they heard Lloyd was in fact a general, but he had been dismissed from the Court of Cologne. Now while in the employ of England he was seeking to join the Russians in their new war with Turkey. Alessandro told Pietro to forget Lloyd, who had so compromised him. Alessandro Verri to Pietro Verri, Roma, 20 settembre 1769, XXX(237), vol. 3 of *Carteggio,* 73–74; and same to same, Roma, 16 dicembre 1769, LX(259), vol. 3 of *Carteggio,* 134–35.

111. Lloyd had fought with a tailor, carriage-maker, and porter of a theater, and with Frisi's help attempted to dismiss charges of misconduct. All this information prompted Pietro to distance himself from the "uneasy" Lloyd, who he believed willingly compromised his friends. Pietro Verri to Alessandro Verri, Milano, 13 maggio 1769, CXXXVIII(202), vol. 2 of *Carteggio*, 272. Alessandro concurred. Alessandro to Pietro, Roma, 31 maggio 1769, CLI(205), vol. 2 of *Carteggio*, 302.

112. Ibid., 55–6. Same to Same, Milano, 14 febbraio 1770, LXXXVIII(225), vol. 3 of *Carteggio*, 181.

113. Hannibal Lloyd, *Memoir of General Lloyd*, 5. Hannibal, Henry and Mary's son born in 1772, erroneously wrote they married in Milan in 1776. He was mistaken. Such a situation would have been unconscionable for either parent's reputation. The fact that Mary was living with Lloyd on his second excursion to Milan makes it likely they married in 1769/1770. Garnett was also the eldest daughter of John Garnett of the Bank of England and grand-niece on her mother's side to the Chevalier James de Johnstone of Jacobite fame. Her mother reportedly so resembled the Young Pretender that on one occasion London authorities arrested her on suspicion that she was Prince Charlie in disguise! Lloyd had abandoned his political ties with Jacobitism, but retained his social relationship.

114. Wilkes was later cleared of all charges and died in 1797, a respectable Tory and ex-Lord Mayor of London. The classic examination of the "Wilkes and Liberty" movement is George Rudé, *Wilkes and Liberty: A Social Study of 1763 to 1774* (Oxford: Clarendon Press, 1962). A more recent biography is Peter D. G. Thomas, *John Wilkes: A Friend to Liberty* (Oxford: Clarendon Press, 1996).

115. Pietro Verri to Alessandro Verri, Milano, 23 settembre 1769, XXIX(240), vol. 3 of *Carteggio*, 73.

116. Lloyd used the pseudonym "Cato" with *An Essay on the English Constitution* (London: Published for the Author, and Sold by J. Almon, 1770). Note the publisher. Almon was an ardent friend and supporter of Wilkes as well as being the foremost "radical" publisher in his day. Lloyd presented a manuscript version of the book to the King, but received no response. John Calcraft to John Almon, Ingress, 18 September 1770, in John Almon, *Memoirs of a Late Eminent Bookseller* (London, 1790), 77. For Almon's career see Deborah D. Rogers, *Bookseller as Rogue: John Almon and the Politics of Eighteenth-Century Publishing*, American University Studies, series IV, English Language and Literature, vol. 28 (New York: Peter Lang, 1986).

117. Lloyd, *An Essay on the English Constitution*, 3 (hereafter called *EEC*). He added that the book was "part of a more extensive work on the different governments established among mankind, which the author proposes giving to the public in a few months." He was referring to the aforementioned manuscript now at the Fitzwilliam Museum. It was never printed in its entirety.

118. Lloyd, *EEC*, 5–14.

119. Ibid., 44.

120. He asked: "Where is the freedom of Parliament, if it is admitted that any power upon earth has a lawful right to deprive a member of his seat, upon no other foundation, than because a majority, or rather force, has been pleased to do it?" He reasoned that with this logic a majority could expel the minority and obtain absolute power. Lloyd, *EEC*, 50.

121. His replacement was not elected. Lloyd, *EEC*, 51–57.

122. Ibid., 79–83.

123. Ibid., 85–90.

124. Ibid., 95.

125. "They are like glass, which by much handling breaks in your hands, but at the same time cuts it." Ibid., 96. He added that their religious principles and political principles concurred with their love of liberty and hatred of tyranny.

126. Ibid., 96–97. Lloyd also criticized England's policy toward Ireland and called for the abolishment of repressive laws against trade.

127. William Knox, *The Present State of the Nation; Particularly with Respect to its Trade, Finances, &c &c, addressed to the King and both Houses of Parliament* (London: Printed for J. Almon, 1768); Edmund Burke, *Observations on the Late State of the Nation* (London: J. Dodsley, 1769).

128. Lloyd, *EEC,* 101–2.

129. Ibid., 102–3.

130. Ibid., 104. AF = P + Q.

131. Ibid., 104–5. England had 8 million people and their annual production totaled £10 million, thus equaling an absolute force of 18. France's population of 18 million people and annual production of £18 million totaled an absolute force of 38. Lloyd used the same data manipulated by Knox and Burke.

132. See Hamisch M. Scott, "The Importance of Bourbon Naval Reconstruction to the Strategy of Choiseul after the Seven Years' War," *The International History Review* 1, no.1 (January 1979): 17–35.

133. Lloyd, *EEC,* 104. He repeated and enlarged this method of analysis in subsequent works.

134. Ibid., 109–13.

135. Ibid., 117–18.

136. Ibid., 114. He wanted 20,000 troops in Ireland, 11,000 infantry and 5,000 cavalry in England, and 3,000 infantry and 1,000 cavalry in Scotland.

137. Ibid., 114.

138. Lloyd thought England's ties to Germany were too expensive. The only alliance of any worth was with Denmark. Ibid., 119. For an overview of the development of the "Blue Water" policy see Daniel A. Baugh, "Great Britain's 'Blue-Water' Policy, 1689–1815," *The International History Review* X, no. 1 (February 1988): 33–58.

CHAPTER 5

1. His rise to power occurred despite his best efforts to prevent it. See Peter Whiteley, *Lord North: The Prime Minister Who Lost America* (London and Rio Grande: The Hambledon Press, 1996).

2. The entire passage is as follows: "My Lord, Destitute as I am of parliamentary connections, I can neither oppose, nor support your administration; and therefore, have not formed the least expectations from your favour and protection: and the less so, as I am convinced, no English minister can confer an employment upon any man *merely* because he deserves it. The good opinion I have of your Lordship's ability and integrity is my only motive for inscribing the following Essay to you, being persuaded, that if it contains anything useful to the nation, you will adopt and promote it." Henry Lloyd, *An essay on the theory of money,* iii–iv. Lloyd's contempt for the patronage system, veiled in deference and humility, is apparent.

3. His only son, Hannibal Evans Lloyd (1771–1847), was a philologist and translator and worked for the British Foreign Service. He resided in Hamburg most of his

life and married a Ms. Von Schwartzkopff, with whom he had a son and several daughters. One daughter deposited General Lloyd's manuscripts in the Fitzwilliam Museum in 1861. Gordon Goodwin, "Lloyd, Hannibal Evans (1771–1847)," *The Dictionary of National Biograph* (Oxford: Oxford University Press; Humphrey Milford, 1937), 9:1300.

4. William Henry Gloucester, Duke of Gloucester (1743–1805) was a nephew of King George III.

5. Turkey declared war on Russia in October 1768 after Poland's plea for assistance and Russia's violation of Turkish territory. In 1769 Russia invaded the Balkans and overran Moldavia and Wallachia, defeated the Turks in Georgia, and fomented rebellion by Ali Bey, the Ottoman governor of Egypt. The following year after repeated Russian victories in the Balkans the Turkish army retreated past the Danube River. At that time the Russian fleet entered the Mediterranean to support a Greek war for independence and defeated and destroyed the Turkish fleet at Chesme (6 July). In 1771, though little progress had been made in the Balkans a Russian army managed to conquer the Crimea. A truce lasted throughout 1772 and both sides took the time to rest and regain strength rather than seriously prepare for peace negotiations.

6. William (Johnstone) Pulteney was the son of James Johnstone and a near relative of the Chevalier de Johnstone of Jacobite fame. He married, Frances, the eldest daughter of William Pulteney, 1st Earl of Bath (1684–1764) and in 1767 took his father-in-law's surname and estates. An MP for Cromartie and Nairn (1768–74) and Shrewsbury (1775–1805), he was a friend of David Hume and Adam Smith, an opponent of the expulsion of John Wilkes, and a secret peace negotiator with Ben Franklin in 1778–79. His relationship and connection to the British consul in Petersburg is unclear. See Alan Valentine, "Pulteney (Johnstone), William (1729–1805)," in *The British Establishment, 1760–1784: An Eighteenth-Century Biographical Dictionary* (Norman, OK: University of Oklahoma Press, 1970), 2:726–27. Charles Schaw, Lord Cathcart (1721–76) was a Scot with a distinguished record in the British army. He was an aide to the Duke of Cumberland at Fontenoy, where he was severely wounded and made prisoner of war. In 1758 he acquired the rank of major general, and lieutenant general in 1760. A Scottish peer, one-time high commissioner of the Church of Scotland, and Knight of the Thistle (1763), he served as ambassador to Russia (1768–72), after which he became Rector of Glasgow University. Alan Valentine, "Cathcart, Charles Schaw (1721–76)," *The British Establishment*, 1:154.

7. He considered the £500 salary inadequate because living expenses in Russia at that time were much higher than in Britain. Catherine probably granted his condition because his wife and child lived in London. Henry Lloyd to Henry Clinton, Petersburg, 5 June 1772, *CPC*, 8:25; Romance de Mesmon, "Précis sur la Vie et le Caractère de Henri Lloyd," xxxvi. Hannibal Lloyd did not mention the interview but claimed Catherine wrote for his help after the disastrous campaign of 1773. This may be true, but his employment began in 1772. See Hannibal Lloyd, *Memoir of General Lloyd*, 6.

8. Joseph Karl, Fürst von Lobkowitz to Wenzel Anton, Fürst von Kaunitz-Rietburg, St. Petersburg, 18 Juni 1772 (no. 31), *Sbornik imperatorskogo russkago istoricheskogo obshchestva*, vol. 125 (St. Petersburg: Imperatorskoe Russkoe Istoricheskoe Obshchestvo, 1906), 73 (hereafter *SIRIO*).

9. Christopher Duffy, *Russia's Military Way to the West: Origins and Nature of Russian Military Power, 1700–1800* (London, Boston, and Henley: Routledge & Kegan Paul, 1981), 145–47. Matthew Smith Anderson, "British Officers in the Russian Army in the Eighteenth and Early Nineteenth Centuries," *Journal of the Society for Army Historical Research* XXXVIII, no. 156 (December 1960): 168–73. Patrick Gordon, who had helped crush the revolt of the *streltsy* in 1698, and James Keith were two prominent Scots. Franz Moritz Lacy's father, Peter, had become a field-marshal in 1736, thus establishing a "dynasty" of Irish soldiers in Russian service.

10. John P. LeDonne, "Outlines of Russian Military Administration, 1762–1796, Part II: The High Command," *Jahrbücher für Geschichte Osteuropas* 33, no. 2 (1985), 184. The High Command was reserved for the leading Russian families because it was the avenue to political power.

11. Isabel de Madariaga, *Russia in the Age of Catherine the Great* provides the best English overview of the diplomacy and conduct of the war. A general overview is also found in Nicholas V. Riasanovsky, *A History of Russia*, 5th ed. (New York: Oxford University Press, 1993). Both Christopher Duffy, *Russia's Military Way to the West*, and Jeremy Black, *War and the World: Military Power and the Fate of Continents, 1450–2000* (New Haven, CT: Yale University Press, 1998) provide succinct accounts of the military operations.

12. David L. Ransel, *The Politics of Catherinian Russia: The Panin Party* (New Haven, CT: Yale University Press, 1975), 233.

13. Matthew Smith Anderson, "Great Britain and the Russo-Turkish War of 1768–74," *The English Historical Review* LXIX, no. 270 (January 1954): 39–40. Hamish M. Scott, "Great Britain, Poland and the Russian Alliance, 1763–1767," *The Historical Journal* 19, no. 1 (March 1976): 53–74, provides an excellent account of the early years of the treaty discussions. Additional Russian demands for a peacetime subsidy and a free hand in Poland were demands to which Britain would not concede. For a general overview of Anglo-Russian relations see David B. Horn, *Great Britain and Europe in the Eighteenth Century,* especially Chapter 8: "Russia and Poland," pp. 201–35.

14. Ransel, *The Politics of Catherinian Russia*, 116–28. His northern system comprising Russia, Denmark, Prussia, and Great Britain was intended to counter the Habsburg-Bourbon southern system. In 1763 a Russo-Prussian alliance was signed, and a Russo-Danish defensive alliance was worked out in 1765. The Russo-Turkish War (1768–74) found Russia without any military support from its allies and marked the failure of Panin's foreign policy.

15. Henry Lloyd to Henry Clinton, Petersburg, 5 June 1772, *CPC*, 8:25. With the resignation of Henry Seymour Conway from the Ordnance Department Lloyd feared losing his pension and implored Clinton to recommend him to the master general of ordnance, George Townshend (1724–1807). See Henry Lloyd to Henry Clinton, 6 August 1774, *CPC*, 8:31.

16. Robert Gunning (1731–1816) was a career diplomat. From 1765–68 he served as minister resident and envoy extraordinary at the court of Denmark. In 1771 he was assigned to the Prussian court, and in 1772 he arrived at his new post in Petersburg with orders to offer British mediation in the Russo-Turkish War and support Catherine's policy in Poland. James M. Rigg, "Gunning, Sir Robert (1731–1816)," *Dictionary of National Biography,* 8:348–49.

17. Robert Gunning to Henry Howard, 12th Earl of Suffolk, St. Petersburg, 27 September/8 October 1772 (No. 155), Most Secret and Confidential, *SIRIO* 19 (1876), 325–29. Gunning reported that Chernyshev, through Lloyd, had sent word of Russian interest in an alliance. But Gustavus's coup d'état ended any hope of opening talks, and convinced Gunning that Panin was not as pro-British as previously believed. For instance, Lord Cathcart had asked Panin to write a memoir of his conduct while ambassador in order to justify his own policies to the British government. Panin sent the document to him through Lloyd, who after reading it warned Cathcart that if made public it might alienate the two countries. Cathcart promptly returned it to Panin. Abbé Antoine Sabatier de Cabres to Emmanuel Armand de Vignerot du Plessis de Richelieu, duc d'Aiguillon, Pétersbourg, 4 septembre 1772 (no. 312), *SIRIO* 143 (1913), 482. Howard, skeptical of the entire episode, sent Gunning's intelligence to the King. Henry Howard, 12th Earl of Suffolk to George III, Elford, 15 September (no. 1130), *The Correspondence of King George the Third from 1760 to December 1783,* ed. John Fortescue, printed from the original papers in the Royal Archives at Windsor Castle (London: Macmillan and Co., Limited, 1927), 2:394–95.

18. Henry Lloyd to Henry Clinton, 6 August 1772, *CPC,* 8:31. Lloyd used a Mr. Richardson as a go between with Clinton and asked him to address all correspondence to Gunning.

19. Graf Victor Friedrich Solms, Conseiller Privé de Légation to Frederick II, Petersburg, 19 Februar 1773, and Frederick II to Solms, Potsdam, 6 mars 1773 (both under No. 21856), *Politische Correspondenz Friedrichs des Grossen,* ed. Gustav Berthold Volz (Berlin: Alexander Duncker Verlag, 1909), 33:338–39. Solms discovered that Lloyd initiated these talks without the authority of Panin, which leads one to suspect he was actually working under orders of the British government. Frederick dismissed it as such and lectured Solms that Russia would never concede to an Anglo-Russian alliance under British terms.

20. For Russian defense planning see John P. LeDonne, "Outlines of Russian Military Administration, 1762–1796, Part I: Troops Strength and Deployment," *Jahrbücher für Geschichte Osteuropas* 31, no. 3 (1983): 321–47. *A Documentary Chronicle of Sino-Western Relations (1644–1820),* pt. 1, compiled, trans. and annotated by Lo-Shu Fu, The Association for Asian Studies: Monographs and Papers, No. XXII, ed. Delmer M. Brown (Tuscon, AZ: The University of Arizona Press, 1966) 266–70, provides details of Sino-Russian friction during this time period.

21. Jacques Abraham Durand d'Aubigny to Emmanuel Armand de Vignerot du Plessis de Richelieu, duc d'Aiguillon, Pétersbourg, 25 novembre 1772 (no. 345), *SIRIO* 143 (1913), 524.

22. Durand d'Aubigny to Duc d'Aiguillon, Pétersbourg, 26 decembre 1772 (no. 361), *SIRIO* 143 (1913), 546–47.

23. Madariaga, *Russia in the Age of Catherine the Great,* 231–34. For a contemporary narrative see "History of Europe, Chapter II," *The Annual Register, or a View of the History, Politics, and Literature, for the Year 1773* (London: Printed for J. Dodsley, 1774), 11–23.

24. Joseph Karl, Fürst von Lobkowitz believed initially that Lloyd was dismissed. In any case, he reported Lloyd's Russian career was over. Lobkowitz to Wenzel Anton, Fürst von Kaunitz-Rietburg, St. Petersburg, 10 August 1773 (no. 103), *SIRIO* 125 (1906), 255; same to same, St. Petersburg, 17 August 1773 (no. 104), *SIRIO* 125 (1906), 257. Lobkowitz later reported that Lloyd's supporters in

the Russian court had fallen from power. Lobkowitz to Kaunitz, St. Petersburg, 2 November 1773 (no. 116), *SIRIO* 125 (1906), 282.

25. Frederick II to Cambellan, comte de Matzan in London, Potsdam, 20 decembre 1773 (no. 22626), *Politische Correspondenz Friedrichs des Grossen,* ed. Gustav Berthold Volz (Berlin: Alexander Duncker Verlag, 1910), 34:346. Frederick resented British duplicity in his dealings with Danzig. Russia's failure to side with Britain in this affair revealed to Britain Prussia's influence at Catherine's court. Anderson, "Great Britain and the Russo-Turkish War of 1768–74," 53.

26. Hannibal Lloyd, *Memoir of General Lloyd,* 6. He did not receive command of an entire army as his son asserted. Rather, he was to join the Russian army in Moldavia and take command of a division under Field-Marshal Rumiantsev.

27. Lloyd, *CHLWG,* 105.

28. Gunning, reporting from St. Petersburg, was not optimistic about the upcoming campaign. For instance the Russian army lacked forage. Rumiantsev would have to wait " 'till the Season is far advanced," to begin operations. Robert Gunning to the Earl of Suffolk, St. Petersburg, 17/28 January 1774 (no. 10), Public Record Office, State Papers 91/95, fol. 79.

29. Henry Clinton, "Journal of Trip to Moldavia in 1774," Henry S. Clinton Papers, The John Rylands University Library of Manchester, Manchester, England, notebook 3:6. (Hereafter cited as *JRULM*).

30. Ibid., notebook 3:11. General Clinton remarked that Lloyd's party resembled a press gang.

31. Ibid., notebook 3:12. Henry Clinton, "Memoranda [1774]," volume 286, *CPC*.

32. Clinton, "Journal of Trip to Moldavia in 1774," *JRULM,* notebook 3:13–14; idem, "Memoranda [1774]."

33. Clinton, "Memoranda [1774]."

34. Ibid.

35. Henry Clinton to Henry Fiennes Pelham Cinton, 2d Duke of Newcastle, Frankfurt, 2 May 1774 (no. 41), NeC 2377, Newcastle Family Papers, The Hallward Library, Nottingham, England.

36. Henry Clinton to the Henry Fiennes Pelham Cinton, 2d Duke of Newcastle, Vienna, 12 May 1774 (no. 47), NeC 2383, Newcastle Family Papers; Same to same, Vienna, 19 May 1774 (no. 46), NeC 2382; Clinton, "Memoranda [1774]."

37. Robert Gunning to the Earl of Suffolk, St. Petersburg, 13/24 June 1774 (no. 48), Public Record Office, SP 91/95, fol. 105; Same to Same, St. Petersburg, 15/26 July 1774 (no. 56), In Code, SP 91/95, fol. 156. Gunning explained the restrictions were intended to keep out French observers.

38. Clinton, "Memoranda [1774]."

39. Henry Clinton to the Duke of Newcastle, Hermanstadt, Transylvania, 6 June 1774, NeC 2379/1, Newcastle Family Papers; Same to Same, Cronstadt, 1/12 June 1774 (no. 42), NeC 2378.

40. Henry Clinton, "Russian Journal, 8 June 1774," *CPC,* 9:28; Henry Clinton to the Duke of Newcastle, Camp on the Danube, 9/20 June 1774 (no. 44), NeC 2380, Newcastle Family Papers; Robert Gunning to the Earl of Suffolk, St. Petersburg, 15/26 July 1774 (no. 56), Public Record Office, SP 91/95, fol. 156. Rumiantsev, ignorant of the order not to allow entry to volunteers, apologized to the Empress. Robert Gunning to the Earl of Suffolk, St Petersburg, 5/15 August 1774 (no. 63), Public Record Office, SP 91/97, fol. 52.

41. Henry Clinton to the Duke of Newcastle, Camp on the Danube, 9/20 June 1774 (no. 44), NeC 2380, Newcastle Family Papers. At the same time Gunning in St. Petersburg reported that the campaign would probably not "render the Turks more tractable." Robert Gunning to the Earl of Suffolk, St. Petersburg, 20 June/ 1 July 1774 (no. 50), Public Record Office, SP 91/95, fol. 112.

42. The breakdown of the truce was due to the new Sultan Abdul Hamid's insistence that there would be no peace without British mediation. Anderson, "Great Britain and the Russo-Turkish War of 1768–74," 51. Rumiantsev's army totaled nearly 52,000. He commanded the 1st Corps (16,747), Ivan Saltykov the 2nd Corps (15,191), Carl Christer von Ungern-Sternberg the 3rd Corps (7,614), and Grigorii Potemkin the Reserve (11,612). LeDonne, "Outlines of Russian Military Administration, 1762–1796, Part II: The High Command," 179.

43. Henry Clinton to Robert Murray Keith, Camp on the Danube, 9/20 June 1774, The British Library, Addit. MSS 35,507, fol. 176; Robert Gunning to the Earl of Suffolk, St. Petersburg, 24 June/5 July 1774 (no. 51), Public Record Office, SP 91/95, fol. 115; Same to Same, St. Petersburg, 1/12 July 1774 (no. 53), fol. 125.

44. There are only a handful of secondary sources on the war in English. See Duffy, *Russia's Military Way to the West,* 168–78; Virginia Aksan, "The One-Eyed Fighting the Blind: Mobilization, Supply, and Command in the Russo-Turkish War of 1768–1774," *The International History Review* XV, no. 2 (May 1993): 221–38; Philip Longworth, *The Art of Victory: The Life and Achievements of Field-Marshal Suvorov, 1729–1800* (New York Holt, Rinehart and Winston, 1965), 92–96; and Madariaga, *Russia in the Age of Catherine the Great* (especially chapters 12 and 13, pp. 187–214). The standard survey of the war remains Richard Ungermann, *Der Russisch-türkische Krieg, 1768–1774* (Wien und Leipzig: Wilhelm Braumüller, 1906). For a contemporary chronicle see "History of Europe, Chapter I," *The Annual Register, or a View of the History, Politics, and Literature, for the Year 1774* (London: Printed for J. Dodsley, 1775): 1–11.

45. For a map of the area see William Roberts, "Plan of Silistria with the Attack made by Major General Lloyd," The Fitzwilliam Museum, Cambridge, England. It is mounted on the end page of a copy of *An Essay on the English Constitution* located in the Founder's Library. During the campaign Lloyd befriended Roberts, an English agent, and had "great affections" towards his family. He urged Clinton to protect and advance the interests of Roberts' son David, who served in the British Army. Henry Lloyd to Henry Clinton, 10 March 1781, *CPC,* 149:3.

46. Gunning reported that the Russian troops, having blocked Silistria, were in an advantageous position. Robert Gunning to the Earl of Suffolk, 15/26 July 1774 (no. 56), Public Record Office, SP 91/95, fol. 154.

47. Clinton, who accompanied Rumiantsev in the advance, was convinced that the campaign would be successful and spoke well of the Russian army's effectiveness. Henry Clinton to the Duke of Newcastle, Camp in Bulgaria, 16/27 June 1774 (no. 49), NeC 2376, Newcastle Family Papers.

48. Lloyd and Major Carleton observed the fight and appreciated the conduct of the squadrons. Lloyd, *CHLWG,* 58.

49. Ungermann, *Der Russisch-türkische Krieg,* 241–42. A few details of the siege are contained in William B. Willcox, *Portrait of a General,* 33–35. Clinton later remarked that he had not seen anything at Silistria as "hot" as his experience in Luxembourg during the Seven Years' War. Robert Murray Keith to Thomas Brad-

shaw, Vienna, 15 September 1774, *Memoirs and Correspondence (Official and Familiar) of Sir Robert Murray Keith, K.B., Envoy Extraordinary and Minister Plenipotentiary at the Courts of Dresden, Copenhagen, and Vienna, from 1769–1792; with a Memoir of Queen Carolina Matilda of Denmark, and an Account of the Revolution there in 1772,* ed. Gillespie Smyth (London: Henry Colburn, Publisher, 1849), 1:475.

50. Henry Clinton to the Duke of Newcastle, July 1774, *CPC*, 9:40.

51. Hannibal Lloyd claimed his father disagreed with Russia's rush to peace because he believed they could have easily marched on Constantinople. The decision was due more to concerns over the Pugachev Revolt than to any missed opportunity. Hannibal Lloyd, *Memoir of General Lloyd*, 6.

52. William C. Fuller, Jr., *Strategy and Power in Russia, 1600–1914* (New York: The Free Press, A Division of Macmillan, Inc., 1992), 105–14; Virginia Aksan, "The One-Eyed Fighting the Blind," 222; and Jeremy Black, *War and the World*, 101.

53. Lloyd claimed Russia had raised 300,000 troops during the war, but only had 36,000 troops in the final campaign; a testament to the long lines of supply that plagued the Russian war effort. Lloyd, *CHLWG*, 65.

54. Madariaga, *Russia in the Age of Catherine the Great*, 207; Aksan, "The One-Eyed Fighting the Blind," 222–34. Aksan argues that both the Russian and Ottoman armies faced similar difficulties, but suffered different fates due to Russia's command superiority. First, the Russian army had developed a General Staff in 1763. Next, the Turks failed to secure centralized control over the large numbers of feudal troops and Tartar cavalry, which inhibited any coherent operational strategy or tactical efficiency. Thus, she discards the standard argument that the Ottomans lost due to a backward society. For a statement of that view see Alexander Balisch, "Infantry Battlefield Tactics in the Seventeenth and Eighteenth Centuries on the European and Turkish Theatres of War: The Austrian Response to Different Conditions," *Warfare and Tactics in the Eighteenth Century: Some Recent Research,* edited by Karl Schweizer, special issue of *Etudes d'Histoire et de Politique* 3 (1983–84): 43–60.

55. Duffy, *Russia's Military Way to the West*, 168–76; Bruce W. Menning, "Russian Military Innovation in the Second Half of the Eighteenth Century," *War & Society* 2, no. 1 (1984): 31–34.

56. Duffy, *Russia's Military Way to the West*, 169; Menning, "Russian Military Innovation," 33–34.

57. He wrote: "Marshal Romanzow [Rumiantsev] is a man of great merit, and among his many good qualities as a general, he studies and knows the genius and character of his enemies." Also, he predicted that Suworow [Suvorov] would one day attain great honors. Lloyd, *HLWG2*, 90.

58. Henry Lloyd to Robert Murray Keith, Warsaw, 18 November, 1774, The British Library, Addit. MSS 35,508, fols. 147–48. Lloyd commented he had been ill for four months and was too weak to travel. In addition he hoped Keith would talk with Marshal Lacy and inquire about possible military employment.

59. Romance de Mesmon, "Précis sur la Vie et le Caractère de Henri Lloyd," xxxvii.

60. H. Arnold Barton, "Russia and the problem of Sweden-Finland," *East European Quarterly* V, no. 4 (January 1972): 447. Gustavus planned to seize Norway from Denmark, a move that required Russian neutrality.

61. The 1772 negotiations collapsed because of Britain's insistence that the Russian officers take an oath of allegiance to King George III. David B. Horn, *Great Britain and Europe in the Eighteenth Century,* 218. See George III to Lord Frederick North, Queen's House, 3 November 1775, vol. 1 of *The Correspondence of King George the Third with Lord North from 1768 to 1783,* ed. W. Bodham Donne, edited from the originals at Windsor, with an introduction and notes (London: John Murray, 1867), 282.

62. Hannibal Lloyd, *Memoir of General Lloyd,* 7; Romance de Mesmon, "Précis sur la Vie et le Caractère de Henri Lloyd," xxxvii–xxxix. He had already been harassed by court lackeys at Silistria when he threatened to throw them in the Danube River. The reason for his sudden departure is obscure. Mesmon relates that he received word that a friend required his assistance in London and that Lloyd had been denied the Order of the Empress. Hannibal Lloyd wrote that he was set to receive the Order of St. George, but resigned before its presentation. In any case, Panin's subsequent fall from power makes Lloyd's decision to leave foresighted.

63. Catherine created the Order of St. George specifically for veterans of the Turkish War. Worth an annuity of £8,000, it is improbable that Lloyd would have turned it down solely because of wounded pride. Court intrigue probably kept it from him, and with that knowledge he resigned. For Catherine's military orders see Duffy, *Russia's Military Way to the West,* 147–52.

64. John Drummond wrote that he encountered Lloyd in London in 1776, the last time they met. Drummond, "Mr. Drummond's Letter to the Editor," xvi.

65. Hannibal Lloyd, *Memoir of General Lloyd,* 7.

66. Alfred Temple Patterson, *The Other Armada: The Franco-Spanish Attempt to Invade Britain in 1779* (Manchester: Manchester University Press, 1960), 40. Spain's threat to mediate a peace between Britain and its colonies was an additional incentive for France to invade.

67. Robert Keith in Vienna did not believe an invasion was probable. "The French talk much upon the Continent of invading you this summer," he wrote, "but I hope that no man of sense in England can ever dread any serious consequences from the common bugbear of invasion." Robert Murray Keith to Andrew Drummond, Vienna, 12 June 1779, *Memoirs and Correspondence (Official and Familiar) of Sir Robert Murray Keith,* 1:89–90.

68. He arrived from Brussels in late July with important information for the King. George's secretary, Charles Jenkinson, relayed the information but did not think "His intelligence had made much Impression on me; and I should have doubted whether I ought to have sent it to your Majesty, if it had not been for the Character of Genl. Lloyd and the very earnest and confident manner, in which the Genl. Deliver'd this Intelligence." Charles Jenkinson to George III, Addiscombe Place, 1 August 1779, no. 2730, vol. IV of *Correspondence of King George the Third from 1760 to December 1783,* ed. Fortescue, 404. North and John Robinson of the Treasury of the exact composition of the Franco-Spanish fleet: 66 vessels of the line plus 50 gunships. Jeremy Bentham to William Petty, 2d Earl of Shelburne, 17 September 1779, vol. 2 of *The Correspondence of Jeremy Bentham,* ed. Timothy L. S. Sprigge (London: The Athlone Press, 1968), 291. Bentham met Lloyd aboard a packet ship.

69. Hannibal Lloyd, *Memoir of General Lloyd,* 8.

70. Patterson, *The Other Armada,* is the best work on the subject.

71. Hannibal Lloyd, *Memoir of General Lloyd,* 9; Romance de Mesmon, "Précis sur la Vie et le Caractère de Henri Lloyd," xxviii–xxix. Eliott once served in the Prussian army and met Lloyd during the Seven Years' War. He became Governor of Gibraltar in 1777 and because of his successful defense against French and Spanish force (1779–83) he was made full general, Knight of the Bath, and given the title Baron Heathfield. Valentine, "Eliott, George Augustus (1717–90)," *The British Establishment,* 1:293. See Stetson Conn, *Gibraltar in British Diplomacy in the Eighteenth Century* (New Haven, CT: Yale University Press; London: Humphrey Milford, Oxford University Press, 1942).

72. According to a Mr. O'Connel, he received 500 pounds sterling, but might have received upwards of 100,000 *ecus* had he sold it to France. Romance de Mesmon, "Précis sur la Vie et le Caractère de Henri Lloyd," xlii.

73. Hannibal Lloyd, *Memoir of General Lloyd,* 8; Henry Lloyd, *A Rhapsody on the Present System of French Politics; on the Projected Invasion, and the Means to Defeat It,* 28. His inscription read: "Pro aris et focis" (for alter and hearth). He dedicated the book to Lieutenant General Robert Clerk for the many favors he conferred upon him. Robert Clerk (or Clerke, Clark, or Clarke) (d.1797) was a Scots military engineer who had risen in the ranks of the British army from spy to Lieutenant General by 1777. See pt. 1 of *Horace Walpole's Correspondence with Henry Seymour Conway, Lady Ailesbury, Lord and Lady Hertford, Mrs. Harris,* eds. Wilmarth Sheldon Lewis, Lars E. Troide, Edwine M. Murty, and Robert A. Smith, vol. 37 of *The Yale Edition of Horace Walpole's Correspondence,* 574 (no. 4).

74. Lloyd, *Rhapsody on the Present System of French Politics,* 31–33 (hereafter called *Rhapsody*).

75. Ibid., 41–45.

76. Patterson, *The Other Armada,* 133–44.

77. Lloyd, *Rhapsody,* 45–48. Lloyd had personally reconnoitered the Isle of Wight after he arrived at Portsmouth.

78. Ibid., 49.

79. Patterson, *The Other Armada,* 107–9, 122–24.

80. Lloyd, *Rhapsody,* 50.

81. Ibid., 51.

82. Ibid., 52–56.

83. Ibid., 68*–71*. Pages with asterisks were inserted prior to publication between the originally numbered pages.

84. Ibid., 65.

85. He wrote: "[H]ave you seen also a Pamphlet written by a General Lloyd, who went to Paris last year as a Spy, offering himself to go to America whilst He was in the Pay of the British King? It is entitled a Rhapsody on French Politics and Invasions; the book was soon bought up by the Government which makes me desire to see it, I have sent to England for it to be got coute que coute." Edmund Jennings to John Adams, Brussels, 5 March 1780, vol. 9 of *The Papers of John Adams,* eds. Gregg Lint, Joanna M. Revelas, Richard Alan Ryerson, Celeste Walker, and Anne M. Decker (Cambridge, MA: The Belknap Press of Harvard University Press, 1996), 20; John Adams to Edmund Jennings, Paris, 12 March 1780, Ibid., 35.

86. George Townshend, "Observations upon General Lloyd's Rhapsody," Townshend Papers, 1779–1783, The British Library, Addit. Mss. 50,008, fol. 83; Col. James Branham, "From G. Lloyd's Rhapsody (c.1781)," Public Record Office,

WO 30/81, fols. 1–15. I thank Mark Danley of Kansas State University for providing a copy of this document.

87. Unlike 1779, William Pitt the Younger's ministry saw no harm in its publication. Hannibal Lloyd, *Memoir of General Lloyd,* 8–9. See Appendix A for the reprint editions. See also "Review of *A Political and Military Rhapsody on the Invasion and Defense of Great Britain and Ireland,* by the Late General Lloyd," *The Monthly Review; or, Literary Journal* 5, 2d ser. (August 1791): 459–61; and "Review of *A Political and Military Rhapsody on the Invasion and Defense of Great Britain and Ireland,* 2d ed., by the Late General Lloyd," *The Monthly Review; or, Literary Journal* 9, 2d ser. (October 1792): 209.

88. The French translation is *Mémoire politique et militaire sur l'invasion et la défénse de la Grand Bretagne* (Limoges: Barrois l'aîné, An IX [1801]). It was also a propaganda tool and was followed by an extended critique, Jacques François Louis Grobert, *Observations sur les mémoire du général Lloyd concernant l'invasion et la defense la Grande-Bretagne* (Paris: Pougens et Magimel, an XI [1803]). Grobert refuted many of Lloyd's claims, especially his assertation that France could not successfully invade Great Britain. First, he argued that the French navy could defeat the British navy and land troops, especially if it took advantage of good fortune such as strong winds or storms. He scoffed at Lloyd's belief that once landed a French army could not advance inland. The French army during the Revolution and under Napoleon had overcome many obstacles and won many victories, and it would do the same against Great Britain as long as it retained the morale gained from its recent glory. In any case, Grobert believed that the army could land nearer London (at perhaps Dover) and avoid seizing a coastal depot. Then it could launch a lightning strike against the capital, which would alleviate the need for mass supplies. Gaius Julius Caesar and William the Conquerer had succeeded, and Grobert boasted that France could as well (especially if it benefitted from luck or good fortune). A spirited critique, Grobert's belief in the intervention of fortune and France's moral superiority was a poor substitute for Lloyd's detailed analysis.

89. General George S. Patton, Jr. owned a copy of the 1792 edition (which he read). It is now housed in the Special Collections Department of the U. S. Military Academy Library, West Point, New York. Steve E. Dietrich, "The Professional Reading of General George S. Patton, Jr.," *The Journal of Military History* 53, no. 4 (October 1984): 394 (no. 16).

90. Lloyd, *Rhapsody,* 10.

91. Ibid., 13–17.

92. Ibid., 27.

93. See Don Higginbotham, *The War of American Independence: Military Attitudes, Policies, and Practice, 1763–1789,* The Macmillan Wars of the United States, gen. ed. Louis Morton (New York: The Macmillan Company; London: Collier-Macmillan Ltd., 1971). The Continental Army's Pennsylvania Line and three New Jersey regiments mutinied in January 1781. By the time the war ended in 1783, the Continental Congress was bankrupt, and was hard-pressed to sustain Washington's army. For a succinct assessment of Britain's strategic failings see Ira D. Gruber, "British Strategy: The Theory and Practice of Eighteenth-Century Warfare," *Reconsiderations on the Revolutionary War: Selected Essays,* ed. Don Higginbotham, Contributions in Military History, no. 14 (Westport, CT: Greenwood Press, 1978), 14–31.

94. Hannibal Lloyd, *Memoir of General Lloyd*, 9.

95. Willcox, *Portrait of a General*, 365. In 1780, Lloyd had pressed John Dalrymple, 5th Earl of Stair (1720–89), for the appointment of Lieutenant General of Provincials (Loyalists), but those requests were turned down by Amherst.

96. Amherst argued that the position should go to an officer of the Provincials already in North America. William Dalrymple to George Germain, London, 7 December 1780, *CPC*, 139:5; Leonard Morse to Benjamin Thompson, Whitehall, 1 January 1781, *CPC*, 139:6 (both letters filed under 4 January 1781).

97. Jennings sent a copy of his letter to France's foreign minister, Charles Gravier, comte de Vergennes. He cautioned Adams and urged "him be Watch'd, if He [Lloyd] is there pray give Notice to the Minister [Vergennes] that he may be attended to." Edmund Jennings to John Adams, Brussels, 22 April 1780, vol. 9 of *The Papers of John Adams*, 227.

98. He published a more detailed military plan as "New Plan to conquer America, by Major General Lloyd," *The Public Advertiser*, no. 14583 (Saturday, 7 July 1781), 3.

99. Hannibal Lloyd, *Memoir of General Lloyd*, 9–10. I have found no corroborating evidence to support his son's claim. Shelburne had been an opponent of the North ministry and its colonial policy. A Lieutenant General he formed a cabinet in July 1782, which lasted until April 1783, when his terms for peace were rejected by the new Charles James Fox-Lord North coalition.

CHAPTER 6

1. Henry Lloyd, *Continuation of the History of the Late War in Germany; Between the King of Prussia, and the Empress of Germany and Her Allies*, part ii (London: Printed for the Author, and Sold by S. Hooper, 1781). The title misrepresents its contents. It is the cumulative expression of his philosophy of war and not a continuation of the historical narrative of the Seven Years' War first published in 1766 (although a reprint edition of that history accompanied this new volume). Lloyd informed Clinton of its summer publication and indicated that a third volume covering the operations in Westphalia would soon follow. Henry Lloyd to Henry Clinton, 10 March 1781, Henry S. Clinton Papers, William L. Clements Library, Ann Arbor, Michigan, 149:3. An English review criticized the title and took offense that its author had once served the "illiberal" princes of the continent. Alexander Jardine, "Of the Philosophy of War," [review of Henry Lloyd's *Continuation of the History of the Late War in Germany, Between the King of Prussia, and the Empress of Germany and Her Allies*], *The Monthly Review; or, Literary Journal* 66 (April 1782): 281.

2. Ibid., 76.

3. Ibid. One anecdote helps illustrate Lloyd's experience with the aristocratic military culture. After his return from Russia he traveled to Belgium (then the Austrian Netherlands) to visit Prince Charles of Lorraine, Austrian General and Viceroy in the Netherlands. The royal valets prevented Lloyd, wearing a red uniform of his own design, from entering the Prince's residence and told him they had never heard of him. Insulted by their behavior, Lloyd remarked, "I, sir, don't want anything," and departed. Germain Hyacinthe, marquis de Romance de Mesmon, "Précis sur la Vie et le Caractère de Henri Lloyd," foreword to *Mémoires militaires et politiques du Général Lloyd, servant d'introduction à l'histoire de la guerre en Allemagne en*

1756, entre le Roi de Prusse et l'Imperatrice reine avec ses alliés, by Henri Lloyd, traduits et augmentés de notes et d'un précis sur la vie et le caractère de ce Général, par un officier Français (Paris: Magimel, An IX [1801]), xxxviii.

4. The French army had understood the need to recruit and refine talented men (albeit largely nobles) years before the French Revolution. Attempts at reform, often inspired by Enlightenment thought, met with little success. The *École militaire* established in 1751 educated poor nobles who demonstrated some ability. It closed in 1776 with its cadets dispersed throughout the traditional provincial schools. See David D. Bien, "The Army and the French Enlightenment: Reform, Reaction and Revolution," *Past & Present: A Journal of Historical Studies,* no. 85 (August 1979): 68–98.

5. Immanuel Kant, *Critique of Judgment,* 2d rev. ed., trans. with introduction and notes by J. H. Bernard (London: Macmillan and Co., Limited, 1914), 191; originally published as *Kritik der Urteilskraft* (Berlin unde Libau: Bey Lagarde und Friedrich, 1790). For a modern study of the idea of genius or "creative imagination" during the eighteenth century see James Engell, *The Creative Imagination: Enlightenment to Romanticism* (Cambridge, MA: Harvard University Press, 1981).

6. Denis Diderot, "Article GÉNIE," in *Œuvres Esthétiques,* ed. Paul Vernière (Paris: Éditions Garnier Frères, 1959), 16.

7. Alexander Gerard, *An Essay on Genius* (London: Printed for W. Strahan, T. Cadell, and W. Creech, 1774; reprint, ed. Bernhard Fabian, Munich: Wilhelm Fink, 1966), 68; Duff, *An Essay on Original Genius and Its Various Modes of Exertion in Philosophy and the Fine Arts, Particularly in Poetry,* 171.

8. Lloyd, "Reflections on the general principles of war," 169; idem., *HLWG,* 6[unnumbered]; idem., *CHLWG,* vii–viii.

9. Carl von Clausewitz, "On Military Genius," bk 1, chap. 3 of *On War,* ed. and trans. Michael Howard and Peter Paret, with introductory essays by Peter Paret, Michael Howard, and Bernard Brodie, with a commentary by Bernard Brodie (Princeton, NJ: Princeton University Press, 1976), 100–12; originally published as *Vom Kriege,* 3 vols. (Berlin: F. Dümmler, 1832–34). For a concise summary of Clausewitz's conception of genius see Thomas H. Killion, "Clausewitz and Military Genius," *Military Review* LXXV, no. 4 (July–August 1995): 97–100.

10. Lloyd, *CHLWG,* 72.

11. Ibid., 73–78. He continued his criticism of imitating Prussian training and discipline. The French army's instructions for infantry in 1774 and 1775 had advocated rigorous fire drill on the Prussian model, no doubt influenced by Baron de Pirch's *Mémoire raisonné sur les parties les plus essentielles de la tactique* (1773), which called for the adoption of the Prussian military system.

12. Ibid., 79.

13. Ibid., 80–82. Lloyd, unlike Helvetius, did not believe that the satisfaction of social passions fulfilled animal needs. Rather, the desire to fulfill social passions for social needs distinguished humans from the rest of the animal kingdom.

14. Ibid., 14.

15. Ibid., 85.

16. Ibid., 88.

17. Ibid., 89.

18. Ibid., 92–93.

19. Ibid., 92.

20. Ibid., 90.

21. Ibid., 98–104.

22. Ibid., 99–100.

23. Ibid., 106–13. The Ségur Law of 1781 prohibited non-nobles from entering the French officer corps.

24. Ibid, 14.

25. Ibid., 114.

26. Ibid., 115–16.

27. Ibid., 120–21.

28. Ibid, 117. He first introduced an analysis of the "analogy between the form of government and the state of war" in his treatise on the invasion and defense of Great Britain. In that work, he compared each political system to a river. A despotism was simply a violent torrent with no system; a monarchy was a majestic river "singularly adapted to war;" and a republic was a "great river, formed by a multiplicity of springs and rivulets" that were difficult to control. Henry Lloyd, *Rhapsody on the present system of French politics; on the projected invasion, and the means to defeat it,* illustrated with plans, on three copper plates (London: Printed for W. Faden, 1779), 21–26.

29. A short review is in *Die Militair-Bibliothek* (Hanover: Gebrüdern, 1782), 1:105. The extended summation and essay is in volume 4 (1784), 99–116. Scharnhorst joined the Prussian army in 1801. A pupil of Friedrich Wilhelm Ernst, Graf zu Schaumburg-Lippe, he was particularly interested in the moral political forces of war and passed on those concerns to his future student, Carl von Clausewitz. For Scharnhorst's efforts to professionalize the Prussian army see Charles Edward White, *The Enlightened Soldier: Scharnhorst and the* Militärische Gesellschaft *in Berlin, 1801–1805* (New York: Praeger, 1989). For Lloyd's influence on Scharnhorst see p. 11.

30. Clausewitz, *On War,* 89. He suggested that the people, the army, and the government paralleled the paradoxical trinity of primordial violence, the play of chance and the creative spirit, and the subordination of war to policy.

31. Lloyd, *CHLWG,* 65. The War of the Spanish Succession (1701–14); The War of the Austrian Succession (1740–48); and the Seven Years' War (1756–63). He added: "Forty years peace and a good government will not atone for the calamities and losses of a six years war."

32. Jean Colin disputed the political explanation of "limited war" in the eighteenth century nearly ninety years ago, calling it "an absurd thesis if ever there were one." Jean Colin, *The Transformations of War,* trans. L. H. R. Pope-Hennessy (London: H. Rees, 1912; reprint, Westport, CT: Greenwood Press, Publishers, 1977, 198); originally published as *Les transformations de la guerre* (Paris: E. Flammarion, 1911).

33. Colin explained the problem in similar terms: "Neither the handling of weapons nor the science of marches derives from the general character of operations; on the contrary, weapons determine the manner of fighting and the evolutions; from this result the general structure of the battle, the form of maneuvres that prepare it, and finally the general character of the operations—the physiognomy of the entire war." Colin, *The Transformations of War,* 199–200.

34. Lloyd, *CHLWG,* 14. For a similar argument see Jean Colin, *The Military Education of Napoleon,* trans. Richard U. Nicholas (n.p., n.d.), 39; originally published as *L'education militaire de Napoleon* (Paris: R. Chapelot et ce, 1901).

35. Ibid., 12.

36. Ibid., 1–3.

37. Ibid., 7–11.

38. Ibid., 13.

39. Ibid., 17.

40. Ibid., 16.

41. We have no contemporary studies on the effectiveness of smoothbore muskets. In theory these weapons allowed a 500-man battalion with a 150–yard frontage to fire at a rate of six to ten shots per minute up to 100 yards. Factoring in battlefield uncertainties, which Lloyd emphasized, the accuracy of fire probably dropped from 40 percent for well-trained infantry to perhaps 10–20 percent. Basil Perronet Hughes, *Firepower: Weapons effectiveness on the battlefield, 1630–1850* (New York: Charles Scribners Sons, 1974; reprint, New York: Sarpedon, 1997), 26–29, 59–65.

42. Lloyd, *CHLWG,* 21. Jeremy Black argues that the adoption of the flintlock musket actually increased tactical flexibility and that "indecisiveness" was a matter of degree and perspective. Black, *European Warfare, 1660–1815,* 39, 67–72.

43. Lloyd, *CHLWG,* 23–28.

44. David Chandler, *The Art of War in the Age of Marlborough* (London: Batsford Ltd., 1976; reprint, New York: Sarpedon, 1994), 19–23. Chandler focuses on the infrastructure of transportation and logistics as the primary factors of the problem, not army organization. Geza Perjés first used the term "crisis of strategy." For his analysis and the best overview of the logistics-based strategy of the seventeenth and eighteenth centuries see Geza Perjés, "Army Provisioning, Logistics and Strategy in the Second Half of the 17th Century," *Acta Historica Academiae Scientiarum Hungaricae* XVI (1970): 1–52.

45. Lloyd, *CHLWG,* 27–32. Liegnitz was possibly the key to Lloyd's and Siškovíc's quarrel.

46. Ibid., 33–4. Lloyd ridiculed the typical officer's understanding of the line deployment: "His army is like a set of china-ware on a chimney-piece; it must not be touched or moved, for fear of breaking it.

47. Ibid., 14, 35.

48. See Weigley, *The Age of Battles.*

49. Jacques-François Maximo de Chastenet, marquis de Puységur, *Art de la guerre par principes et par règles,* 2 vols. (Paris: Claude-Antoine Jombert, 1748), emphasized the need for the historical study of war and argued that firearms had become the superior form of armament for infantry. For the tactical reform in the French army see Robert S. Quimby, *The Background of Napoleonic Warfare.* For a general overview of tactics as they evolved during the first half of the eighteenth century see Brent Nosworthy, *The Anatomy of Victory: Battle Tactics, 1689–1763* (New York: Hippocrene Books, 1990). Another useful survey is Jean Colin, *L'Infanterie au XVIIIe siècle: La Tactique* (Paris: Berger-Levrault & Co., 1907).

50. François-Jean de Graindorge Dorgeville, baron de Mésnil-Durand, *Projet d'un ordre françois en tactique, ou la phalange coupée et doublée soutenue par le mélange des armes* (Paris: De l'Imprimerie d'Antoine Boudet, 1755).

51. Jacques Antoine Hippolyte, comte de Guibert, *A General Essay on Tactics,* 2 vols. (London, 1781); originally published as *Essai général tactique, précéde d'un discours sur l'état de la politique & de la science militaire in Europe,* rev. ed. (London: Libraires Associés, 1773).

52. The resistance to firearms befuddled Jean Colin, who argued that firepower was more effective than shock tactics when attacking an enemy's flank. Colin, *The Transformations of War*, 17, 111.

53. Paul Gédéon Joly, comte de Maizeroy, *Cours de tactique, théorique, practique, et historique*, 2 vols. (Paris: C. A. Jombert, 1766).

54. François-Jean de Graindorge Dorgeville, baron de Mésnil-Durand, *Fragments de tactique, ou six mémoires* (Paris: C. A. Jombert, 1774).

55. Quimby, *The Background of Napoleonic Wafare*, 233–44.

56. Jacques Antoine Hippolyte, comte de Guibert, *Défense du système de guerre moderne, ou, Réfutation complette du système de M. de M.-D.*, 2 vols. (Neuchatel: [s.n.], 1779).

57. Quimby, *The Background of Napoleonic Wafare*, 302–6.

58. It first surfaced in *A rhapsody on the present system of French politics; on the projected invasion and the means to defeat it, by a Chelsea pensioner* (London: W. Faden and T. Jeffreys, 1779), 72*–74, as a proposed reform for the British army.

59. For example John Shy, "Jomini," in *Makers of Modern Strategy from Machiavelli to the Nuclear Age*, 143–85. Shy relies on the conclusions of Napoleon Bonaparte to characterize Lloyd's entire philosophy of war as representative of the backward ways of Old Regime warfare. In fact, Napoleon criticized those parts of Lloyd's theory that were innovative and counter to existing military traditions.

60. Lloyd, *CHLWG*, 35–64.

61. Colin, *The Military Education of Napoleon*, 44. The French army never formally adopted Broglie's "divisions," and it was left to the French Revolutionary armies to develop the modern combat division that contained all three military arms. See Steven T. Ross, "The Development of the Combat Division in Eighteenth-Century French Armies," *French Historical Studies* 4, no. 1 (Spring 1965): 84–94.

62. Lloyd, *CHLWG*, 37–42. Lloyd confessed that the breastplate was more for morale purposes than for actual protection.

63. Ibid., 47–49.

64. Ibid., 41

65. Ibid, 44, 53, 149–50.

66. Ibid., 43–44.

67. Ibid., 56–62.

68. Ibid., 45–46.

69. Ibid., 49–52.

70. Ibid., 63. He wrote: "To increase this activity [receiving the enemy], the general, as well as the soldier, seem to place all their confidence in the artillery, rather than in the valour of the soldier; accordingly the cannon is become the soul of our military establishments."

71. Napoleon, during his exile on St. Helena, rejected the pike revival because he believed firepower was everything in war. Napoleon I, *Notes inédites de l'Empereur Napoléon Ier sur les Mémoires Militaires du Général Lloyd*, edited by Ariste Ducaunnès-Duval, extrait du tome XXXV des "Archives Historiques de la Gironde" (Bordeaux: G. Gounouilhou, 1901), 12–13. This is sample marginalia found on the 1784 edition published in Brussels (this is the source Shy used for Napoleon's monosyllabic analysis). In more detailed notes he confessed if infantry could be armed with both pikes and guns the system would be perfected. Napoleon I, "Notes sur l'Introduction de la Guerre en Allemagne en 1756, entre le Roi de Prusse

et l'Impératrice-reine et ses Alliés, etc., par la Général Lloyd," in vol. 31 of *Corre-spondance de Napoléon Ier* (Paris: Henri Plon, 1870), 422. Of course, that is what Lloyd wanted to do. Simon François, baron Gay de Vernon reflected the contem-porary consensus against Lloyd's pikemen, although he admitted many problems plagued modern firearms. His conclusions were transplanted to the United States Army in a translation of his military treatise published in 1817. Simon François, baron Gay de Vernon, *Treatise on the Science of War and Fortification: Composed for the Use of the Imperial Polytechnik Schools,* trans. for the War Department for the use of the Military Academy of the United States to which is added a summary of the principles and maxims of grand tactics and operations by John Michael O'Connor (New York: Printed by J. Seymour, 1817), 1:62; originally published as *Traité élémentaire et de fortification, à l'usage des éléves de l'École polytechnique, et des éléves des écoles militaire,* 2 vols. (Paris: Allais, 1805). The most effective critic was Jomini who disliked the fourth rank of pikemen because it would make the line too unwieldy and weak against musket fire. Henri Jomini, *The Art of War,* trans. from the French by G. H. Mendell and W. P. Craighill (Philadelphia: J. B. Lip-pincott & Co., 1862); reprint, The West Point Military Library, eds. Thomas E. Greiss and Jay Luvaas (Westport, Connecticut: Greenwood Press, Publishers, 1971), 266. For the French Revolutionaries use of pikes see John A. Lynn, "French Opin-ion and the Military Resurrection of the Pike, 1792–1794," *Military Affairs* 41, no. 1 (February 1977): 1–7.

72. He was not trying to create a universal theory of war; he was applying what he believed to be universal principles of theory to the material constraints and realities of his time. It should be noted that even with the invention of high-powered artillery, rifles, and machine guns, the belief in morale over material lived on, espe-cially in the French army with Marshal Ferdinand Foch.

73. Again Napoleon criticized Lloyd's devaluation of cavalry as "quite absurd" and listed several examples during his career where cavalry charges did make a great dif-ference in the outcome of a battle. Gay de Vernon emphasized Lloyd's dislike of cav-alry but did not explain how Lloyd's cavalry was to be used. Jomini took a similar line and condemned the intervals between the divisional lines because enemy cav-alry could surround and annihilate them. Thus, he ignored Lloyd's allocation of cav-alry and light troops or simply misrepresented his theory. Napoleon I, *Notes inédites de l'Empereur Napoléon Ier,* 18–19; Idem, "Notes sur l'Introduction de la Guerre en Allemagne en 1756," 426–27; Gay de Vernon, *Treatise on the Science of War and Fortification,* 97; Jomini, *The Art of War,* 266.

74. Peter Paret, *Yorck and the Era of Prussian Reform, 1807–1815* (Princeton, NJ: Princeton University Press, 1966), 41, credits Lloyd as the pioneer in the new use of light infantry.

75. In an undated and unfinished essay on artillery Lloyd reiterated his conviction that the scientific spirit of Vauban had infected warfare to its detriment. Artillery for example was not a precise science and one had to rely as much on experience as on ballistic tables. Henry Lloyd, "An essay on the artillery," Henry Lloyd Papers, The Fitzwilliam Museum, 1–4. In another irony, it was the trained engineer who became the foremost critic of the "science of war." For the diffusion of the scientific spirit in military institutions of that era see Henry Guerlac, "Science and War in the Old Regime: The Development of Science in an Armed Society," (Ph.D. diss., Harvard University, 1941); and Howard Rosen, "The Système Gribeauval: A Study of Tech-

nological Development and Institutional Change in Eighteenth Century France," (Ph.D. diss., The University of Chicago, 1981, UMI Order Numer AAT T-28084).

76. Lloyd, *CHLWG*, 63.

77. A translation of Guibert's *Essai général tactique* appeared in 1781 dedicated to Charles Stanhope, 3d earl of Harrington (1753–1829), who had been aide-de-camp to Burgoyne at Saratoga. The anonymous translator apologized for any defects in the translation due to his many years service overseas in foreign armies. While it is only conjecture, perhaps Lloyd was more closely associated with Guibert than the record reveals.

78. He wrote: "The line which connects these points, on which every army must act, is called *The Line of Operation*." Lloyd, *CHLWG*, 134. He appears to have been the first theorist to use that term when he first introduced it in his 1779 treatise on the defense of Great Britain. He explained: "An army, like a traveller, must necessarily depart from any given point, and proceed to a given point in the enemy's country. The line which unites these points, I call *The Line of Operation*." Lloyd, *A rhapsody on the present system of French politics; on the projected invasion and the means to defeat it, by a Cheslea pensioner,* illustrated with a chart of the opposite coasts of England and France (London: W. Faden and T. Jeffreys, 1779), 35.

79. Lloyd, *CHLWG*, 137.

80. Lloyd wrote: "when the respective forces and abilities of the commanders are nearly equal, those who act on the shortest line, must from that circumstance alone prevail in the end, because being nearer their depots, they can open the campaign sooner, act with more vigour and activity, and for a longer time than those whose line of operation is at a greater distance." Ibid., 154.

81. Lloyd, *CHLWG,* 66–67. The French army enacted a similar reform in 1776 with the establishment of sixteen zones or divisions superimposed on France. Each division served as an administrative zone and permanent military garrison from which regiments were recruited, trained, and organized. This was the origin of the permanent military organization called the division used with great success during the French Revolutionary and Napoleonic wars. See Steven T. Ross, "The Development of the Combat Division in Eighteenth-Century France," 85–86.

82. Lloyd, *CHLWG,* 65. The difficulties that Russia experienced in reinforcing and resupplying its armies during the Turkish War disturbed Lloyd. The perpetual military colonies would serve as "advance bases" for military operations and insure the continual stream of logistics required by modern warfare.

83. Ibid., 153.

84. Ibid., 154–57.

85. Ibid., 167. George Hanger, a pro-French British soldier, adopted Lloyd's lines of operation and military geography in an analysis of the Austrian loss of Brabant in 1792. Karl Wilhelm Ferdinand, Herzog von Brunswick's failure to advance into France illustrated the importance of the rules of lines of operations. His line had been far too long for any chance of success. See George Hanger, *Anticipation of the Freedom of Brabant, with the Expulsion of the Austrian Troops from that Country; with some Remarks on the Future Extension of the French Frontier to the Rhine: Investigated according to the Principles laid down in the Works of General Lloyd; together with some Military Observations on the Late intended March of the Duke of Brunswick to Paris* (London: Printed for J. Debrett, 1792), 51–67.

86. Ibid., 169–71.

87. Ibid., 172–73.

88. Ibid., 176–77.

89. Ibid., 138–41.

90. Ibid., 182–84.

91. Ibid., 185; Henry Lloyd, "New Plan to Conquer America, by Major General Lloyd," *The Public Advertiser,* 7 July 1781, no. 14583, 3. Those four provinces were Massachusetts, Rhode Island, New York, and Connecticut.

92. Lloyd, *CHLWG,* 185–86; Lloyd, "New Plan to Conquer America," 3.

93. Ibid., 145.

94. Ibid., 143–45.

95. Ibid., 147.

96. David G. Chandler, *The Campaigns of Napoleon* (New York: The Macmillan Company, 1966). See "Part Three: Napoleon's Art of War," 161–78. See also the insightful historiographic overview, Albert M. J. Hyatt, "The Origins of Napoleonic Warfare: A Survey of Interpretations," *Military Affairs* 30, no. 4 (Winter 1966–67): 177–85.

97. Lloyd, *CHLWG,* 147–48.

98. Lloyd did not use the word "strategy" when defining his concepts, but the idea of strategy as different from tactics was not unknown. Maizeroy had differentiated between the two levels of war in *Théorie de la guerre* (Paris: Claude-Antoine Jombert, 1777).

99. Jean Colin, *The Military Education of Napoleon,* 64, 77, 107; Chandler, *The Campaigns of Napoelon,* 179. Whereas Colin suggests that Lloyd's operational methods had particular affect on the Emperor, Chandler argues that his tactical and grand tactical ideas had more influence.

100. Colin, *The Military Education of Napoleon,* 107. Basil Liddell Hart, "Some Extracts from a Military Work of the 18th Century," *Journal of the Society for Army Historical Research* XII, no. 47 (Autumn 1933): 139.

101. For these editions see the Appendix. Lloyd's influence, nearly impossible to ascertain, is diffuse but widespread. Henry Clinton in his old age digested Lloyd's theory; his commentary is contained in notebooks dated 1791. See Henry Clinton, "Lloyd's Book," in Notebook 14 of the Henry S. Clinton Papers, The John Rylands University Library of Manchester, Manchester, England.

102. Lloyd, *CHLWG,* 12.

CONCLUSION

1. "Historical Chronicle," *The Gentleman's Magazine* vol. LIII, part 2, no. 3 (September 1783): 803; Romance de Mesmon, "Précis sur la Vie et le Caractère de Henri Lloyd), xliii. Lloyd's anti-Catholic orientation and possible involvement with the Belgian separatist movement, *Pro ari et focis,* may help explain the disinterment. Joseph Michaud, Jr. and Alfred Maury, "Lloyd (Henri-Humphrey-Évans)," vol. 24 of *Biographie Universelle (Michaud) Ancienne et Moderne,* new ed. (Paris: Chez Madame C. Desplaces; Leipzig: Librairie de F. A. Brockhaus, n.d.), 635. The seized papers included a copy of his defense of Great Britain and history of the Seven Years' War published as volume two in 1790.

2. Adam Heinrich Dietrich, Freiherr von Bülow, *The Spirit of the Modern System of War,* with a commentary by C. Malorti de Martemont (London: Sold by

T. Egerton, 1806); originally published as *Geist des neuern Kriegssystem* (Hamburg: Benjamin Gottlieb Hofmann, 1799).

3. The title of chapter 5 reveals his basic geometric approach to strategy: "Of lines of Operation which, proceeding from the Extremities of the Base in a right line, forms, in meeting at the Object, a right Angle, or an obtuse one; and of those whose Base is the segment of a Circle of 90 Degrees or more." Ibid., 58.

4. He wrote: "That if a base is too long, that the two lines of operations from its extremities, form in meeting the object of operation, an angle 90 degrees, an army may advance perfect safety; but if not, that it would be imprudent." Ibid., 50.

5. Ibid., 45, 187.

6. Ibid., 81, 83.

7. Ibid., 191–229.

8. Ibid., 245.

9. For example, Azar Gat placed Bülow after Lloyd in his survey of military thought, thereby implying the natural progression of ideas. The evolutional methodology is suspect because it presupposes that each writer simply added to or expanded upon the work of their predecessor within a grand process of creating a universal theory of war. In fact, there is little evidence in the works themselves that such a project existed or was meant to exist. In any case, Bülow's theory was never accepted as sound, and he died in a Prussian prison an eccentric and refuted figure.

10. See the spirited critique of Jomini by John R. Elting, "Jomini: Disciple of Napoleon?," *Military Affairs* 28, no. 1 (Spring 1964): 17–26. Lloyd never had the chance to answer his critics or modify his final ideas.

11. Henri Antoine, baron de Jomini, *The Art of War*, new ed. with appendices and maps, trans. George Henry Mendell and William Price Craighill (Philadelphia, PA: J. B. Lippincott & Co., 1862; reprint, The West Point Military Library, eds. Thomas E. Greiss and Jay Luvaas (Westport, Connecticut: Greenwood Press, Publishers, 1971); originally published as *Tableau analytique des principes combinaisons de la guerre: et de leurs rapports avec la politique des états pour servir d'introduction au traité des grandes opérations militaires*, 2d ed. (St. Pétersbourg: Chez Bellizard, 1830); idem., *Traité des grandes opérations militaires, contenant l'histoire critique campagnes de Frédéric II comparées à celles de l'empereur Napoléon, avec un recueil des principes généraux de l'art de la guerre*, 2d ed., 8 vols. (Paris: Magimel, 1811–1816).

12. Jomini, "Strategy," chp. 3 of *The Art of War*, 65–162.

13. Elting, "Jomini: Disciple of Napoleon?," 25.

14. For a general overview of the development of American military thought see Russell F. Weigley, *Towards an American Army: Military Thought from Washington to Marshall* (New York: Columbia University Press, 1962). For Jomini's pervasive influence in the early United States Army see Bruno Colson, *La Culture Stratégique Américaine: L'influence de Jomini* (Economica: Paris, 1993); see especially pp. 11–14 for Lloyd's influence on Jomini.

15. Henry Wager Halleck, *Elements of Military Art and Science; or, Course of Instruction in Strategy, Fortification, Tactics of Battles, &c.; Embracing the Duties of Staff, Infantry, Cavalry, Artillery, and Engineers* (New York: D. Appleton & Co.; Philadelphia, PA: G. S. Appleton, 1846). See especially pp. 38–60 for Lloyd's influence.

16. Peter von Wahlde, "A Pioneer of Russian Strategic Thought: G. A. Leer, 1829–1904," *Military Affairs* 35, no. 4 (December 1971): 149–50; Max Jähns, *Das*

XVIII Jahrhundert seit dem Auftreten Friedrichs des Großen, 1740–1800, vol. 3 of
Geschichte der Kriegswissenschaften vornehmlich in Deutschland Munchen und
Leipzig: R. Oldenbourg, 1891; reprint, New York: Johnson Reprint Corporation;
Hildesheirr: Georg Olms, 1965), 2113–14. Leer published selections of Lloyd's military writings in the monthly Journal of the War Ministry. See Genrikh A. Leer,
"Voennoe dlo v XVIII vk: Lloid kak voenniy pisatel. Ego voennie I politicheskie
memuari," *Voennyi Sbornik* no. 10 (1864): 175–234; idem. "Voennoe dlo v XVIII
vk: Lloid, kak strategicheskii pisatel," *Voennyi Sbornik* no. 11 (1865): 3–32.
17. Svechin helped develop Soviet military policy in the 1920s and subsequently
died in the purges of the 1930s. He viewed Lloyd as the progenitor of operational
theory. See Alexandr A. Svechin, "Strategy and Operational Art," in *Operational
Art, 1927–1964,* vol. 1 of *The Evolution of Soviet Operational Art, 1927–1991:
The Documentary Basis,* trans. Harold S. Orenstein, with a forward and introduction by David M. Glantz (London: Frank Cass, 1995), 7. Svechin's larger work
is *Strategy,* edited by Kent Lee, introductory essays by Andrei A. Kokoshin,
Valentin V. Larionev, Vladimir N. Lobov, and Jacob W. Kipp (Minneapolis, MN:
East View Publications, 1991); originally published as *Strategiia* (Moscow: Voennyi
vestnik, 1927).
18. Fuller's synthesis of the principles of war, modeled after Lloyd's theory, remains
their standard statement. Brian Holden Reid, "Colonel J. F. C. Fuller and the
Revival of Classical Military Thinking in Britain, 1918–1926," *Military Affairs* 49,
no. 4 (October 1985): 192.
19. John Frederick Charles Fuller, *The Foundations of the Science of War* (London:
Hutchinson & Co. (Publishers), LTD, 1926), 21; Idem, "Major General Henry
Lloyd: Adventurer and Military Philosopher," *Army Quarterly* 12 (1926): 300–14.
20. Ibid., 82, 147, 154.
21. Ibid., 98. He quotes Lloyd in support of his notion of genius.
22. Carl von Clausewitz, *On War,* edited and translated by Michael Howard and
Peter Paret, with introductory essays by Peter Paret, Michael Howard, and Bernard
Brodie, with a commentary by Bernard Brodie (Princeton, NJ: Princeton University
Press, 1976), 131; originally published as *Vom kriege,* 3 vols. (Berlin: F. Dümmler,
1832–34).
23. Ibid., 136.
24. Ibid., 133–39.
25. In Book 3: "On Strategy in General," pp. 177–224, several chapters discuss elements of strategy and principles of war not unlike Lloyd's historical analysis. In
Book 5: "Military Forces," 279–356, Lloyd's basic operational approach using lines
of communication and terrain is preented in a Clausewitzian, and thereby abstract,
format. For the argument that Clausewitz was an enlightened *philosophe* closely
connected with the eighteenth-century tradition, see Amos Perlmutter, "Carl von
Clausewitz, Enlightenment Philosopher: A Comparative Analysis," *The Journal of
Strategic Studies* 11, no. 1 (March 1988): 7–19. Azar Gat argues the contrary. He
sees in Clausewitz the embodiment of the Counter-Enlightenment that cast aside the
limited military theory of the Enlightenment, which was tied to the Greco-Roman
past, and embraced the changes wrought by the Napoleonic period in warfare and
intellectual life. See Azar Gat, *The Origins of Military Thought from the Enlightenment to Clausewitz,* 139–250.

26. Rudolf von Caemmerer, *The Development of Strategical Science during the Nineteenth Century*, trans. Karl von Donat (London: Hugh Rees, LTD., 1905), 28; originally pulished as *Die Entwickelung der Strategie-Wissenschaft im 19 Jahrhundert* (Berlin: W. Baensch, 1904).

27. Ibid., 1–4, 22–26. Caemmerer argued that Austria's defeats in the 1859 war with France and Italy and 1866 war with Prussia and Italy at their root were caused by the reliance on the traditional methods of Archduke Karl and Marshal Daun.

28. Hans Delbrück, *The Dawn of Modern Warfare*, vol 4 of *History of the Art of War within the Framework of Political History*, trans. Walter J, Renfroe, Jr., Contributions in Military History, no. 9 (Westport, CT: Greenwood Press, 1985), 314; originally published as *Neuzeit*, vol. 4 of *Geschichte der Kriegkunst im Rahmen der Politischen Geschichte* (Berlin: G. Stilke, 1920).

29. Clausewitz viewed iconoclasm and opposition to intellectual authority as the hallmark of his new military theory. Eighteenth-century predecessors, most notably Lloyd and Guibert, had been defenders of the old order and were unable to discard the intellectual straightjacket of conformity. Peter Paret, *Clausewitz and the State* (Oxford: Clarendon Press, 1976), 357.

Selected Bibliography

UNPUBLISHED PRIMARY SOURCES

Arquivo do Conde de Lippe. Arquivo Histórico-Militar. Lisbon, Portugal.

Clinton, Henry S. Papers. The John Rylands University Library of Manchester. Manchester, England.

———. Papers. William L. Clements Library. Ann Arbor, Michigan.

Donoughmore Family. Papers. Trinity College Library. Dublin, Ireland.

Kriegsarchiv. Österreichisches Staatsarchiv. Vienna, Austria.

Lloyd, Henry. Papers. The Fitzwilliam Museum. Cambridge, England.

Newcastle Family. Papers. The Hallward Library. Nottingham, England.

Schaumburg-Lippe Family. Papers. Niedersächsisches Staatsarchiv. Bückeburg, Germany.

United Kingdom. The British Library. London, England.

———. Public Record Office. Kew, England.

PRINTED PRIMARY SOURCES

"Account of the action between the allied Army and that of France, near Tournay, the 11th of May, N.S. 1745, with the names of the general and other Officers, and number of private men, and horses, that were killed, wounded and missing in each Regiment." *The Gentleman's Magazine* 15 (May 1745): 246–53.

Almon, John. *Memoirs of a Late Eminent Bookseller.* London, 1790.

Bell, Robert Fitzroy, ed. *Memorials of John Murray of Broughton Sometime Secretary to Prince Charles Edward, 1740–1747.* Edinburgh: Printed at the University Press by T. and A. Constable for the Scottish History Society, 1898.

Berkenhout, John. Review of *The History of the Late War in Germany*, by Henry Lloyd. *The Monthly Review; or, Literary Journal* 35 (August 1766): 81–87.

Blaikie, Walter Biggar, ed. *Origins of the Forty-Five and Other Papers Relating to that Rising*. 1916. Reprint, Edinburgh: Scottish Academic Press, 1975.

Bülow, Adam Heinrich Dietrich, Freiherr von. *The Spirit of the Modern System of War*. With a Commentary by C. Malorti de Martemont. London: Sold by T. Egerton, 1806. Originally published as *Geist des neuern Kriegssystem*. Hamburg: Benjamin Gottlieb Hofmann, 1799.

Burke, Edmund. *Observations on the Late State of the Nation*. London: J. Dodsley, 1769.

Casati, Carlo, ed. *Lettere e scritti inediti di Pietro e di Alessandro Verri*. 4 vols. Milan: Giuseppe Galli, 1879–81.

Clausewitz, Carl von. *On War*. Edited and Translated by Michael Howard and Peter Paret. With Introductory Essays by Peter Paret, Michael Howard, and Bernard Brodie; with a Commentary by Bernard Brodie. Princeton, NJ: Princeton University Press, 1976. Originally published as *Vom Kriege*. 3 vols. Berlin: F. Dümmler, 1832–34.

"Description of Bergen-Op-Zoom." *The Gentleman's Magazine*. 17 (July 1747): 328–29.

Donne, W. Bodham, ed. *The Correspondence of King George the Third with Lord North from 1768 to 1783*. Edited from the Originals at Windsor with an Introduction and Notes. London: John Murray, 1867.

Drummond, John. "Mr. Drummond's Letter to the Editor." Foreword to *A Political and Military Rhapsody, on the Invasion of Great Britain and Ireland*, by Henry Lloyd. 2d ed. To which is annexed, a Short Account of the Author, and a Supplement by the Editor. London: Sold by Debrett; Sewell; Clark; Mayler, 1792: xi–xvi.

Duff, William. *An Essay on Original Genius and Its Various Modes of Exertion in Philosophy and the Fine Arts, Particularly in Poetry*. London: Printed for Edward and Charles Dilly, 1767. Reprint, Edited with an Introduction by John L. Mahoney. Gainesville, FL: Scholars' Facsimiles & Reprints, 1964.

"End of the Siege of Bergen-op-Zoom." *The Gentleman's Magazine* 17 (September 1747): 50.

English Volunteer. *An authentic journal of the remarkable and bloody siege of Bergen-op-Zoom, by the French, under M. de Lowendahl: begun July 14, and ended Sept. 16, N.S. 1747: when the place was taken by storm, after as brave a defence and desperate an attack, of two months and two days, as ever was known*. London: Printed for the Proprietors; and Sold by R. Griffiths, Publisher, 1747.

"Extract of a letter from a burgomaster of Bergen-op-zoom, Jan. 31." *The Gentleman's Magazine* 17 (July 1747): 346.

"Farther relation of the battle of Fontenoy, dated Paris, May 24." *The Gentleman's Magazine* 15 (June 1745): 313–17.

Feuquières, Antoine Manassès de Pas, marquis de. *Memoirs Historical and Military*. 2 vols. London: Printed for T. Woodward and C. Davis, 1735–6. Reprint, Westport, CT: Greenwood Press, 1968. Originally published as *Memoires sur la guerre: ou, l'on a rassemblé les maximes les plus necessaires dans les operations de l'art militaire*. Amsterdam: François Changuion, 1731.

Forbes, Robert. *The Lyon in Mourning, or a Collection of Speeches, Letters, Journals, etc. Relative to the Affairs of Prince Charles Edward Stuart.* 3 vols. Edited from his Manuscript, with a Preface by Henry Paton. Edinburgh: Printed at the University Press by T. and A. Constable for the Scottish History Society, 1895. Reprint, Edinburgh: Scottish Academic Press, 1975.

Fortescue, John, ed. *The Correspondence of King George III from 1768 to 1783.* 6 vols. Printed from the original papers in the royal archives at Windsor Castle. London: Frank Cass, 1927–28.

Frederick II. *Posthumous Works of Frederic II, King of Prussia.* 13 vols. Translated from the French by Thomas Holcroft. London: Printed for G. G. J. and J. Robinson, 1789.

Frisi, Paolo. "Estratto del Libro Intitolato *An Essay on the Theory of Money.*" Appendix to *Meditazioni sulla Economia Politica,* by Pietro Verri, 237–53. 6th ed. Livorno: Nell Stamperia dell'Enciclopedia, 1772.

Gay de Vernon, Simon François, baron. *Treatise on the Science of War and Fortification: Composed for the Use of the Imperial Polytechnik School, and Military Schools.* 2 vols. Translated for the War Department, for the Use of the Military Academy of the United States to which is added a Summary of the Principles and Maxims of Grand Tactics and Operations by John Michael O'Connor. New York: Printed by J. Seymour, 1817. Originally published as *Traité élémentaire d'art militaire et de fortification, à l'usage des élèves de l'École polytechnique, et des élèves des écoles militaire.* 2 vols. Paris: Allais, 1805.

Gerard, Alexander. *An Essay on Genius.* London: Printed for W. Strahan, T. Cadell, and W. Creech, 1774. Reprint, Edited by Bernhard Fabian. Munich: Wilhelm Fink, 1966.

Greppi, Emanuele, and Alessandro Giulini, eds. *Carteggio di Pietro e di Alessandro Verri dal 1766 al 1797.* 12 vols. Milan: Casa Editrice L. F. Cogliati, 1910–44.

Grobert, Jacques François Louis. *Observations sur les mémoire du général Lloyd concernant l'invasion et la defense la Grande-Bretagne, par le chef de brigade Grobert, s.inspecteur aux révues et à l'administration des troupes.* Paris: Pougens et Magimel, an XI [1803].

Guibert, Jacques Antoine Hippolyte, comte de. *Défense du système de guerre moderne, ou, Réfutation complette du système de M. de M.-D.* 2 vols. Neuchatel: [s.n.], 1779.

———. *A General Essay on Tactics.* 2 vols. London, 1781. Originally published as *Essai général tactique, précéde d'un discours sur l'état de la politique & de la science militaire in Europe.* New Edition Revised. London: Libraires Associés, 1773.

Halweg, Werner, ed. *Schriften-Aufsätze-Studien-Briefe: Dokumente aus dem Clausewitz- Scharnhorst- und Gneisenau-Nachlaß sowie aus öffentlichen und privaten Sammlungen.* 2 vols. Göttingen: Vandenhoeck & Ruprecht, 1990.

Hanger, George. *Anticipation of the Freedom of Brabant, with the Expulsion of the Austrian Troops from that Country; with some Remarks on the Future Extension of the French Frontier to the Rhine: Investigated according to the Principles laid down in the Works of General Lloyd. Together with some Military Observations on the Late intended March of the Duke of Brunswick to Paris.* London: Printed for J. Debrett, 1792.

Helvetius, Claude Adrien. De l'Esprit *or Essays on the Mind and Its Several Faculties.* New Ed. Translated from the French. 1810. Reprint, New York: Burt Franklin, 1970. Originally published as *De l'Esprit.* Paris: Durand, 1758.

"Historical Chronicle." *The Gentleman's Magazine.* 53 Part II, no. 3 (September, 1783): 803.

Historical Manuscripts Commission. 12th Report. *Manuscripts of His Grace the Duke of Rutland, K.G., Preserved at Belvoir Castle.* 4 vols. London: Eyre and Spottiswoode, 1888–1905.

"History of Europe, Chapter I." *The Annual Register, or a View of the History, Politics, and Literature, for the Year 1774.* London: Printed for J. Dodsley, 1775: 1–11.

"History of Europe, Chapter II." *The Annual Register, or a View of the History, Politics, and Literature, for the Year 1773.* London: Printed for J. Dodsley, 1774: 11–23.

Hume, David. *Philosophical essays concerning human understanding.* London: Printed for A. Millar, 1748.

———. *Four Dissertations.* London: Printed for A. Millar, 1757.

———. *Essays Moral, Political, and Literary.* 2 vols. Edited by T. H. Green and T. H. Grose. New York: Longmans, Green, and Co., 1912.

Jardine, Alexander. "Of the Philosophy of War." [Review of Henry Lloyd's *Continuation of the History of the Late War in Germany, Between the King of Prussia, and the Empress of Germany and Her Allies.*] *The Monthly Review; or, Literary Journal* 66 (April 1782): 275–85.

Johnstone, James Johnstone, chevalier de. *A Memoir of the Forty-Five.* Edited with an Introduction by Brian Rawson. London: Folio Society, 1958. Originally published as *Memoirs of the rebellion of 1745 and 1746.* London: Printed for Longman, Hurst, Rees, Orme, and Browne, 1820.

Jomini, Henri. *Traité des grandes opérations militaires, contenant l'histoire critique campagnes de Frédéric II comparées à celles de l'empereur Napoléon, avec un recueil des principes généraux de l'art de la guerre.* 2d ed. 8 vols. Paris: Magimel, 1811–16.

———. *The Art of War.* A New Edition, with Appendices and Maps. Translated from the French by George Henry Mendell and William Price Craighill. Philadelphia, PA: J. B. Lippincott & Co., 1862. Reprint, The West Point Military Library, eds. Thomas E. Greiss and Jay Luvaas. Westport, CT: Greenwood Press, Publishers, 1971. Originally published as *Tableau analytique des principes combinaisons de la guerre: et de leurs rapports avec la politique des états pour servir d'introduction au traité des grandes opérations militaires.* 2d ed. St. Pétersbourg: Chez Bellizard, 1830.

Knox, William. *The Present State of the Nation; Particularly with Respect to its Trade, Finances, &c &c, addressed to the King and both Houses of Parliament.* London: Printed for J. Almon, 1768.

"Letter from an Officer in Bergen-op-Zoom, when it was taken." *The Gentleman's Magazine* 17 (September 1747): 410.

Lewis, Wilmarth Sheldon, ed. *The Yale Edition of Horace Walpole's Correspondence.* 48 vols. New Haven, CT: Yale University Press; London: Oxford University Press, 1937–83.

Lindsay, Colin. *Extracts from Colonel Tempelhoffe's* History of the Seven Years' War; *His Remarks on General Lloyd; On the Subsistence of Armies; and on the March of Convoys.* 2 vols. London: Printed for T. Cadell, 1793.

Lloyd, Ernest M., ed. "Two Despatches Relative to the Battle of Fontenoy." *The English Historical Review* 12, no. 312 (April 1897): 523–30.

Lloyd, Henry. *Lists of the Forces of the Sovereigns of Europe &c. viz. Ranks, Uniforms, Numbers of Officers, Private Men &c. of each Nation.* Methodized by J. Millan & Engraved by the best hands. London: Printed for J. Millan, 1761.

———. "Reflections on the general principles of war; and on the composition and characters of the different armies in Europe." *The Annual Register, or a View of the History, Politics, and Literature, For the Year 1766.* 7th ed. London: C. Baldwin, 1816: 169–77.

———. *The History of the Late War in Germany; Between the King of Prussia, and the Empress of Germany and Her Allies.* London: Printed for the Author; and Sold by R. Horsfield; L. Hawes and Co.; J. Dodsley; J. Walter; T. Davies; W. Shropshire; and E. Easton, 1766.

———. *An Essay on the English Constitution.* London: Published for the Author, and Sold by J. Almon, 1770.

———. *An essay on the theory of money.* London: J. Almon, 1771.

———. *A rhapsody on the present system of French politics; on the projected invasion and the means to defeat it, by a Chelsea pensioner.* Illustrated with a Chart of the Opposite Coasts of England and France. London: W. Faden and T. Jeffreys, 1779.

———. *Continuation of the History of the Late War in Germany; Between the King of Prussia, and the Empress of Germany and Her Allies.* Part II. London: Printed for the Author, and Sold by S. Hooper, 1781.

———. "New Plan to conquer America." *Public Advertiser,* no.14583, Saturday, 7 July, 1781.

———. *The History of the Late War in Germany; Between the King of Prussia, and the Empress of Germany and Her Allies: Containing the Campaigns of 1758, and 1759, with a correct Military Map of the Seat of War; and Plans of the Siege of Olmütz, and the Battles of Zornsdorf, Hochkirchen, Paltzig, Cunnersdorf, or Frankfurt, and Maxen.* vol. 2. Published from the General's Manuscripts, under the Inspection of an English Officer, and Illustrated with Notes Critical, Historical, and Explanatory. London: Printed for T. and J. Egerton, 1790.

Locke, John. *An Essay Concerning Human Understanding.* Edited with an Introduction, Critical Apparatus and Glossary by Peter H. Nidditch. Oxford: At the Clarendon Press, 1975. Originally published as *An essay concerning human understanding.* 4th ed. London: A. and J. Churchil, and S. Manship, 1700).

Lockhart, George, ed. *The Lockhart Papers: Containing Memoirs and Contemporaries upon the Affairs of Scotland from 1702 to 1715, by George Lockhart, Esq. Of Carnwath, His Secret Correspondence with the Son of King James the Second from 1718 to 1728, And his other political Writings; Also, Journals and Memoirs of the young Pretender's Expedition of 1745, by Highland Officers in his Army.* 2 vols. Published from the Original Manuscripts in the Possession of Anthony Aufrere, Esq. London: Printed by Richard and Arthur Taylor for William Anderson, 1817.

Lowendal, Ulric Fréderic Waldemar, comte de. "Letter from Count Lowendahl to Marshal Saxe. From the camp under Bergen-op-zoom, Sept. 17." *The Gentleman's Magazine* 17 (September 1747): 438–39.

Luvaas, Jay, ed. and trans. *Frederick the Great on the Art of War*. New York: The Free Press; London: Collier-Macmillan Limited, 1966.

Mina, Jaime Miguel de Guzmán, marqués de la. *Máximas para la guerra, sacadas de las obras del excelentisimo Sr. marqués de la Mina con un epitome de su vida*. Vich: Pedro Mosera, 1767.

Montecuccoli, Raimondo. *Le opere di Raimondo Montecuccoli*. 2 vols. Edited by Raimondo Luraghi. Rome: Stato maggiore dell'Esercito, Ufficio storico, 1988.

Montesquieu, Charles Louis de Secondat, baron de La Brède et de. *The Spirit of the Laws*. Translated and Edited by Anne M. Cohler, Basia Carolyn Miller, and Harold Samuel Stone. Cambridge Texts in the History of Political Thought, eds. Raymond Guess, Quentin Skinner, and Richard Tuck. Cambridge, MA: Cambridge University Press, 1989. Originally Published as *L'Esprit des lois*. 2 vols. Genève: Barillot et fils, 1748.

Murray, John, ed. *The Autobiographies of Edward Gibbon*. 2d ed. With an Introduction by John Holroyd, Earl of Sheffield. London: John Murray, 1897.

Napoleon I. *Correspondance de Napoléon Ier*. 32 vols. Paris: Henri Plon, 1858–70.

———. *Notes inédites de l'Empereur Napoléon Ier sur les Mémoires Militaires du Général Lloyd*. Edited by Ariste Ducaunnès-Duval. Extrait du Tome XXXV des "Archives Historiques de la Gironde." Bordeaux: G. Gounouilhou, 1901.

Ochwadt, Curd, ed. *Graf zu Schaumburg-Lippe: Schriften und Briefe*. 3 vols. Frankfurt am Main: Vittorio Klostermann, 1976–83.

Officer who served in the British Force. *The operations of the allied army, under the command of His Serene Highness Prince Ferdinand, Duke of Brunswick and Luneberg, during the greatest part of six campaigns, beginning in the year 1757, and ending in the year 1762*. London: Printed for T. Jeffreys, geographer to the King, 1764.

"Progress of the Siege of Bergen-Op-Zoom." *The Gentleman's Magazine* 17 (August 1747): 401–2.

Puységur, Jacques-François Maximo de Chastenet, marquis de. *Art de la guerre par principes et par règles*. 2 vols. Paris: Claude-Antoine Jombert, 1748.

Rees, Abraham. Review of *An Essay on the Theory of Money*, by Henry Lloyd. *The Monthly Review; or, Literary Journal* 46 (January 1772): 75–76.

Remarks on the military operations of the English and French armies, commanded by His Royal Highness the Duke of Cumberland, and Marshal Saxe, during the campaign of 1747; to which are added, I. Military Principles and Maxims drawn from the remarks; II. The Siege of Bergen-op-Zoom. London: Printed for T. Becket, 1760.

Review of *A Political and Military Rhapsody on the Invasion and Defense of Great Britain and Ireland*, by Henry Lloyd. *The Monthly Review; or, Literary Journal* 5, 2d ser. (August 1791): 459–61.

Review of *A Political and Military Rhapsody on the Invasion and Defence of Great Britain and Ireland*, 2d ed., by Henry Lloyd. *The Monthly Review; or, Literary Journal* 9, 2d ser. (October 1792): 209.

Romance de Mesmon, Germain Hyacinthe, marquis de. "Précis sur la Vie et le Caractère de Henri Lloyd." Foreward to *Mémoires militaires et politiques du Général Lloyd, servant d'introduction à l'histoire de la guerre en Allemagne en 1756, entre le Roi de Prusse et l'Imperatrice reine avec ses alliés,* by Henri Lloyd. Traduits et augmentés de notes et d'un précis sur la vie et le caractère de ce Général. Par un Officier Français. Paris: Magimel, An IX [1801]: vii–xliv.

Rousseau, Jean-Jacques. *Discours sur l'origine et les fondemens de l'inégalité parmi les hommes.* Amsterdam: Marc Michel Rey, 1755.

Santa Cruz de Marcenado, Alvaro Navia Osorio, marqués de. *Reflexiones Militares.* Madrid: Imprenta de Enrique Rubiños, 1893. Reprint, Oviedo: Principado de Asturias, Instituto de Estudios Asturianes, 1984.

Saxe, Hermann Maurice, comte de. *Reveries on the Art of War.* Translated and Edited by Thomas R. Phillips. Harrisburg, Pennsylvania: The Military Service Publishing Company, 1944. Originally published as *Mes rêveries; ou Mémoires sur l'art de la guerre.* La Haye: Pierre Gosse, 1756.

————. *Lettres et mémoires choisis parmi les papiers originaux du maréchal de Saxe.* 4 vols. Paris: J. J. Smits et Compagnie, 1794.

Sbornik imperatorskogo russkogo istoricheskogo obshchestva. 148 vols. St. Petersburg: Imperatorskoe Russkoe Istoricheskoe Obshchestvo, 1867–1914.

Scharnhorst, Gerhard Johann David. *Die Militair-Bibliothek.* 4 vols. Hanover: Gebrüdern Helwing, 1782–84.

Sedgwick, Romney, ed. *Letters from George III to Lord Bute, 1756–1766.* London: Macmillan and Co. LTD., 1939.

"Select Relations concerning the loss of Bergen-Op-Zoom." *The Gentleman's Magazine* 17 (September 1747): 409–12.

"Series of Proofs that Bergen-op-Zoom was Surprised." *The Gentleman's Magazine* 17 (September 1747): 412.

Smyth, Gillespie, ed. *Memoirs and Correspondence (Official and Familiar) of Sir Robert Murray Keith, K.B., Envoy Extraordinary and Minister Plenipotentiary at the Courts of Dresden, Copenhagen, and Vienna, from 1769 to 1792; with a Memoir of Queen Carolina Matilda of Denmark, and an Account of the Revolution there in 1772.* 2 vols. London: Henry Colburn, Publisher, 1849.

"Some of the Severe Orders from the French Army before Bergen-op-Zoom." *The Gentleman's Magazine* 17 (August 1747): 378.

Sprigge, Timothy L. S., and Alexander Taylor Milne, eds. *The Correspondence of Jeremy Bentham.* 10 vols. London: The Athlone Press, 1968–94.

Syrett, Harold C., ed. *The Papers of Alexander Hamilton.* 20 vols. New York: Columbia University Press, 1961–74.

Taylor, Robert J., ed. *The Papers of John Adams.* 10 vols. Cambridge, Massachusetts and London, England: The Belknap Press of Harvard University Press, 1977–96.

Tempelhof, Georg Friedrich von. *Geschichte des Siebenjährigen Krieges in Deutschland zwischen dem Könige von Preussen und der Kaiserin Königen mit ihren Alliirten, vom General Lloyd.* 6 vols. Aus dem Englischen neue übersetzt mit verbesserten Planen und Anmerkungen. Berlin: J. F. Unger, 1783–1801.

Thucydides. *The Peloponnesian War.* 4 vols. Translated by Charles Forster Smith. Loeb Classical Library, ed. George P. Goold, nos. 108–10, 169. 1919–23.

Reprint, Cambridge, Massachusetts: Harvard University Press; London: William Heinemann LTD, 1975–80.

Thümmler, Lars-Holger, ed. *Die Österreichische Armee im Siebenjährigen Krieg: Die Bautzener Bilderhandschrift aus dem Jahre 1762.* Berlin: Brandenburgisches Verlagshaus, 1993.

Tielke, Johann Gottlieb. *An Account of Some of the Most Remarkable Events of the War between the Prussians, Austrians, and Russians, from 1756 to 1763: and a Treatise on several Branches of the Military Art, with Plans and Maps.* 2 vols. Translated by Charles and Robert Crauford. London: Printed for the Translators; and Sold by J. Walter, 1787–8. Originally published as *Beyträge zur Kriegs-Kunst und Geschichte des krieges von 1756 bis 1763: mit Plans und Charten.* 6 vols. Freyberg: Gedrunckt mit Barthelischen Schriften, 1775–86.

Townshend, George Townshend, marquis of. *A Brief Narrative of the Late Campaign in Germany and Flanders, in a Letter to a Member of Parliament.* London: Printed for J. Lion, 1751.

Vauban, Sébastien le Prestre, marquis de. *The new method of fortification as practised by Monsieur de Vauban, Engineer-General of France: with an explanation of all terms appertaining to the art.* Translated by A. Swall. London: Printed for Abel Swall, 1691.

———. *De l'attaque et de la defense des places.* 2 vols. La Haye: Pierre de Hondt, 1737–42.

———. *A manual of siegecraft and fortification.* Translated by George A. Rothrock. Ann Arbor: University of Michigan Press, 1968.

Verri, Pietro. *Reflections on Political Economy.* Translated from the Italian by Barbara McGilvray in Collaboration with Peter D. Groenewegen. Fairfield, N.J.: A. M. Kelley, 1993. Originally published as *Meditazioni sull economia politica.* Venizia, 1771.

Volz, Gustav Berthold, ed. *Politische Correspondenz Friedrichs des Grossen.* 46 Volumes. Berlin: Alexander Duncker Verlag, 1879–1939.

SECONDARY SOURCES

Aksan, Virginia. "The One-Eyed Fighting the Blind: Mobilization, Supply, and Command in the Russo-Turkish War of 1768–1774." *The International History Review* XV, no. 2 (May 1993): 221–38.

Alger, John I. *The Quest for Victory: The History of the Principles of War.* Contributions in Military History, no. 30. Foreword by Frederick J. Kroesen. Westport, CT: Greenwood Press, 1982.

Allmayer-Beck, Joseph Christoph. "The Establishment of the Theresan Military Academy in Wiener Neustadt." In *East Central European Society and War in the Pre-Revolutionary Eighteenth Century,* eds. Gunther E. Rothenburg, Béla K. Király and Peter F. Sugar, 115–21. War and Society in East Central Europe, vol. 2. East European Monographs, no. 122. Boulder, CO: Social Science Monographs, 1982.

Anderson, Matthew Smith. "Great Britain and the Russian Fleet, 1769–70." *The Slavonic and East European Review* XXXI, no. 76 (December 1952): 148–63.

———. "Great Britain and the Russo-Turkish War of 1768–74." *The English Historical Review* 69, no. 270 (January 1954): 39–58.

————. "Samuel Bentham in Russia, 1779–1791." *The American Slavic and East European Review* XV, no. 2 (April 1956): 157–72.

————. "British Officers in the Russian Army in the Eighteenth and Early Nineteenth Centuries." *Journal of the Society for Army Historical Research.* 38, no. 156 (December 1960): 168–73.

————. *War and Society in Europe of the Old Regime, 1618–1789.* New York: St. Martin's Press, 1988.

————. *The War of the Austrian Succession, 1740–1748.* London: Longman, 1995.

Balisch, Alexander. "Infantry Battlefield Tactics in the Seventeenth and Eighteenth Centuries on the European and Turkish Theatres of War: The Austrian Response to Different Conditions." *Warfare and Tactics in the Eighteenth Century: Some Recent Research.* Edited by Karl Schweizer. Special Issue of *Etudes d'Histoire et de Politique* 3 (1983–84): 43–60.

Banaschick-Ehl, Christa. *Scharnhorsts Lehrer, Graf Wilhelm von Schaumburg-Lippe, in Portugal: die Heeresreform, 1761–1777.* Studien zur Militärgeschichte, Militärwissenschaft und Konfliktsforschung, ed. Werner Halweg, Band 3. Osnabrück: Biblio Verlag, 1974.

Bangert, William V. *A History of the Society of Jesus.* St. Louis: The Institute of Jesuit Sources, 1972.

Barker, Thomas M. *The Military Intellectual and Battle: Raimondo Montecuccoli and the Thirty Years' War.* Albany, NY: State University of New York Press, 1975.

————. *Army, Aristocracy, Monarchy: Essays on War, Society, and Government in Austria, 1618–1780.* War and Society in East Central Europe, vol. 7. Boulder, CO: Social Science Monographs, 1982.

Barton, H. Arnold. "Russia and the Problem of Sweden-Finland, 1721–1809." *East European Quarterly* V, no. 4 (January 1972): 431–55.

Baugh, Daniel A. "Great Britain's 'Blue-Water' Policy, 1689–1815," *The International History Review* X, no.1 (February 1988): 33–58.

Baumer, Franklin L. "Intellectual History and its Problems." *The Journal of Modern History* 21, no. 3 (September 1949): 191–203.

Bécker, Jerónimo. "La Embajada del Marqués de la Mina, 1736–1740." *Boletin de la Real Academia de la Historia* 83, no. 6 (December 1923): 364–78; 84, no. 2 (February 1924): 184–96; no. 4 (April 1924): 393–402; 85, no. 1 (July 1924): 5–14; 86, no. 1 (January–March 1925): 42–115.

Bérenger, Jean. "Le Marechal de Belle-Isle, General et Homme d'Etat a l'Epoque des Lumieres (1684–1761)." In *Soldier-Statesmen of the Age of the Enlightenment: Records of the 7th International Colloquy on Military History, Washington, D.C., 25–30 July 1982,* edited by Abigail T. Siddall, 181–210. Manhattan, KS: Sunflower University Press, 1984.

Beretti, Francis. *Pascal Paoli et l'image de la Corse au dix-huitième siècle le témoignage des voyageurs britanniques.* Studies on Voltaire and the Eighteenth Century, no. 253. Oxford: The Voltaire Foundation at the Taylor Institution, 1988.

Bien, David D. "Military Education in Eighteenth Century France: Technical and Non-Technical Determinants." In *Science, Technology and Warfare: Proceedings of the Third Military History Symposium, United States Air Force Academy, 8–9 May 1969,* edited by Monte D. Wright and Lawrence J. Paszik,

51–59. Washington: Office of Air Force History, United States Air Force Academy, 1971.

———. "The Army and the French Enlightenment: Reform, Reaction and Revolution." *Past & Present: A Journal of Historical Studies* no. 85 (August 1979): 68–98.

Biographie Universelle (Michaud) Ancienne et Moderne. 45 vols. New ed. Paris: Chez Madame C. Desplaces; Leipzig: Librairie de F. A. Brockhaus, 1854–65.

Black, Jeremy. "Eighteenth-Century Warfare Reconsidered." *War in History* 1, no. 2 (July 1994): 215–32.

———. *European Warfare: 1660–1815.* New Haven, CT: Yale University Press, 1994.

———. *Culloden and the '45.* London: Grange Books, 1997.

———. *War and the World: Military Power and the Fate of Continents, 1450–2000.* New Haven, CT: Yale University Press, 1993.

Bois, Jean-Pierre. *Fontenoy, 1745: Louis XV, arbitre de l'Europe.* Paris: Economica, 1996.

Bromsley, John S. "Britain and Europe in the Eighteenth Century." *History: The Journal of the Historical Association.* 66 (1981): 394–412.

Browning, Reed. *The War of the Austrian Succession.* New York: St. Martin's Press, 1993.

Büsch, Otto. *Military System and Social Life in Old Regime Prussia, 1713–1807: The Beginnings of the Social Militarization of Prusso-German Society.* Translated by John G. Gagliardo. Atlantic Highlands, NJ: Humanities Press, 1997. Originally published as *Militärsystem und Socialleben im alter Preussen, 1713–1807: die Anfänge der Socialen Militarisierung der preussisch-deutschen Gesellschaft.* Berlin: De Guyter, 1962.

Cadell, Robert. *Sir John Cope and the Rebellion of 1745.* Edinburgh and London: William Blackwood and Sons, 1898.

Caemmerer, Rudolf von. *The Development of Strategical Science during the Nineteenth Century.* Translated by Karl von Donat. London: Hugh Rees, LTD., 1905. Originally published as *Die Entwickelung der Strategie-Wissenschaft im 19 Jahrhundert.* Berlin: W. Baensch, 1904.

Carter, Alice C. "The Dutch Barrier Fortresses in the Eighteenth Century, as shewn in the de Ferraris map." In *La Cartographie au XVIIIe Siecle et l'Œuvre du Comte de Ferraris (1721–1814).* International Colloquium, Spa, 8–11 September 1976, 259–71. Brussels: Crédit communal de Belgique, 1978.

Cassirer, Ernst. *The Philosophy of the Enlightenment.* Translated by Fritz C. A. Koelln and James P. Pettegrove. Princeton, NJ: Princeton University Press, 1951. Originally published as *Die Philosophie der Aufklärung.* Tübingen: Mohr, 1932.

Chagniot, Jean. *Le Chevalier de Folard: la Stratégie de l'incertitude.* Manaco: Éd. de Rocher, 1997.

Chandler, David G. *The Campaigns of Napoleon.* New York: The Macmillan Company, 1966.

———. *The Art of Warfare in the Age of Marlborough.* London: Batsford LTD., 1976. Reprint, New York: Sarpedon, 1994.

Colin, Jean. *The Military Education of Napoleon.* Translated by Richard U. Nicholas. [n.p., n.d.]. Originally published as *L'education militaire de Napoleon.* Paris: R. Chapelot et ce, 1901.

————. *L'Infanterie au XVIIIe siècle: La Tactique*. Paris: Berger-Levrault & Co., 1907.

————. *The Transformations of War*. Translated by L. H. R. Pope-Hennessy. London: H. Rees, 1912. Reprint, Westport, CT: Greenwood Press, Publishers, 1977. Originally published as *Les transformations de la guerre*. Paris: E. Flammarion, 1911.

Colson, Bruno. *La Culture Stratégique Américaine: L'Influence de Jomini*. Paris: Economica, 1993.

Conn, Stetson. *Gibraltar in British Diplomacy in the Eighteenth Century*. New Haven, CT: Yale University Press; London: Humphrey Milford, Oxford University Press, 1942.

Corrasco-Labadia, Miguel. *El Marqués de Santa Cruz de Marcenado; noticias historicas de su vida, sus excritas y le celebración en 1884*. 2d ed. Madrid: Impr. y litografia de Depósito de la Guerra, 1889.

Corvisiér, André. *Armies and Societies in Europe, 1494–1789*. Translated by Abagail T. Siddall. Bloomington, IN: Indiana University Press, 1979. Originally published as *Armées et sociétés en Europe de 1494 à 1789*. Paris: Presses Universitaires de France, 1976.

Craig, Gordon A. *The Politics of the Prussian Army, 1640–1945*. New York: Oxford University Press, 1956.

Creveld, Martin van. *Technology and War from 2000 B.C. to the Present*. New York: The Free Press, A Division of Macmillan, Inc.; London: Collier Macmillan Publishers, 1989.

Cust, Edward. *Annals of the Wars of the Eighteenth Century, Compiled from the most Authentic Histories of the Period*. 3d ed. 5 vols. London: John Murray, 1862–69.

Dawson, Doyne. "The Origins of War: Biological and Anthropological Theories." *History and Theory: Studies in the Philosophy of History* 35, no. 1 (February 1996): 1–28.

Delbrück, Hans. *History of the Art of War within the Framework of Political History*. 4 vols. Translated from the German by Walter J. Renfroe, Jr. Contributions in Military History, no. 9. Westport, CT: Greenwood Press, 1975–85. Originally published as *Geschichte der Kriegkunst im Rahmen der Politischen Geschichte*. 4 vols. Berlin: G. Stilke, 1900–20.

Dietrich, Steve E. "The Professional Reading of George S. Patton, Jr." *The Journal of Military History* 53, no. 4 (October 1989): 387–418.

Duffy, Christopher. *The Army of Maria Theresa: The Armed Forces of Imperial Austria, 1740–1780*. New York: Hippocrene Books, 1977.

————. *Russia's Military Way to the West: Origins and Nature of Russian Military Power*. London: Routledge & Kegan Paul, 1981.

————. "The Seven Years' War as a Limited War." In *East Central European Society and War in the Pre-Revolutionary Eighteenth Century*, eds. Gunther E. Rothenburg, Béla K. Király and Peter F. Sugar, 67–74. War and Society in East Central Europe, vol. 2. East European Monographs, no. 122. Boulder, CO: Social Science Monographs, 1982.

————. *The Fortress in the Age of Vauban and Frederick the Great, 1660–1789: Siege Warfare Volume II*. London: Routledge & Kegan Paul, 1984.

————. *The Army of Frederick the Great*. 2d ed. Chicago, IL: Emperor's Press, 1996.

————. *The Military Experience in the Age of Reason.* New York: Atheneum, 1988.

————. *Instrument of War.* Volume 1 of *The Austrian Army in the Seven Years' War.* With the Support of the Austrian Army Museum (Heeresgeschichtliches Museum), Vienna. Rosemont, IL: The Emperor's Press, 2000.

Elting, John R. "Jomini: Disciple of Napoleon?" *Military Affairs* 28, no. 1 (Spring 1964): 17–26.

Erickson, Arvel B. "Abolition of Purchase in the British Army." *Military Affairs* 23, no. 2 (Summer 1959): 65–76.

Fabel, Robin F. A. "Born of War, Killed by War: The Company of Military Adventurers in West Florida." In *Adapting to Conditions: War and Society in the Eighteenth Century,* edited by Maarten Ultee, 104–16. Tuscaloosa, AL: The University of Alabama Press, 1986.

Fitzmaurice, Edmond. *Charles William Ferdinand, Duke of Brunswick: An Historical Study.* London, New York, and Bombay: Longmans, Green, & Co., 1901.

Fortescue, John W. *A History of the British Army.* 2d ed. 13 vols. London: Macmillan and Co., Limited, 1910–30.

Fuller, John Frederick Charles. *The Foundations of the Science of War.* London: Hutchinson & Co. (Publishers), LTD, 1926.

————. "Major General Henry Lloyd: Adventurer and Military Philosopher." *Army Quarterly* 12 (1926): 300–14.

Fuller, William C., Jr., *Strategy and Power in Russia, 1600–1914.* New York: The Free Press, A Division of Macmillan, Inc.; Toronto: Maxwell Macmillan Canada; New York: Maxwell Macmillan International, 1992.

Gat, Azar. *The Origins of Military Thought from the Enlightenment to Clausewitz.* Oxford: Clarendon Press, 1989.

Gay, Peter. *The Enlightenment: An Interpretation.* 2 vols. New York: Alfred A. Knopf, 1966–69.

Gilbert, Arthur N. "Military Recruitment and Career Advancement in the Eighteenth Century: Two Case Studies." *Journal of the Society for Army Historical Research* 57, no. 229 (Spring 1979): 34–44.

Goyder, Arnold G. "David Morgan and the Welsh Jacobites." *The Stewarts* 10 (1955–58): 286–93.

————. "Welsh Jacobite Societies." *The Stewarts* 11 (1960): 16–21.

Gregg, Edward. "Monarchs without a Crown." In *Royal and Republican Sovereignty in Early Modern Europe: Essays in Memory of Ragnhild Hatton.* Edited by Robert Oresko, G. C. Gibbs and H. M. Scott, 382–422. Cambridge, MA: Cambridge University Press, 1997.

Groenewegen, Peter. "Pietro Verri's Mature Political Economy of the *Meditazioni*: A Case Study in the Highly Developed International Transmission Mechanism of Ideas in Pre-Revolutionary Europe." In *Political Economy and National Realities: Papers presented at the Conference held at the Luigi Einauldi Foundation (Palazzo d'Azeglio, Turin, September 10–12, 1992),* edited by Manuela Albertone and Alberto Masoero, 107–25. Torino: Fondazione Luigi Einauldi, 1994.

Gruber, Ira D. "British Strategy: The Theory and Practice of Eighteenth-Century Warfare." *Reconsiderations on the Revolutionary War: Selected Essays,* edited by Don Higginbotham, 14–31. Contributions in Military History, no. 14. Westport, CT: Greenwood Press, 1978.

———. "The Education of Sir Henry Clinton." *Bulletin of the John Rylands University Library of Manchester.* 72, no. 1 (Spring 1990): 131–53.

Guerlac, Henry. "Science and War in the Old Regime: The Development of Science in an Armed Society." Ph.D. diss., Harvard University, 1941.

———. "Vauban: The Impact of Science on War." Chapter 4 in *Makers of Modern Strategy from Machiavelli to the Nuclear Age,* edited by Peter Paret with the collaboration of Gordon A. Craig and Felix Gilbert, 64–90. Princeton, NJ: Princeton University Press, 1986.

Hall, Thad E. *France and the Eighteenth Century Corsican Question.* New York: New York University Press, 1971.

Hargreaves-Mawdsley, William N. *A History of Academical Dress in Europe until the End of the Eighteenth Century.* Oxford: At the Clarendon Press, 1963.

———. *Eighteenth-Century Spain, 1700–1788.* Totowa, NJ: Rowman and Littlefield, 1979.

Hazard, Paul. *European Thought in the Eighteenth Century: From Montesquieu to Lessing.* New Haven, CT: Yale University Press, 1954. Originally published as *La pensée europeene au 18e siècle de Montesquieu à Lessing.* Paris: Boivin & Cie, 1946.

Hegeland, Hugo. *The Quantity Theory of Money: A Critical Study of Its Historical Development and Interpretation and a Restatement.* Göteborg: Elanders Boktryckeri Aktiebolag, 1951.

Herrmann, Otto. *Über die Quellen Geschichte des siebenjährigen Krieges von Tempelhoff: Inaugural-Dissertation zur erlangung der Doctorwürde von der philosophischen Facultät der Friedrich-Wilhelms-Universität zu Berlin genehmigt nebst den beigefügten Thesen öffentlich zu vertheidigen am 6 November 1885.* Berlin: Buchdruckerei von Gustav Schade (Otto Francke), 1885.

Higginbotham, Don. *The War of American Independence: Military Attitudes, Policies, and Practice, 1763–1789.* The Macmillan Wars of the United States, ed. Louis Morton. New York: The Macmillan Company; London: Collier-Macmillan LTD., 1971.

Higonett, Patrice Louis-René. "The Origins of the Seven Years' War." *The Journal of Modern History* 40, no. 1 (March 1968): 57–90.

Horn, David Bayne. *Great Britain and Europe in the Eighteenth Century.* Oxford: Clarendon Press, 1967.

Howard, Michael. "Jomini and the Classical Tradition in Military Thought." In *The Theory and Practice of War: Essays Presented to Captain B.H. Liddell Hart,* edited by Michael Howard, 3–20. London: Cassell & Company LTD, 1965.

———. *War in European History.* Oxford and New York: Oxford University Press, 1976.

Hughes, Basil Perronet. *Firepower: Weapons effectiveness on the battlefield, 1630–1850.* New York: Charles Scribners Sons, 1974. Reprint, New York: Sarpedon, 1997.

Hutchison, Terence. *Before Adam Smith: The Emergence of Political Economy, 1662–1776.* Oxford: Basil Blackwell, 1988.

Hyatt, Albert M. J. "The Origins of Napoleonic Warfare: A Survey of Interpretations." *Military Affairs* 30, no. 4 (Winter 1966–67): 177–85.

Hytier, Adrienne D. "Les Philosophes et le problème de la guerre". In *Studies on Voltaire and the Eighteenth Century,* ed. Theodore Bestermann, vol. 127, 243–58. Banbury; Oxfordshire: The Voltaire Foundation, Thorpe Mandeville House, 1974.

Jacob, Margaret C. *The Radical Enlightenment: Pantheists, Freemasons and Republicans.* London: George Allen & Unwin, 1981.

Jähns, Max. *Geschichte der Kriegswissenschaften vornehmlich in Deutschland.* 3 vols. München und Leipzig: R. Oldenbourg, 1891. Reprint, New York: Johnson Reprint Corporation; Hildesheirr: Georg Olms, 1965.

James, George P. R. *Memoirs of the Great Commanders.* 2 vols. Philadelphia: E. L. Carey & A. Hart; Boston: W. D. Ticknor, 1835.

Jany, Curt. *Geschichte der Preußischen Armee vom 15 Jahrhundert bis 1914.* 2d ed. 4 vols. Osnabrück: Biblio Verlag, 1967. Originally published as *Geschichte der königlich Preussischen Armee bis zum Jahre 1807.* 4 vols. Berlin: K. Siegismund, 1928–33.

Jenkins, Geraint H. *The Foundations of Modern Wales, 1642–1870.* Oxford: Clarendon Press; University of Wales Press, 1987.

Jespersen, Knud J. V. "Claude Louis, Comte de Saint-Germain (1707–1778): Professional Soldier, Danish Military Reformer, and French War Minister." In *Soldier-Statesmen of the Age of the Enlightenment: Records of the 7th International Colloquy on Military History, Washington, D.C., 25–30 July 1982,* edited by Abigail T. Siddall, 305–21. Manhattan, Kansas: Sunflower University Press, 1984.

Jesse, John Heneage. *Memoirs of the Chevalier, Prince Charles Edward, and their Adherents.* 2d ed. 2 vols. London: Richard Bentley, 1846.

Kaegi, Jr., Walter Emil. "The Crisis in Military Historiography." *Armed Forces and Society* 7, no.2 (Winter 1981): 299–316.

Kaiser, David. *Politics and War: European Conflict from Philip II to Hitler.* Cambridge, MA: Harvard University Press, 1990.

Keegan, John. *The Face of Battle.* New York: The Viking Press, 1976.

Keep, John. "Feeding the Troops: Russian Army Supply Policies during the Seven Years' War." *Canadian Slavonic Papers* XXIX, no. 1 (March 1987): 24–44.

Keller, Ludwig. *Graf Wilhelm von Schaumburg-Lippe: Ein Zeitgenosse und Freund Friedrichs des Grossen.* Berlin: Wiedmann, 1907.

Killion, Thomas H. "Clausewitz and Military Genius." *Military Review* LXXV, no. 4 (July–August 1995): 97–100.

Klein, Hans. *Wilhelm zu Schaumburg-Lippe: Klassiker Abschreckungstheorie und Lehrer Scharnhorsts.* Osnabruck: Biblio Verlag, 1982.

Knight, Isabel F. *The Geometric Spirit: The Abbé de Condillac and the French Enlightenment.* New Haven, CT: Yale University Press, 1968.

Koch, Hannsjoachim W. *A History of Prussia.* New York: Longman Group Limited, 1978. Reprint, New York: Dorset Press, 1987.

Kotasek, Edith. *Feldmarschall Graf Lacy: Ein Leben für Österreichs Heer.* Horn: F. Berger, 1956.

Lanir, Zvi. "The 'Principles of War and Military Thinking." *The Journal of Strategic Studies* 16, no. 1 (March 1993): 1–17.

LeDonne, John P. "Outlines of Russian Military Administration, 1762–1796, Part I: Troop Strength and Deployment." *Jahrbücher für Geschichte Osteuropas* 31, no. 3 (1983): 321–47.

———. "Outlines of Russian Military Administration, 1762–1796, Part II: The High Command." *Jahrbücher für Geschichte Osteuropas* 33, no. 2 (1985): 175–204.

Leer, Genrikh Antonivich. "Voennoe dlo v XVIII vk: Lloid kak voenniy pisatel. Ego voennie i politicheskie memuari." *Voennyi Sbornik* no. 10 (1864): 175–234.

———. "Voennoe dlo XVIII vk: Lloid, kak strategicheskii pisatel." *Voennyi Sbornik* no. 11 (1864): 3–32.

Lenman, Bruce. *The Jacobite Risings in Britain, 1689–1746*. London: Methuen, 1980.

Liddell Hart, Basil. "Some Extracts from a Military Work of the 18th Century." *Journal of the Society for Army Historical Research* XII, no. 47 (Autumn 1933): 138–54.

Lloyd, Hannibal Evans. *Memoir of General Lloyd, Author of the* History of the Seven Years War, *etc. etc.* London: Printed for Private Circulation, 1842.

Lloyd, John Edward, and Robert T. Jenkins, eds. *The Dictionary of Welsh Biography Down to 1940*. London: B. H. Blackwell, Ltd., 1959.

Lloyd, Richard Douglas. *Pride, Prejudice & Politics: A History of the Lloyd Family in Wales, Pennsylvania, and Ontario*. 3 vols. Toronto: Genealogical Pub. Co., 1992.

Longworth, Philip. *The Art of Victory: The Life and Achievements of Field-Marshal Suvorov, 1729–1800*. New York; Chicago; San Francisco: Holt, Reinhart and Winston, 1965.

Luvaas, Jay. "Frederick the Great: The Education of a Great Captain." In *The John Biggs Cincinnati Lectures in Military Leadership and Command, 1986*, edited by Henry S. Bausum, 23–37. Lexington, VA: The VMI Foundation, Inc., 1986.

Lynch, John. *Bourbon Spain, 1700–1808*. Oxford; Cambridge: Basil Blackwell, 1989.

Lynn, John A. "French Opinion and the Military Resurrection of the Pike, 1792–1794." *Military Affairs* 41, no. 1 (February 1977): 1–7.

———. "The Evolution of Army Style in the Modern West, 800–2000." *The International History Review* 18, no. 3 (August 1996): 505–35.

———. "The Treatment of Military Subjects in Diderot's *Encyclopédie*." *The Journal of Military History* 65, no. 1 (January 2001): 131–65.

Madariaga, Isabel de. *Russia in the Age of Catherine the Great*. New Haven and London: Yale University Press, 1981.

Manners, Walter E. *Some account of the military, political, and social life of the Right Hon. John Manners, marquis of Granby*. London: Macmillan and Co., Limited, 1899.

Manuel, Frank E. *The Eighteenth Century Confronts the Gods*. Cambridge, MA: Harvard University Press, 1959.

McLynn, Frank J. *France and the Jacobite Rising of 1745*. Edinburgh: Edinburgh University Press, 1981.

———. "Issues and Motives in the Jacobite Rising of 1745." *The Eighteenth Century: Theory and Interpretation* 23, no. 2 (Spring 1982): 97–133.

Mears, John Ashley. "Count Raimondo Montecuccoli: Practical Soldier and Military Theoretician." Ph.D. diss., University of Chicago, 1964.

Meek, Ronald L. *Social Science and the Ignoble Savage*. Cambridge: Cambridge University Press, 1976.

Menning, Bruce W. "Russian Military Innovation in the Second Half of the Eighteenth Century." *War & Society* 2, no. 1 (1984): 23–41.

Michel, Francisque. *Les Écossais en France, les Français en Écosse*. 2 vols. London: Trübner and Co., 1862.

Monod, Paul Kleber. *Jacobitism and the English People, 1688–1788*. Cambridge: Cambridge University Press, 1989.

Morais, A. Faria de. "O Documento Lloyd (1765)." *Separata do Boletim do Arquivo Histórico Militar*, no. 21 (1951).

Morris, A. *Merionethshire*. Cambridge County Geographies, ed. Francis H. H. Guillemard. Cambridge: At the University Press, 1913.

Neill, Donald A. "Ancestral Voices: The Influence of the Ancients on the Military Thought of the Seventeenth and Eighteenth Centuries." *The Journal of Military History* 62, no. 3 (July 1998): 487–520.

Nicholas, Donald. "The Welsh Jacobites." *The Transactions of the Honourable Society of Cymmrodorian* (1948): 467–74.

Nosworthy, Brent. *The Anatomy of Victory: Battle Tactics, 1689–1763*. New York: Hippocrene Books, 1990.

Nuccio, Oscar. Introduction to *An Essay on the Theory of Money*, by Henry Lloyd. Ristampe Anastatiche di Opere Antiche e Rare XCIV. Rome: Edizioni Bizzarri, 1968.

O'Neal, John C. *The Authority of Experience: Sensationist Theory in the French Enlightenment*. Literature & Philosophy, ed. A. J. Cascardi. University Park, PA: The Pennsylvania State University Press, 1996.

Orenstein, Harold S., trans. *The Evolution of Soviet Operational Art, 1927–1991: The Documentary Basis*. 2 vols. With a Foreword and Introduction by David M. Glantz. London: Frank Cass, 1995.

Outram, Dorinda. *The Enlightenment*. Cambridge: Cambridge University Press, 1995.

Owen, Richard H. "Jacobitism and the Church in Wales." *Journal of the Historical Society of the Church in Wales* 2 (1953): 111–9.

Palmer, Robert R. "The French Jesuits in the Age of Enlightenment: A Statistical Study of the *Journal de Trévoux*." *The American Historical Review* 45, no. 1 (October 1939): 44–58.

———. *Catholics and Unbelievers in Eighteenth-Century France*. Princeton, NJ: Princeton University Press, 1939.

———. *The Age of the Democratic Revolution: a Political History of Europe and America, 1760–1800*. 2 vols. Princeton, NJ: Princeton University Press, 1964.

———. "Frederick the Great, Guibert, Bülow: From Dynastic to National War." In *Makers of Modern Strategy: Military Thought from Machiavelli to Hitler*, edited by Edward Meade Earle, 49–74. Princeton, NJ: Princeton University Press, 1943. Reprint, *Makers of Modern Strategy from Machiavelli to the Nuclear Age*, edited by Peter Paret with the collaboration of Gordon A. Craig and Felix Gilbert, 91–119. Princeton, NJ: Princeton University Press, 1986.

Paret, Peter. *Yorck and the Era of Prussian Reform, 1807–1815*. Princeton, New Jersey: Princeton University Press, 1966.

———. *Clausewitz and the State*. Oxford: Clarendon Press, 1976.

Patterson, Alfred Temple. *The Other Armada: The Franco-Spanish Attempt to Invade Britain in 1779.* Manchester: Manchester University Press, 1960.

Pennant, Thomas. *Tours in Wales.* 3 vols. London: Printed for Wilkie and Robinson; J. Nunn; White & Co., 1810.

Pereira Sales, Ernesto Augusto. *O conde de Lippe em Portugal.* Vila Nova de Famalicão: G. Pinto de Sousa & Irmao, 1986.

Perjés, Geza. "Army Provisioning, Logistics and Strategy in the Second Half of the 17th Century." *Acta Historica Academiae Scientiarum Hungaricae* XVI (1970): 1–52.

Perlmutter, Amos. "Carl von Clausewitz, Enlightenment Philosopher: A Comparative Analysis." *The Journal of Strategic Studies* 11, no. 1 (March 1988): 7–19.

Petrie, Charles. *King Charles III of Spain: An Enlightened Despot.* New York: The John Day Company, 1971.

Petter, Wolfgang. "Zur Kriegkunst im Zeitalter Friedrichs des Großen. In *Europa im Zeitalter Friedrichs des Großen: Wirtschaft, Gesellschaft, Kriege,* edited by Bernhard R. Kroener, 245–96. München: R. Oldenburg Verlag, 1989.

Pieri, Piero. *Guerra e Politica negli Scrittori Italiana.* Milan e Napoli: Riccardo Ricciardi Editore, 1955.

Quimby, Robert S. *The Background of Napoleonic Warfare: The Theory of Military Tactics in Eighteenth Century France.* New York: Columbia University Press, 1957. Reprint, New York: AMS Press, 1979.

Ransel, David L. *The Politics of Catherinian Russia: The Panin Party.* New Haven, CT: Yale University Press, 1975.

Reid, Brian Holden. "Colonel J.F.C. Fuller and the Revival of Classical Military Thinking in Britain, 1918–1926." *Military Affairs* 49, no. 4 (October 1985): 192–97.

Riasanovsky, Nicholas V. *A History of Russia.* 5th ed. New York; Oxford: Oxford University Press, 1993.

Ribalta, Pere Molas. "The Early Bourbons and the Military." Chapter 2 in *Armed Forces and Society in Spain, Past and Present,* edited by Rafael Bañón Martínez and Thomas M. Barker, 51–80. Boulder, CO: Social Science Monographs; New York: Distributed by Columbia University Press, 1988.

Robitschek, Norbert. *Hochkirch: Eine Studie.* Wien: C. Teupen, 1905.

Robson, Eric. "The Armed Forces and the Art of War." In *The New Cambridge Modern History,* vol. 7, *The Old Regime,* edited by J.O. Lindsay, 163–89. Cambridge: At the University Press, 1963.

Rogers, Deborah D. *Bookseller as Rogue: John Almon and the Politics of Eighteenth-Century Publishing.* American University Studies. Series IV, English Language and Literature, vol. 28. New York: Peter Lang, 1986.

Ropp, Theodore. *War in the Modern World.* Rev. ed. New York: Collier Books, 1962.

Rosen, Howard. "The Système Gribeauval: A Study of Technological Development and Institutional Change in Eighteenth Century France." Ph.D. diss., The University of Chicago, 1981. UMI Order Number AAT T-28084.

Ross, Steven T. "The Development of the Combat Division in Eighteenth-Century French Armies." *French Historical Studies* 4, no. 1 (Spring 1965): 84–94.

Rothenburg, Gunther E. "Maurice of Nassau, Gustavus Adolphus, Raimondo Montecuccoli, and the "Military Revolution" of the Seventeenth Century." Chapter 2 in *Makers of Modern Strategy from Machiavelli to the Nuclear Age*, edited by Peter Paret with the collaboration of Gordon A. Craig and Felix Gilbert, 32–63. Princeton, NJ: Princeton University Press, 1986.

Rudé, George. *Wilkes and Liberty: A Social Study of 1763 to 1774*. Oxford: Clarendon Press, 1962.

Sánchez de Arco, Manuel. *El marqués de Santa Cruz de Marcenado*. Madrid: Editora Nacional, 1945.

Savory, Reginald A. *His Britannic Majesty's Army in Germany during the Seven Years War*. Oxford: The Clarendon Press, 1966.

Schrijver, Elka. "Bergen op Zoom: Stronghold on the Scheldt." *History Today* 26, no. 11 (November 1976): 749–52.

Schukking, W. H. "Menno van Coehoorn (1641–1704) et la 'Fondation' qui porte son nom." *Revue Internationale d'Histoire Militaire* No. 19 (1957): 332–43.

Schweizer, Karl. "The Seven Years' War: A System Perspective." Chap. 10 in *The Origins of War in Early Modern Europe*, edited by Jeremy Black, 242–71. Edinburgh: John Donald Publishers LTD, 1987.

Scott, Hamish M. "Great Britain, Poland and the Russian Alliance." *The Historical Journal* 19, no. 1 (March 1976): 53–74.

———. "The Importance of Bourbon Naval Reconstruction to the Strategy of Choiseul after the Seven Years' War." *The International History Review* 1, no. 1 (January 1979): 17–35.

Showalter, Dennis E. *The Wars of Frederick the Great*. London: Longman, 1996.

Shy, John. "Jomini." In *Makers of Modern Strategy from Machiavelli to the Nuclear Age*, edited by Peter Paret with the collaboration of Gordon A. Craig and Felix Gilbert, 143–85. Princeton, NJ: Princeton University Press, 1986.

Sinety, André Louis Woldeman Alphée, marquis de. *Vie du maréchal Lowendal*. 2 vols. Paris: Librairie Bochelin-Deflorenne, 1867–68.

Skrine, Francis Henry. *Fontenoy and Great Britain's Share in the War of the Austrian Succession, 1741–48*. With an Introduction by Frederick Sleigh Roberts, Earl of Kandahar and Waterford. Edinburgh and London: William Blackwood and Sons, 1906.

Smith, Charles Hamilton, trans. *The History of the Seven Years' War in Germany, by Generals Lloyd and Tempelhoff, with observations and maxims extracted from the* Treatise of Great Military Operations *of General Jomini*. Vol. 1. Translated from the German and French by Captain Charles Hamilton Smith. London: Printed for R. G. Clarke, [n.d.].

Stephen, Leslie, and Sidney Lee, eds. *The Dictionary of National Biography: From the Earliest Times to 1900*. 22 vols. London: Oxford University Press; Henry Milford, 1937–38.

Storrs, Christopher, and Hamish M. Scott. "The Military Revolution and the European Nobility, c. 1600–1800." *War in History* 3, no. 1 (January 1996): 1–41.

Strachan, Hew. *European Armies and the Conduct of War*. London: George Allen & Unwin, 1983.

Sutherland, Lucy S. *The University of Oxford in the Eighteenth Century: A Reconsideration*. Oxford: Oxford University Press, 1973.

Svechin, Aleksandr Andreevich. *Strategy.* Edited by Kent Lee. Introductory Essays by Andrei A. Kokoshin, Valentin V. Larionev, Vladimir N. Lobov, and Jacob W. Kipp. Minneapolis, MN: East View Publications, 1991. Originally published as *Strategiia.* Moscow: Voennyi vestnik, 1927.

Szechi, Daniel. *The Jacobites: Britain and Europe, 1688–1788.* Manchester: Manchester University Press, 1994.

Thadden, Franz-Lorenz von. *Feldmarschall Daun: Maria Theresias grössten Feldherr.* Wien und München: Herold, 1967.

Thibault, Edward A. "War as a Collapse of Policy: A Critical Evaluation of Clausewitz." *Naval War College Review* 25, no. 5 (May/June 1973): 42–56.

Thirsk, Joan, ed. *The Agrarian History of England and Wales.* 8 vols. Cambridge: Cambridge University Press, 1967–91.

Thomas, Peter D.G. "Jacobitism in Wales." *The Welsh History Review* 1, no. 3 (1962): 279–300.

———. *John Wilkes: A Friend of Liberty.* Oxford: Clarendon Press, 1996.

———. *Politics in Eighteenth-Century Wales.* Cardiff: University of Wales Press, 1998.

Travers, Tim. "The Development of British Military Historical Writing and Thought from the Eighteenth Century to the Present." In *Military History and the Military Profession,* edited by David A. Charters, Marc Milner, and J. Brent Wilson, 23–44. Foreword by Anne N. Foreman. Westport, CT: Praeger, 1992.

Ungermann, Richard. *Der Russisch-Turkische Krieg, 1768–1774.* Wien und Leipzig: Wilhelm Braumüller, 1906.

Vagts, Alfred. *A History of Militarism: Civilian and Military.* Rev. ed. New York: Meridian Books, 1959.

Valentine, Alan. *The British Establishment, 1760–1784: An Eighteenth-Century Biographical Dictionary.* 2 vols. Norman, OK: University of Oklahoma Press, 1970.

Valeri, Nino. *Pietro Verri.* Firenze: Felice Le Monnier, 1969.

Varnhagen von Ense, Karl August. *Biographische Denkmale.* 5 vols. Berlin: G. Reimer, 1845–6.

Vaughn, Herbert M. "Welsh Jacobitism." *The Transactions of the Honourable Society of Cymmrodorian* (1920–21): 11–39.

Venturi, Franco. *Le Vite incrociate di Henry Lloyd e Pietro Verri.* Torino: Editrice Tirrenia-Stampatori, 1977.

———. "Le 'Meditazioni sulla economia politica' di Pietro Verri: Edizioni, echi e discussioni." *Rivista Storica Italiana* 90, no. 3 (October 1978): 530–93.

———. "Le Avventure del Generale Lloyd." *Rivista Storica Italiana* 91, nos. 2–3 (April–September 1979): 369–433.

———. *The End of the Old Regime in Europe, 1768–1776.* Edited by R. Burr Litchfield. Princeton, NJ: Princeton University Press, 1989. Originally published as *Settecento riformatore, III: La prima crisi dell'Antico Regime (1768–1776).* Turin: Giulio Einaudi editore, 1979.

———. *The End of the Old Regime in Europe, 1776–1789.* 2 vols. Edited by R. Burr Litchfield. Princeton, NJ: Princeton University Press, 1991. Originally published as *Settecento riformatore, IV: La caduta dell'Antico Regime (1776–1789).* 2 vols. Turin: Giulio Einauldi editore, 1984.

————. *L'Italia dei Lumi (1764–1790)*. Vol. 5, pt. 1 of *Settecento riformatore*. Turin: Giulio Eunaudi editore, 1987.

Waddington, Richard. *Le Guerre de sept ans: histoire diplomatique et militaire*. 5 vols. Paris: Firmin-Didot & cie, 1899–1914.

Wahlde, Peter von. "A Pioneer of Russian Strategic Thought: G. A. Leer, 1829–1904." *Military Affairs* 35, no. 4 (December 1971): 148–53.

Weigley, Russell F. *Towards an American Army: Military Thought from Washington to Marshall*. New York: Columbia University Press, 1962.

————. *The Age of Battles: The Quest for Decisive Wafare from Breitenfeld to Waterloo*. Bloomington, IN: Indiana University Press, 1991.

Western, John R. "War on a New Scale: Professionalism in Armies, Navies and Diplomacy." Chapter 6 in *The Eighteenth Century: Europe in the Age of Enlightenment*, edited by Alfred Cobban, 182–216. New York: McGraw Hill Book Company, 1969.

White, Charles Edward. *The Enlightened Soldier: Scharnhorst and the* Militärische Gesellschaft *in Berlin, 1801–1805*. New York: Praeger, 1989.

White, Jon Manchip. *Marshal of France: The Life and Times of Maurice, Comte de Saxe [1696–1750]*. Chicago, IL: Rand McNally & Company, 1962.

Whiteley, Peter. *Lord North: The Prime Minister Who Lost America*. London and Rio Grande: The Hambledon Press, 1996.

Whitworth, Rex. *Field Marshal Lord Ligonier: A Story of the British Army, 1702–1770*. Oxford: The Clarendon Press, 1958.

————. *William Augustus, Duke of Cumberland: A Life*. London: Leo Cooper, 1992.

Willcox, William B. *Portrait of a General: Sir Henry Clinton in the War of Independence*. New York: Alfred A. Knopf, 1964.

Wilson, Peter H. "War in German Thought from the Peace of Westphalia to Napoleon." *European History Quarterly* 28, no. 1 (January 1998): 5–50.

Winter, Georg. *Die Kriegsgeschichtliche Überlieferung über Friedrich den Großen: Kritisch geprüßt an dem Beispiel der Kapitulation von Maxen*. Historische Untersuchungen, ed. J. Jastrow, vol. 7 (Berlin: R. Gaertners Verlagsbuchhandlung; Hermann Heyfelder, 1888).

Wrede, Alphons Freiherrn von. *Geschichte der K. und K. Wehrmacht: Die Regimenter, Corps, Branchen und Anstalten von 1618 bis Ende des XIX. Jahrhunderts*. 5 vols. Wien: L. W. Seidel & Sohn, 1898–1905.

Wright, John W. "Sieges and Customs of War at the Opening of the Eighteenth Century." *The American Historical Review* 39, no. 4 (July 1934): 629–44.

————. "Military Contributions during the Eighteenth Century." *The Journal of the American Military Institute* 3, no. 1 (Spring 1939): 3–13.

Zwitzer, H. L. "The Dutch Army during the Ancien Régime." *Revue Internationale d'Histoire Militaire*, no. 58 (1984): 15–36.

Index

NOTE: Numbers set in *boldface italics* indicate illustrations.

Adams, John, 91–92
Aix-la-Chapelle, Treaty of, 38
Alexander III, the Great, of
    Macedon, 96
American Revolution, 88, 92, 100,
    112–13
Amherst, Gen. Sir Jeffery, Baron,
    89, 91–92, 181nn.96
Aranjuez, Treaty of, 88
Aristotle, 8
Arrian, 8, 46
Auerstädt, battle of, 55
Augusta, Princess, 57, 161nn.1
Austrian army, 42, 150–51nn.5–6,
    165nn.57
Austrian Succession, War of the,
    12, 20, 38

Bath, William Pulteney, 2d Earl of,
    81, 172nn.6
Bayle, Pierre, 63
Beccaria, Cesare, 64

Belle-Isle, Marshal, 40
Bentham, Jeremy, 64
Bergen-op-Zoom, siege of, 34–37,
    36, 97, 149nn.94, 98
Blue-Water Strategy, 77–78
Bonaparte, Napoleon, 2, 15,
    96, 112, 114, 119,
    185–86nn.71, 73
Boščovíc, Ruggiero Giuseppe, 11
Boyd, Maj. Gen. Robert, 81
Bragança, Dom João Carlos,
    duque de, 43
Branham, Col. James, 91
Brett, Capt. Peircy, 27
Brunswick, Karl Wilhelm
    Ferdinand, Hereditary Prince
    of, 55, 57, 161nn.1
Brunswick, Prince Ferdinand of,
    55, 57, 125
Bülow, Adam Heinrich Dietrich,
    Freiherr von, 2, 118–121,
    189nn.9

Burgoyne, Maj. Gen. John, 88,
    92, 112
Burke, Edmund, 76–77

Cadwaladr, 5
Caemmerer, Rudolf von, 120
Campbell, Lt. Gen. Sir James, 22
Carleton, Maj. Thomas, 84
Cathcart, Charles Schaw,
    4th Baron, 81–82
Catherine II, the Great, of Russia,
    3, 81–84, 87
Chandler, David G., 114
Charles V of Spain, 12
Chauvelin, François-Claude,
    marquis de, 70
Chernyshev, Count Ivan, 82
Clausewitz, Carl von, 2, 96, 101,
    114, 118–20, 157nn.101,
    190nn.25, 191nn.29
Clerk, Lt. Gen. Robert, 81
Clinton, Henry, 58, 81–82, 92,
    155nn.59
    journey to Silistria with Lloyd,
    83–85
    Lloyd's appeals to for
    employment, 58, 60–61
Clinton, Thomas Pelham, 83
Coehoorn, Emmo van, 16, 34
Colin, Jean, 114, 183
Condorcet, Marie-Jean-Antoine-
    Nicholas de Caritat, marquis
    de, 11
Continuation of the History of the
    Late War in Germany,
    95–115, 181nn.1
Cope, John, 28–31
Corsican Revolt, 70–71, 166nn.79
coup d'œil, 5, 43, 50
    definition of, 136nn.5
Cromwell, Oliver, 6
Cronström, Isaac Kock, Baron, 34
Crown Prince Frederick of
    Britain, 59–60
Culloden, battle of, 32

Cumberland, William Augustus,
    duke of, 32–33
    in Fontenoy campaign, 20–25,
    144nn.22
Cwm Bychan, 6

Daun, Leopold Josef, Reichsgraf
    von, 40, 43, 53
    Lloyd's critique of, 52
D'Eau, Capt., 28
Delbrück, Hans, 47, 121
Diderot, Denis, 4, 11, 96
Dorth, Johan Adolf, Baron van, 21
Drummond, James, 28–29
Drummond, John, 20, 27, 32–33,
    35, 38, 136nn.4
Drummond, Lord John, 20, 28, 31
Duff, William, 96, 138nn.28
Dutens, Vincent-Louis, 74, 169nn.107

École Militaire, 15, 140–41nn.54
Edward I, 6
Effende, Reis, 84
Eliott, Lt. Gen. George Augustus, 89
Encyclopédie, 4
Enlightenment
    basic outlook of, 62
    Counter-, 114
    and genius, 96
    Milanese, 61–62, 152nn.15
    Military, 3–4
    relationship to Jesuits, 11–12
    "Essai philosophiques sur les
    gouvernements," 62–72,
    162nn.10
Essay on the English Constitution,
    75–78, 170nn.116–17
Essay on the Theory of Money,
    72–74, 81, 168nn.97, 171 nn.2

Falkirk, battle of, 32
Felipe V of Spain, 12
Fermor, Count William, 51
Feuquières, Antoine de Pas,
    marquis de, 16, 104

Finck, Friedrich August von, 53
Fitzwilliam, Richard, 84, 161
Folard, Jean-Charles, chevalier de, 17, 105
Fontenoy, Battle of, 21–25, *23*
Forty-Five, 27–33, 147nn.60, 69
France, 10, 20
Frederick II, the Great, of Prussia, 16, 38, 50, 101, 117
  in battle of Hochkirch, *55*
  in battle of Kolin, 51
  in battle of Leuthen, 51
  genius of, 96
  invades Saxony, 40
  Lloyd's critique of, 47
  preference for Junker nobility, 10
Frederick William, the Great Elector, of Prussia, 13
Frederick William I of Prussia, 10, 160nn.136
French Classicism, 48, 155nn.60
French Revolution, 2, 96, 105, 114, 121
Frisi, Paolo, 62
Frontiers of Europe, 111–12
Fuller, John Frederick Charles, 120

Garnett, John, Bishop of Clogher, 74
Garnett, Mary, 74, 81, 88, 170nn.113
George I of Britain, 27
George II of Britain, 20, 27
George III of Britain, 57, 61, 75, 89
Gerard, William, 96
Germain, Lord George, 92
Gibbon, Edward, 3
  at Oxford, 7
Gibraltar, 88–89, 166
Golitsyn, Count Dmitry Aleksandrovich, 84
Granby, John Manners, marquis of, 58, 60–61, 74, 80
Great Britain, 79–80
Great Northern War, 14

Grenville, George, 75–76, 80
Guibert, Jacques Antoine Hippolyte, comte de, 2, 105, 110, 114
Gunning, Robert, 82, 173nn.16
Gustavus III of Sweden, 83, 87
Gwynedd, Maelgwyn, 6

Halleck, Henry Wager, 119
Halley, Edmond, 8
Hardy, Admiral Charles, 89
Harvey, Maj. Gen. Edward, 81
Harvey, William, 72
Hawley, Lt. Gen. Henry, 32
Helvetius, Claude Adrian, 64
Herodotus, 8
History of the Late War in Germany, The, 45–57, 60, 112, 155nn.58
Hochkirch, battle of, 53–55, *56,* 102, 128
Hume, David, 62, 164nn.46, 165nn.52
Huy, 92

indecisiveness of warfare, 101
Ingoldsby, Brig-Gen. Richard, 22, 24, 144nn.22

Jacobites, 81
  aborted 1744 invasion of England, 20
  in exile, 27
  at Oxford, 7
  military service in foreign armies, 10, 81, 173nn.9
  Scottish, 20
  Welsh, 31–32
Jennings, Edmund, 91–92
Jesuits, 10
  and education, 11, 14, 139nn.40
  relationship to Enlightenment, 11–12, 161nn.6
  suppression of, 11, 62
Jesus College, 7–8

Johnson, Samuel, 7
Johnstone, James, chevalier de Johnstone, 28
Jomini, Antoine Henri, baron de, 119
Joseph I, King of Portugal, 57
Joseph II, Holy Roman Emperor, 84

Kamenskii, Gen. Mikhail, 84
Kant, Immanuel, 3
Karl, Archduke, of Austria, 121
Karl I, Herzog von Brunswick, 45, 57–58
Kaunitz-Rietberg, Wenzel Anton, Reichsgraf von, 40, 84
Keith, James, 38
Knox, William, 76–77
Kolin, battle of, 51, 125–26, 157nn.89
Königsegg und Rothenfels, Lothar Dominik, Graf von, 22
Königsegg-Rothenfels, Maximilian Friedrich von, Elector and Archbishop of Cologne, 58
Kozludzhi, battle of, 84–85
Kunersdorf, battle of, 53
Kutchuk-Kainardji, Treaty of, 85

La Mettrie, Julian Offray de, 19, 64
Lacy, Franz Moritz, Graf von, 40, 150nn.4, 151nn.14
   in battle of Hochkirch, 55, 106
   in battle of Maxen, 53–55, 106
   and Generalquartiermeister corps, 40–41
   relationship with Lloyd, 43–44, 152nn.30
Laffeld, battle of, 33
Leer, Genrikh Antonovich, 119, 190nn.16
Leuthen, battle of, 51–53, 102, 126–27

Liegnitz, battle of, 104
Ligonier, Sir John, 22, 57
Limited War, 2–3
Lindsay, Lt. Gen. David, 90
Lists of the Forces of the Sovereigns of Europe, 38, 150nn.102
Lloyd (Llwyd) family, 5, 135nn.3
Lloyd, Hannibal Evans, 81, 171–72nn.3
Lloyd, Henry Humphrey Evans, 1
   anti-clericalism of, 98, 162nn.17
   appointed honorary major general by Elector of Cologne, 58
   in Austrian service, 41–45, 152nn.29, 32
   at battle of Fontenoy, 21–25
   at battle of Maxen, 53–55, 54
   in Brunswickian service, 45, 55–58
   commoner status of, 1, 10, 13, 97
   conducts siege of Silistria, 85
   death of, 117
   educated by Jesuits, 11
   educated at Oxford, 8–10
   in French service, 40
   on genius, 96, 156nn.64
   historical method, 45–47
   influence of, 117–121
   influence of battle of Prestonpans on, 31
   influence of classical literature on, 8–9, 46
   influence of Marshal Saxe on, 25–26
   and invasion scare of 1779, 88–91
   in Italy, 61–62, 70–71, 74
   in Jacobite service, 27–33
   legacy of, 121

on lines of operation, 53,
    110–11, 127
marriage to Mary Garnett, 74
military sociology of, 66,
    97–99, 117
on National Character, 67–68, 117
"New System" of, 105–10,
    107, 114
with Pietro Verri in the Seven
    Years' War, 42–44
plans for recruiting for British
    army, 57
plans for Sino-Russian War, 83
plans for winning American
    Revolution of, 112–13
on political nature of war,
    99–101, 183nn.28
on principles of war, 47–55,
    123–28, 155nn.63, 158nn.108
in Prussia, 10
in Prussian service, 38
on religion, 62–64
romantic nature and "genius"
    for war, 9, 33, 43, 92,
    138nn.29, 154nn.49
in Russian service, 81–88,
    174nn.17, 19, 24,
    178nn.62–63
Russo-Turkish War's influence
    on, 87, 99
in siege of Bergen-op-Zoom,
    35–38
in Spanish service, 12–17
in support of Paoli's revolt,
    70–71, 166nn.78–79
upbringing in Wales, 5–7, 135
works of, 129–31
Liechtenstein, Joseph Wenzel
    Laurenz, Fürst von, 40, 45
Lloyd, John, Rev., 5–6
Locke, John, 62

Lorraine, Karl Alexander, Prince of,
    1, 157nn.93
Loudon, Gideon Ernst, 44
Louis XIV of France, 10, 13–14,
    16, 95
Louis XV of France, 20, 25, 37, 100
Louvois, François Michel le Tellier,
    marquis de, 13
Lowendal, Frédéric Waldemar,
    comte de, 21, 148
    conducts the siege of Bergen-
    op-Zoom, 34–37, 149nn.87
Loyola, Ignatius of, 11

Machiavelli, Niccolò, 46
Mahan, Dennis Hart, 119
Maizeroy, Paul Gédéon Joly, comte
    de, 105
Maxen, battle of, 53–55, *54*, 102,
    106, 127–28
*Memoirs on the Present State of
    Portugal*, 58–59
Merioneth, 5–6, 135nn.2
Mésnil-Durand, François-Jean de
    Graindorge Dorgeville, baron
    de, 105
Migazzi zu Wall und Sonnenthurn,
    Christoph Bartholomäus
    Anton, Graf, 40
military education, 18th century,
    13–17
military engineers, 14–15
Mina, Jaime Miguel Guzmán,
    marques de, 12, 17, 40
Monckton, Lt. Gen. Robert, 90
Montazet, Antoine de, 43
Montecuccoli, Raimondo, 16
Montesquieu, 3, 66–67, 164nn.32
Münnich, Field-Marshal Burkhard
    Christoph, Graf von, 85, 150
Murray, Lord William, 29

Ney, Marshal Michel, 119
Norris, Admiral John, 20
North, Frederick North, Lord,
    80–81, 88–89

O'Connor, John Michael, 119
O'Hagarty, Ignatius, 84
Olmütz, siege of, 125, 156nn.86
Orvilliers, Louis Guillouet, comte
    de, 88–89
Oxford University, 7–10
    classical curriculum of, 8–9
    and Jacobitism, 7, 136nn.11
    Laudian Statutes of, 8, 137nn.17
    reputation of, 7, 137nn.13

Paltzig, battle of, 51, 125–26
Panin, Nikita Ivanovich, 82–83, 87
Paoli, Pasquale, 70–71
Paris, Peace of (1763), 57
Paris, Treaty of (1782), 92
Parma, 74
Pasha, Grand Vizier Muhsinzade
    Mehmed, 84
Pattinson, Thomas, 31
Peloponnesian War, 45, 100
Peter the Great of Russia, 14, 85
Plato, 8
Poltava, battle of, 21
Polybius, 8, 46
Ponte-Nuovo, battle of, 71
Prague, siege of, 125
Prestonpans, battle of, 29–31, 30,
    147nn.61
Prussia, 10
Pugachev Revolt, 82
Puységur, Jacques-François Maximo
    de Chastenet, marquis de, 104,
    110, 184nn.49

quantity theory of money, 72

Reichenberg, battle of, 125
Rhapsody on the Present System of
    French Politics, A, 89–92,
    179nn.73, 85, 86, 180nn.87–89
Richelieu, Louis François Armand
    du Plessis, duc de, 32,
    147nn.61
Rocoux, battle of, 33
Romance de Mesmon, Germain
    Hyacinthe, marquis de, 114,
    135nn.4
Roquefeuil, Jacques-Aymar, comte
    de, 20
Rossbach, battle of, 103
Rousseau, Jean-Jacques, 3
    Lloyd's critique of, 68–69,
    165nn.62
Roy, Col. William, 89
Royal Écossais, 20, 27, 31
Rumiantsev, Field Marshal Count
    Petr Aleksandrovich, 83–87,
    106, 108, 177nn.57
Russo-Turkish War, 81–87, 106,
    169nn.108, 172nn.5,
    176nn.42, 177nn.54
Ryswick, Peace of, 14

Saint-Germain, Claude Louis,
    comte de, 68
Saltykov, Gen. Peter, 51
Saltykov, Ivan, 85
Santa Cruz de Marcenado, Alvaro
    Navia Osorio, marques de, 17
Saxe, Hermann Maurice, comte de,
    2, 20, 26, 33–34, 37
    in Fontenoy campaign, 21–25,
    145nn.40
    Mes Rêveries, 25–26
Saxony, Xavier Auguste, prince of, 45
Scharnhorst, Gerhard Johann
    David von, 101, 183nn.29

Schaumburg-Lippe, Friedrich
Wilhelm Ernst, Graf zu,
57–58, 159nn.117
sensationist theory of knowledge,
64, 163nn.30
Seven Years' War, 45, 76, 91, 106
end of, 57
influence on Lloyd, 110–11
outbreak of, 39
Shelburne, William Fitzmaurice
Petty, 2d Earl of, 92, 113
Shumla, 84–85
Silistria, siege of, 85, 86, 176nn.45
Siškovíc, Josef, Graf von, 44, 97, 104
Solms, Victor Friedrich, Graf von,
83, 174nn.19
Spain, 12, 15, 88
Spanish Succession, War of the,
14–15
Squillacci, Leopoldo di Gregorio,
marchese de, 62, 161nn.6
Stuart, Charles Edward, the Young
Pretender, 26, 147nn.61
leads Forty-Five, 27–33
Stuart, James Francis Edward, the
Old Pretender, 26, 143nn.1
Suvorov, Gen. Aleksandr
Vasilevich, 84
Svechin, Alexandr Andreevich, 119,
190nn.17
Swiss Confederation, 100

Tacitus, Cornelius, 6
Tempelhof, Georg Friedrich von,
47, 117, 119, 154nn.55
Thucydides, 45, 153nn.43
Tillot, Guillaume-Léon du, 74
Townshend, George, 90–91
Turenne, Henri de la Tour
d'Auvergne, 25
Turkish army in Balkans, 87

utilitarianism, 65–66

Valmy, battle of, 55
Vauban, Sébastien le Prestre,
marquis de, 14–16, 37, 109
Vaux, Noël Jourde, comte de,
71, 88
Venice, 10, 12
Verboom, Jorge Prospero de, 15
Verri, Alessandro, 61–62, 74,
161nn.3
Verri, Pietro, 9, 41, 81, 135nn.4,
151nn.15
with Lloyd in Seven Years'
War, 42–44
Meditazioni sulla economia
politica, 72
relationship with Lloyd in Italy,
61–62, 74, 167nn.89,
169nn.110, 170nn.111
Voltaire, François-Marie Arouet de,
3, 11, 63

Waldeck, Karl August Friedrich,
Fürst von, 22, 144nn.17
Wales, 5–7
Wall, Ricardo, 12
Walpole, Horace, 24
Walsh, Capt. Antoine, 27
War of the Roses, 6
Wedell, Lt. Gen. Johann von, 51
Welianow, Maj., 85
Wilkes, John, 74–75
Wunsch, Prussian Gen., 52, 126
Württemberg, Ludwig, Fürst von, 43

Xenophon, 8–9, 46, 157nn.89

Zorndorf, battle of, 51, 125–26

About the Author

PATRICK J. SPEELMAN teaches history at the College of Charleston in Charleston, South Carolina.

Recent Titles in
Contributions in Military Studies

The Battle of Ap Bac, Vietnam: They Did Everything but Learn from It
David M. Toczek

The Emperor's Friend: Marshal Jean Lannes
Margaret Scott Chrisawn

An Uncertain Trumpet: The Evolution of U.S. Army Infantry Doctrine, 1919–1941
Kenneth Finlayson

Death Waits in the "Dark": The Senoi Praaq, Malaysia's Killer Elite
Roy Davis Linville Jumper

War Wings: The United States and Chinese Military Aviation, 1929–1949
Guangqiu Xu

A Navy Second to None: The History of U.S. Naval Training in World War I
Michael D. Besch

Home by Christmas: The Illusion of Victory in 1944
Ronald Andidora

Tides in the Affairs of Men: The Social History of Elizabeth Seamen, 1580–1603
Cheryl A. Fury

Battles of the Thirty Years War: From White Mountain to Nordlingen, 1618–1635
William P. Guthrie

A Grateful Heart: The History of a World War I Field Hospital
Michael E. Shay

Forged in War: The Continental Congress and the Origin of Military Supply
Lucille E. Horgan

Tricolor Over the Sahara: The Desert Battle of the Free French, 1940–1942
Edward L. Bimberg